"Games hold a much-loved and important place in human society and, in our history they usually receive no more than a footnote on their commercial success. *Hobby Games: The 100 Best* gives some of the game industry's most creative minds the opportunity to explore the importance of games beyond the retail dollar. It is a fascinating look at the true role of games in our culture and in our lives."

— SHERI GRANER RAY, author of *Gender Inclusive Game Design*

"*Hobby Games: The 100 Best* is a definitive record of an artform that reached an extraordinary creative peak toward the end of the 20th century, rather than the pedestrian, consensus-driven listing of the top 100 games implied by its title. Collectively authored by many of the designers who produced the greatest games the field has to offer, these essays offer a critical appreciation of the most inspired, the most elegant, and the most plain damn fun games. James Lowder has assembled a collection that richly rewards the reader's perusal, ranging from seminal, all-but-forgotten titles (*Lensman, Stalingrad*) to *succès d'estime* (*Empires of the Middle Ages, Once Upon a Time*) to inspired cross-genre designer/game combinations (Stafford on *Kingmaker*, Garfield on brown-box *D&D*). The DNA of hobby games is pervasive throughout today's computer and entertainment culture, in disciplines as diverse as technical manuals and cosplay; *HG100* is an excellent guide to the source material, not to mention a roadmap to thousands of hours of enjoyment."

— ERIC GOLDBERG, designer of *Paranoia, Kursk*, and *MadMaze*

"There's never been a better time to look back at the history of adventure gaming. *Hobby Games: The 100 Best* assembles an impressive roster of our best and brightest designers, to talk about the games that make the hobby what it is."

— ROBIN D. LAWS, author of *Feng Shui* and *40 Years of Gen Con*

HOBBY GAMES
THE 100 BEST

Edited by James Lowder

Foreword by Reiner Knizia
Afterword by James F. Dunnigan

GREEN RONIN
PUBLISHING

Please address questions and comments concerning this book, as well as requests for notices of new publications, by mail to:

Green Ronin Publishing
PO Box 1723
Renton, WA 98057-1723

Visit us online at www.greenronin.com.

10 9 8 7 6 5 4 3 2 1

Stock number GRR4001, September 2007.

ISBN 10: 1-932442-96-0
ISBN 13: 978-1-932442-96-0

Printed in the United States.

CONTENTS

FOREWORD

by Reiner Knizia

WHEN I RECENTLY VISITED a BIG international game company to discuss the publication of one of my new designs, I was told: "Gameplay is mostly invisible to marketing. It is virtually impossible to communicate gameplay on the box. To reach the consumer, we need TV-able games where people grasp instantaneously what the game is about, ideally with a unique gimmick that stands out." This may very well be right when it comes to selling games on a global level, but. . . .

That does not mean that gameplay is not important. On the contrary, I believe gameplay, also called game mechanics or game system, is the most important aspect of most family and adult games. Gameplay is the engine that drives the game, creates tension, and brings us back to play the game over and over again. Even the BIG game companies will agree that gameplay is critical to a game's continued success.

Clearly, the artwork and the game components are important, very important. We want the game to look nice and to feel nice. We want the presentation of the game to be appealing and inviting.

Ignoring some ingenious abstract board games, the theme or setting of the game is also important, vitally important. The theme creates the atmosphere of the game. It establishes the world we populate and the role we play. It defines our life in the world of gaming. We can be Tutankhamun, a little Hobbit, a formula motor racing driver, a modern art dealer, a spy, a princess, a pirate. . . . With so many games on offer, you can literally be almost anything you ever wanted to be.

The artwork, the components, the theme, or even an intriguing gimmick are all important. But all these aspects mean little if they are not bound together and ignited by good gameplay. If there is no exciting gameplay, there is no exciting game to play.

SO HOW DO YOU find exciting gameplay if you can't see it in advertising and if it is difficult to identify it on the box?

I have three suggestions for you:

First, you can read this book. It is all about gameplay, written by enthusiastic gamers who love games so much that they became designers and publishers, most of them now as full-time professionals. And none of them were allowed to write about their own products. They love the games here so much that they are even willing to praise one of their competitor's products. What more can you ask for?

However, please keep in mind that essentially all the contributors to this book are intense game players and their needs and favorites may go further than what casual gamers are used to. Hence, if you are already a gamer, here is a treasure of new games from many different genres for you. If you are a casual player or novice, this book will give you an impressive overview of what is out there beyond what you will find in the mass-market stores or advertised on TV — but you may feel a little overwhelmed. It is, though, a good place to start your search.

Next, you can visit a specialist game shop, where people care about their products passionately. These retailers know their products inside out. They love games and will be eager to tell you all about them. If you tell the shop assistant the names of a few games that you enjoy playing or express your interest in a genre of games, he or she will be able to recommend some new games from the shelves that should be just right for you.

Yes, specialist game shops are not the cheapest and you may have to pay a little bit extra compared to the prices in the BIG stores, but what is the point in randomly picking a cheap game from the shelf that may bring you zero enjoyment? There are many, many wonderful games around. The challenge is to find those games that are right for you. Advertising will not tell you the whole story. Internet information may help. But specialist shops will do the job and many of them have areas dedicated to gaming, offering you the opportunity to meet other players.

Finally, the very best way to be introduced to new games that interest you, particularly if you suspect you may be overwhelmed by too much specialized information, is to play with experienced players. Reading or talking about a game is one thing, reading the rules may be quite another, and successfully playing and finally mastering the game is yet another thing.

The fast track into a new game is to play it with others who already know it well. (You don't know other game players? Ask your local retailer or run an Internet search for game clubs or game conventions in your area!) Not only will experienced players give you a smooth introduction into the game and answer any questions you may have, but even more significantly, by playing with them — or even by simply watching them play — you will soon understand what the game is all about. Mastering a game moves you beyond the written rules and the handling of the components. Mastering a game means entering the zone where you play "in character" and focus on the choices and options your game role offers you at the very moment. You are in the *now* of gaming.

PLAYING A GAME IS the *only* way to find out what a game is really all about. I have designed more than 400 new games in my career, as well as having played many thousands of games. This statement is still as true for me today as it was when I played my first game. During the design process, every new creation needs countless playtest sessions to shape and fine-tune the gameplay. Only once in a blue moon will all these factors fall into place from the outset. Usually, it takes a long time and many alterations to create a finished design. Only when the game is robust enough so that the fun and excitement will literally jump out of the box when you open it, will the game be released to the publisher and the market.

Take my word for it: Opening the box and playing a game is the only way to find out what a game and gaming is all about. Use this book to find your games, and then go and *play*!

REINER KNIZIA was born in Germany and now lives in the U.K. He gained a Master of Science from Syracuse University in the United States and a doctorate in Mathematics from the University of Ulm in Germany. After managing a two-billion-dollar financial company, he now dedicates his time solely to designing games. With more than 400 published games and books, which have sold more than 10 million copies in numerous countries and languages, Dr. Knizia is arguably the world's most prolific games designer. He is currently represented with nine games in the 2006 Games 100. His international awards include four German Game Prizes, three French Grand Prix du Jouet, three Austrian Game Awards, two Japan Board Game Prizes, the Swiss Game Award, and five European Children's Game of the Year Awards. Further information can be found at www.knizia.de.

INTRODUCTION

by James Lowder

YOU WON'T AGREE WITH every single entry in this discussion of 100 of the best hobby games ever published.

Hypothetically, I suppose, there could be *someone* who will agree wholeheartedly with everything here, a lone soul in Cahirciveen, Ireland or the Ogasawara Islands in Japan or San Narciso, California who will pick up this tome at some out-of-the-way bookshop and find every single game discussed herein perfectly corresponds to his or her tally. (If that's you, I hope you plan on buying several copies.) But the table of contents doesn't reflect my list of the 100 best, or the publisher's list, or that of any of the several dozen participating authors. It won't match yours, either.

That's by design.

Hobby Games: The 100 Best is not intended as a consensus report. The games listed are not the result of an Internet poll or voting among the writers. The participants were asked to rank three or more hobby games they thought deserved to make the list of "the best" and then write an essay championing their top pick. Some got their second or third choice, since their first one or two had already been reserved. For anyone who asked, the working definition of a "hobby" game was one that invited repeated play and depth of strategy. They tend to be available through specialty retailers, though they might also be found in big box stores, as the mass-market success of *Heroscape* and *Pokémon* attests. More than one author convinced me to include a title I did not, at first, consider a hobby game, so it's safe to say the rules had some flex to them.

Not so with the rules limiting the authors' relation to their subjects. To avoid conflicts of interest, writers had to select a game designed by someone else. Neither could they pick a property in which they have a direct financial stake, as author or publisher. (You won't see any Green Ronin titles here for similar reasons.) This led to some surprising revelations, as designers selected games completely unlike the work for which they are known. Creators of horror RPGs chose military miniatures games. Card game designers selected unusual roleplaying games.

And their essays reveal some interesting connections between the seemingly incongruous games they create and the ones they play.

I also asked that everyone keep the tone of the essays positive. The point of the book is to say why the games discussed deserve attention, not explain why the ones you don't see here are less than worthy. If a game's not here, it just wasn't chosen as a top pick by an invitee. Several games were near misses — the second choice for a half-dozen writers. Their champions, though, never stepped forward. Another set of authors would have chosen some very different titles to discuss.

As they worked, the essayists were totally unaware of the full list of games being covered by their peers. They didn't know if someone had selected one of their creations. No one even saw the table of contents until the essays were complete and the book typeset. When they did finally get their preview, several designers expressed some bemusement at a particular favorite not making the cut, or surprise at the topic an old friend chose, or pleasure at the fact that a secretly beloved game had also caught the eye of someone else. So the final list encapsulates the opinions and biases of the individuals involved, but should not be misconstrued as a catalog endorsed in its entirety by any one person.

To understand why someone chose a particular game, you're going to have read his or her essay. Every writer participating in this project entertains a different idea of what *best* means, and when asked to single out a hobby game to praise, they all applied a personal vision to the task. As editor, I might have tried to limit the discussion to a narrow criterion for excellence. With the brilliant and opinionated people involved in this book, I wouldn't have taken a bet on my chances to get everyone marching in step. If I'd succeeded, though, the outcome would have been a collection of tediously uniform essays and a blandly predictable games list. The book still would have been biased, too — colored by my imposed definition, rather than the authors' individual viewpoints.

So I left it up to the writers to decide precisely what the word *best* meant for this project. The initial invitation offered some suggestions on qualities to consider. Innovative rules count for a lot, obviously, but also positive impact on the hobby as a whole. A game that redefines the relationship between the publisher and the player, or the player and the game itself, should be worth a serious look. Historical significance can be a factor, as should the simple, but overlooked notion of play value. Fun matters.

So, too, the game's personal significance for its self-declared champion.

Why should that hold any weight? Well, the men and women writing these commentaries are designers and publishers. If you don't know their names, take this opportunity to learn them. They've created many of the most popular and successful hobby games of the past five decades. They're the founders of the companies that continue to publish those properties all over the world. Every effort was made to include the widest variety of voices and as many of the titans of the hobby game field as I could track down. Deadlines prevented a few designers from joining in, and a staff non-competition policy ruled out participation by the current full-time employees at one major corporation. (Plenty of their games are covered, though.) Still, the collective experience of the writers gathered between these covers represents a significant portion of the industry's little-understood history. The products that inspired these VIPs impact you each and every time you sit down at the gaming table with one of their creations.

Many of the essays reveal quite a lot about their authors, too. Nostalgia colors more than one critical commentary. This might appear a bit self-indulgent.

Gaming, though, is a social occasion, and the games we play connect us in very special ways to the people gathered around that table with us. The better the game, the more likely it is to forge particularly strong connections. Little surprise, then, that discussing a beloved title conjures vivid and powerful memories.

My own history with the hobby — the winding path that brought me to first propose this project at Gen Con 2006 — originates in the 1970s, with my high school gaming group. Gatherings of friends and fellow enthusiasts compose the waymarks along the road from there. Playing *Dungeons & Dragons* in a house behind the now-defunct King's Castle Land kiddie amusement park in Whitman, Massachusetts. (There's nothing quite like playing *D&D* in the shadow of a fairy tale castle, a hundred yards or so from a gigantic dragon statue that actually belches flame.) Being introduced to *Kremlin* and a bunch of other great games at one of Warren Spector's open house Labor Day gamefests. Or spending lunchtimes in the library at TSR, talking about brilliant wargames and card games and RPGs, and coaxing others to give them a try.

Like those lunches in the TSR games library, this book has provided me the chance to get together with both old and new friends, and learn more than a little about the hobby. There are games discussed in these pages I'd never heard of before writers requested them as topics, and others I'd never seriously considered playing — that is, until one of the essays convinced me that I was missing out on something great. Through the book I've also come to recognize the profound interrelation of the hobby game and computer game industries. Take a look at the author biographies and you'll see what I mean.

So *Hobby Games: The 100 Best* is a guide to great games you might have missed, and a reminder of why you love the games you play time and time again. It's also a chance for you to catch up on the industry's history and an introduction to the people behind your favorite titles (or those you'll be breaking out at an upcoming game night).

It's also an invitation.

Everyone involved in this book loves games. They love to create them. They love to play them. They love to share their enthusiasm and introduce new people to the titles they treasure.

So *Hobby Games: The 100 Best* is also an invitation to an industry get-together, the sort that takes places after the exhibit hall closes at the Origins game fair, when plans for the best projects for the coming year are hatched over a drink or ten, and designers casually chat about how much they enjoy and admire *Castle Falkenstein* or *Caylus* or *Age of Steam*. It's a chance to jump back a couple of decades and pull up a chair in the games library at TSR (where, no doubt, several of the authors participating in this book are cheerfully handing me my head in the latest session of *Machiavelli* or *Empires of the Middle Ages*). The discussion will quickly turn to the newest issue of *Berg's Review of Games* and the most obscure titles in Steve Winter's collection that everyone will have to try next week.

It's expected that you'll continue the discussion started here with your own gaming group, or your family, or the regulars at the local hobby shop, or, thanks to the Internet, with other, more far-flung enthusiasts through the auspices of RPG.net and BoardGameGeek.com, Grognard.com and TheMiniaturesPage.com. The website of our publisher, greenronin.com, will have some forum space set aside for you, too.

In the meantime, though, welcome to the conversation. Sit back and let us tell you about some games we love. The ones we think of as the *best*, whatever that multifaceted word means to each of us.

This is going to be fun, and, as I said a little earlier, fun matters.

James Lowder has authored several bestselling novels, including *Prince of Lies* and *Knight of the Black Rose*, and written game material, comic book scripts, feature articles, and book and film reviews for many different publishers. He's helmed more than a dozen critically acclaimed anthologies, with subjects ranging from Arthurian Britain to zombies. He's been a finalist for the Stoker Award and International Horror Guild Award, and is a two-time Origins Award winner. In his six-plus years at TSR, he never won a single game of the many he played in the library at lunchtime. Those games were still the best part of the job.

GAME CREDITS AND EDITIONS

GAME DESIGN AND PUBLISHING are sometimes solitary pursuits, but often they are not, and that makes assigning credit a tricky business. For the essay headers, we have chosen the phrase "key designers" to indicate the game's creators and, in some cases, other significant developers. (See James F. Dunnigan's afterword for a description of the developer's role in board game and wargame publishing.) Space limitations preclude identifying all the editors, artists, graphic designers, playtesters, and the multitude of other people who play crucial roles in making a game a success. Take the time to read the full credits published in your favorite games, or any of the games you seek out because of this book.

If we have failed to assign credit where credit is due, please contact the editor, in care of the publisher, at the address on the copyright page. We will strive to make all necessary corrections in future printings and editions.

Many of the games discussed in these pages have been released in various editions, often by different publishers. With each new edition, the game may have undergone revision, sometimes minor, sometimes quite radical. Third edition *Dungeons & Dragons*, for example, is very different from first edition. So, where it matters to the essay, the header indicates a specific edition. For games that originally appeared in languages other than English, the first English-language edition is listed. Otherwise, headers identify the game's first or only edition.

For more information on how to locate the games and editions covered in *Hobby Games: The 100 Best*, see the appendix "Finding Hobby Games."

Bruce C. Shelley on

ACQUIRE

KEY DESIGNER: SID SACKSON

3M (SECOND EDITION, 1966)

I WAS INTRODUCED TO *Acquire* in the middle 1970s at a university game club where it was played at almost every weekly meeting. It was a good three- and five-player game when few of those were around. It was often a warm-up game, played while we waited for the regulars to assemble and start the new, cool game of the month. Those new games usually fell out of favor but *Acquire* remained a staple and I have often pondered why that was so.

Central to its success are four factors: simple rules, deep strategy, short game length, and a modest luck element. The rules are minimal and anyone can get playing quickly. But the strategy is deceptively deep and playing well depends mainly on making good decisions that have important downstream ramifications. There is an element of luck in tile draws and the actions of other players, giving even relative newcomers a chance to win. The luck element keeps the game from becoming a rigorous math exercise. A relatively short game length — an hour or so — and easy take-down/set-up give players a big payoff in entertainment versus their investment of time and energy.

Acquire is a competitive finance game that represents the building and financing of hotel chain empires. Tiles placed on a grid board represent hotels; groups of adjacent tiles become hotel chains. The rules to the game changed quickly after the first 3M Bookshelf Games edition was published in 1962, but have remained largely unchanged thereafter. The winner is the wealthiest player at the end. Wealth equals cash, plus the value of shares you hold in existing hotel chains, and cash bonuses for holding the most or second-most shares in existing chains.

Play consists of placing a tile on the grid board and then buying up to your limit of shares in existing hotel chains from the bank. The placing of a tile may occasionally create a new hotel chain (there are seven possible chains) or force a merger between existing chains.

Strategy is dictated by the tiles you have picked up randomly, and continue to pick each turn. Early on, you want to start new hotel chains — you get a free share for doing so — and buy shares to establish first- or second-place ownership positions in existing companies. Cash flow is critical; when you exhaust your starting cash you can't buy shares and defend your majority positions. As the game continues and the board fills up, your focus changes to establishing controlling positions in companies that are "safe" — that is, can no longer merge — and growing those companies to increase the value of their shares and bonuses at game's end.

Decisions you make have big consequences as the game unfolds. Do I buy shares in a company likely to grow or one likely to merge? Do I take my last money to bolster an existing holding or speculate in another? When to merge, how to spend the last little money you have, and whether to trade, sell, or retain shares (in hope of restarting the company) at the moment of merger are examples of the interesting decisions players face.

You must play a tile on your turn and every placement can have consequences. Sometimes there are no good choices. Sometimes you play to spoil someone else's plan, if you can't do something positive for your own position. If I add a tile to my chain, the shares I own increase in value (as does any bonus I qualify for), but my chain may become too big for me to merge.

Company mergers provide the most dramatic element of play. If another chain merges into mine, the majority owners of the disappearing company get cash bonuses immediately (providing them with cash to continue buying shares) and can trade their shares 2-for-1 for the shares of my company, assuming there are any shares left in the bank. I can suddenly lose control of the largest company on the board by such a trade and an immediate purchase by the player who played the tile.

The second sweetest move in the game is to merge a less expensive, $200-per-share chain (called Luxor or Tower) into a $400-per-share chain (Continental or Imperial), then trade a bunch of those cheap shares 2-for-1 for shares that are now worth a minimum of $700, and take control of a majority position. The single sweetest move is to be the sole share holder of a Continental or Imperial chain, merge it, and pocket both the first- and second-place bonus ($6,000, the same amount everyone starts the game with). Players who let you get away with that deserve to lose. I've seen it done with a single $400 share purchase.

Believe me, the tension mounts as players run out of cash, hotel chains creep closer to each other with each tile played, and everyone waits for the first merger to break open play again. The late purchase of a single share of stock can make a big difference when that isolated company finds itself acquired suddenly and you get the second-place bonus. If you don't get any bonus cash out of the first merger, the pressure increases to find a way to raise cash to keep up.

There are two variants of the basic game: The shares a player owns are held open for everyone to see or are held secret, like a poker hand. My groups always went for secrecy, while many people think the game in its "pure" form requires holdings to be played in the open. Because there are 25 shares for each company, the numbers 13 (guarantee of first place) and 8 (guarantee of at least a tie for second) became significant. Being able to keep track of what shares have been taken and who had controlling interest of the various chains can prove very useful, but isn't easy to do. I try to keep track of the holdings of the chains in which I have an interest, but that's my limit.

Acquire has been published by several companies over the years and occasionally goes out of print entirely, which is too bad. I understand that we are in the digital age, but part of the fun of *Acquire* is the social interaction, banter, and negotiating that accompanies play. I own a nice Avalon Hill version with plastic pieces; the most sought-after version by collectors is from 3M, with wooden pieces. The latest version, from Hasbro, changes the hotels to high-tech corporations and includes some suitably modern 3-D pieces. I know people who have filched tile stands from *Scrabble* to hold their tiles from older sets and added a cloth bag to hold the unplayed tiles. Other friends have played the game so much they've had to replace badly worn share certificates.

I consider *Acquire* the masterwork of Sid Sackson (1920 – 2002), one of the most prolific game designers of the 20th century. He designed uncounted games and wrote about them regularly in books and magazines. His apartment in New York was stuffed with shelves stacked to the ceiling with his legendary game collection. I met him once and he grilled me on other games that I played and why I liked them. I have played many, many excellent games over the years, but this is one of the very best. Thanks for *Acquire*, Sid.

In 1980, BRUCE SHELLEY joined friends from the University of Virginia game club to help start Iron Crown Enterprises (original publishers of the *Middle Earth Role Playing* series). Following a brief stint at Simulations

Publications, Inc. (commonly known as SPI), he spent nearly six years at Avalon Hill, where he designed several titles and developed such classics as *1830*, *Titan*, and *Britannia*. In 1988, he joined Microprose Software, where he managed and contributed to the design of many projects. He was Sid Meier's assistant designer on the original editions of *Railroad Tycoon* and *Civilization*. After working briefly as a freelance writer of game strategy guides, in 1995 he joined another old friend from the Virginia game club, Tony Goodman, who was starting Ensemble Studios (ES) to make computer games. At ES, Shelley helped establish the company's development process and create the Age of Empires series. He continues to serve on the studio management team and act as spokesman for the company and its games. He has been invited to speak about game design on five continents and served for six years on the board of directors of the Academy of Interactive Arts and Sciences.

Nicole Lindroos on

AMBER DICELESS

KEY DESIGNER: ERICK WUJCIK
PHAGE PRESS (1991)

WHEN I NOTICED *AMBER* Diceless Role-Playing back in 1991 it seemed on the surface an unlikely development. Author Erick Wujcik was best known for his work on Palladium Games' rules-intensive Megaversal System. Other game designs of the era focused on the problem of adjudicating player actions by attempting to cover all conceivable contingencies with comprehensive rules, almost always involving a wide variety of polyhedral dice. Attacking a monster in *Dungeons & Dragons*? Roll a 20-sided die. Are you using a sword or a dagger? Is the monster large or small? Those different circumstances require different dice to determine damage. *Warhammer Fantasy Roleplay* featured many charts that required the roll of percentile dice, but some that used 12-sided dice instead. It could take a whole handful of six-sided dice to determine a character's success in *Shadowrun*. Other roleplaying game designs that could be called "diceless" substituted other randomizing elements, such as playing cards, or determined outcomes through cross-referencing charts and tables. *Amber* proved to be different from all of these.

Amber Diceless Role-Playing brings the world of Roger Zelazny's classic fantasy novels, with their vivid settings and massively powerful, world-shaping characters, to the game table, affording players the chance to create their own stories of glory and intrigue. The setting of the Amber Chronicles is explicitly an infinite universe. Unlike other licensed properties of the time, which quite literally and purposely had a finite number of characters acting in a finite number of locations (all of which could be mapped, described, and defined in their entirety), the setting of Amber includes anything and everything its powerful, reality-shaping characters can conceive. The expansiveness of the novels' universe defies traditional notions of roleplaying game design and practically demands the radical departure that *Amber Diceless Role-Playing* eventually took.

Amber characters often don't know what they're capable of accomplishing until some crisis causes them to throw their force of will and the power of their blood against the problem. Surprising new powers can manifest suddenly, and a character may be just as amazed as everyone else to discover that she can control the weather or regenerate from deadly wounds. *Amber* could not realistically provide rules for everything a character might attempt, from fighting adeptly with a weapon she's never seen before to summoning an army of spiny, red-eyed demonic minions or reshaping the world by sabotaging the Primal Pattern that makes up the universe. So Wujcik did not try. The result was a charmed match between system and setting, and a game fully deserving of a place among the top hobby games.

The first phase of character creation in *Amber Diceless* reinforces the setting's aggressive politics and backbiting by starting the players off with an attribute auction. Characters have only four attributes. Every action a character may take will be helped or hindered by one of these scores, but the score itself is not what is at stake in the auction. The auction is ultimately about rank. Rank is the tie-breaker, the ever-so-slight edge that a character will hold over others in a contest. (First-ranked characters will win a head-to-head competition; you can't beat the master of warfare in a martial contest.) Players bid against each other from their pool of character creation points to secure the ranking they desire. Spend too many points to win that ranking in warfare and you're left with fewer points to flesh out the rest of your character. Cutthroat bidding wars during an auction often lay the groundwork for character rivalries, central to Zelazny's stories, before a single scene of action is played out.

In this way *Amber* diverges significantly from games that rely on dice or other randomizing elements. In a game where players roll dice to determine the outcome of their actions, the character-defining scores can sometimes be completely overshadowed by the results of a roll. With the right kind of lucky roll, a character whose stats define her as a puny weakling can land a killing blow with a dart. Conversely, a catastrophic failure on the dice can cause a trained duelist to not just botch a simple sword thrust, but somehow mortally wound herself in the process.

Amber characters are represented by attribute levels that are much more broadly defined, by the descriptions Human, Chaos, or Amber. The difference between these levels is so broad as to be similar to comparing a toddler at the baby gym to an Olympic athlete. Just as a toddler has no chance to best an Olympic athlete on the rings, so are characters in the game divided by their attribute ranks. This mechanic is a brilliant reinforcement of the novels' universe, where characters know precisely which brother is the unbeatable master of warfare or which sister cannot be bested in a contest of endurance. Armed with this knowledge, Zelazny's characters must rely on trickery, alliances, and strategy, and *Amber Diceless* applies its mechanics to reinforce the same style of gameplay. If your opponent in a wargame is a naval powerhouse, you'll do better to force her into a land battle; if your opponent in *Amber* is the strongest character ever known, you'll do better to shift the contest to one where endurance is the key to victory.

To encourage players to be creative in their approach to in-game politics, contests, and challenges, Wujcik's rules involve them in the metagame — how the players interact with the rules and the game itself — through the addition of Stuff. Characters with Good Stuff have a few extra points they haven't spent elsewhere and are naturally harmonious and lucky. Characters with Bad Stuff have gone into karmic debt for more points, so luck does not break their way. Good Stuff is earned not through a character's actions, but through a player's contributions outside of the story. Creating character diaries (logs of game events from a character's perspective), campaign logs (logs of game events from a neutral perspective), art, or fiction can gain Good Stuff. Even assisting the game master with chores such as making photocopies can help.

While many campaigns for other roleplaying games have benefited from enthusiastic individuals who contribute maps, art, or session write-ups, *Amber* encourages this style of play by rewarding it. The results can be a remarkable sense of community. An artist in one of my *Amber* campaigns drew beautiful portraits of each character for us to use as Trumps, the mechanism by which psychic contact between characters is possible. Another kept a character diary purposely seeded with falsehoods, in the hope that players and characters alike might be misled into believing versions of events that benefited him or worked to the detriment of his character's rivals. Some elements of his diaries long accepted as truths in the lore of our campaign were revealed as utter fabrications only after the campaign wrapped up.

Through the smartly written rulebook, Wujcik provides ample support and enthusiastic encouragement for this style of play. This not only removes the burden for building the game community from the game master's shoulder, but gives all *Amber* players the foundation of a skill set that not only apply to *Amber Diceless* in particular, but to roleplaying games nearly across the board.

Within this atmosphere of codified communal storytelling, *Amber* fans have developed a strong network. Phage Press published supplementary inspirational material in its *Amberzine*, and national and regional Ambercons have been held annually around the world since the game's initial publication in 1991. In this time of social networking sites, email lists, and online message boards, it's easy to take for granted the idea of a community developing around something of interest to a far-flung group of people. The appeal of *Amber Diceless Role-Playing* was so strong, its fans achieved this without the aid of today's ubiquitous technology.

Other diceless games and conversions have appeared in the years since *Amber*'s release. Designers have borrowed aspects of *Amber*'s system for dice-based and diceless systems alike, be it the idea of auctions, player contributions, or skill ranks. Yet each of these efforts has lacked the simplicity and natural cohesion of the game that originally brought diceless roleplaying to the consciousness of mainstream hobby enthusiasts.

Plans for a new edition of the game have been announced by Diceless by Design, which is great news. *Amber Diceless Role-Playing* remains unmatched and still sets the standard by which all other attempts at diceless roleplaying are judged.

NICOLE LINDROOS lives in Seattle, Washington, with her husband Chris and daughter Katherine, who share her passions for good food and fun games. Though she twice went as far as applying to culinary school, Nicole entered the game industry in 1989 and has applied her talents to bring board games, card games, roleplaying games, periodicals, and support products of various sorts to market ever since. She's helped found three companies (two of them successful!), worked on two magazines, written numerous articles, and contributed everything from editorial assistance to graphic design for companies including Atlas Games, White Wolf, FASA, Wizards of the Coast, and Green Ronin Publishing. She has volunteered on the board of directors of the Game Manufacturer's Association, the Origins Awards committee, and as the chairman of the Academy of Adventure Gaming Arts and Design. Nicole still clings stubbornly to the belief that an individual can make a difference.

Ian Livingstone on

AMUN-RE

KEY DESIGNER: REINER KNIZIA

RIO GRANDE GAMES (ENGLISH EDITION, 2003)

FOR OVER TWO DECADES, I have served as secretary of the Games Night Club that has a fixed membership of just six. They are Steve Jackson (U.K.), Peter Molyneux, Clive Robert, Skye Quin, Mark Spangenthal, and me. Incidents, observations, comments, letters, and the league table are all dutifully recorded in the not-to-be-taken-seriously newsletter written by the secretary. Points are scored for games played, and the Pagoda Cup (named after the road where the club was founded) is kept by the champion for a year. Double points are scored for those games defined as a "game of substance." These are proper games and have to earn their status at Games Night.

A game of substance has to be easy to learn but hard to master and hard to win. It must have significant replay value, have an innovative or compelling mechanism, and present the players with lots of choice, decisions, and tactical options. It should be absorbing, with never a dull moment, and take around two hours to play, with lots of player interaction and negotiation. Finally the game must be balanced to allow those who got off to a slow start the chance to win. One such game of substance is *Amun-Re*.

The good news is that *Amun-Re* is a classic when played by five players. The bad news is that our group is usually six, so we don't play it as often as we would like. For us it is rather annoying that games designed for six players seem to be a thing of the past these days, and I'm not sure why that is. Do publishers think that it is impossible for six people to get together to play games in the frantic world in which we live? Or do designers think games are best played by four or five players? Who knows, but I digress.

In my opinion, Reiner Knizia is the best game designer in modern times. In fact he is probably the best ever. As well as *Amun-Re*, he has designed such classics as *Tigris & Euphrates, Taj Mahal, Lost Cities, Through the Desert, Ra,* and *Tutenkhamun.* For future reference, you may conclude that if a game he created has a camel, river, or a desert in it, then it's likely to be brilliant! He is certainly the most prolific designer ever and has probably won more awards than anybody else. He has had more than 400 games and books published in numerous languages and countries. The awards he's won include the German Game Prize in 1993, 1998, 2000, and 2003; the Austrian Game Prize in 2003, 2004, and 2006; the Spanish Game Award in 2006; the Swiss Game Prize in 2004; the French Grand Prix du Jouet in 2000, 2003, and 2004; the Dutch Toy of the Year Award in 2001; Japan's Board Game Prize in 2004 and 2005; the International Gamers Award in 2000 and 2003; five Children's Game of the Year Awards; and more. Impressive stuff.

Reiner is a mathematician and it shows. His designs are both elegant and clever. He always comes up with innovative mechanics and then wraps a suitable theme around them. *Amun-Re* was released in 2003, originally by German publisher Hans im Glück, and came with the usual high production values many have come to associate with the company. It is a wonderfully entertaining game of strategy that thrives on its superb bidding system. It's not particularly complex, but it's hardly an end-of-the-evening filler game, either.

Amun-Re is set in ancient Egypt and players act as competing pharaohs vying for control of the Nile valley. This is done by bidding for land, employing farmers to gain income, and building pyramids for victory. There are lots of good things to say about the mechanics, of which there are several, each affecting the game in different ways as play unfurls, with several twists, through its various stages.

The board is divided into 15 provinces and split in two by the Nile. Players seek to gain control of the provinces by bidding for them, but each location has different attributes. Some produce lots of farmers or building stones for use in constructing pyramids. Others allow the purchase of power cards or contain valuable temples. Each province is different and is therefore worth a different amount to each player, depending on needs and strategy. It's important for each player to secure the province that adds real value to his kingdom, and that is why the game's bidding system is so effective.

The number of provinces available is equal to the number of players, and they can only buy one each. Players take it in turn to bid on a province and must decide, according to their available resources, whether or not to make a large, preemptive bid for their first choice; if they are subsequently outbid, they next have to bid on a different province. If they wait long enough, they might get a province for free, but it might not be of much use to them. (In *Amun-Re*, it's usually a case of "you get what you pay for. . . .") It's a simple yet great system, one that makes the game exciting and competitive right from the start.

Once the bidding is over, the pharaohs improve their provinces. This is done by spending gold on farmers, stones to build pyramids, and so on. But therein lies another clever design twist, as the cost of each resource rises rather than falls when more of each are bought. Then comes the fun of each pharaoh simultaneously and secretly offering gold to the sun god, Amun-Re, to gain favors, with the highest reward going to the ruler who made the biggest sacrifice. If the collective sum offered is high, Amun-Re will be happy and the reward will be a bumper harvest. If it is low, times will be tough for a while. Finally, income is received by each player according to his province's yield after the sacrifice to the sun god.

This bid-buy-develop-sacrifice-yield turn sequence is repeated twice, by which time all the provinces will be owned. Then civilization falls apart and everything is wiped from the board (apart from any pyramids constructed) before a new kingdom begins. Three more turns are played in the same way as before, but obviously with different incentives because of the pyramids already in place. After that comes the big tally of points, and a winner is declared.

For me, *Amun-Re* achieves about the perfect levels of complexity and fun. It has fantastic mechanics — the bidding and sacrifice phases, and the old and new kingdom dynamic — that keep players interested at all times. The theme, too, is built brilliantly into the mechanics in a believable and logical way. You really get the sense that the game simulates life in ancient Egypt by entertaining gameplay relating to the relationship between harvests, farmers, construction, and the Nile. The game encourages great player interaction, and features many tough decisions to make and multiple ways to win (although I'm still not sure if there is a single "correct" way). It also has great replay value; no two games are ever the same.

Over the years I've learned to treat *Amun-Re* well and he is now my friend. He looks after me, rewards me with gifts, and thoroughly deserves a place in my top ten of favorite games.

IAN LIVINGSTONE is creative director at Eidos, the U.K.'s largest publisher of video games, where he secured many of the company's major franchises, including *Tomb Raider* and *Hitman*. In 1975 he founded Games

Workshop, Ltd. with Steve Jackson, and launched *Dungeons & Dragons* in Europe and the Games Workshop retail chain. Ian launched *White Dwarf* in 1977 and served as the magazine's editor for five years. In 1982, again with Steve Jackson, he wrote *The Warlock of Firetop Mountain*, the first release in the Fighting Fantasy series of interactive gamebooks. He subsequently wrote *Deathtrap Dungeon* and many other popular volumes in the series. Ian has also invented several board games, including *Boom Town*, *Judge Dredd*, *Automania*, *Legend of Zagor*, and *Dragonmasters*. His awards include an Honorary Doctorate of Technology; a BAFTA Special Award; and an OBE, which he received in the 2006 New Year's Honours List for his contribution to the computer games industry.

Stewart Wieck on

ARS MAGICA

KEY DESIGNERS: JONATHAN TWEET, MARK REIN•HAGEN

LION RAMPANT (FIRST EDITION, 1987)

RETROSPECT FINDS *ARS MAGICA* at the epicenter of the web of roleplaying games for the past 20 years, which is where one of the most innovative and lauded roleplaying games ever created belongs.

Consider the game's publishing history. Originally created in 1987 by a pair of intellectually ambitious designers for their own small, upper-Midwest game company, Lion Rampant, *Ars Magica* made the rounds of the game industry before returning to its roots. Lion Rampant produced two editions, but a third and much-expanded edition of the game was published by White Wolf, Inc. In its time with White Wolf, *Ars Magica* gained access to a wider audience because the company itself was experiencing a great deal of success. As the hobby game industry continued to see a level of growth unknown since the original heyday of *Dungeons & Dragons*, *Ars Magica* seemed poised to take the next step with the new industry behemoth, Wizards of the Coast. Wizards published some supplements for *Ars Magica* but never published a fourth edition. That edition saw *Ars Magica* return to the upper Midwest, this time in the hands of an equally intellectually ambitious game designer, John Nephew (who, coincidentally, had written material for *D&D* since his high school years). Nephew's small company, Atlas Games, also published the fifth edition in 2004. Since Nephew had also been part of the early Lion Rampant crew, it could be said that *Ars Magica* truly had returned to its roots.

Or consider the creators of the game. Mark Rein•Hagen and Jonathan Tweet parted ways after the game's initial publication, with Hagen retaining ownership of Lion Rampant. Shortly after moving the company to Atlanta, Hagen helped form White Wolf, Inc., where he would co-create *Vampire: The Masquerade* and the World of Darkness. Tweet also remained within the hobby game industry's orbit and would, a decade later, be one of the co-designers of the overhauled third edition of *Dungeons & Dragons* at Wizards of the Coast. So the innovative approach both authors took in their early work on *Ars Magica* remains on display throughout their later work, with the two top roleplaying publishers and the industry's top game lines.

Most important, consider the game itself. With an allegiance to its historical setting and a dedication to characters balanced between realism and romance, *Ars Magica* (Latin for "the art of magic") takes for its premise that magic is real in 13th-century Europe and is practiced and studied by magi ("wizards") with monastic dedication and alchemical rigor in bastions of enlightenment called covenants. These covenants exist outside the mundane spheres of political and religious influence.

The hallmark of the game's mechanics is the magic system, but *Ars Magica*'s innovations go beyond that. Of particular note is its emphasis on troupe-style roleplaying, which is most strongly presented in the game's early editions.

The typical roleplaying game relies on a game master, the player who creates the adventures and generally acts as narrator for the ongoing events for all the other players. In *Ars Magica*'s troupe-style play, the role of the game master — here called a storyguide — is shared in turn by all the players. This format serves to heighten *Ars Magica*'s already strong emphasis on storytelling. With a variety of narrators working together, just as their characters "on the other side of the screen" cooperate, a palpable environment of communal storytelling results.

The wide range of options and stories that this troupe-style creates is not limited to just the storyguides. Each player creates three characters: a magus, a companion, and a grog. The magi are the game's focus. These workers of magic are like monastic elders within the covenant. Their ambitions and scholarship form the heart of everything that unfolds. But each player also creates a companion — a warrior, diplomat, scholar, or virtually any other role that tends to interact more with the outside world than the introverted magi. Finally, each player creates a grog (or even several grogs). These are the convenant's servants — the cooks, footsoldiers, messengers, and other, more mundane workers.

Interestingly, the grog characters are shared among all the players, so in a game one night, I might end up playing the grog you created, a minor scribner. That same night, you could be playing your magus, while another friend takes on the role of storyguide. When there's a break or end to his story, I could take over as the next storyguide, while you play your companion character and our friend plays his magus, who comes back into the narrative after finishing a three-month-long research project in his laboratory.

The presence of these humble and eccentric characters marks *Ars Magica* as very different from the typical fantasy roleplaying game. Virtually all other RPGs encourage the creation of the deadliest warrior or mightiest wizard, and it's difficult to fault a player for pursuing that ultimate hero in a game where you have a single character who must survive against long odds and dangerous enemies. Still, the result is often character retreads where all the warriors are fierce barbarians or shining knights. Troupe-style play creates a much more democratic environment, where the characters reasonably reflect the setting's entire population instead of just the elite. It's easy to imagine the dynamic, story-rich environment that can result when a group of creative players begin to cooperate in such myriad ways.

Ultimately, a game called "The Art of Magic" will be a dud if the mechanics for the magic system don't live up to the promise of the game's setting and conceits. Fortunately, *Ars Magica* offered the most exciting magic system available at the time of its release, and one that remains among the most interesting to this day.

Dungeons & Dragons, and virtually every other fantasy game to that time (and even most today), utilized a tactical miniatures-based approach to magic, where a spell's specific range and effects are outlined in rather rigid detail. *Ars Magica*, on the other hand, offered a flexible system that allowed magus characters to cast spells spontaneously, to tailor an enchantment to perfectly suit the story's circumstances. Players with characters who had suffered the cavern-filling explosion of a classic *D&D* fireball, with effects determined by the rule set rather than the wizard, quickly came to appreciate the ability to craft a spell's details.

Sometimes referred to as a verb-noun system, the *Ars Magica* magic system is divided into fifteen different aspects of five verbs and ten nouns. A magus has ratings in each of these fifteen categories and, by combining his ratings in a verb and a noun, the magus can determine what kind of effect he may create. Like the title of the game, these verbs and nouns are used in-game in Latin. All part of that cloak of verisimilitude.

The verbs: *creo* (create), *intélligo* (perceive), *muto* (transform), *perdo* (destroy), and *rego* (control). The nouns: *animál* (animal), *aquam* (water), *auram* (air), *corpus* ([human] body), *herbam* (plant), *ignem* (fire), *imáginem* (image/illusions), *mentem* (mind), *terram* (earth), and *vim* (power).

Through scholarship and laborious study, the magi of *Ars Magica* created a number of formulaic spells (like those in *D&D*, with set effects). To cast these a character requires ratings in these magic arts. But a magus need not depend on those spells alone. He may create whatever effect he desires, within the limits of his knowledge of the arts — be that create fire, control an animal, or even a combination effect, like transform flesh to stone. Unlike that *D&D* fireball, which can be so dangerous to its own creator, an *Ars Magica* fireball can be sized appropriately. In fact, a skilled enough magus might even create fire that burns the forest (*herbam*), which has come alive to threaten him, while sparing himself and his comrades (*corpus*).

It's an intuitive system that, importantly, makes magic part of the story itself, rather than simply an accoutrement.

Ars Magica stands among the best roleplaying games because it takes itself and the rich traditions of storytelling seriously. The game has its detractors, who suggest it takes itself *too* seriously, but to hold that view is to purposefully ignore the game's innovations and its central conceit that, like storytelling of old, the narrative process within a roleplaying game should be collaborative. Truly, which game takes itself too seriously — the one where you might play a one-armed grog in the service of a magus so absentminded he's forgotten the secret ingredient he's now scouring the forest to locate, or all those others, where your character, Dirk Nightcleaver, is a master ninja-wizard seeking the Ultimate Artifact of Power, just like every other master ninja-wizard in the world?

A game designer and author for over 20 years, STEWART WIECK's career in roleplaying games began as a freelance writer, but his accomplishments are primarily associated with the company he co-founded in 1986, White Wolf Publishing, later White Wolf, Inc. Stewart co-created the World of Darkness and devised much of the mythology that's central to *Vampire: The Masquerade* (1991), but his most personal game design was *Mage: The Ascension* (1993). An author of four novels and a number of short stories, Stewart continues to design games, most recently *Long Live the King* (2006).

Thomas M. Reid on

AXIS & ALLIES

KEY DESIGNER: LARRY HARRIS
MILTON BRADLEY (SECOND EDITION, 1984)

AXIS & ALLIES, **PERHAPS** the best-known World War II board game ever to grace store shelves, is a wonderful addition to any game library. The true beauty of this classic lies in its role as a bridge between the casual game player and the dedicated wargamer. Though not a strategic combat simulation in the truest sense, *Axis & Allies* introduces all the fundamental elements of the wargame mindset in a high-production-value board game with an easy-to-learn set of rules and genuine replay value.

Larry Harris and others first wrote and developed *Axis & Allies* for a company called Nova Game Design, who initially produced it with all-paper components. Milton Bradley eventually acquired the rights to the title from Nova, intent on publishing it as part of their Gamemaster series of strategic games. They made a few minor modifications to the rules and upgraded all the components, which included a three-panel game board with a full-color map broken up into color-coded land or sea zones and showing national capitals. The game also featured a multitude of color-coded plastic military units, two sets of six-sided dice, cardboard territory control markers, abstract paper money in various denominations, a couple of reference charts, and a 32-page rulebook. The 1984 edition became the bestselling title in the Gamemaster series and the version of the game most widely recognized today.

Axis & Allies offers the casual board-game fan a glimpse into the world of true war simulations without overwhelming him. The object of the game is to conquer enemy territory while protecting the home front and trying to manage a military budget at the same time. Two to five people can play, each assuming the role of military leaders for one or more of the five principal participants in World War II. Players must develop attack and defense strategies based on the terrain they hold, their offensive objectives and defensive liabilities, and the limited resources at their disposal each turn. Victory comes down to an individual commander's ability to take and hold enemy territory, factories, and ultimately, capitals.

Much like chess, the game is simple to learn but a fun challenge to master. With a little tutoring from a more experienced player, a novice can get the gist of the rules in a matter of a few minutes. He can even work through the example-laden rulebook himself and be ready to play in less than an hour. Most of the time, a complete game can be finished in a matter of two to three hours, rather than the days or weeks that more traditional wargames require.

Furthermore, many of the esoteric and intimidating conventions of traditional wargames are absent from *Axis & Allies*. Odd-looking cardboard squares covered with confusing data, often referred to as "chits" or "units" in wargaming parlance, are dismissed in favor of nice, high-quality plastic figures with plenty of visual and tactile appeal, also known in the industry as "toy value." They really do look like miniature WWII-era troops and artillery marching across the world, just like the old black-and-white footage of the war everyone grew up with. There are no complicated charts to reference, no need to fret over obscure terms like "depleted units," "zones of control," or "lines of sight" that are found in most true wargames. Attacking and defending is as simple as rolling a few six-sided dice, counting the number of appropriately low results, and removing plastic figures from the map board. That lack of complexity lessens the intimidation factor that many would-be wargame enthusiasts feel when confronting more realistic wargames.

Even in its simplicity, though, *Axis & Allies* introduces enough basic concepts of war simulations to expose a newcomer to the broader hobby. People who enjoy Parker Brothers' *Risk* board game might recognize the basic premise of conquering territories, but *Axis & Allies* offers much more in the way of military strategy. For example, players learn the value of combined-arms tactics. Every unit has strengths and weaknesses in some combination of offensive firepower, defensive strength, and/or cost. Infantry is a mainstay on land for holding onto the territory already in one's possession, but tanks and fighters are paramount to taking ground. On the seas, transports, carriers, and their fighters need to be protected at all costs, but losing a battleship in the process is always a tough pill to swallow. Reinforcements must be purchased before a turn starts, but not placed on the board until the end of it, so astute planning has to go into how much a potential new territory should "cost" in armaments. In addition to those tactical considerations, some thought must be devoted to spending for additional strategic resources. Perhaps investing in bombers to strike at opponents' industrial centers and cripple their manufacturing capabilities is the way to go, or maybe spending precious currency on researching newer, more powerful weapons is the better choice. How those decisions are made can have a profound effect upon a game.

Hardcore wargamers should also find much to enjoy in *Axis & Allies*, even though some of the game will feel inaccurate to a military history scholar. For example, the rules state that the game begins in the spring of 1942, but the initial set-up places Japan in a position to strike at Hawaii once again and Germany is deep into Soviet territory with a significant force, neither of which is historically accurate. Clearly, balance of play is a consideration here, but for some, the discrepancies are irritating. Also, during combat, there is a tendency for players to first expend the cheapest units — such as infantry — regardless of tactical appropriateness. Furthermore, play is most balanced when each participant works individually, attempting to claim the most territory without teaming up with other historical allies — the United States with Great Britain, for example. In practice, however, partnered players often assist one another, which may offer a more historically appropriate feel to the game, but which tips the balance of play noticeably in favor of the Allies.

Despite these minor shortcomings, seasoned players come back to *Axis & Allies* again and again. Enthusiasts have spent countless hours over the years debating the finer tactical points of effective play. Every game is different, so a true strategist can spend a lifetime testing different theories. Numerous *Axis & Allies* clubs and online communities exist, populated by lifelong fans who play and discuss the game regularly.

Without a doubt, *Axis & Allies* stands as one of the best means of introducing new players to the larger world of war-simulation gaming. Many longtime wargame buffs got their start in the hobby through this classic, and many more have used it as a gateway through which they shepherd others into the fold. But *Axis & Allies* is also loads of fun in its own right. Like *Monopoly*, it is a game that families and friends can — and do — pull off the shelf again and again.

THOMAS M. REID has been an award-winning roleplaying game designer and editor in the hobby industry for over 15 years. He is the author of more than a dozen short stories and novels, including *Insurrection*, the second title in the *New York Times* bestselling War of the Spider Queen series. He currently lives on a quarter-acre cat ranch in the Texas Hill Country with his wife and three boys. In his spare time, Thomas enjoys playing hobby games with his kids and traveling to wargaming conventions with his friends. You can learn more about Thomas's work at www.thomasmreid.com.

BATTLE CRY

KEY DESIGNER: RICHARD BORG

AVALON HILL (2000)

IF YOU TOOK MY father and separated him into different halves, you would have my brother and me. Gerry is an attorney; I am a fantasy novelist and game designer. My brother is a Civil War buff; I was vaguely aware of there being some trouble between the North and the South back in the 1800s, something about Lincoln and a speech I had to memorize in junior high and slavery, and that the North won. Gerry could recount every battle of the war and all of its implications. I could tell you about *Gone With the Wind*. On the other hand, I could master a complex set of simulation game rules handily and run a 600-page RPG rules set without breaking a sweat; Gerry's eyes would glaze over at the mere thought of a 20-sided die, and the idea of playing through the entirety of World War II by pushing around cardboard squares with numbers on them sounded, to him, like a torture to rival Andersonville. Though both of us were raised on *Monopoly* and *Life* as regular family events, card games at all reunions, and even a rather embarrassing afternoon of *Mystery Date* with my cousin Tammy — so far as games were concerned, we couldn't be further apart.

One game — the game I admire most — brought my brother and me together. *Battle Cry* calls itself "the Exciting Civil War Battlefield Game," but it defies neat categorization. It could be considered a simulation game, although the technical detail of its rules set is so simple that the simulation is very broad. It is perhaps more of a miniatures game, since the game pieces are represented by legions of Civil War infantry, artillery, and cavalry and the terrain is laid out on a hexagonal grid. But its rules set is so straightforward, elegantly simple, and intuitive in its resolution as to almost qualify it as a family board game. Educational without being pedantic, this is the game that fired my interest in the War Between the States. Detailed while at the same time elegantly straightforward in design, *Battle Cry* also achieved the seemingly impossible: It proved enjoyable for both my brother and me.

The game was designed by Richard Borg. Whether he is a genius or savant I leave up to you, but either way his design is an inspiration. The game is built around his Command and Colors System, a root game mechanic that handles all the complexities of the usual simulation or wargame charts and tables with a set of specialized dice, the number of figures in each unit, and a deck of cards. Any simulation complexities are submerged in this deceptively elegant arrangement. If there is one game designer that I admire, it's Richard Borg.

You set up a game of *Battle Cry* according to one of several historical scenarios. By placing geomorphic tiles representing trees, buildings, hills, rivers, rail fences, or cornfields on the blank battlefield, you recreate the setting for Antietam, Sharpsburg, or a host of other battles. Then you get to play with the amazing number of plastic figures, each unit of infantry represented by four soldiers, each artillery unit by two cannons, and each mounted cavalry unit by three horses. Arrayed on the board they are an impressive sight, particularly after such an easy set-up. Shuffle the cards and distribute them between the players according to the scenario you've chosen, and it's time to begin.

Here is where the game becomes truly great. You play a card; choose which units will move and/or fight, according to what the card says; and roll the number of dice indicated by the unit attacking, minus one die for every hex of distance to your target. Take one miniature figure away from the unit for every die rolled that shows the target unit's symbol. If the last figure is eliminated, give it to the attacking player. As soon as one player has eliminated six of his opponent's units, he wins. If no one has won yet, take another card. Play passes to the other player.

It's amazing to me that, in the above paragraph, I've taught you just about all you need to know to play *Battle Cry*. The genius in this design is that you can teach anyone to play in less than five minutes and be up and fighting it in less than 10. One of the biggest problems facing game players is finding someone willing to play with them. Who, except the most hardcore game enthusiast, wants to sit down and read a 64-page manual printed in nine-point type, with rules, charts, tables, and a turn sequence that is 36 phases long? One of the underappreciated strengths of *Battle Cry* is that its streamlined design means it can be enjoyed by both veteran game enthusiasts and casual board game players with equal felicity.

Borg's Command and Colors System has been used successfully for other games, too. In 2004, Days of Wonder produced *Memoir '44*, a World War II game that I enjoy tremendously. 2006 brought both GMT's *Command and Colors: Ancients* and Days of Wonder's *BattleLore*. The former depicts historical warfare from 3000 B.C. to the opening of the Middle Ages, while the latter is a very well-reviewed fantasy battle game. Each of these incarnations has introduced welcome refinements to the system.

For me, however, it is my experience with my brother that places *Battle Cry* at the top of my list. It is this aspect of the game that I appreciate the most — its remarkable ability to connect hobby gamers with "the rest of the world." *Battle Cry* brings people together, teaches us something true, and does so with grace and elegance. That, for me, is the very definition of the perfect game.

It was in 1981 — between jobs and looking for money to buy shoes for his children — that TRACY HICKMAN approached TSR, Inc. about buying two of his game modules he had written with his wife . . . and ended up with a job instead. That job lead to his association with Margaret Weis and their first publication together, the Dragonlance Chronicles, in 1985. Since that time, they have jointly authored over 40 books. Tracy's first two solo novels, *Requiem of Stars* and *The Immortals* were published in the spring of 1996. More recently, he and his wife Laura have fulfilled a longtime dream by once again writing together. Their first joint novel, *Mystic Warrior*, was published in 2004 and they look forward to a long and exciting career together. Tracy remains highly active in his church and pursues a number of hobbies. He currently resides in St. George, Utah.

Philip Reed on

BATTLETECH

KEY DESIGNERS: JORDAN WEISMAN, L.R. "BUTCH" LEEPER,
FOREST G. BROWN, WM. JOHN WHEELER, L. ROSS BABCOCK III

FASA CORPORATION (SECOND EDITION, 1985)

TODAY, *BATTLETECH* IS A large, grandiose game world defined by roleplaying games, computer games, a collectible card game, a collectible miniatures game, toys, a short-lived animated series, a massive selection of novels, and, of course, the tabletop game that was my original introduction to the chaos of warfare of the 30th century. Billed as "A Game of Armored Combat" on the second edition box cover — my first and favorite edition of the game — *BattleTech* takes place in a feudalistic, dark future in which giant robotlike vehicles dominate the battlefields.

Giant robots fighting? How could I not fall in love with this game?

My first encounter with the *BattleTech* universe took place in early 1987, during my freshman year in high school. You see, our custom on the weekends was for several of us to get together for all-night gaming — camped out in a friend's backyard in a makeshift tent city, within which we played game after game, ate far too many snacks, and drank more carbonated beverages than is recommended for any living thing to consume. A fairly typical gathering of friends.

It was at one such get-together that a friend of a friend, I wish I could remember his name today, pulled out a couple of boxes and started laying out colorful map sheets. Seeing as how my previous experience with map sheets were with the simple, black-and-white road sections from *Car Wars* — a game that we played too much of, at the time — my attention was captured immediately upon viewing these heavy, full-color sheets. In looking back on them today, they're really not all that colorful, but at the time it was an astounding sight to my rather inexperienced gamer eyes.

As he set up the map sheets, we started flipping through the rulebooks. My eyes got wider still as I stared at the sharp artwork, found the section on critical hits, *and* — best of all — located the section on designing 'Mechs. In flipping through the rules today and comparing them to similar material in newer games,

I find these 'Mech design rules still hold up as a masterful display of minimalism; they require only four pages and a single page of tables.

That night I was handed the counter and record sheet for a Shadow Hawk — a 55-ton BattleMech — and started a love of *BattleTech* that has continued to this day. The game was everything I loved about *Car Wars* and more. After all, we're talking giant robots here, people! Taking control of the Shadow Hawk, I marched across the battered landscape depicted on the map sheet, going head-to-head with a pair of Locusts and narrowly avoiding death.

It was in that first session that I learned all about heat, a system by which the game's designers — I realize only today, after my own experience as a designer — maintain its balance. Heavy, powerful weapons generate heat, and if a battle 'Mech's heat level grows too high, bad, bad things begin to happen. The concept of heat in *BattleTech* is so important that even today, when playing *MechAssault* on my Xbox, the 'Mech's heat level is something I have to keep an eye on.

So why is the second edition of *BattleTech* my favorite? Primarily, I suppose, a mix of nostalgia — a dangerous reason — and respect for the fact that it's a relatively uncluttered, easy-to-play tabletop combat game. The array of potential *BattleTech* material available for player use is daunting, but by sticking with the second edition, *CityTech* (a boxed supplement that introduces city fighting and new 'Mechs), and a couple of other small supplements, the game is easily manageable and loaded with options. For those of you who, like me, enjoy games that you can dive into and start playing quickly, a set-up like the original *BattleTech* is far superior to a thick, meaty tome of rules options. There's something liberating about a smaller rulebook, and it definitely cuts down on rules arguments.

So what's a game of *BattleTech* like? Fast, brutal, and loaded with tons of smack talk and dice rolling, which makes it like a lot of games I find myself playing these days. Though the 'Mech design rules were one of the first things to draw me to the game, today I find that selecting from the predesigned 'Mechs — there are 14 different designs in the original game — greatly speeds play. For the most basic game described in the rules, each player selects a 'Mech of comparable sizes and then start fighting. The system is simple, using a series of phases for movement and combat. The winner is the player with last functioning 'Mech.

MOVEMENT: 'Mechs turn and move across the hex-gridded map by expending movement points. Heat, as described earlier, builds up when the 'Mechs move and can start to slow the machine down. (The first time a *BattleTech* player finds that he can't move his 'Mech due to heat damage, he learns to pay close attention to his heat level.) Some 'Mechs can also jump, which builds up heat faster but can be a hell of a lot of fun as you leap over — or on top of! — an opponent. Death From Above, a maneuver in which a 'Mech jumps onto another 'Mech, is a favorite among all the *BattleTech* players I've gamed with.

COMBAT: Once the 'Mechs on the board have moved, they open fire with their lasers, missiles, and machine guns. All the weapons in the game — nine different types in the second-edition boxed set — have various range limitations and base to-hit numbers. Establishing the range between a 'Mech and its unfortunate target is a simple matter of counting hex grids (that's part of the reason I prefer miniatures games with maps to games that require rulers), but the act of firing those weapons builds heat. (There's that dreaded heat again.) Damage is resolved by determining on a table which part of the targeted 'Mech was hit, and then the weapon's damage is subtracted from the armor in that location. Shots can blow off a 'Mech's limbs or rip holes in heads. Really lucky shots can nail the 'Mech's engine. What's really fun is that combat, after your first few times playing the game, runs as quickly as movement.

MOVEMENT AND COMBAT REPEAT until one 'Mech stands victorious. In my experience, a battle between two 'Mechs can be over in as short a time as 15 minutes. More complex fights — those involving dozens of 'Mechs on the table — can take hours to play. When starting a game, just decide how much time you have to play and set up your own battle conditions accordingly.

So the next time you're looking for a new game, and you have an interest in giant robots or just ridiculously enjoyable combat games, give *BattleTech* a try. The newest editions — a collectible miniatures game published by WizKids and *Classic BattleTech*, from Catalyst Game Labs — are easily found in most hobby stores. You may also want to seek out a copy of the second edition *BattleTech* rules, if you want to try my favorite version of the game. Copies appear frequently on eBay and typically go for $10 or less; which is a very low price to pay for a game that can provide two decades of fun.

PHILIP REED has been working professionally in the roleplaying game industry since 1995. In that time, he has worked for such companies as West End Games, Privateer Press, and Atlas Games. Today, Philip spends his days with Steve Jackson Games and his nights running Ronin Arts. To learn more about Philip Reed — and Ronin Arts — please visit www.philipjreed.com and www.roninarts.com.

Justin Achilli on

BLOOD BOWL

KEY DESIGNER: JERVIS JOHNSON
GAMES WORKSHOP (THIRD EDITION, 1994)

I'M GIVEN TO UNDERSTAND that the field of overlap between hobby game nerds (like me) who are sports nerds (like me) is a fairly small cross-section of either community. Specifically, I'm a football nerd — and when I say "football," I mean American football, with all of its arena-chanting glory, its broken limbs, and its larger-than-life on-field personalities.

I've broken up with girlfriends because they didn't like football. Moreover, I've broken up with girlfriends because they liked the wrong football team. Honestly, who can even consider the idea of kissing a Ravens fan? No one sensible.

Consider my thrill, then, to discover that someone had designed a game just for me. Okay, not just me, thereby disproving the theory that mutual sports and hobby game nerds are a hopeless minority. To the point, though, I discovered *Blood Bowl*.

Blood Bowl is a jovial hybrid: a decidedly English spoof of American football that commingles the cartoonish violence often ascribed to the sport with the signature flair of the *Warhammer* setting. It's an interesting amalgam of miniatures army building and board game objectives. *Blood Bowl* has all the tactical trappings of a wargame, adding to it the meta-goal of scoring in-game points. Elude the other fiends on the field to enter the end zone with the (spiked) ball in your possession to score one of those points.

Blood Bowl doesn't attempt to be taken seriously, but instead throws a pair of competitors into a head-to-head gridiron brawl with their choice of athletic styles. Indeed, it isn't even necessary to score to win. If your team manages to disembowel enough players on the opposing side, the opposing side will have no choice but to forfeit. The game doesn't distinguish formally between offense and defense, with such niceties as turns of possession. Rather, the ball bounces randomly onto the field and whichever player-figure has enough movement allowance on his turn to reach the ball and make the dice roll to pick it up is ostensibly on offense. That is, at least until the other side can pummel the poor slob holding the ball and take it away.

Most importantly, *Blood Bowl* is a joy to play. Fantasy races add their own distinct flavor to the game, in a twist on the familiar *Warhammer* idiom, making it a darkly humorous epic struggle between civilized cultures and marauding monsters. The humans are average in all their game stats. Orcs lack finesse but excel at brute strength. The mutated fiends devoted to Chaos often aren't so good with the scoring but are excellent at reducing other teams to quivering goo. The undead may revive fallen players. Elves dance elusively around tackles. Dwarfs plow relentlessly up the field.

The game also distills the positions of American football, which can sometimes seem arcane to the casual watcher, into easy archetypes that convey the sport (and the lampoon thereof) with panache. Throwers throw, much like quarterbacks. Catchers function like wide receivers, skillful but fragile. Linemen either try to punch holes through a gaggle of defenders so the figure with the ball can run for the end zone (in an offensive role), or put the hurt on anyone with the bad fortune to stand near them (in a defensive role). Blitzers are somewhat like running backs, but more like roving thugs.

Customizability also plays a large part in *Blood Bowl*'s success. Each coach can use one of the prefab teams that came with the set or may, in grand Games Workshop tradition, buy his own unique team. Customization allows coaches to refine their rosters, adding players to key positions in order to allow for distinct styles of point scoring. The whole thing balances with the notion of a salary cap, whereby specialty players cost more than stock grunts, as any player of point-build army miniatures games will recognize.

Where the game truly goes above and beyond is in its implementation of league rules and seasonal play, available in the *Death Zone* supplement. Whereas one game is an amusing pastime, a league season is the stuff of legend, easily as exciting as a convention tournament but stretched out over a number of days or weeks. League and season rules accommodate "star players," who gain experience on the field and additional abilities, and "underdogs," so a less experienced team isn't necessarily broken into bloody giblets the moment they take the field against a superior opponent. *Death Zone* also offers special play cards, reflecting magical items, in-game cheating, and other rules-bending bits of freakishness that make the *Blood Bowl* world so entertaining. For example, the right card played at the right time could make a character's wound suffered on the field fatal, or a scroll of fumble-fingeredness might find a sure-handed player dropping the ball at a crucial moment.

The whole beautiful mess comes together most advantageously in large leagues, where the inclinations of each team blend with the . . . um . . . personality traits (ahem) of the individual coaches. The notorious Wolf Blight League, played at the White Wolf offices, featured a team of entirely naked human females, a pack of subliterate rat-men, high elves with all the social grace of a nosebleed, traditionally blood-soaked Chaos mutants, wood elf skinhead hippies (seriously), artistically deviant Chaos dwarfs, orcs who self-immolated, quasi-Canadian humans who didn't quite understand what was going on, Proustian undead, and a gang of mutants who were . . . er, never mind. Just be glad you weren't in their locker room at "goat time."

If the game has a flaw, it's the common one that reductivism yields whenever Games Workshop arises as the subject of conversation. That is, it all boils down to who rolls the most sixes and the fewest ones. All of the pretty, painted miniatures and high-concept tactics are only set dressing to the toss of a pair of dice.

To hell with reductivism, though. *Blood Bowl* is a ridiculous amount of fun that revels in its own absurdity with infectious abandon. It's the sort of stupid fun that's built on a legitimate principle, a game in which "BITE HIM IN THE CROTCH UNTIL HE DIES!" is a valid — and effective — action. It's not a football simulation, nor is it a skirmish-level wargame. It's an amusing synthesis of what make both of them appealing.

I'm gushing, I know. But the game is that good. When you're a fan of both venues, it's easy to find fault with either of the factors and declare the game broken, unevocative, or a failure. *Blood Bowl* is none of those. It succeeds as a clever twist on the *Warhammer* universe as well as fluid, idealized football send-up.

JUSTIN ACHILLI has worked at White Wolf since 1995. He developed *Vampire: The Masquerade* and *Vampire: The Requiem*, as well as contributing to *Werewolf, Mage, Promethean, Changeling, Ravenloft*, and other titles. He's currently part of the design team for an MMO that has not yet formally been announced, but you can probably guess what it is.

BOHNANZA

KEY DESIGNER: UWE ROSENBERG
RIO GRANDE GAMES (ENGLISH EDITION, 1997)

BOHNANZA IS THE BEST card game ever written about bean farming.

Wait, okay, that's not the most impressive claim. Let me try again.

Bohnanza is the best card game ever written. And it just happens to be about bean farming.

I fell in love with Uwe Rosenberg's little classic on a two-day luxury train ride from Seattle to Los Angeles in 1998, when my wife and I only packed entertainment that could fit in a handbag. Between the wine- and cheese-tastings, we logged something like 50 games of *Bohnanza* on that trip down the Pacific coast, and 50 more on the way back.

What kept us riveted, long after the novelty of cartoon beans wore off, was a brilliant card mechanic that requires you to keep your cards in the order you drew them. This causes you all sorts of headaches, which in turn gives you all sorts of opportunities. Here's how it works:

You get a handful of bean cards. At the start of your turn, you must plant the first card in your hand (and the second, if you want) into your precious two bean-fields. Each beanfield can contain only one type of bean.

Now you draw two cards. You have to either plant them or trade them. Remember, you only have two beanfields, so those two cards will rip up the beans you already have there, assuming they're not the same types. So you have to get rid of unwanted beans by trading them, and maybe trading other cards from your hand. This is where the rule about keeping your cards in order matters. If you can't get rid of the beans that you don't want, you will later have to plant them and destroy the beans you care about.

Then it comes time to harvest beans, if you want. The beans have up to four numbers of coins on them. For example, the Sauerbohne (stink bean) has the number 3 under one coin, the number 5 under two coins, the number 7 under three coins, and the number 8 under four coins. That means you can harvest three Sauerbohnen for one coin, five Sauerbohnen for two coins, and so on. You need to become a bean-trading genius, or you'll never harvest enough beans of one type to make big bank.

Here's where my other favorite mechanic comes in: On the backs of the cards are coin symbols. As you harvest beans, you flip them over to represent your money. But you're also taking those beans out of the deck, and so the type of beans you just harvested become rarer. You go through the deck three times (the third time very quickly), and then whoever has the most coins wins. That trip through the deck goes so quickly that you don't realize you've played through a hundred turns and made several hundred unique decisions. That's why you're exhausted at the end of the game, and still raring to play again.

Bohnanza sets you up to be underwhelmed — "I'm sorry, the game's about what now?" — and then overwhelms you with its simplicity, elegance, and lightning-fast interactivity. It's everything that the classic *Pit* wanted to be when it grew up. If you liked saying, "I've got two! Two!" as a kid, you'll like saying, "Who wants my kidney bean?" just as much as an adult.

That's another key point: *Bohnanza* is a resource-management game as much as *The Settlers of Catan* and *Monopoly* are. Unlike those games, though, the commodities in *Bohnanza* are funny. The Augenbohne (black-eyed bean) is dressed like a boxer . . . with a black eye. The Sojabohne (soy bean) is a hippie. The Rotebohne (red bean) is embarrassed at being naked, if you can believe that. As a subgenre, resource-management games tend to scare people because of their gravitas, *Bohnanza* welcomes everybody in.

And everybody eventually does come in. For the 10 years after its release in 1997 — this sentence blows my mind — *Bohnanza never* fell out of the top 20 current sellers at one of the top board and card game e-tailers. That's not overall sales through a game's lifetime, it's what's selling that week. If you check the list now, *Bohnanza*'s probably still in the top 20 this week. No other board or card game can say that, not *Puerto Rico*, not *Settlers*, not my precious *Axis & Allies*, nothing. In its own way, *Bohnanza* is the equivalent of *Magic: The Gathering* or *Dungeons & Dragons*: In its category, there is no game that can unseat it from the mountaintop.

Rosenberg and his co-designers have rolled out a dozen expansions since the first bean hit the market. They've made games about cowboy beans (*High Bohn*) and fairy tale beans (*Rabohnzel*) and pirate beans (*La Isla Bohnita*) and Napoleonic beans (*Bohnaparte*) and gangster beans (*Al Cabohne*). They're all fun little refried variants, but I keep coming back to my original German set, which is the most addictive card game I own.

And yet, there's still a large number of people who won't touch *Bohnanza* because of its theme. They play games with tanks and games with dragons and games with seriousness etched into their souls. And I say, how misguided. It takes a serious gamer to play a serious bean-farming game. Let go of your pretensions, and pick up a copy of *Bohnanza* from your favorite store. You won't be the last to do so, I assure you.

I'll end on a personal note. I don't know Uwe Rosenberg, but I do know his sidekick, Hanno Girke, who co-designed some of the *Bohnanza* expansions. In 2002, Hanno had the honor of standing next to me when I broke my arm curling. Yup, the sport with the brooms. Ice is hard.

Anyway, I told Hanno earlier that day that the reason I liked *Bohnanza* was the reason I liked curling. It's not a glamour game. It's not an epic battle of wits. It's an ungainly looking little thing with a premise that you can't believe is fun. And then, when you try it, you realize it's a hoot and a half, and you want to keep playing it till they turn out the lights.

Only, unlike curling, I haven't broken my arm playing *Bohnanza*. But not for lack of trying.

MIKE SELINKER is a game and puzzle designer from Seattle. He is the co-designer of such board and card games as *Gloria Mundi*, *Key Largo*, *Risk Godstorm*, *Pirates of the Spanish Main*, and *Stonehenge*. At Wizards of the Coast, he helped revitalize *Axis & Allies* and *Dungeons & Dragons*. He also writes puzzles for the *Chicago Tribune*, the *New York Times*, and *Games* magazine. He runs the game design studio Lone Shark Games (www.lonesharkgames.com) alongside a happy crew of mercenaries, including fellow *100 Best* writers James Ernest and Teeuwynn Woodruff.

Tom Dalgliesh on

BRITANNIA

KEY DESIGNER: LEWIS PULSIPHER
FANTASY FLIGHT GAMES (REVISED EDITION, 2005)

BRITANNIA SHOULD NOT WORK. I've designed a lot of games over the years and this one violates most of my "cherished principles." But the designer of *Britannia* had his own principles. Let me tell you about his masterpiece.

The game was created by Lewis Pulsipher under the working title *Invasions*. It was published in England as *Britannia* in 1986 by Gibsons Games after development by Roger Heyworth, and nominated for a 1987 Charles S. Roberts Award. A German-language version was released by Welt der Spiele, and the game was later republished in the United States by Avalon Hill. The sale of that company to Hasbro sent the rights back to the designer, who then revised it for publication by Fantasy Flight Games in 2005.

One reason I enjoy *Britannia* is the subject matter. I'm British (and Canadian and American) and the game covers a thousand years of chaotic British history. It starts with the Roman invasion of 43 A.D. (led by Claudius, of *I, Claudius* fame) and then brings on the Saxons, first invited by the Romans as mercenaries to defend the "Saxon Shore" but who overstayed their welcome. Then come the Angles, whose "Angleland" eventually became the name for England; the Jutes from Jutland (Denmark), who also had their way with red-haired Celtic maidens and other treasures; and the Scotti from Ireland, who somehow managed to tame the fearsome blue-painted Picts to found Scotland.

Somewhere in the middle of all this pushing and shoving, a semi-legendary king called Arthur arose and did his part to prevent the collapse of Romano-British civilization. He did well for a few years, but it was a hopeless task. Most of Britain succumbed to the waves of invaders, except for the less desirable bits of Cornwall (one potential location of Camelot) and Wales (another potential location of Camelot) and Scotland (never, as yet, claimed to be the location of Camelot). Indeed, the Kingdom of Strathclyde, centered on Dunbarton — the "fort of the Britons" — lasted well into the seventh century and would be a more respectable Camelot than any other pile of rock currently claiming the title.

From the sixth to eighth centuries the invasions declined while the earlier squatters battled it out for supremacy. Obviously, the Angles and Saxons got the upper hand, or at least the bragging rights, because England became an Anglo-Saxon realm.

Then the trouble started anew with invasions by Norwegians (Vikings), more Danes, and finally the Normans, who were only slightly civilized northmen themselves. 1066 and all that!

Britannia is a multi-player game that covers all this historical turmoil in just four hours — well, most games last five to six hours. There are scenarios for three and five players, but the game is best for four.

There are 17 nations in the game, divided among the players. Each player has one color (blue, green, red, or yellow) but controls different nations at different times of the game. For example, the blue player controls the Belgae, Picts, Angles, and Normans, all of them blue counters with distinctive identity symbols. This player will start the game fending off a Roman invasion, then fight for control of Scotland and northern England, and end fighting the Saxons for control of southern England. Sometimes, the blue player can keep the Belgae around for two or three centuries, and the Picts have actually been known to stay alive to dance with the Normans.

The game begins with one army each in five separate areas of Britain: the Brigantes (red), Belgae and Picts (blue), and Welsh and Caledonians (green). A force of Romans (yellow), who begin in the English Channel, are the first nation to move. Through their superior fighting power and mobility the Romans soon come to dominate most of Britain, but eventually withdraw, leaving behind a few beleaguered Romano-Britons. New nations invade and rise or fall according to the skill of their guiding players, who must continually weigh short-term gain against long-term benefit, never forgetting the looming threat of the Danes and Normans.

The game is played over 16 rounds. Nations mostly score points for holding different areas of Britain during five special scoring rounds: V, VII, X, XIII, and XVI. Nations also score points by achieving a *Bretwalda* (King) at various times, and for meeting or exceeding the fixed goals given on their nation cards.

Britannia works best with four skilled players. Points are accumulated at different rates throughout the game. This means the player actually winning is not always immediately obvious. Novices often have trouble determining who's in the lead and attack players who pose no real threat, giving the true leader an easier victory. But because novice players are never eliminated from the game, they learn after a session or two what the typical scores are at the different stages and so soon figure out what's really going down.

At the end of the game all four players will have the chance to become king of England through their control of Harold the Saxon, William of Normandy, Harald of Norway, or Svein the Dane. However this in itself will not determine who wins. To achieve victory, a player must accumulate points by good play throughout the *entire* game.

Britannia is an unusual game. Players must overcome their natural instincts to bash a neighbor and, instead, roleplay the strengths and weaknesses of each nation. Some nations have the advantage of numbers. Some have good position. Others have good timing, since their relative strength peaks at an opportune moment. You need to invest several sessions in the game to learn the basics, preferably once with each color. But the payback is hundreds of hours of great gaming.

The new version by Fantasy Flight Games is the best edition to date. The components are top quality and the rules finally get it right. Minor tweaks by Lewis Pulsipher have given *Britannia* some new life, although the new "VP tokens" are tedious to use. Keeping track of points the old way on paper was just fine by me, but perhaps new players will like them.

At the beginning of this essay I noted, somewhat pompously, that *Britannia* violated most of my "cherished principles." What are those principles? Well, they have changed over time, but they can all be reduced down to "let the players play." By that I mean a good game should set the stage and provide simple rules, and then the designer should get out of the way. *Diplomacy* is a great example of the art, as is *Acquire*. With a play time of four to six hours, highly scripted events, and a 24-page rulebook, *Britannia* doesn't even come close to matching that ideal.

But it works. Every game has the same events, yet every game is different. And one of the great appeals of *Britannia* is that you are never eliminated from play. Each period brings you another nation to direct and the final outcome is often in doubt until the very end. That means, of course, the designer did a great job assigning and balancing the nations.

Britannia is an epic journey through history, highly entertaining and possessing immense flair. It's one of the best four-player games out there. Rule *Britannia*!

★   ★   ★

Born in Scotland, TOM DALGLIESH is the owner of Columbia Games and a designer of many popular wargames. He began his career playing poker as a midshipman in the British Merchant Navy, then emigrated to Canada in 1967. Along with Lance Gutteridge, Tom founded Gamma Two Games in 1972 and Columbia Games in 1982. Tom's designs, starting with *Quebec 1759*, include *War of 1812*, *Napoleon*, *Slapshot*, *Klondike*, *Smoker's Wild*, *Bobby Lee*, *Sam Grant*, *Dixie*, *Eagles*, *Victory*, *Pacific Victory*, and *Liberty*. He also co-designed *Wizard Kings* with his son Grant, *EastFront* with Craig Besinque, and *Hammer of the Scots* and *Crusader Rex* with Jerry Taylor. Tom now lives in Washington (state), a few miles south of the Canadian border, and enjoys sailing as a hobby.

Greg Stolze on

BUTTON MEN

KEY DESIGNER: JAMES ERNEST

CHEAPASS GAMES (1999)

JAMES ERNEST'S *BUTTON MEN* is a successful game, based on any measure short of enabling its designer to retire. It's mechanically elegant, it won Origins Awards, it's been a fan favorite, and I'd guess it had a pretty sweet profit margin.

Button Men earns its accolades through brilliance, and it's brilliant on several levels. First off, it has sharp mechanics. It's simple, it's easy to learn, but it has enough variety that it holds interest for a long time. It possesses the elusive quality of emergent complexity: Its simple rules synergize to produce more complicated interactions, and understanding those interactions lets a player optimize his chances to succeed.

On the surface, it's simple: Players roll dice. The size of the die rolled — from a common six-sided cube up through a 20-sided polyhedron or down to a two-sided "d2" — yields a result. You and your opponent take turns applying your results in order to capture dice from each other. Capturing larger dice gets you more points, but the interesting twist is that you can apply your results one of two ways. A "power attack" rewards high single results. A "speed attack" works by combining results. Picking tactics on the fly requires strategy. On the other hand, it is possible to simply roll a lousy set of results, no matter how good you are. Far from being a flaw, the luck element keeps the game exciting — and holds out the possibility of an underdog victory to inexperienced players.

The best games, like chess, have emergent complexity. The moves are simple enough to learn, but the field of play lets those simply moving pieces form vast permutations. *Button Men* does the same.

Unlike chess, *Button Men* is expandable, a quality that really only developed in hobby games. You're never going to get a new type of piece in classic chess, but in *Magic: the Gathering* there's always a new card to, y'know, gather. *Button Men* expanded by introducing Poison Dice, Trip Dice, Shadow Dice, and other variations on its core theme. Shadow Dice, for example, capture single dice that are larger than their result, up to a maximum number. Instead of hoping for a big number on a big die (which helps the power attack) or a series of varied results (which combine into good speed attacks) the player now hopes for a low result on a single large Shadow Die. This gradually rising complexity extended the game's replay value by keeping it perpetually new, without changing so swiftly that players couldn't keep up with tactics. *Button Men* — and any other game that grows its rules — stays on the edge of the players' learning curve. That's how they remain fresh and interesting.

The elegance of *Button Men* had a powerful influence on my own design of *Meatbot Massacre*. The core design concepts I learned from *Button Men* were that: 1) dice selection could be made interesting by giving different dice types balanced and varied qualities, and 2) dice could serve as semiotic markers. That is, each die could have a different meaning, as opposed to, say, *D&D* damage dice, which all do the same thing — bring pain — just in different amounts. In *Meatbot Massacre*, you can pick a d4 to move faster, a d6 to defend, or a d12 to attempt some insane grandstand maneuver. In *Button Men*, you can pick a d20 for Hulk Smash, or a d4 to seize initiative and give yourself small numbers to fine-tune finesse attacks.

The cleverness went deeper than the game's design. When it became apparent that *Button Men* was selling, other companies got in on the act. James Ernest's Cheapass Games licensed the game to other companies, using the system (both the rules and the marketing concepts) to push their properties and create awareness of their images and concepts. For example, the publisher of *Legend of the Five Rings*, a juggernaut card- and roleplaying-game property, cooperated to produce *Button Men* with their signature characters on them. Atlas Games did the same thing to promote the eerie graphics of their card game *Lunch Money*. It was a sharp cross-marketing strategy that got *L5R* fans buying *Button Men* and *Button Men* fans buying *L5R* merchandise. Everybody won.

It came at the right time, too. Released in in the late 1990s, collectible card games were ruling the marketplace, but it was clear that they could fail — and when a CCG fell, it usually landed hard on the company that produced it. At the same time, the established card games were reaching a level of complexity that, while compelling for the serious players who'd followed a game from the beginning, intimidated people who wanted casual play without spending dozens of hours to learn rules and hundreds of dollars to gain the cards they needed to approach parity with the veterans.

Button Men cut with and against that prevailing paradigm. It resembled trading card games. There were a lot of small, nifty, varied, and beautiful pieces you could get. Collectors could easily try to get 'em all (to paraphrase the phenomenon soon to follow). At the same time, it was a breath of fresh air to people who weren't collectors or who didn't have lots of money and attention to devote to a game. The buttons were largely balanced. Even if Button A had a situational advantage against Button B, it was paid for by a weakness against Button C. Besides, the varied tactics for using random results ensured that even if there was an advantage before dice hit table, it was a slim one once the numbers were up.

Most importantly, you only used one button at a time. No matter how many you owned, the rest of your *Button Men* collection didn't impact an individual game. You picked one and went against one, unlike card games where you might pick 60 cards out of 500, and go against a deck built of the best 40 cards out of a couple thousand. The one-on-one aspect appealed to card gamers used to getting demolished by opponents with sample cases of rare, powerful, expensive, or highly specialized cards.

Like the card games of the time, *Button Men* was well presented from the beginning. Brian Snoddy's art was gorgeous and evocative. The flavor text describing the fighters' personalities ("Hammer is a vicious, sweaty man with a garbage can on his head") was irreverent and funny. The small size of the package, its low cost point, and its accessible appearance meant barriers for entry were as low as a line painted on the floor. On top of that, there was the promise of instant community. Walking around big conventions, like Gen Con or Origins, you could see a stranger, recognize the *Button Man* on his satchel, and not only have a reason to go start a conversation ("Hey, wanna throw down?") but also get some small idea of his favored tactics. ("Hmmm . . . a Zeppo player, eh?") The cool-looking button wasn't just a game, it was a fashion accessory and a group signifier. By wearing it, you showed other players that you were ready to play, a secret meaning inaccessible to people who weren't in the know. Neat!

There's no way of knowing how many personal connections started with pickup games of *Button Men*, but in the long term those connections may well be the best measure of its impact. *Button Men* isn't just a good game, it's a remarkably clever tool for creating community through fun.

GREG STOLZE started gaming before his voice changed, and started writing game stuff for pay in the early 1990s. Best known for designing the role-playing game *Unknown Armies* with John Tynes, he has also created traditional strategy board games (*Elemental*, from Kenzer & Co.), and wargames (*Meatbot Massacre*). He has worked on big lines from big companies (both iterations of *Vampire* from White Wolf) and has produced small, independent games (*Executive Decision* and . . . *in Spaaace!*). He's currently working on *Reign*, a game for his One Roll Engine. You can visit him online at www.gregstolze.com to download free games and learn more about his work.

Monte Cook on

CALL OF CTHULHU

KEY DESIGNER: SANDY PETERSEN

CHAOSIUM (FIRST EDITION, 1981)

SINCE THE EARLY DAYS of the hobby, if you were to ask virtually any role-player what *other* game should be on the ideal RPG shelf (other than the ubiquitous *Dungeons & Dragons*), it's likely the answer would be *Call of Cthulhu*. As a counterpoint to the games that preceded it, and the vast majority of those that came later, this horror game does not stress character improvement and gaining wealth or power. Instead — like the mythos created by H.P. Lovecraft, the writer upon whose works the game is based — this dark game thrives upon madness, deterioration, and even character death. And yet, because of these things, not despite them, the game has cemented itself as one of the most enjoyable play experiences in the hobby.

Howard Phillips Lovecraft's relatively small body of work has been extraordinarily influential on 20th- and 21st-century horror and fantasy. Virtually every tentacled beastie that rears a bulbous eye from the murky brine owes at least a nod of gratitude to Lovecraft and his most famous creation, the monstrous Cthulhu. Although not without their literary flaws, Lovecraft's stories evoke a unique mood of nihilistic gloom — a horror that comes as a gradual realization of the truth rather than as a sudden shock. They present us with a world where man does not even begin to comprehend the true nature of his universe, and he's the better for it. Lovecraft's horrors are vast, unknowable beings that as likely as not possess no more awareness of us than a man is aware of the anthill he accidentally crushes as he walks to work. Still, as groundbreaking as these stories were, it is sometimes surprising that they, published in disposable pulp magazines such as *Weird Tales*, managed to survive the irresistible pull toward the pit of obscurity that has consumed the work of so many of Lovecraft's contemporaries from the 1920s and 1930s. In fact, it is likely that the roleplaying game itself has become the major contributor to Lovecraft's enduring popularity, introducing new generations to his dark visions of cosmic horror.

Game designer Sandy Petersen was a fan of Lovecraft's work, and imagined a means to capture the mood of his most famous stories. The result of his labors was the first horror roleplaying game, creating a legacy which would influence hundreds of designers after him. The game has gone on to become Chaosium's flagship product, selling hundreds of thousands of copies in its various editions.

Lovecraft's tales are set primarily in the 1920s, and thus so is the game (although, eventually, the game spread to other eras). *Call of Cthulhu* turns the traditional power fantasies found in RPGs — where characters attain godlike might, rule entire kingdoms, and slay dragons with a single stroke of a sword — on their collective ears. Characters are designed to get worse as time goes on, not better. Things that make characters more powerful in the game, such as books of forbidden spells or the amassing of lore about the dark secrets of the universe (in the form of a skill simply called Cthulhu Mythos) carry with them great dangers. In fact, these items and skills almost always end up spelling an early end for the characters who utilize them.

Mechanically, *Call of Cthulhu* is deceptively simple. The game uses a percentile-based system taken from Chaosium's *Basic Role-Playing* — itself a simplified version of their *RuneQuest* game — for most task resolution, integrating combat and non-combat skills in a cohesive framework. Rather than the hulking warriors, mighty wizards, roguish starship captains, and masked superheroes of other games, *Call of Cthulhu* characters are fragile things. Many are not just average folk, but are in fact bookish professors and bespectacled investigators with extensive knowledge of history, archeology, and obscure languages, but rarely any grounding in combat or survival skills.

The true genius of the game's mechanics, however, lies in its handling of sanity. Each character has a sanity score (or SAN), like hit points. This same score is the number you must roll under to avoid losing more points when witnessing terrible events and encountering supernatural entities. However, as one loses SAN, this roll becomes more difficult, which means one quickly loses more SAN, which, of course, means that the roll becomes still more difficult, and so on — a so-called "sanity death spiral."

The game's continued appeal owes as much to the self-effacing dark humor of the devoted players as it does to game mechanics. While the gameplay itself is deadly serious, when people talk about the game they typically tell you about their characters' deaths and bouts of insanity with a manic glee rarely seen in other play experiences. It's become a sort of rite of passage among gamers to have some ululating eldritch horror tear their character apart in a grisly way or drive them insane, so that they race about, cavorting madly, while the world ends or sit catatonic while the eldritch horror devours their comrades.

For many people, *Call of Cthulhu* is the perfect "alternative" game. In between longer campaigns of other, more traditional RPGs, they enjoy a "one-shot" *Call of Cthulhu* game as a break. These usually play out like a single horror story or movie. The characters are normal people who come upon something extraordinary and then try to escape with lives and sanity intact. No matter what the group's regular game, *Call of Cthulhu* is almost certainly a change of pace, one that encourages a different play style because the characters are likely doomed to short, unpleasant lives. Players need not feel attached to their characters, and can revel in, rather than rue, their demise. This brief, but intense style of play also lends itself well to games run at conventions, which is likely another contributor to the game's enduring success.

Ironically, though, *Call of Cthulhu*'s supplements include some of the best campaign-length adventures ever published, for any game, in particular the excellent *Masks of Nyarlathotep* by Larry DiTillio, Lynn Willis, and others. The dedicated *Call of Cthulhu* player appreciates campaigns as much, or more, than short adventures, but they are notoriously difficult to create, since the horror must be revealed slowly. In *Masks of Nyarlathotep*, like many archetypal *Call of Cthulhu* campaigns, the heroes begin by investigating the possibly mundane plots of mad cultists, only to encounter more and more of the unexplainable — Omar Shakti, a sorcerer who casts real spells; then monsters such as zombies and fire vampires; and eventually an avatar of the dread Outer God, Nyarlathotep — until they can no longer deny that what they face is supernatural in origin and entirely antithetical to humanity. They cannot hope to best it, only stave it off. But in *Call of Cthulhu*, even these small victories are enough.

Over the years, various versions of the game have been published, setting the action in different eras but maintaining the same atmosphere of cosmic horror. Publishers beside Chaosium have produced licensed, compatible material for the game, most notably Pagan Publishing. In 2001, when given the opportunity to show off their new open game license by converting another game to the d20 System, *Dungeons & Dragons* publisher Wizards of the Coast chose *Call of Cthulhu*. *Call of Cthulhu d20*, for which I served as lead designer, was created as a bridge product to give *D&D* players a taste of this very different setting and style of play.

In the end, however, it is the original version of the game that belongs on any list of the top hobby games of all time. Having broken new gaming ground when it first emerged, *Call of Cthulhu* still shines brightest when cleaving as closely to Lovecraft's own stories as possible, with Jazz Age investigators facing weird horrors they can never entirely understand, let alone defeat. In the face of such darkness, the best stories are created and players have the most fun.

MONTE COOK is an award-winning veteran of the game industry, best known for his work as one of the designers of the third edition of *Dungeons & Dragons*. Other notable works include *Dead Gods*, *Return to the Temple of Elemental Evil*, *D20 Call of Cthulhu*, *Monte Cook's Arcana Evolved*, and *Ptolus: Monte Cook's City by the Spire*. These latter two titles are among the dozens of books published by his own design studio, Malhavoc Press. A graduate of the Clarion Science Fiction and Fantasy Writer's Workshop, Monte has published several novels and a number of short stories.

Steven E. Schend on

CARCASSONNE

KEY DESIGNER: KLAUS-JÜRGEN WREDE
RIO GRANDE GAMES (ENGLISH EDITION, 2000)

THE GAME *CARCASSONNE* TAKES its name from the southern French city of Carcassonne, famous for its surviving Roman and medieval architecture and fortifications. In an abstract way, the gameplay emulates the changing fortunes and rulership over a medieval countryside — the Carcassonne region, a strategic trade location between the Atlantic and the Mediterranean. Since history plays no role in this game, the designers could have used any medieval city for the game title. While it would still work as *Prague* or *York* or *Vienna*, using a place equal in European and Mediterranean influences focuses on the gameplay without distractions of national or historical themes.

Originally published in Germany by Hans im Glück, *Carcassonne* is fast on its way toward classic status, even after only seven years in print. It's a resource-management game with a striking variety of play, thanks in large part to its lack of a set board. Each player helps build the playing surface by laying down tiles and creating cities, rivers, and road systems. In essence, you make a different board each time you play.

Every turn, a player draws and places a tile, connecting land or water features with previously laid tiles. Then, the player may place a follower — called a "meeple" by some fans, a portmanteau word for "my people" — on that tile. Where the follower is placed determines both its role (farmer, knight, monk, and thief) and how it scores points for its player (based on the size of its farm, city, or road). As the game progresses, there are many ways to shift the lay of the land and change the score of one or more players. Rarely is the game's outcome a foregone conclusion. Two players can start building separate cities only to have subsequent tiles merge the cities, allowing both players to gain points from the construction.

The high quality of its components makes *Carcassonne* a pleasure to use. The sturdy wooden meeples are now so recognizable as to be virtual symbols for the entire subgenre of European-style resource-management games. The 74 land and 12 river tiles are clean, die-cut pressboard squares with a light semi-gloss coating.

Even with extensive use, the tiles don't fray along the edges and the images don't curl up off the tile. The artwork is finely detailed color drawings rather than simplistic graphics. This is a game designed for repeated play.

On average, games last between 40 minutes and an hour, depending on the number of players. A good range of players, for game balance and variety, is three or four. *Carcassonne* plays equally well with two players as it does with five or six, though tactics change with the number of competitors. With fewer players, each individual gets more tiles to control, so cities, roads, and fields tend to grow larger; with more players, cities and roads stay small, to help ensure they can be completed and scored. There is no optimal number, honestly — the game entertains no matter how many are at the table.

There are many attractions to *Carcassonne* that make it one of the best hobby games, but I'll look at two primary points: its easy learning curve and its flexibility in play style. Both of these factors helped *Carcassonne* win the 2001 Grand Prize Spiel des Jahres, a German game of the year award.

Carcassonne is a quick game to learn and easy to teach to others. You can pick up the basics in less than five minutes, but there are tricks to tile and follower placement that take longer to master. Many new players tend not to use their meeples as farmers, since farmers are stuck on their farms once placed and meeples used to claim other things are freed for re-use once their castle or road or cloister is completed. After a few games, though, most players realize that farmers score a lot of points in the endgame and can be a key to winning.

Whether your tastes run toward strategy games or more conventional board games, *Carcassonne* uses elements of both to keep things interesting on different levels for different styles of play. You can play aggressively and place tiles to shorten other players' farmland, roads, or cities. *Carcassonne* even can be played like chess, if you like to plan multiple moves ahead, but this is quite tricky with the random tile draw mechanic.

Since its initial release, *Carcassonne* has seen seven expansions, all of which use or bulwark the core rules with new mechanics and new strategies. None are crucial to enjoying the game, but they all complicate the central mechanics and strategies in interesting ways.

Of all the expansions, I find the first two supplements — *Traders & Builders* and *Inns & Cathedrals* — the best; together, they expand the number of players to six and add the most balanced rules additions without slowing down gameplay.

The *Traders & Builders* supplement provides city tiles with trade goods, which add points in the endgame. The goods motivate other players to help build cities, since the person who finishes a city gets the trade goods, not necessarily the person who controls (or gains points from) the city. The *Inns & Cathedrals* supplement increases the points gained by certain roads and cities. *Inns & Cathedrals* also adds a larger "super-meeple" — known in our house as Mongo — which counts for two followers in whatever role it adopts.

Carcassonne boasts five stand-alone variants that use the original's core mechanics, but with slightly different themes, whether it's exploration of new lands (*The Discovery*), constructing forests and herding wildlife (*Hunters & Gatherers*), or building an individual city (*The Castle*). The latter, designed by Reiner Knizia, is a two-player game that is suitable for younger audiences and provides a great introduction to resource-management games in general.

Carcassonne's success — both as a single game and as a game franchise — reveals its popularity and its ability to entertain many people in different ways.

Last, but hardly least for me, I treasure this game as the first one I played with the woman who became my wife. We discovered this game at our first Gen Con together and bought every expansion we could the day after we first played it. We've shared the game with many couples and family members, all of whom are now avowed fans.

So give *Carcassonne* a try. It's certain to be a perennial favorite in your house, just as it is in ours.

Since 1990, STEVEN E. SCHEND has designed or edited scores of roleplaying games for TSR, Inc., Wizards of the Coast, and other publishers. At present, Steven has published one novel and five short stories, with another novel, a novella, and two short stories due in 2008. Living in Grand Rapids, Michigan, Steven works as a bookseller and writes tales crossing worlds from the Forgotten Realms to his own contemporary fantasies. If he's not busy, expect him to be playing games like *Scrabble*, *Kill Doctor Lucky*, *The Great Khan Game*, or *Space Hulk*. Luckily, his wife likes to play most of these, as well.

Jeff Tidball on

CAR WARS

KEY DESIGNERS: CHAD IRBY, STEVE JACKSON
STEVE JACKSON GAMES (SECOND EDITION COMPENDIUM, 1990)

DRIVE OFFENSIVELY! THOSE WERE the first two words on the back of the original edition of *Car Wars*, published in 1980 and released in the ziplock-baggie format common to so many Steve Jackson Games designs of that era. The basic concept, described so succinctly in the game's name, was nearly the perfect expression of the pop culture zeitgeist that had seen the release of *Mad Max* the year before, and *Death Race 2000* not too long before that. What could be more American than the violent fusion of cars and guns?

In *Car Wars*, each player controls one or more vehicles, each a rectangular cardboard counter, on a paper map. Although sometimes seen at conventions played with miniatures of the Matchbox or Micro Machine scale, *Cars Wars* has always been, first and foremost, a paper game. Early editions of the rules used a square grid to regulate movement, while later revisions were more freeform, with measured ranges and movement governed by an inventive turning key. The vehicles, naturally, bristle with weaponry, from rocket launchers to machine guns, smokescreens to ram plates. The cars' statistics can be complex, describing weaponry, armor, speed, and maneuverability in great detail.

Scenarios range from arena-based duels — think of Roman gladiator games, but with armed cars — to scenes in the wider *Car Wars* world, where, for example, the law-abiding (but well-armed) residents of a Midwestern town might have to defend themselves from a marauding cycle gang, or a convoy of 18-wheelers protect itself over dangerous highways.

A very successful release, the *Car Wars* line saw relentless expansions, first in Steve Jackson Games's baggie and pocket-box formats, and eventually in full-sized boxed sets. The cars and motorcycles of the original game were eventually joined by trikes, trucks, buses, boats, tanks, hovercraft, helicopters, airplanes, and more. New weaponry and vehicular accessories — and their attendant rules — were printed both in these expansions and in the pages of *Autoduel Quarterly*, the journal of the American Autoduel Association. The AADA was both an in-game organization of professional car-fighters and a real-world club for the game's fans. All these new options and rules were revised and reprinted many times over in a series of editions and compendiums.

This pattern of expansions highlights the game's greatest strength. From the first release of the first edition, players were empowered to create and arm their vehicles from the ground up, and they had lots of options. They were free to obsess over such minutiae as the weight and cost of the individual rounds with which their recoilless rifles were armed. And not for nothing; trading a bit of ammo for a point or three of armor could spell the difference between life and death in the arena! By the time the various — and definitive — boxed *Deluxe Editions* were released in the mid-'80s to early '90s, the game burst with options, from flaming oil slicks to tank guns, laser-reactive webs to fake passengers.

Such deep but structured creative opportunities — long before collectible card games made "customizable" a design buzzword — gave *Car Wars* the effectively solo gameplay mode of vehicle creation, and also a mode of "extroverted" meta-play — the sharing of car designs, fan to fan, via *Autoduel Quarterly*, club newsletters, and, later, the Web. Of course, there was also a practical application; players could "share" their designs with their opponents, in combat! But if extensive customizability was *Car Wars*' greatest strength, it was also its most damning liability. Just as high start-up costs — both mental and monetary — plague today's collectible games, it hurt *Car Wars*, as well. With myriad choices came the necessity to understand those choices, and to make them.

There was, however, a community to offer support. The AADA presaged the explosion in organized play that surrounds today's collectible games. It preceded organizations like the DCI, the sanctioning body for *Magic: The Gathering*, or Decipher's Game Management Authority by a decade or more; perhaps the only comparable organization at the time was the RPGA, but since that group was primarily concerned with roleplaying, the AADA did not tread the same ground. One additional difference was that many members of the AADA organized themselves into local chapters — there were more than 50 such groups at one point — who hosted games, held club championships, and so forth. Some chapters were as small as a single playing group, while others had dozens of members. Some chapters still meet to play *Car Wars* today, even though the central AADA organization has been inactive for some time. At the club's height, though, SJG printed 11,400 copies of *ADQ*, just over 2,000 of which were mailed directly to subscribers.

Along with the support of stores, convention play, and sales of *ADQ*, serious enthusiasm among the staff at Steve Jackson Games fueled the club's expansion and kept it vital. SJG corresponded actively with the club's chapters, offered them playtest material, and listened to their feedback on the state of the game. Fan excitement, in turn, kept the staff energized.

In 2002, the fifth edition of *Car Wars* was released. It was a major re-envisioning of almost everything about the game. The rules were stripped and streamlined to near their first-edition length. The game's playing time was greatly reduced, and with very little loss of the fluid, ebullient fun previous editions had possessed. Even the release format was different; rather than lengthy tomes of rules, each retail release was a two-car game pack, with all the material needed for play. However, the rules for vehicle customization never saw release, which is why the *Car Wars Compendiums* — in their various incarnations — remain the definitive editions for most of the game's hardcore fans today.

The most critical component of *Car Wars'* success over the years — and the reason the game remains so damn much fun — goes back to the idea encapsulated in the game's title: It's a *war* . . . with *cars*. It's almost certain that anyone who's ever climbed behind the wheel for a morning commute or grocery-store errand can identify with the impulse to (paraphrasing from the back cover of the *Compendium*) "trigger the rear rocket-launchers one more time and teach *him* not to tailgate!"

JEFF TIDBALL is an Origins Award-winning game designer whose credits include *Cthulhu 500*, *Cults Across America*, and *Pieces of Eight*. He's served as line developer for *Ars Magica*, *Feng Shui*, and Decipher's *The Lord of the Rings Roleplaying Game*, and currently works as the senior developer and editor for the board and card game departments at Fantasy Flight Games. Jeff holds an MFA in screenwriting from the University of Southern California, and lives with his wife, son, and dog in the Twin Cities area. He hopes you will use the word *AmeriTreasure* rather than *AmeriTrash* as a counterpoint description to German-style board games, was the runner-up in the AADA World Championships of 2046, and invites you to visit his website at jefftidball.com.

Bill Bridges on

CHAMPIONS

KEY DESIGNERS: STEVE PETERSON, GEORGE MACDONALD
HERO GAMES (REVISED EDITION, 1982)

THE REVISED EDITION OF *Champions* was subtitled "The Super Hero Role Playing Game," and that's exactly what it was — *the* superhero roleplaying game. While it wasn't the first game on the market that let you play superheroes and duke it out with supervillains, using earth-shattering powers, it was the most innovative. The major roleplaying games of the time involved characters stalking monsters in dungeons; the heroes in *Champions* delivered knockout blows to archnemeses — all while speaking the requisite inspiring soliloquies.

Champions wasn't just a roleplaying game, it was a revelation. While that might seem like an overstatement, it accurately describes how the game changed the way my group thought about roleplaying games, about their possibilities. (And it wasn't just my group, but many gamers across the country, judging by the influence it exerted on subsequent designs.) *Champions* didn't just give us the chance to get out of the dungeon and don capes, or provide an entirely new way to make a character. It did more than that. It colonized our brains and rewired how we looked at comics, books, movies, and even the world — everything could be seen in terms of character traits and how many points they cost your character to buy them. You know when the Hulk stomps and everybody falls to the ground? How can my character do that? Easy: Apply a modifier to his strength score that allows his blows to have an area effect, but only when he strikes the ground.

The rules provide the pieces for the jigsaw puzzle that is your character.

Before *Champions*, nothing else on earth could have made me love fractions and math. I *needed* them now. How else was I going to afford that walloping energy blast without the cost break provided by tying it to a mystic amulet?

What *Champions* does is to make players think like game designers. While you aren't actually designing rules — the rulebook does that for you, with its wonderfully simple yet capable-of-great-complexity rules architecture — you're designing *characters*. Character design becomes a game in itself.

The process certainly has some of the hallmarks of designing a game: it's fun, it's challenging, and it stokes the imagination. One of my fellow players wanted to riff off a name in a Frank Zappa song; his character, the Decentral Scrutinizer, was a robot that could break off pieces of itself and so be in multiple places at once. It took some clever thought, but the player managed to build the character to the satisfaction of the game master. While the powers he needed weren't obvious in the rules, they could be coaxed out of them by the proper combination of traits. This imaginative quest beyond the surface of the rules to find the possibilities latent within them makes character creation a rewarding challenge.

Like a game designer, you have to consider game balance in your character design choices, reinforced by the point-buy system. Character traits and powers are purchased with points, and they each have varying costs. You can use a variety of tricks to shave off some of the costs here and there, but there are also tweaks that might raise the cost — say, transforming an energy blast from its normal ranged mode into an area-effect attack. To get the character you want, you not only have to be clever about his limitations, you have to be honest about your own. Sometimes, you simply can't get everything you want with the number of points you're given. This highlights the foibles of superheroes themselves; they are defined by their limits as much as by their strengths.

So why is *Champions* still a great game, multiple editions since its premiere? Freedom. Flexibility. Balance.

Champions expertly captures its genre, which is no easy task. It has to present rules that do justice to both supernatural characters, like Doctors Strange and Fate, and scientific heroes, such as Iron Man or Mr. Fantastic. It needs to make a street vigilante as interesting as a teleporting visitor from another dimension. And the rules rise to the challenge.

One of the game's real innovations is "effects-based" powers, rather than the usual "cause-based" ones. The rules deal with the actual *effect* a power has, and leaves it to the player to describe how the power works. With cause-based powers, you need rules for each different power a superhero might possibly possess, differentiating a laser blast from a fire blast or mystic blast. The blast's source might also trigger its own rules — one hero shoots from his eyes, another hero from his hands, but a villain might fire his blast from a gun. None might act the same way. With effects-based powers, you simply figure out how many dice you roll for damage. It's such a simple and expedient answer. It doesn't matter whether you are shooting optic blasts or bullets — the source of the power is eye candy.

Because of this brilliant design, you have access to every power dreamt of in comics — all in an 80-page book, for the second edition. (The latest edition consists of a 592-page *Hero System* rulebook and a companion, 216-page genre book for superhero play: "Any Superhero . . . Any Power . . . Any Adventure!")

And about that damage — oh, that wonderful damage. *Champions* uses six-sided dice instead of an array of polyhedrals, but most characters can cause you to roll an awful lot of them in a battle. Eight, 10, even 14 dice aren't uncommon. Think of the sheer tactile pleasure of dropping a dozen six-sided dice onto a table. You then get to count them up and deliver a mass of hurt to a villain. The moments in which you count the results of your roll often provides breathless suspense for the other players, as they wait to hear your result.

Champions isn't perfect; no game is. The play experience can get bogged down, especially with characters who possess super-speed and can take many actions in a turn. If any of the players don't know the rules well, the poor game master can get stuck with some extra work, making sure every character acts when their speed rating says they can. But these are minor flaws.

Successive editions have plugged rules holes and stripped away ambiguity. In some cases, however, the ambiguity wasn't a bug so much as a feature (intentional or not) that gave players the excuse, and the urge, to create their own solutions. After all, the game made them feel like game designers. And there was something pure and beautiful about a vast cosmos fitting into an 80-page book.

As has been said about Golden-Age comic books: "All in color for a dime!" The second edition of *Champions*, like the comics that inspired it, packed a lot of value into a small space.

BILL BRIDGES is the lead designer of White Wolf's *Mage: The Awakening* and *Promethean: The Created* roleplaying games, along with the Storytelling system rules for all of the World of Darkness games. He previously developed *Werewolf: The Apocalypse* and co-created the *Fading Suns* science-fiction setting and roleplaying game for Holistic Design. He has written gaming-based novels, including *The Silver Crown*, and scripts for a number of computer games. He co-chairs the presenter programming for the bi-annual Mythic Journeys conferences in Atlanta, Georgia.

CIRCUS MAXIMUS

KEY DESIGNERS: MICHAEL MATHENY, DON GREENWOOD

AVALON HILL (REVISED EDITION, 1980)

THERE ARE A LOT of very good racing games out there, set against a wide variety of interesting backdrops, everything from cavemen riding dinosaurs through Formula One racers on real-world tracks and on to spaceships hurtling through interstellar space. So what is it that makes *Circus Maximus* stand out as, far and away, my favorite of the bunch? Is it the Imperial Roman setting? The elegant mechanics? The way the game encourages players to work together while still competing? I can't really say that it's any of those things, but rather that it's *all* of those things together.

I suppose that an important bit of starting information is that I never actually played the original Battleline publication of *Circus Maximus*. The version that I am familiar with — and I dare say that, in this, I am like most current fans of the game — is the Avalon Hill edition, first published in 1980. The original *Circus Maximus* was a chariot-racing game and a gladiatorial arena combat game in one package. When Avalon Hill obtained the rights, they promoted the personal combat rules into their own game, *Gladiator*. After additional development by Donald Greenwood, *Circus Maximus* was released in its current form — a game focused completely on chariot racing.

My first interaction with *Circus Maximus* was at a Gen Con, where I happened past a table at which an oversized version of the game was being played on an incredibly detailed diorama. While the craftsmanship of the board and the concept of a chariot-racing game pulled me in, the subtle elegance of the rules kept me there, watching, for well over an hour. I was fascinated by the simple tension between deciding how hard to drive your horses and not knowing when you would be able to act.

As with most racing games, the tactics in *Circus Maximus* revolve around drivers jockeying for position, trying to get and hold the lead while making it difficult for the other drivers to pass. You start each turn deciding how fast you want your team to go, how many spaces on the board you're going to move. In this you have complete control, by which I mean that you can choose exactly the number of spaces you want to move — with the possibility of adding a small random bonus by "whipping" your horses — as opposed to many other race games, where you choose a speed range and use dice or some other randomizing factor to determine exactly how fast you go within that range. What you don't know, however, is *when* you will be able to act. *That* is determined randomly each round.

This, I think, forms the heart of what makes *Circus Maximus* such a great game. There is no "perfect strategy." There certainly are good plays and bad plays, but at any point in the game the quality of an individual decision cannot be known until the round plays out. The same strategy that wins one race may cause you to crash in the next race — based *not* on the luck of the dice, but rather on the actions of your opponents. You might be all set to sprint out into the lead, but if an opponent goes first and positions his chariot directly in front of yours or, worse, a group of opponents move before you and set up a blocking screen, your earlier decision to drive your horses all-out may come back to haunt you. If there is nowhere for your team to go, you'll have to use your driver's brute strength and endurance in an attempt to hold them back. Otherwise, you'll ram into the blocking racer, something that could injure your horses or even cause you to wreck.

Of course, a wreck in this case is a flipped chariot, which still leaves you being pulled headlong around the track by the reins strapped to your wrist. The beauty of the game's theme is that it adds a visceral excitement to all the various interactions and obstacles of the Circus Maximus. You have a team of horses that make up your "engine," but the animals each matter individually, too. A particular horse can become exhausted or injured. It can also be the target of attacks by other drivers, either with whips or the bladed wheels of their chariots. For that matter, the driver himself may be targeted by these attacks, giving the whole game a much more up-close and personal feeling.

In fact, a significant portion of the *Circus Maximus* fanbase maintains that the game is *intended* to be one of chariot combat rather than racing — something like an Imperial Roman version of *Car Wars*. It is to the game's further credit that it serves both functions equally well. In general, a racer will beat a fighter, but a game composed of a racer and three or four fighters working in tandem can make for an interesting competition.

Another of the game's assets is that a single three-lap race of *Circus Maximus* takes somewhere between 60 and 90 minutes, so it is certainly possible to play more than once in an evening — a distinct advantage for such a competitive game. If a group of players is feeling particularly ambitious, there are robust rules for running a campaign. Each player has five separate chariots, drivers, and horse teams, of which he may enter up to two in any given race. While your goal remains winning each race, the overall campaign is won by the player who gathers the most sesterces — Roman coins — through wagers placed on the race results. (You must always place at least half of your bets on your *own* teams.) Between races, you may spend some of your sesterces to improve your resources or on skullduggery to sabotage an opponent.

I've met very few people who have ever actually played in a *Circus Maximus* campaign. I highly recommend giving it a try, especially if you already have a feel for the game. The additional options and expanded milieu will, I'm sure, give you an entirely new appreciation for what already is one of the most elegant and robust games ever published.

STAN! has been publishing cartoons, games, and fiction professionally since 1982. He's authored two novels, 15 short stories, and more than 50 game products, plus innumerable comics and cartoons. He has been lucky enough to earn Origins Award nominations in all his chosen disciplines: Best Roleplaying Supplement (*Heroes of Sorcery*), Best Game-Related Short Fiction ("The Insurrection That Never Was"), Best Graphic Fiction (*Bolt & Quiver: Back to Basics*), and twice for Best Roleplaying Game (*SAGA Fate Deck* and *Pokémon Jr. Adventure Game*). Currently, Stan! is the creative content manager for Upper Deck Entertainment, the creative vice president for The Game Mechanics, and a freelance cartoonist/writer. He also sings a lot of karaoke. Stan! lives in Vista, California, and hopes to one day soon be the owner of a Sony Aibo robot dog. Visit him online at www.stannex.com or www.doodle-a-day.com.

Tom Jolly on

CITADELS

KEY DESIGNER: BRUNO FAIDUTTI

FANTASY FLIGHT GAMES (ENGLISH EDITION, 2002)

I WAS INTRODUCED TO *Citadels* when it was called *Ohne Furcht und Adel*. I couldn't read the German text on the cards, and one of my good friends, knowing what an excellent game it was, produced a version of it with each separate card painstakingly altered with the addition of a glued-on English translation of the text. He was unaware that, while he was doing this, an English-language version came out from Fantasy Flight Games in 2002.

I never did play the German version, being happily absorbed by the English version, and inexplicably felt guilty for my friend's wasted effort, except for the fact that he proved to me what a great friend he was to have.

There are a number of criteria I use to decide whether a game is truly great. *Citadels* fits them all. *Citadels* is amazingly easy to learn, but infinitely variable. The rules are short, and it only takes five to ten minutes to teach. Each time you play it, you learn something new about the best strategies. And, it has a unique game mechanic that plays incredibly well. Finally, the theme is very strong and well imbedded into the gameplay.

Each player acts as leader of a rival medieval city, trying to build up his holdings to enhance his power and prosperity. Using a variety of characters as tools, players strive to acquire money (gold tokens) and create new districts (cards). The base of the game revolves around eight character cards you can choose from. Each has a unique way to acquire gold, which can then be used to buy district cards (or prevent other players from doing so). At the start of a round, beginning with the player who held the King card on the prior round, players select one of the eight characters, then pass the remainder to the left. Then that player selects one and so on, until each has a different character card.

The characters' abilities are activated in numerical order. The King, of course, always gets the right of first action. The Assassin can sneak through a kingdom's back alleys to do in an unsuspecting victim. The Thief surreptitiously relieves someone of his hard-earned gold. The Merchant happily brings in gold from his businesses, while the Architect busily constructs new buildings. The Bishop, Warlord, and Magician also add to the game's theme, putting you in the middle of a medieval town where all the characters are plotting against one another in various ways. Each round your character changes, your choices limited to the cards the previous player passes you.

The object, simply enough, is to buy eight district cards before anyone else does, playing them face up in front of you from your card hand. You do this by paying the gold for them. A few of the district cards give you special abilities when you acquire them, but they aren't the core of the game. On your turn, you can get two gold or draw two district cards into your hand, keeping one of them. After that, you can pay to build a district (of various colors and costs), if you can afford to do so. And, most importantly, you can use your character's ability.

There are ten additional characters, which originally comprised an expansion set to the game, *Citadels: The Dark City*, but are now part of the basic Fantasy Flight Games edition. The expansion lets you swap out two of the original characters with new ones that instigate novel interactions between the players and demand new strategies.

The idea of character cards with an array of different powers isn't groundbreaking. Games such as *Dune* and *Cosmic Encounter* let you play a fixed character with a unique power for the whole game. But if one player lands an overwhelming ability, particularly in *Cosmic Encounter*, they can run away with the game; the main source of balance in that case is the ability of the other players to gang up on the obvious leader.

The balance in *Citadels* comes from the fact that character cards rotate and players get a chance to play any character during the game. It's hard for anyone to gang up on the leader because you don't know for certain what character they've picked for the round. As the cards go around the table each round, you know what's already been taken (except for one character discarded at the start of the round), which helps you plot against others. Likewise, the players before you know what they've passed you and what your options are. The last players to choose often display a look of stunned disbelief when they see what cards remain after all the other players have had their picks. To cope, they'll need to think quickly and adjust their strategies, but such dealing with temporarily foiled plans is an important part of *Citadels*, as it is many of Bruno Faidutti's best designs.

In fact, Bruno has a bit of a reputation for making chaotic games — that is to say, games in which the interactions of the components are so complicated or seemingly random that it's difficult to plan ahead or predict an action's outcome. Faidutti's *Democrazy* is one such game, wherein players essentially vote to determine what the rules are going to be, resulting in play so cheerfully chaotic that it's nearly useless to plot your actions too far ahead. *Citadels* doesn't go to that extreme, of course, but gives you enough options and challenging twists of play that it carries that familiar stamp of chaos about it.

Character-selection mechanics are a particular favorite for Faidutti, too. In his rules for *Citadels*, he credits *Verräter*, designed by Marcel-André Casasola Merkle, as an inspiration for his multi-character selection process. And since the release of *Citadels*, he's worked with other designers to craft a number of excellent variations on the mechanic. In *Fist of the Dragonstones*, co-designed by Faidutti and Michael Schacht, players bid for various characters. In *Queen's Necklace*, co-designed with Bruno Cathala, they buy them. For *Mission: Red Planet*, again by Faidutti and Cathala, each player starts with a common stack of characters, choosing which to use on their turn, very much like *Citadels*, yet different because two or more of the same character types can appear together. With Faidutti and Cathala's *Mystery of the Abbey*, they give the mechanic a twist by creating a board game wherein each room allows a different action, instead of different characters triggering this effect. The result is a very entertaining merger of *Citadels* with *Clue*.

Yet *Citadels* remains the king of Faidutti's character-selection games; it's easy to learn, steeped in theme, and never the same game twice when you play. (It's also a good game with as many as seven players, something very hard to find in hobby game circles.) It boasts a smart balance of theme and originality, chaos and strategy, art and packaging. *Citadels* is, in short, a meld of everything I want from a hobby game.

Tom Jolly is an obscure game designer who is self-deprecating almost to the point of martyrdom, not truly worthy of writing about other great game designers. He assumes the blame for designing *Wiz-War*, *Drakon*, *Cave Troll*, *Light Speed*, *Camelot*, *Cargo*, and co-designing *Diskwars* and *Vortex/Maelstrom*. He still designs new games assiduously, hoping to lure young, unsuspecting gamers away from their computers into an intellectually stimulating and socially compelling environment. He lives in California with his wife of 28 years, horses, cats, dog, and lots of oak trees, and works as an electrical engineer at a humongous aerospace company in his spare time.

CIVILIZATION

KEY DESIGNER: FRANCIS TRESHAM
AVALON HILL (FIRST U.S. EDITION, 1981)

IN ITS TIME, *CIVILIZATION* was something of a rarity among strategy games, in that it did not focus on war and combat. Indeed, with *Civilization* it was all about trade and cooperation. That isn't to say that war and combat had no place in the game. After all, the whole point of *Civilization* was to simulate the rise and fall of ancient peoples. To that end, each player controls one of nine possible civilizations as it wrestles with everything from infrastructural development and colonization, to population explosions and natural (and man-made) disasters. In order to flourish, a civilization needs to master certain visionary principles: architecture, law, literacy, metalworking, democracy, philosophy, and so on. Each new development helps a society better cope with adversity and opens the door to opportunity for new advancements. These boons are financed by imperial expansion. To win the day, a society has to surpass all others in terms of knowledge and development.

For me, the best games are always cutthroat affairs that rely upon lying, cheating, stealing, and generally being a no-good, rotten . . . okay, not *quite* that bad, but the entries on my list of top games all share a strong core of unpredictable deceit. In terms of strategy, the ability to read a player should outweigh any need to grasp more than the game's basic mechanics.

What set *Civilization* apart from the other games my friends and I were playing at the time was the theme. It was quite simply genius — a game about the rise and fall of civilizations, not merely empires duking it out across Theatre Europe. Beyond that, I loved the fact that it concentrated on trading for victory — indeed, it was impossible to win without some serious wheeling and dealing. The game suggested that no society could develop within a vacuum. (A lesson that could still be learned by a politician or two, if you ask me). As with any game, personalities come into it, of course, and I was blessed in those days with a great circle of gaming friends. The Wednesday Gang was about as disparate a set of fellows as you could get, which meant that when it came to diplomacy, trading, and alliances, there was always a fair share of bullying and backstabbing to be had.

Despite its scope, *Civilization* always struck me as quite an intimate game. How you play can reveal a lot about your closely held personal beliefs and politics. Do you value philosophy and democracy over physical crafts like engineering and metallurgy? Will you pursue law before poetry? In the Wednesday Gang, we all had our ideas about which path worked best, but then, we were a bunch of earnest young men studying politics, religion, and engineering, so it was hardly surprising that we each played the game differently.

And that's *Civilization* at its best. Even with the relative simplicity of the game's mechanics, each society can pursue the path to enlightened stability in its own unique way. Of course, that leads to some very interesting interaction. Although you can play the game with anything from two to seven players, it's usually at its best with a full complement, maximizing the chance for countless mini-games and personal competitions to spring up within the framework of the larger contest.

With all the potential for duplicity and diplomacy, it should come as no surprise that a game of *Civilization* is an investment of life — 4,000 years of history do not fly by. Our games would run eight to 12 hours, but that time was not slow to pass. We would frequently forget the basics of sustenance, chain-smoking over the chits as the games became truly Machiavellian affairs. Players were regularly heard cackling with delight over some scheme or other coming to fruition — or in one player's case, chortling and tenting the tips of his fingers as he traded you papyrus instead of food, leaving your populace to starve while he made like a shepherd and got the flock out of there. It was all very Walt Disney villain stuff.

Thinking about it now, another interesting implication of the treachery in our games of *Civilization* was that it seldom came to blows. Rather, it affected other alliances and sanctions, causing victims to unite and power-players to grow ever more nervous as the turns advanced.

That's not to say there was no fighting.

In the game, every society invariably goes through its own aggressive expansion phases, but actually eliminating another society through combat is just about impossible to achieve, even for the most vindictive of us.

I think I just gave myself away there, didn't I?

Okay, I'll admit it. There were epochs when I would rumble on about striking infidels down and teaching my enemies a thing or two about Babylonian justice. I was young and fueled up on caffeine. With enough determination I could lay them low, but their humbling never lasted more than a turn or two before balance re-asserted itself. In other words, my opponents would invariably profit as my precious Babylonians suffered calamities of their own, including, but not limited to volcanic eruptions, famine, floods, civil war, epidemics, civil unrest, heresy, and worse.

And the other civilizations stopped trading with me, so we stagnated.

From a game mechanics standpoint, this simple conceit is actually quite brilliant, not least because it hones the players' attention. It forces them to concentrate on what is truly important to win the game — knowledge being fundamental to the rise and fall and rise of civilizations over time. But it's also clever because it never truly allows a single society to maintain an advantage through all of the game's various epochs. Unlike *Risk* — in which General Bigwig will undoubtedly win the day by hiding out somewhere in Australasia, recouping his losses and building strength — *Civilization* takes a different path pretty much every time it's played. The treachery factor comes in there, too, at least with the Wednesday Gang's sessions, since we were always trying to come up with different ways to screw each other. . . .

I did say we were untrustworthy so-and-so's, didn't I?

In terms of gauging *Civilization*'s influence, originality, and, heck, even its importance, I'd argue that you only have to look at the army of clones that have followed in its wake. There's good reason it's become a household name in hobby circles. Ask a random gamer to name three board game classics off the top of his head and the odds are good he'll list *Civilization* as one of them.

Of course, it should be noted that part of *Civilization*'s brand-recognition value comes, only somewhat mistakenly, from Sid Meier's cult computer game of the same title, which borrowed rather heavily from the board game's core concept. And in return for that and the use of the name, the computer game contained fliers for the Avalon Hill edition of board game.

After that, the interaction between the board game and the computer game — and the companies behind them — became a tangled web of maneuvers and machinations that is easily a match for anything the Wednesday Gang ever came up with, including court injunctions against Activision for *Civilization: Call To Power* and a legal battle that weakened Avalon Hill and Microprose (the original manufacturer of the computer game) to the extent that Hasbro managed to snaffle them up for a song in a hostile takeover, which, a year later, resulted in *Civilization II: Test of Time*. Then along came Infogrames, which picked up Hasbro Interactive in 2001, and *Sid Meier's Civilization III* was born.

The ultimate irony has to be that, early in 2002, Microprose refugee and founder of Eagle Games, Glenn Drover, announced the development of *Sid Meier's Civilization: The Board Game*. And thus the cycle continues, from paper to pixel and back again.

It's the original Francis Tresham design that deserves your attention, though. With *Civilization*, he created a thinking gamer's game, one that deserves to be played around a table with friends — especially the cheerfully scheming sort, like my own Wednesday Gang.

STEVEN SAVILE started out writing and reviewing play-by-mail games in the U.K. in the late 1980s, then launched his own company, Pheonix Games (yes, it was spelled incorrectly by mistake), before working for Games Workshop. He has written several novels, including *Inheritance*, *Dominion*, and *Retribution*, all set in the Warhammer world, as well as fiction connected to *Slaine*, *Dr. Who*, and most recently, *Torchwood*.

COSMIC ENCOUNTER

KEY DESIGNERS: BILL EBERLE, JACK KITTREDGE, PETER OLOTKA

EON (FIRST EDITION, 1977)

THE LATE 1970S AND early 1980s was when I discovered gaming, and they were simple yet exciting times. My friends and I had copies of *Hare and Tortoise*, *Jockey*, *Scotland Yard*, and *Acquire*. Those were clever and challenging games, precursors of what would become the "German school" in game design, but nothing I considered really *fun*. At the opposite end of the spectrum, we had *Junta*, and later *Illuminati* and *Battlecars*, which were more fun but fiddly, with rules more convoluted than felt necessary.

Then we discovered two games, almost simultaneously, and it proved difficult to make a choice between them, to decide which was the most important. Those two games were *Cosmic Encounter* and *Dungeons & Dragons*. Being a student, I managed, like most of my friends, to find time for both. But it was *Cosmic Encounter* that would later impact my own game designs the most profoundly.

Cosmic Encounter was the first design by the Future Pastimes team of Bill Eberle, Jack Kittredge, and Peter Olotka. All they really knew of board games when they began work was *Risk*, so they took *Risk* and first reduced it to its central element — battles to conquer your opponent's territories — then added all the stuff they could mine from their twisted minds and any other handy source — the zany books they had read (think Douglas Adams and the like), their parents' attics, local shopping malls, and the era's oddball television shows (and there was plenty of goofy stuff on TV in the late '70s). The result was a game both terribly simple and incredibly convoluted.

Cosmic Encounter is grounded upon some really simple rules. Each player controls five planets and, on your turn, you attack a randomly determined opponent. To do this, you take tokens from your planets, call for allies, and play a numbered card face down. Your opponent also calls for allies and plays a card. You both reveal your cards, then add the number on it to the total number of tokens on your side. The highest total wins, either capturing the planet or repelling the would-be invaders. The first player to conquer five planets wins the game. That's all.

But there's much more to it, when you get beyond the basic concept, and in this "much more" lurks almost everything that would inspire revolutions in both German-style board games and American-style collectible card games.

The mark of *Cosmic Encounter* can be seen on many of the successful card and board games published in the wake of its 1977 release, including Richard Garfield's remarkable *Magic: The Gathering*. Of my own designs, *Citadels*, *Fist of Dragonstones*, and *Dragon's Gold* all proudly show the game's influence.

The essential characteristic of *Cosmic Encounter* — what makes it innovative and, in a special way, a perfect reflection of the spirit of the late 1970s — is its openness. The basic rules are only a rough sketch, and the rest of the mechanics can be viewed as a kind of "game generator," one refined and developed in many expansions — nine official Eon expansions, and many more that could be found on the Web, even in the very first years of the Internet.

In terms of gameplay, *Cosmic Encounter*'s open system manifests like this: Each player in the skirmish for territories is a different alien race, and each of those races possesses a different, rule-twisting power, one that makes the tokens and cards interact in dozens of strange ways. The twists started with simple things. Virus multiplies the number on his card by the number of tokens in the fight, instead of adding them together. Macrons are giants, so each of their tokens count for four instead of one, like those belonging to the other aliens. Later expansions added substantial wackiness. Schizoid changes the goal of the game. Hurtz rents game elements not in use at the time. Butler requests a fee to handle cards or tokens, and so on. There are also dozens of different action cards — edicts — that impact play, as well as blanks for players to use in designing their own cards. Moons add hundreds of zany effects, so zany some players don't use them at all.

With so many different elements driving the game in unexpected directions, powers and cards whose interaction are usually not covered in the rules, *Cosmic Encounter* is a completely new game every time you play. I've seen a game won in 20 seconds, and another last for more than 10 hours.

As the presence of blank cards suggests, the designers of *Cosmic Encounter* openly encouraged customization, and many players twist the game in their own ways, selecting and tailoring the use of alien powers, moons, and edict cards to suit their needs. This makes playing with another person's copy of the game an interesting experience. My copy, for example, has a really fun "Three-Cards Ante" alien, and challenge cards that copy the opponent's card, or whose value is equal to the opponent's age or the number of minutes since the last hour. I bet there are some homemade edict cards in Richard Garfield's copy that later found a home in *Magic: The Gathering*.

The Future Pastimes team designed a few other unusual games, including *Dune* (Avalon Hill, 1979), which is a kind of *Cosmic Encounter* Lite and was obviously playtested with a *CE* set; *Darkover* (Eon, 1979), based on the Marion Zimmer Bradley books and boasting the zaniest combat system ever designed; *Quirks* (Eon, 1980), an evolution game that is, of course, quirky; *Borderlands* (Eon, 1982), which introduced a resource-building system that would be later developed in *The Settlers of Catan*; *Runes* (Eon, 1981), a word game where you actually construct your letters; and *Hoax* (Eon, 1981), a kind of perverted *Clue* where you can lie to your opponents. All were fun, all were new, but none of them had the wild appeal of *Cosmic Encounter*.

Cosmic Encounter can now be played online, but that means the game had to be more formally codified, so it's definitely not the same experience. No more crazy house rules and homemade aliens; less beer — and other substances — at the gaming table. The game has grown old and responsible, as have we all, and I'm not sure that's a good thing.

The box for Eon's first edition of *Cosmic Encounter* proclaimed "the science-fiction game with everything." And, indeed, long before today's collectible card games, live-action roleplaying games, and massively multi-player online RPGs, *Cosmic Encounter* was the game with everything.

Born in 1961, BRUNO FAIDUTTI studied law, economics, and sociology, eventually earning a doctorate in History by writing about the scientific debate in the Renaissance on the reality of the unicorn. His favorite authors are Pynchon, Joyce, Proust, Rushdie, and Eco, his favorite movie, Andrei Tarkovsky's *Andrei Roublev*. He came into the world of hobby gaming through *Cosmic Encounter* and roleplaying games, and was one of the first French *D&D* players. Bruno has created and published over 40 board and card games, sometimes in collaboration with other designers. Among his best known titles are *Knightmare Chess* and *Citadels*.

Andrew Looney on
COSMIC WIMPOUT

KEY DESIGNERS: THE COSMIC WIMPOUT CLUBHOUSE

C3, INC. (1976)

COSMIC WIMPOUT IS ONE of my very favorite games, as you can tell by look-ing in the little purple gamebag I carry (like a purse) most everywhere I go. Aside from some standard playing cards, the only gaming equipment in my bag that wasn't made by Looney Labs is a set of *Cosmic Wimpout* dice.

This wonderfully portable game consists simply of a special set of five dice, marked with mystic symbols instead of plain pips: four white dice, plus the black "Flaming Sun" die. Everyone from a couple to a crowd can play, with no other equipment but a method of keeping score.

Cosmic Wimpout is a press-your-luck-style game. During each turn, you roll the dice to get points. As long as you successfully score, you can keep rolling again, adding more to your total for that turn. Sometimes you are required to con-tinue rolling, but when you decide to stop, the points you've accumulated during that turn are added to your official total. However, if you "wimpout" with a roll that scores nothing, your turn ends and you get a zero for that round. This creates a fascinating dynamic in which it's technically possible — though obviously very difficult — to win the game with a single series of really lucky rolls.

Cosmic Wimpout is like TV's *Deal or No Deal*: There's a lot of luck involved, but, really, it's all about timing. You want to keep playing as long as you can, to maximize your score, but you also have to know when it's time to be happy with what you've got, and stop. Push it too far, and you'll lose it all.

Cosmic Wimpout has a clean, elegant rules set that allows losing players to feel they still have a chance at a come-from-behind victory. This makes *CW* a game you can jump into at almost any point and still have a shot at winning.

Another really good *CW* rule has to do with getting started. Until you've actu-ally gotten onto the scoreboard — "into the club," as we like to say — you can-not bank a score of less than 35 points. This rule elegantly encourages good play with a subtle lesson in the importance of taking some risks: If you always try to play it safe, you'll never even get into the game, much less win.

While playing *Cosmic Wimpout*, you needn't pay any attention to the action unless and until it's your turn. I like this because it allows you to slip away for a few moments without penalty (and if you don't return in time, the other players can just skip your turn, and it's the same as if you'd scored nothing). Being a dedicated multi-tasker, I try to include these considerations in my own designs. However, multi-tasking with addictive games can be risky.

For example, when I first discovered *CW*, I was preparing to appear in my high school's Senior Class Play. (I was Luther Billis in "South Pacific.") We played *Cosmic Wimpout* to pass the time backstage, when it wasn't our scene. During one performance, I was so eager to get back to the game that I forgot I was in the very next scene. What's more, I was the only character on stage at that particular moment! Thus, for like a full minute, *nothing at all* was happening on stage, until someone found me and I went running back to the waiting audience.

As it turns out, my wife (and co-founder of Looney Labs) got into *Cosmic Wimpout* at around the same time as I did. Kristin, too, was instantly drawn to its mystical look, its arcane mythos, and its compelling fun factor. (Plus, she had this thing about cube-based toys. In 1981, she was certified as the fastest Rubik's Cube solving girl in the nation. But that's another story. . . .)

Anyway, when Kristin and I first got together, and my own ideas for a mystical set of gaming pieces were congealing in my brain, we discovered our common fondness for *Cosmic Wimpout*. We played it during our lunches at NASA, and talked about how we'd both carried our cubes everywhere, had found our way onto the mailing list for C3's *Occasional Newsletter*, and so on. We both really admired how this tiny company was doing the entrepreneurial thing out in the mountains of New England. I think part of the game's special appeal was the fact that it wasn't made by a giant corporation, and that you had to seek it out. We were also inspired by C3's fan-outreach program, cool hand-drawn catalogs, annual tournaments (which we later imitated), and even ideas like using a minimally sized, clear plastic box for packaging. When I add everything up, I would say that *Cosmic Wimpout* is the single most influential game I've ever played.

I loved the company's sense of humor, and the way the staff's fun personalities could be seen in everything from their marketing materials to the cool felt game boards they sold for keeping score. I enjoyed the way they urged you to "pick up and hold the cubes" while you read about how to use them. I dug how they insisted that *Cosmic Wimpout* wasn't just a game, it was an "Experience."

Perhaps the most important part of the *Cosmic Wimpout* Experience was this little note at the end of the instruction sheet called "The Guiding Light — Rules for Creating House Rules." These few short sentences about how to alter the rules to a game — even while you're in the middle of playing it! — provided me with an important bit of mind-expansion. (The first step toward designing my own games was creating new rules for the games we were already playing. . . .)

Who created *Cosmic Wimpout*? That's kind of shrouded in mystery. The company's founders shun personal credit, preferring to use nicknames like Maverick, Argo, and Cargo. They explain the history of the game thusly:

> *Cosmic Wimpout* originated in the forests of the Pacific Northwest. Two travellers came upon the game and liked it so much that they shared it with people everywhere they went. People everywhere made up and added their own rules until it became what it is today: an ever-changing game that's as original as the people who play it.

Digging deeper into the history, *Cosmic Wimpout* is clearly based on an old French dice game called *Dix Mille* (*Ten Thousand*), played with six dice and an inflated point system. Other names for versions of this game include *Five Thousand*, *Zilch*, *Bupkis*, *Greed*, *Farkle*, and *Zonk*. (The last includes extra rules for the imbibing of certain intoxicants.)

You could dismiss *CW* as being just a commercial version of a classic dice game with funky symbols, but that's like saying *Uno* is nothing more than *Crazy Eights* with special cards. It's the funky symbols and special cards that set these products apart, make them more than just another game you can play with dice or cards. It may seem a small point, but mystic symbols instead of typical boring pips were an important part of what first hooked me, and the reason why I still carry *Cosmic Wimpout* dice in my gamebag, instead of trying to get the same fun from a set of five ordinary dice.

Like many luck-oriented games, *Cosmic Wimpout* is not for everyone. "Must-win-to-prove-my-worth" gamers will be frustrated by its relaxed, non-competitive spirit, but if you enjoy chaotic fun — like the action of my games — then give these dice a roll.

★　　★　　★

ANDREW LOONEY is the chief creative officer for Looney Labs, and the designer of *Fluxx*, *Chrononauts*, *Aquarius*, *Nanofictionary*, *IceTowers*, *Treehouse*, and *Martian Coasters*. Andy is also a photographer, a cartoonist, a video-blogger, and a marijuana-legalization advocate. Andy lives with his wife Kristin (and their housemate Alison) somewhere near Washington, DC. Andy is a Hippie, a Trekkie, and a Geek. He's been an Eagle Scout and a NASA engineer. He's gotten patents and won awards. He's written a novel. He designed and coded a videogame. And he once watched as his software was launched into space. Andy loves cake.

Skip Williams on

DAWN PATROL

KEY DESIGNER: MIKE CARR

TSR, INC. (SEVENTH EDITION, 1982)

BOARD GAMES FEATURING WORLD War I air combat have been popular among game designers, if not game fans, for decades. Entries in the field include *Blue Max* from Game Designers' Workshop, *Richthofen's War* from Avalon Hill, *Wings* from Yaquinto, and, most recently, *Wings of War* from Fantasy Flight. The granddaddy of them all, however, is *Dawn Patrol*.

Originally published as *Fight in the Skies* in a 25-copy private effort back in 1968, *Dawn Patrol* has provided a legion of players with camaraderie and a sense of derring-do for nearly 40 years. Designer Mike Carr and scores of dedicated fans constantly work to add new aircraft and other expansions to the rules, a fact reflected in the steady steam of new editions that have seen publication throughout the game's history.

Like many great games, *Dawn Patrol* is remarkably easy to learn. Aircraft move on a square grid, with each 10-miles-per-hour of the plane's speed translating into one square of movement. A plane moves one square in the direction that its nose points, and can turn 45 degrees left or right after it moves. The game offers a series of standard maneuvers — all based on actual maneuvers World War I pilots used in combat — that allow aircraft to bend the basic movement rules somewhat. These maneuvers range from a simple bank, in which the aircraft slides along diagonally, to the dramatic Immelmann (named after Max Immelmann, a German ace of 1916) in which the aircraft abruptly reverses direction.

Any player who can perform the game's selection of maneuvers can handle a plane as well as any ace in the Great War could. This ease of flight is one of the game's strong points. Players needn't worry about the intricacies of handling a vintage aircraft — anyone wishing to enjoy that experience is much better off trying out a computer-based flight simulator. Instead, *Dawn Patrol* allows players to concentrate on the challenging task of handling an aircraft in battle and wringing out every ounce of its fighting capacity.

Several things about the game have inspired a fervent devotion in its fans.

Though the rules are easy to grasp, *Dawn Patrol* requires years to master. A simple sheet of notes holds all the information a player must handle in order to keep an aircraft flying. The player must track the plane's throttle setting, its altitude (a vital record because the game handles combat in three dimensions on a two-dimensional board), ammunition supply, state of the guns (WWI machine guns had a bad habit of jamming after a few bursts), and any damage the craft has sustained.

Novice players soon learn how to maneuver into position for a shot, and they also quickly discover that staying higher than a foe gives a pilot a decided advantage. Truly great players understand that *Dawn Patrol* is a game of position and teamwork.

In a swirling dogfight, it's all too easy to become separated from your wingmen and find yourself at the mercy of enemy guns. The rules simulate the chaos of an air battle though a simple initiative system, in which dice rolls determine the movement order for each turn. Players with higher rolls must move first, which leaves them vulnerable to attack when foes move later on. A player who has been dominating the game can go from the hunter to the hunted with a single dice roll. In addition, whenever bullets strike a plane there's a slight chance that something truly important — such as the engine, a control cable, or the pilot himself — will become damaged, crippling the aircraft. A plane riddled with bullets can also suffer a series of malfunctions that doom it.

Canny players are constantly aware of these dangers and they learn to fight aggressively, even while leaving themselves an out in case the tide of battle turns against them. For example, a veteran knows to attack from above — to maintain an altitude advantage over foes — firing from a "nose down" position. (This is a game term that simply means the pilot has briefly pushed forward his stick and made the front of his machine dip down long enough for a shot before resuming level flight.) A truly crafty player also angles the plane's nose on the square grid so that foes must turn — and lose speed — to attack, in case his initiative number requires an early move during the following game turn. The best players also pay close attention to what their wingmen are doing and take care to keep their friends close by. Two or more planes fighting together are considerably more deadly than a lone machine.

Dawn Patrol has several other appealing elements. First, the game supports almost any number of players. The largest recorded *Dawn Patrol* game had 42 participants, though most fans agree than six to 10 players are best. A single game lasts two hours or less, which means that a group can stage several sessions over the course of an afternoon or evening.

The game also includes set-up charts that allow for a virtually infinite number of scenarios. Though one can simply create a scenario, you can randomly generate the battle's date and location (which, in turn, determines the sorts of aircraft than can be involved), altitude level, prevailing weather, and type of mission, such as fighter versus fighter, escort mission, balloon attack, ground attack, and so on.

Finally, each player develops a roster of fictional pilots who fly each type of plane in the air services of Germany, Austria-Hungary, England, France, Italy, Belgium, or the United States. A new pilot must have a name — *Dawn Patrol* players soon develop appetites for lists of period names — and starts as a vulnerable rookie. If the pilot survives several missions or accumulates a string of victories, he gains new abilities that make him better in combat. He might even win a medal. After only a few games, any player boasts a solid collection of pilots, each with his own tales of narrow escapes and improbable victories. Such pilots inevitably develop personalities that make gameplay even more memorable.

This last element adds a strong roleplaying flavor to an otherwise completely tactical combat game. In fact, TSR, Inc. briefly touted *Dawn Patrol* as a roleplaying game during the early 1980s. *Dawn Patrol*'s claim to roleplaying game status shouldn't be lightly dismissed. Players create fictional personae who face the dangers of a game world and who get better with experience. Personal rivalries between fictional pilots frequently develop, and many players alter their playing styles just a bit to suit their best pilots' temperaments. Most roleplayers, however, crave more flexibility in creating characters than simply recording a name and nationality, and many (if not most) would like their characters to do more than just fight.

Dawn Patrol remains a staple at the famous Gen Con game convention. There have been *Dawn Patrol* or *Fight in the Skies* events at every Gen Con gathering held in the Midwest, all the way back to the very first convention in 1968. The Fight in the Skies Society, founded in 1969, runs a full slate of events at Gen Con every year. It also sponsors several "fly-ins" around the United States. The offerings include an invitational Masters Game every two years, in which the best players pit their skills against each other in a ferocious last-man-flying dogfight. The winner receives a silver cup as a trophy. This practice is modeled after the custom in German Jagdstaffels, where aces were awarded silver cups to commemorate their victories. In the alternating years, the society offers the Society Open, in which all members are invited to join an aerial clash that can rage for hours. They also organize an annual team event and a mini-con, held each spring somewhere in the Midwest, and publish the quarterly *Aerodrome* magazine, which recently saw the release of its 150th issue.

The longevity of *Aerodrome* speaks volumes about the dedication of *Dawn Patrol*'s many fans, and the quality of Mike Carr's classic design. If you want to get a better sense of the game that's earned their devotion, the best way to do so is grab some dice and get up and at 'em!

SKIP WILLIAMS is an unofficial member of the "older than dirt" club, having worked in the game industry since the mid-1970s, when he started as a clerk in TSR, Inc.'s Dungeon Hobby Shop. Skip wore many other hats during the next several decades. He ran the Gen Con Game Fair in Kenosha and Milwaukee, wrote reams of pages about *Dungeons & Dragons* (Skip is the co-author of blockbuster third edition of *D&D*), and worked as an organizer and editor for the Role-Playing Game Association. Skip also holds a coveted *Dawn Patrol* Master's Cup and can paint a pretty good-looking miniature. Skip and his wife Penny live in rural Wisconsin in a century-old farmhouse surrounded by several acres of abandoned farmland, none of which, Skip reports, is suitable for landing a wounded aircraft.

Alan R. Moon on

DESCENT

KEY DESIGNER: KEVIN WILSON

FANTASY FLIGHT GAMES (2005)

I'VE ALWAYS BEEN A fan of dungeon-crawl games. Seems like I buy every new one that comes out and give it a try, each time hoping it will finally be the one. Then, in March 2006, I played *Descent: Journeys in the Dark*.

In dungeon-crawl games most of the players take the roles of heroes who set out to explore a dungeon (or something similar, like a cave or tomb). There, the heroes must defeat lots of monsters, hunt for treasure, and possibly rescue someone or satisfy some other type of quest, all the while trying to increase their abilities for the next adventure. In some dungeon-crawl games, one of the players takes the role of the dungeon master (or DM). He is like the manager of a sports team, running the monsters and springing traps and doing anything else he can to thwart the heroes. In other dungeon-crawl games, there is no DM and the players just play against the game system.

Descent comes with a booklet of nine scenarios. In each scenario, the heroes start with a number of conquest tokens. They can gain additional tokens in the dungeon by finding treasures and sometimes in various other ways. The heroes lose tokens when they die, each hero having a separate value. If the heroes ever run out of conquest tokens, the DM wins. The heroes win by fulfilling the victory conditions set forth in the scenario being played.

Designer Kevin Wilson succeeds with *Descent* where so many others have failed for a number of reasons. Number one among them is the clever mechanic that drives the DM's play. He first draws a number of threat tokens equal to the number of players. Then he draws two cards from his own deck. The DM then moves and attacks with any or all of the monsters on the board, playing cards if and when possible.

Each card has two values on it: the cost in threat tokens to play the card and the threat token value of the card, meaning that if the DM discards the card without playing it, he gains that many threat tokens. The cards are mostly: 1) spawn cards, which allow the DM to bring more monsters into the game at the start of his turn; 2) battle cards, which allow him to upgrade the dice for a monster, give him rerolls, attack with a monster during a hero's turn, and the like; 3) movement cards, which allow the DM some sort of bonus movement for one or more monsters; or 4) traps, which can be played during a hero's turn when a hero moves, opens a door, or opens a chest. The best cards, though, are ones that provide a lasting effect for the whole game. My particular favorites are Doom, which gives the DM an extra die every time a monster attacks; Evil Genius, which lets the DM draw three cards each turn instead of just two; and Trapmaster, which reduces the cost on all future trap cards by one threat token and adds two to any damage a hero receives from traps.

In each scenario, the dungeon is divided into areas separated by doors. The heroes can only see the parts of the dungeon they have already entered. Every time the heroes open a new door, a new area of the dungeon is revealed. The DM then puts the pieces of the dungeon, the monsters, treasures, and other items in the new area into play. Usually, each area has a portal (called a glyph). The heroes can use the portals to travel between town and the dungeon. For instance, when a hero is killed, he starts back in the town and can then enter the dungeon via any portal, usually electing to enter through the portal deepest into the dungeon. Heroes also use portals to go back to town to heal, to buy items, or just to reorganize before reentering the dungeon.

Descent bucks a lot of trends for me. I typically don't like games where one player plays against all the others. I also usually don't enjoy cooperative games, but here being part of a band of heroes works so well, it's just too much fun for me to even concern myself with the cooperative factor. (I should note that in many other dungeon-crawl games, the players compete not only against the DM but against each other.) I generally don't like games where you spend lots of time fighting battles, many of them similar, or games that take more than 90 minutes. *Descent* features both potentially repetitive battles and a long playing time. If the heroes win, depending on what scenario you're playing, a session can last four to eight hours. Of course, if the DM wins, it can be quite a bit shorter. But all of those factors don't matter to me with *Descent*, which is a testament to just how good a game it is.

Downtime is also a perennial concern for me, downtime being the time between your turns in a game. There is a fair amount of downtime with *Descent*, but it doesn't seem to be a problem. If I'm the DM, it's fascinating to listen to and watch the heroes plan and execute their turns. As a hero, I'm interested in watching the DM take his turn, if I'm not talking to my fellow heroes and planning our next moves.

Another thing that makes *Descent* great is that only two of the players need to know the rules: the DM and one of the heroes. The experienced hero can show the others what weapons, armor, magic items, and potions they should equip at the start of the game. He can then show them how to move and fight on their first turn or two. After that, most players will know the majority of what they need to know to get their hero through the adventure. This makes the game's cooperative factor a plus for me, for perhaps the first time ever!

The heroes won the first six games of *Descent* I played. I thought that meant the game was unbalanced. But in the next bunch of sessions, the DM won almost every time. So the balance is definitely impacted quite a bit by the scenario being played as well as the players' skill. I've tried adding and deleting some rules and/or cards in the game, but I can't say any of those changes made much difference. The multiple variables make it hard to evaluate *Descent*'s balance, but those same variables are also what makes it so much fun.

Fantasy Flight knows fantasy games and knows production quality, with *Descent* just being one example in a whole line of games with tons of top-notch plastic figures. I'd still probably enjoy *Descent* if the heroes and monsters were just cardboard counters, but the large plastic figures make it just that much better. They are eye-catching, so if you play the game in a public area, expect curious passersby to stop and ask what's going on. Yeah, those big boxes of plastic figures cost a lot more than your average game. They may not be for everyone. But I love what Fantasy Flight is doing. *Descent* is worth any amount of money to me. I've already gotten back enjoyment equal to ten times what I spent on the game.

The first expansion for *Descent*, *The Well Of Darkness*, was released in late 2006, and it's a must. It adds more scenarios, more monsters, and some very interesting new elements to the DM's repertoire. Things like rolling boulders (picture Indiana Jones here), traps made of spinning blades, hot lava, and mud. There are lots of new DM cards, too. But the DM doesn't simply add all the new cards to his deck. In each scenario, he gets a certain number of points that he can spend to take on new cards. Lots of tough choices are involved, as almost all of the new cards contribute interesting elements. I've played enough of the different *Well of Darkness* scenarios to know that the heroes seem to have a much tougher time winning with them. The expansion also affords the game more variety, so that, while there is still lots of battling, killing monsters is not the only objective.

A second expansion, *The Altar Of Despair*, was released in March 2007, and it appears to be just as excellent as the first. Fantasy Flight also plans a campaign game, with rules on how to play multiple scenarios with the same characters.

If you want something simpler than *Descent*, or want to start with a more basic dungeon-crawl game, TSR's old *Dungeon* board game, isn't bad at all. In fact, it had been my favorite dungeon-crawl for over 30 years, until *Descent* came along. But my bet is that once you play *Descent*, you won't want to play any other dungeon-crawl game again.

When ALAN MOON was a kid, every Sunday was family day. Along with his father, mother, and brother, Alan would spend the day bowling, playing miniature golf, going to the movies, and then end the day at home playing games. So it wasn't too surprising when he wound up with a career in the hobby game industry. Alan has worked at various times for Avalon Hill, Parker Brothers, and Ravensburger F.X. Schimd USA. He also ran his own company, White Wind, from 1990 to 1997. Since 2000, Alan has been a full-time freelance game designer, with almost 70 games to his credit. His first published game was *Black Spy* (Avalon Hill, 1981), inspired by the classic card game, *Hearts*. But his first game that seemed to get any real attention was *Airlines*, published by the German company Abacus in 1990. Alan has won the coveted Spiel Des Jahres award (Game of the Year in Germany) twice, for *Elfenland* in 1998 and for *Ticket to Ride* in 2004. *Ticket to Ride* has won almost two dozen other awards worldwide. His favorite games are poker, *Twilight Struggle*, *Descent*, *Cosmic Eidex*, spades, *Mystery Rummy: Jack the Ripper*, *Crokinole*, *Hunters & Gatherers*, *Adel Verpflichtet*, and *Liar's Dice*.

Larry Harris on

DIPLOMACY

KEY DESIGNER: ALLAN B. CALHAMER

AVALON HILL (1959)

THE SENSATION IN YOUR back is from the figurative dull, rusty knife protruding there. The pain it causes can be as intense as that brought on by the real thing. Raw human emotions are being toyed with here! A few moments ago you looked into the eyes of the Russian head of state, and you gazed into his soul. You've also known him since the third grade, so you were absolutely certain he was telling you the truth. You were certain he was going to support your move into the Black Sea.

As it turns out, he had other things in mind.

The results of the last turn are called out and the various armies and navies spread across Europe move about the map. But not in the way you were expecting. Your Black Sea gambit has failed. Of course the Russian leader — your childhood best friend — offers up all kinds of reasons for letting you down. Indeed, he can rattle off a long and somewhat logical list of explanations for stabbing you in the back. He also assures you, on the head of a future unborn first child, that he will never do it again.

Such drama! This is fun stuff.

When the phrases "dull, rusty knife" and "the sensation in your back" are uttered together, in the context of a book on brilliant hobby games, many of you know right away that we've come to Allan B. Calhamer's *Diplomacy*. For those who have not yet had the pleasure of experiencing this masterpiece, let me introduce you to it.

As a player in *Diplomacy*, you take on the role of leader for one of seven European countries at the dawn of the 20th century, just prior to World War I. The countries include Austria-Hungary, England, France, Germany, Italy, Russia, and Turkey. The actual game mechanics of *Diplomacy* are wonderfully simple. An army or naval unit can enter a region and take control of it. Pretty straightforward, no? Well, what happens if someone else wants to do the same thing at the same time? Sounds like there's a bit of a conflict of interest to me. And, like all conflicts of interest, this situation can quickly turn into a tense power struggle. Eventually, the player with the most power will win.

Since all the nations start out with pretty much the same number of military units, how does one player get more powerful than another? The best way is by receiving support from other players. How do you do that? You talk to them. You negotiate. You convince them that it's in their best interest to help you. Your currency in this exchange is usually some sort of return favor, a pledge of support for one of your (temporary) ally's endeavors. That's where it gets political and tricky.

Diplomacy uses no dice. Moves are made or thwarted by the decisions you and the other players make. There's no randomizing factor, no lucky die roll to overturn the result of your machinations and deliberations. The sum total of the players' deals — those honored and those broken — decides who wins the day.

The game is a turn-based affair, but all the players are busy doing the same things simultaneously. In the negotiation period, players will . . . well, negotiate. They go off together and talk things over. They make deals. They try to convince their enemies that they're really friends, that their noble people do not have ambitions to take the land belonging to that would-be partner, even as they are hatching plans to do just that. They try to convince their allies to support their intended moves — for this turn, anyway.

A lot of the maneuvering and negotiating centers around the limited number of supply centers located throughout Europe. The more supply centers you control, the more armies and fleets you can place on the map. Guard those centers well! If you lose them, you may be required to reduce (disband) some of your ground or naval forces.

Once negotiations are deemed complete, players write orders for each of their units. An order will command an army or navy unit to move, hold, or support. A move order directs a unit to advance to a specific neighboring region. Hold orders direct units to stay in place. Support means the unit will assist another unit in either moving or holding.

These written orders are "state secrets." How much — or, more typically, how little — they reflect the promises made and deals struck during the negotiations phase isn't revealed until the person serving as game master collects them all and starts to put them into play. The orders often conflict, so it's up to the game master to make sense of this basket of crabs. It can get complicated, figuring out who is trying to move where and who is supporting each move and hold. But based on the rulebook, and no little amount of debate about said rules, the game master eventually adjudicates all the orders. Only then is the map updated and the individual nations left to stew over the latest betrayal and mull over their new, possibly diminished positions in the world.

Even when things are not going your way, though, you can play a role in dictating the fate of early 20th-century Europe, because the great powers will need your help.

Just don't expect them to treat you kindly. Nothing and no one can be trusted in *Diplomacy*. You should know that's the case while you're playing, because you have probably been bending the truth since turn one — at least if you're playing the game the right way. In fact, if you're a veteran *Diplomacy* player, you started lying even before the game started. The spin cycle began when you called up Germany and invited him to play — and promised to be his ally all the way, until the two of you were the only ones left.

Which brings us back to the running-dog, doublecrossing Russian.

Okay, he managed to stab you. For the moment, you're the wronged party. You can take the moral high ground. Play the guilt card or pout. Promise to never trust or negotiate with the scoundrel again. You can even make it public that this recent development can be considered proof positive that you are a willing and trustworthy partner for any anti-Russian plots that the other nations might want to hatch. It is your right — no, your *duty* to get revenge for the injustice delivered to your peace-loving people at the hands of a once-trusted ally.

You've probably heard the saying "Countries don't have friends, they only have self-interest." Well, it can also be said that *Diplomacy* players don't have friends at the table, only (temporary) barriers or bridges to achieving their nation's self-interest.

Few games bring you to the heart of their theme as quickly and forcefully as *Diplomacy*. You live it! That wasn't a real Russian or Italian ruler betraying you, of course, but the players' promises to you were certainly real. And that emotional content makes the game all the more effective. It'd probably be easier to have the stranger running France knife you in the back than that longtime friend, the guy who stood up in your wedding or just helped you move.

In time, you'd think you might become a hardened diplomat and not find yourself so caught up in the game's myriad treacheries. Take it from me, though, no matter how seasoned a *Diplomacy* player you are, it still hurts when you're betrayed. The nature of this diabolically designed game makes it a perfect venue for the study of treachery and deceit, but that also means it's not a game for the thin skinned. Many an annoyed and angry novice player has asked, after a single session, why anyone would want to play the game again. But, more often than not, they come back for more.

Originally released as a board game in 1959, *Diplomacy* became a popular play-by-mail game in the 1960s. Today, of course, it can be found all over the World Wide Web. Still, there is nothing more fun than hand-to-hand — or, should I say, face-to-face — games of *Diplomacy*.

I am convinced that Allan Calhamer's masterpiece should be part of every high school curriculum. Don't tell the kids, but it teaches history, geography, the art of political negotiation, and something else — some healthy critical skepticism. By the time you get into high school, you have a pretty good idea that not everyone always tells the truth. But a good game of *Diplomacy* helps you to understand how skillful some people can be at fooling you!

I know this all sounds rather dark, but what better place to explore this side of human nature than with a game?

Imagine this. All high schools have their rivals. They meet on the gridiron for football. They meet on the track field and the baseball diamond. What if they met in a yearlong, area-wide game of *Diplomacy*? Each school could play a county. Its team would form its own internal decision-making processes and assign its external negotiators. In the middle of it all would be game masters and a communication hub, a community newspaper or website. Each week the hub could cover the latest developments, complete with a current map and commentaries from the school teams themselves. This sort of exercise could teach the kids a lot — and bring this fine game the following it deserves.

I'm very guarded about what I do with my time. I have to feel that I'm not only enjoying myself, but that I'm also learning something — that, as a result of how I just spent the last few hours, I'm somehow a better person, with a better understanding of the world. *Diplomacy* does this for me. It's the ultimate social activity for the 21st century — stabbing you friends in the back with that dull, rusty knife and avoiding the favor returned.

What better way to spend some time?

LARRY HARRIS has had an extensive career working as a game designer. Companies for which he's designed games include Milton Bradley, Mattel, Coleco, Parker Brothers, Hasbro Games Group, Hasbro Interactive, and Infogrames Interactive. He currently runs his own company, Harris Game Design. During 1984 alone, his first year at Milton Bradley, he had no fewer than 13 games of his design featured in the company's catalog. This included the three initial titles in the Gamemaster series: *Conquest of the Empire, Broadsides and Boarding Parties*, and, of course, *Axis & Allies*. He plays lots of board and computer games, and has a particular interest in strategy games and military history. Larry has lived extensively in Europe and even three years in Iran. He speaks fluent French, is an Army veteran with five years service, and has been known to pilot an ultra-light.

Richard Garfield on

Dungeons & Dragons

Key Designers: Gary Gygax, Dave Arneson

TSR, Inc. (first edition, 1974)

I FORGET HOW I first heard about *Dungeons & Dragons*. I was about 14, and it was a few years after the game had been published, in 1974, but just a bit before the second publishing, in 1977 — which is when it split into a beginner's game and *Advanced Dungeons & Dragons*. I was enthralled with descriptions of the game I'd heard from the college students that hung out at Gandalf's Den, the store that supposedly sold *D&D*. I say *supposedly* because they were always sold out and the wait for a copy was interminable. But the stories the college kids told — of fighting monsters, exploring mysterious places, and confronting diabolic traps seemed too exciting to be contained in a game.

I went home and tried to create my own version of *D&D*. Since that time I have recreated many games from descriptions, or portions of play sessions — but never have I fallen so far from the mark. My gaming experiences at the time simply had not equipped me to reconstruct *D&D* from its description. It is like I was living in Flatland and, after having the third dimension described to me, rushing home to try and draw in 3-D, but just ending up with a bunch of squares that in no way resemble cubes. How far off I was is a testament to how outrageously innovative *D&D* was.

My copy eventually arrived. I remember biking back home from the shop and reading all the cryptic little books from beginning to end, trying to gain admission into the world that the college kids had described. It wasn't easy; by any standards the rules were wanting. They contained misspellings, charts with little or no explanation, and hardly any instruction of how to actually play the game. I am sure that this experience is the foundation of my belief that no one except for the most hardened players actually read rules, and those players will get through them no matter what the challenge.

The general way it worked, which was so hard to fathom back then, is known to an extraordinary number of people today. *D&D* built upon a foundation laid out in a set of combat rules titled *Chainmail*, but *Chainmail* was still firmly part of military tabletop gaming. *D&D*, on the other hand, was the first roleplaying game.

The basic framework of a roleplaying game has a game master devising situation that the players confront, typically in a cooperative or semi-cooperative way. The players have characters who change over time, generally growing more powerful. There are a host of ways in which *D&D* influenced future games that I consider secondary to this basic framework: player attributes, experience points and levels, character archetypes, and the fantasy flavor, to name a few. Whether or not these and many other characteristics were original to *D&D*, their presence in that first version of the game — and the way they were dealt with in its pages — has had a far-reaching influence on the hobby game industry. While this legacy is far more than most games will ever achieve, it's secondary. To focus on that aspect is to miss the big picture.

To call *D&D* an innovative game is a bit like calling the Wright Brothers' vehicle an innovative car. The definition of *game* has expanded to include *D&D*, but there is really no reason that a neutral outside observer would categorize it that way. A definition for *game* would previously have been something like: A contest between two or more players or sides, constrained by rules that are understood by all players, which ends in a ranking — of winners and losers, or perhaps a score or exchange of money. Oh, and it is engaged with for entertainment. Now, along comes *D&D*, and what do we have? We may have no winners or losers, the rules may be unknown to the players (only the game master needs to know them) and are often somewhat flexible, and there may be no end to the game. There aren't even clear sides; there are players and the game master, but the players are not exactly on the same side as their fellow players and the game master is neither antagonistic nor usually entirely neutral. The only unambiguous constant with that old idea of *game* is that *D&D* is engaged with for entertainment.

In this way, I don't think it is a stretch to call *D&D* the most innovative game ever. It is possible some other game deserves this title; the first one-player game maybe, or the first game for more than two players, or the first game that used pieces, or the first game designed for gambling. But this isn't going to be a list with bridge or go or *Monopoly* on it; they just aren't in the same league when it comes to innovation.

As more roleplaying games came out, my friends and I moved on from *D&D*, some to *AD&D*, others to different RPGs. There was a sort of snobbish disdain for *D&D*, because these newer games were better. Duh. The airplanes a few years after the Wright Brothers' flight were a lot better, too. It embarrasses me that at one point I critiqued *D&D* at that level, but I was teenager with no perspective on what *D&D* had brought to the world of games. And, in fact, it is astonishing how many of the particulars of the game turned out to be really excellent ideas in the end anyway. For example, class- and level-based systems seemed naive back then, but now it is understood just how powerful and flexible this approach can be.

It wasn't just new roleplaying games I took up after learning *D&D*. I started playing every game I could get my hands on, I engaged in a full-fledged exploration of the world of games. I figured if something as amazing as *D&D* was out there, who knew what else there was to be discovered? Although I fell in love with games, I will confess I was disappointed that I never found a game that gave me the feeling I had when I discovered *D&D*, a feeling of awe about the boundless possibilities of games.

While learning about the vast world of games, I took an ownership of these games that perhaps I wouldn't have, if I hadn't been exposed to *D&D*. After all, the game master is a game designer — creating the challenges for the players, interpreting and creating rules to handle the myriad situations that come up. Often, even the players are engaged in game design as they participate in the collaboration that is roleplaying. It is no surprise then that when I met new games I wasn't afraid to play with the rules, to experiment with variations and combine game ideas. And I am certain I wasn't alone in this regard. I believe that many people — perhaps not directly and perhaps without realizing it — learned to master their own game experience from *D&D*.

So, while no particular game gave me the feeling that *D&D* did when I first met it, games as a whole did feel powerful and unlimited. And in this way, *D&D* fostered a love of games and game design in a generation of players — not just because it was a game they loved, but more important, because it taught them the possibilities of this fantastic pursuit.

RICHARD GARFIELD's first published game, *Magic: The Gathering*, was the first trading card game — now a multi-billion dollar industry worldwide. Since that time, he has produced many award-winning board and card games. In the realm of computer gaming, he has been a game designer and consultant for companies including Electronic Arts and Microsoft. Richard was a professor of mathematics at Whitman College before he left to help start Wizards of the Coast, the original publisher of *Magic*, now currently owned by Hasbro. He holds a doctorate in Mathematics from the University of Pennsylvania, and currently teaches a class titled "The Characteristics of Games" at the University of Washington.

William W. Connors on

DYNASTY LEAGUE BASEBALL

KEY DESIGNER: MICHAEL CIESLINSKI

DESIGN DEPOT (1995)

FEW SPORTS CAN BE captured in tabletop format without the loss of many of the things that make the game special. Baseball, on the other hand, is ideally suited to such adaptations. Games that have tried to replicate the Great American Pastime range from the quick-playing *Inning-A-Minute Baseball* I designed in concert with friend and fellow fan Timothy Brown to the venerable *Strat-O-Matic Baseball*, which has been around so long it may predate the actual sport. For my money, though, it's never been done better than in *Dynasty League Baseball*.

Starting in October of 1989, I had the good fortune to work for TSR, Inc. During most of my time there, many members of the design staff spent our lunch hours playing ongoing leagues of *Dynasty League Baseball* (it was called *Pursue the Pennant* back then). It wasn't unusual to walk into the lunchroom and find three games going on at once, with a few people standing around kibitzing — sometimes even doing the wave! The fact that so many professional game designers and truly avid baseball fans opted for *DLB* as our game of choice should, I think, speak volumes. Even more telling is the fact that we didn't feel the need to rewrite half the rules. To paraphrase Dr. McCoy: "I know (game designers), they love to change things."

Before the game starts, each manager puts together a team of 25 players — usually about 10 or 11 pitchers and 14 or 15 position players. That's the same number you'll find on a typical Major League roster. Starting line-ups are created and pitching match-ups determined. If the game is part of an ongoing series, which is certainly the best way to play, managers need to take into account pitcher fatigue, players who might be nursing a minor injury, and other such subtleties. That done, it's time to . . . play ball!

At its heart, *DLB* (like real baseball) is a deceptively simple game. Only when you look deeper do you understand the strategy and complexity at its heart.

A game of *DLB* is resolved one at-bat at a time, with only the make-or-break payoff pitch being addressed. Each player on your team has a card with a table on it, representing how he actually performed during the season. These are all real players, from real Major League teams, and the information on the cards is painstakingly accurate. Although these cards have a wealth of detailed information on them, they are easy to read and managers quickly master their use.

The outcome of the at-bat is determined when the pitching team's manager rolls three 10-sided dice. These are read like percentile dice, generating a number between 000 and 999. Numbers between 000 and 499 are listed on the batter's card and those between 500 and 999 are on the pitcher's card. (This creates, essentially, one combined table between the two cards.) Generally, rolls on the batter's card favor the batter and rolls on the pitcher's card favor the pitcher. For example, suppose you're playing a classic game from the 1982 season and Paul Molitor is at the plate. The dice are rolled and come up 182. If he's facing a right-handed pitcher, that's a long fly out to center field. On the other hand, if there's a lefty on the mound, Molitor has just hit a shot out of the park.

In some cases, this roll ends the matter right there. If there's no one on base and the result of the roll is a strikeout, pop fly, or routine grounder, that's that. In many situations, however, you'll need to consult a book of other tables to determine additional details. A routine grounder might not be so routine if the offensive manager has called a hit-and-run play. Will the runner be caught off base and thrown out, can he see what's happening in time to hold up, or is he fast enough to make it safely to the next base? The charts to resolve all these things can be a little intimidating at first, but their use is logical and quickly mastered.

Okay, so what's the big deal? That's a cute mechanic, but does it really make *Dynasty League* so much better than all the other baseball games on the market? Nope. But here's what does.

Factored into *DLB*'s tables and charts are all the unusual and often controversial plays that make every at-bat potentially game- or even season-shattering. The ever-present chance of an error can transform a simple dribbler down the line into extra bases or a blown call by the umpire can thwart a manager's best strategy. A hitter who's a terror in the clutch can turn the tide of the game with one swing of the bat, while a pitcher who's tough in a jam can come through to shut down a potentially disastrous rally. And there's every manager's biggest nightmare — the injury table. Having the heart of your batting order or the ace of your staff go down for the season on opening day can bring tears to your eye.

There's also a little entry on one of the cards reading *Bizarre*. When you roll that, everyone sits up and takes notice. This is where *Dynasty League Baseball* really hits it out of the park. All sorts of unusual, one-in-a-million things — drawn from real events of the MLB season — show up here. Line drives or blazing fastballs can hit birds in flight, ceiling tiles can break away from domes and bring games to a premature halt, and bench-clearing brawls can result in one or more players ending up with suspensions. Corked bats, pine tar in the pitcher's palm, and traffic accidents on the way to the ballpark are all possibilities here.

Design Depot releases a new set of cards and charts every year, detailing the previous Major League season. If your team moved to a new stadium, it will be in the charts. If your favorite player had a career year, you'll see it reflected in his new card. *Dynasty League Baseball* is ideal for people who want to draft and manage their own team — trading players, adjusting batting orders, and setting up pitching rotations.

There's so much detail and careful thought in every aspect of *Dynasty League Baseball*, it can only be described as a labor of love. And, to my way of thinking, that's what sets great games apart from good games — the certain knowledge that the designer had as much fun creating it as you do playing it.

I had the chance to introduce the game to my friend Kevin, a designer from another company who was also a hardcore baseball fan. We were playing a game between his favorite Toronto Blue Jays and my home town Pittsburgh Pirates. (This was back when the Pirates were good, so you know it was a while ago!) The game was a good one, with a number of close plays and interesting twists — but we went into the ninth with his Jays ahead of my Bucs by two runs. I was down to my final out, with runners on first and third. I brought in a .200-hitting bat off the bench and was getting ready to congratulate Kevin on the win, when the dice were rolled. POW! The results were right in the middle of a very narrow sweet spot on my batter's card, so the ball just cleared the fence for a three-run walk-off homer. There was silence in the room.

I can't say I was overjoyed, even though things had clearly gone my way. If you want someone to like a new game, it's really best if they win.

But after a second, Kevin stood up and shook his head. "[Expletive deleted], I feel just as upset as I would have at the ballpark!"

How many games can evoke that kind of emotion?

WILLIAM W. CONNORS is a lifelong gamer who's been lucky enough to get paid for it since the mid-1980s. He's worked for a number of companies, either on staff or as a freelancer, including TSR, Wizards of the Coast, id Software, and Hasbro. He is best known as the guiding force behind the Ravenloft game line and currently heads up the entertainment division of Senario, LLC, a Chicago-area entertainment and consumer products company. Although still a baseball fan, it has been supplanted by Rugby Union as his favorite sport. He currently resides in southeastern Wisconsin with his wife Kathryn and two sons, Chris and Patrick.

EL GRANDE

KEY DESIGNERS: WOLFGANG KRAMER, RICHARD ULRICH
RIO GRANDE GAMES (ENGLISH EDITION, 2001)

IN 2001, AS I played *El Grande* for the first time, its design left me awestruck; beneath its simple mechanisms, layer upon layer of strategy and depth lay hidden. It was an epiphany. I was filled with an inspiration that other German titles, even the exceptional *Settlers of Catan*, had failed to instill in me.

Growing up in Denmark, I had been lucky to play a steady diet of "Anglo-style" board games from such legendary publishers as Avalon Hill, Milton Bradley, and Games Workshop. During those years, I was exposed only to a few "German-style" games, such as *Scotland Yard* and *Targui*. Although I found these few German imports enjoyable, I relished the immersion of the more meaty Anglo designs, willingly grinding through dense rule systems to enjoy the simulation and choices they evoked.

It wasn't until the brilliant mechanics of *El Grande* unfurled before me in 2001 that I gained more than a passing appreciation for the invasion of German board games. This invasion had been launched upon U.S. shores in the late 1990s by Mayfair Games and Rio Grande Games, later joined by other publishers such as Überplay, Z-Man, and Fantasy Flight. To be fair, Mayfair Games had been publishing German games for a considerable period of time before the mid-'90s, but their efforts would not have meaningful impact until their publication of *The Settlers of Catan* in 1996.

El Grande showed me the surprising depth that could be achieved by interlocking simple mechanisms — the principle that lies at the heart of the German school of design.

Considered among the heaviest of the great German designs, *El Grande* would be the one game that moved me to appreciate the refreshing European vision of design (although the French racing game *Formula Dé* had come close). Perhaps that was no accident. The comparative weight of *El Grande*'s system, and its plethora of special abilities, makes it arguably the closest of its breed to the Anglo design tradition.

In *El Grande*, players each take the role of a "grande," one of the leading aristocrats in 15th-century Spain, and his cohort of caballeros (knights and members of the lower aristocracy). Players seek to accumulate influence in the form of abstract points, accumulated over three general scoring rounds and through certain action cards.

At its heart, *El Grande* is what connoisseurs call an "area-majority game." I personally consider it the granddaddy — one of the earliest, and certainly the most influential — of the idiom. As the name would imply, the goal of an area-majority game is for players to seek domination of the prevalent (and many times, relatively few) areas of the board. A common feature is that these games allow for units/tokens/pieces of *several*, or even all, players to *share* game board areas, but not dominance of such an area, which is usually granted to the player with the most tokens/power there. Examples of other area-majority games are Martin Wallace's *Struggle of Empires* (2004), Eric Lang's *Midgard* (2007), and Tom Jolly's *Cave Troll* (2002, 2006).

The core objective of *El Grande*, as you would expect in a German design, is simple: To achieve victory, players seek to gain victory points by placing the greater number of caballeros into the various regions on *El Grande*'s game board (gorgeously illustrated by Doris Matthaus). The regions are not equal in value, with some providing more points than others. Fundamentally, this poses the classic player choice between concentration or diversification.

This simple premise provides the foundation for an incredible system of interlaced mechanics. To start, players are provided with identical power decks, each consisting of 13 numbered cards. At the beginning of every round, these cards inversely determine a player's initiative, as well as the number of caballeros he may add to his court. The higher the initiative number played, the more the player improves the likelihood of taking early action. A high number conversely means the player receives proportionally fewer caballeros that round. As caballeros represent the main game resource, this is not an insignificant choice.

The brilliance of the power decks rests not only in the trade-off between initiative and resources, but as each power card is discarded after use, a player must balance this diminishing supply with both long- and short-term goals, while at the same time evaluating what remaining power cards his opponents hold.

Many German designs would have built their entire game experience around a mechanic as interesting as that of *El Grande*'s power decks. Yet, Wolfgang Kramer and Richard Ulrich serve this wonderful initiative/resource mechanic as only one of many tasty dishes in *El Grande*. In fact, the game's true main course is the selection and execution of action cards.

After players have determined initiative and collected their caballeros, as determined by the power cards they selected, the player with the highest initiative proceeds to select and resolve one of the five action cards drawn for that round. This continues until all players have chosen and resolved an action card, after which the round ends.

Like the power cards, *El Grande*'s action cards represent a tradeoff, where players must balance strategic goals with the tactical considerations for the round at hand. Each action card provides its player with a voluntary special ability, as well as the number of caballeros that player may move from his courts onto the game board during his turn. (Caballeros may only be placed in the vicinity of the enormous black "king" token, the movement of which is also influenced by action cards.) Typically, the more powerful the special ability granted by the action card, the fewer caballeros will be allowed to make their journey to the board.

The selection of action cards is central to the delicious agony of choice that *El Grande* executes so brilliantly. Not only must a player consider how many caballeros he wishes to place, he must also consider whether the special ability of an action card justifies fewer caballeros, how to resolve said ability, or whether he should choose a specific action card simply to deprive an opponent of its beneficial effect.

The action card system in *El Grande* was really the harbinger of a new trend in game design, typically referred to as a character-selection system. Following *El Grande*'s success, the core idea of Kramer and Ulrich's action cards was developed by Marcel-André Casasola Merkle in his acclaimed *Verräter* (1998), Bruno Faidutti channels the principle in applying both bluff and game structure to the concept in his brilliant *Citadels* (2000), and Andreas Seyfarth takes Faidutti's notion of game structure further in his *Puerto Rico* (2002). Appreciating this trend, I sought to explore the principle of structure selection, while adding an Anglo design twist, in my *Twilight Imperium, Third Edition* (2005). I strongly believe that as more designers discover the possibilities of this concept, the archaic Anglo phase structure will be a thing of the past. This should pave the way for more organic and interlaced designs that also retain the thematic immersion that is fundamental to the Anglo design style.

In addition to its power cards, *El Grande* features other subsystems that support the central action card mechanism. These smaller systems are evocative, interesting, and interlaced with one another in a way that creates a satisfying organic whole. The castillo, for example, acts as an abstract region where players may dump all or part of their round's caballeros. These caballeros are concealed at the bottom of the castillo — a sturdy wooden tower that is one of the most interesting and just-plain-neat board game components ever made.

A game of *El Grande* game is played over nine rounds, with the various regions on the game board being scored after every third round. This gives the game an interesting three-act dramatic structure. Keeping track of the game rounds is easy with the inspired round track, one of the most beautiful and utilitarian track designs to date. It also imaginatively uses both a Y and an X axis to communicate the round progression, as well as the scoring phase structure; the game's nine rounds are represented by nine descending boxes (the Y axis) while rightward boxes (the X axis) provide players with illustrated chronological steps for the three scoring rounds.

El Grande inspired me to explore the possibility of merging the immersive and thematic experiences of the Anglo-design tradition with the elegance and surprising depth of German-design principles. I first sought to implement this philosophy in my Origins Award-winning *A Game of Thrones* board game, and *El Grande* continues to inspire me in my work today.

This powerful idea of merging Anglo and European game design principles is central to the message I seek to communicate to the developers and designers at Fantasy Flight Games every day. For this vision, and many hours of gaming fun, I am thankful for *El Grande*.

CHRISTIAN T. PETERSEN is the CEO of the Minnesota-based games publisher Fantasy Flight Games, the company he founded in 1995. In addition to his responsibilities as CEO, Christian manages the day-to-day operations of Fantasy Flight's development and design department, and has himself designed many of Fantasy Flight's games throughout the years, including *Twilight Imperium* (all editions), the *A Game of Thrones* board game, *World of Warcraft: The Board Game*, *The Lord of the Rings*

Trivia Game, and many others. His credits as co-designer include *Diskwars* and *Vortex* (also entitled *Maelstrom*) with Tom Jolly, the *A Game of Thrones* CCG with Eric Lang, and *The StarCraft Board Game* with Corey Konieczka. Under Christian's management, Fantasy Flight Games has published more than 400 titles and has grown into one of the most successful publishers in the hobby games industry. Christian lives in Minnesota with the love of his life, Gretchen, and their two children, Lars and Sofie.

Alessio Cavatore on

EMPIRES IN ARMS

KEY DESIGNERS: HARRY ROWLAND, GREG PINDER

AVALON HILL (REVISED EDITION, 1985)

ANYONE WHO KNOWS THE game *Empires in Arms* (*EiA*) would agree that it is a monster. It is one of the longest, most complicated, and most demanding board games that has ever been produced. It's certainly the longest I've ever played, and I've played quite a few. However, *EiA* has also been the most exciting, engrossing, and rewarding board-gaming experience of my life. For those of you who don't know this classic, let me give you a brief description of it.

Empires in Arms is a board game for two to seven players, where each person controls a major power during the Napoleonic era. The available nations are France, Great Britain, Austria, Spain, Prussia, Russia, and Turkey. The game includes a huge and detailed map of Napoleonic Europe, North Africa, and the Middle East, onto which each power moves its own army corps, made up of militia, infantry, guard, cavalry, and artillery, as well as its fleets of warships.

Each game turn represents a month of real time, and players must control their armies during highly detailed military campaigns. They must also engage in intense diplomatic activity, because alliances are vital for success. Not even France can stand alone — not for long at least. . . .

Every three turns/months there's a detailed economic phase, during which the major powers, and the minor powers under their control, gather their money and muster their manpower. Then they can invest these resources into equipping and training larger armies and fleets, or perhaps gain political stability at home by reducing taxation and conscription. They can also curry diplomatic favors abroad with massive loans to fund someone else's military — the British way! In each of these phases, the nations accumulate victory points, based on how well they are doing on a political success chart.

Empires in Arms can be played in several different scenarios or small campaigns, which include only a part of the board and a limited number of powers. Giving these more modest scenarios a try is an essential step in learning the complex rules. However, the game really comes into its own with the Grand Campaign and a full group of seven players. Spanning the decade from January 1805 to December 1815, the Grand Campaign encompasses a walloping 132 turns. If your group plays at an average of three turns per gaming evening, that still comes out to 44 sessions — or nearly one weekly session for an entire year. More realistically, a full Grand Campaign will take well over a year, depending on how quickly your group can play each turn and, especially, how often you can meet.

It's a board game that requires a dedication similar to that of a roleplaying game. Seven players have to find time in their busy lives to spend one night a week poring over complex charts, a massive rules manual, and a map filled with cardboard counters! Another issue the group will have to overcome is space. Someone needs to have a dedicated gaming room, because the game needs to remain set between sessions. This means leaving the huge map, covered with hundreds of counters, laid out horizontally for a year or so.

Difficult to learn and play, difficult to keep going with satisfying regularity, difficult to maintain at home. Is *Empires in Arms* really worth all that trouble? Well, if a gaming group manages to defeat all of the above adversities, the rewards are more than worth it! The games succeeds on many levels, but its two greatest strengths are great game mechanics and the exhilarating diplomatic interaction it requires of its players.

First, the military phases make you feel like a high-ranking general as you study the map with your allies and try to coordinate the strategic movement of your troops across Europe, in an attempt to bring the enemy to battle in the most favorable conditions. On a tactical level, you can identify with the famous military leaders of the time, from Napoleon and his marshals to Kutusov, from Nelson and Wellington to Blücher. It's grand fun trying to outmaneuver your foe on the field, whilst taking into account the many factors that influence the battle, such as morale, reserves, and the abilities of your sub-commanders.

The game's economic phases convey a tantalizing feeling of being in control of the resources of a mighty nation, carefully planning how to invest all that wealth. The most interesting challenge is deciding between support for long-term, expensive investments — building a navy, training Guard units and cavalry — and fulfilling immediate needs with cheap measures. Sometimes you need to raise as much militia as possible, as quickly as possible, to wear down the advancing French!

Finally, the fact that each country must accrue a different quantity of points to win makes it difficult to identify a clear leader at any given point. This helps to avoid the worst of the classic "let's all ally against the guy that's ahead!" syndrome. Instead, players are left to utilize diplomatic efforts to convince the other powers of who *really* is winning. (It's always someone else!) This, to me, is a sign of a masterfully designed game.

Arranging alliances, issuing ultimatums, declaring wars, and negotiating peace terms are all very tense and exciting moments in *Empires in Arms*. Bluffing, intrigue, and many, many moral dilemmas are integral parts of the game. Does the enemy know how my army corps are pitifully under-strength? Should I insist for unconditional surrender or, rather, leave a generous way out for the defeated enemy? After all, in a few years our roles could be reversed. . . .

The players' personalities come into it, too. Will the Austrians (played by "Mad" Dave and therefore utterly unpredictable) respect the neutrality of Bavaria? Can I trust the Russians (methodical and normally reliable Clive) not to switch sides and invade Prussia while the Prussians are besieging Paris with the Austrians and the Spanish? Will the British (craftily commanded by Jervis "tinkering" Johnson) really lift the blockade? Mastering the psychology of the gaming table is vital to your success on the board.

In games that last a single session, one tends to think ahead for just a few moves, a few hours of gaming. With *Empires in Arms*, time dilates, and decisions made today have repercussions lasting for months of real life. To engage with the game fully requires a different mindset than the one you're used to, and only after playing a couple of times does one truly appreciates just how different.

For example, from the experience of normal-length games, one might think that it's a good idea to annihilate an opponent's armies in a bloody war where no quarter is given and only unconditional surrender will do, as this will probably knock the player out of the game. Not so in *EiA*, where a ravaged opponent will instead turn into a relentless enemy — one that will scheme for years, slowly rebuilding its country from the ashes, cementing new alliances and preparing its armies for the time of retribution. Success in *Empires in Arms* requires a lighter touch, a player with as keen a feel for politics as he has for military strategy.

Given the time investment required for a full campaign, it should be no surprise that players often end up roleplaying — speaking with the appropriate accent, exchanging diplomatic e-mails written in period language and signing them "Napoleon" or "Alexander the First." It's immense fun, and anecdotes from the game will often resurface, many years after the campaign's close, still carrying the full emotional impact of the yearlong battle. (I will never trust Dave again in *any* game after the Great Bavarian Betrayal!). This creates a common language and great shared memories — a bond between the players that they will remember for the rest of their lives.

Alessio Cavatore was born in Turin, Italy, on Valentine's Day, 1972. In 1995 he moved to Nottingham (U.K.) to work for Games Workshop, a job he still holds. He wrote several supplements for *Warhammer Fantasy Battle* before heading up the *Lord of the Rings Strategy Battle Game*. In 2004 Alessio was made responsible for all rules material published for the company's three main tabletop systems — *Warhammer*, *Warhammer 40,000*, and *The Lord of the Rings* — and, in 2006, he wrote the rules for the fifth edition of *Warhammer*. In his spare time he designed the game *Cavachess*, which he would love you to publish.

Timothy Brown on

EMPIRES OF THE MIDDLE AGES

KEY DESIGNERS: JAMES F. DUNNIGAN, REDMOND A. SIMONSEN,
ANTHONY F. BUCCINI

SIMULATIONS PUBLICATIONS, INC. (FIRST EDITION, 1980)

EMPIRES OF THE MIDDLE AGES is a strategic level multi-player board game, "a dynamic simulation of Medieval Europe, 771-1467." Historically, that covers the time of Charlemagne through the end of the Dark Ages, just before the Renaissance. Players take the roles of monarchs who administer their lands, collect taxes, wage both diplomatic and military wars against their neighbors, and ultimately try to leave their kingdoms a bit better off than they found them. It's exactly the sort of multi-player resource-management game that I can't resist, and I was delighted to find it possessed such innovative gameplay.

The game is played in a series of highly abstracted yearly turns where each empire's leader applies his three primary attributes — combat, administration, and diplomacy — to improve the realm or, failing that, to keep plague and famine at bay. Cards are drawn and played to determine the result of each yearlong task, and each draw simultaneously introduces a variety of random elements, such as years of plenty or the death of one's monarch. Everyone playing gets to enjoy each other's highs and lows, as famines sweep countries or leaders die heirless!

The game map depicts Europe and the Middle East from Scotland to Jerusalem, divided into graphically depicted regions, where colors and symbols convey different information. A variety of counters are applied to each area, markers that turn each map location into a unique information display and control panel. These show everything from the relative wealth of the region to possible unrest, diplomatic ties and claims to fortifications and the like. For me, a great map can make a game, and the *Empires* map is graphic genius.

The scenarios range from the virtually solitaire Charlemagne and the Frankish Empire to the Crusades to the all-encompassing Grand Scenario. The number of countries, their set-up, and the victory conditions change with each one, but a player can expect to rule over a handful of areas to start each game, unless you're playing a scenario with the somewhat sprawling Holy Roman Empire. Though the initial scenario, Charlemagne and the Frankish Empire, is for just two players (Franks and Byzantines), the game is far more exciting and interactive with the scenarios that support up to eight players, setting the stage for alliances and back-stabbing aplenty!

I first played *Empires of the Middle Ages* at the time of its initial release, and I was immediately struck by how the graphics are so deeply incorporated into the game's functionality, and how they merge seamlessly with so many innovative design concepts.

Take the graphic approach to the game board, for instance. The Iberian Peninsula, by way of example, is divided into seven areas: Leon, Castille, Portugal, Cordova, Granada, Aragon, and Valencia. From color alone one sees that the first five of these speak languages of the Iberian language group, the last two the related, but not-identical Langue d'Oc. One well-placed number shows that both Cordova and Granada have a higher population, making them harder to conquer and control than the other regions. A single symbol denotes all seven areas are of the Roman Catholic religion (unless dictated by the scenario being played — Muslim empires on the march make their presence known in some scenarios). Can you get from Castille to Granada? Not directly, but through Cordova, yes, as the connecting lines clearly indicate.

This wealth of game information is available at a glance. Departing from tra-ditional board designs of the day, such as that found in *Kingmaker*, *Empires of the Middle Ages* boasts a play area informed more by graphic functionality than a slavish devotion to geography, and the game as a whole is strengthened by it. Frankly, the game map is a work of art worthy of display.

Empires was a groundbreaking board game, completely and enjoyably blend-ing the notion of a dynamic, changing character with a strategic situation, ele-ments deservingly copied by many games since. Each country begins the game with a historical leader. In the Millennium Scenario, which begins in the year 976, the kingdom of France is ruled by the universally inept Lothair (rated just 2 in each area — combat, administration, and diplomacy), whereas in the Age of the Crusades Scenario (1136 start), the principality of Poland is ruled by the compar-atively brilliant Boleslav III, also known as "the Wry-mouthed" (rated with 5s across the board). But the start of each scenario is where historicity ends and the game begins, and the life of an *Empires of the Middle Ages* monarch is an uncer-tain one. Monarchs frequently perish, which, at best, means the arrival of a new ruler improved in some attributes and weakened in others, or, at worst, an empire temporarily without a monarch, throwing everything into unrest. New monarchs are "rolled up" randomly, so he may improve in combat and get much worse in administration and diplomacy. Time for a crusade, anyone?

Admittedly, our enjoyment of *Empires*, when we played it regularly in the games library at TSR, was further enhanced by a series of tables letting you randomly roll a historically plausible name for each new monarch. This list was hand-typed and not part of the original game; it was, in fact, an article from the company's files. (Entitled "Color Me Boleslaus," it had been submitted by Gary Anderson to *Strategy & Tactics* or *Moves* magazine in 1983, but never published.) James Lowder (this volume's editor) entertained us all with his uncanny ability to not only draw Poland as his country in game after game, but to consistently roll "Ladislav" as the name of his ruler more than a dozen times in a row.

But even without the name generator, the ebb and flow of nations moves quite quickly and satisfyingly through each game. One can argue that the simulation creates a far more dynamic situation than actually existed, but the balance of success with inevitable disasters makes *Empires* a dynamic game with a believable unfolding of events. Some board wargamers, like the groups I've played with, rely on their knowledge of history to fuel endless witty repartee, which, of course, only adds to the fun.

Fortunately, I've been part of three different game groups since *Empires of the Middle Ages* was released by SPI in 1980, and the game has risen to a position among the top five choices for play in every one of them, a strong testament to its appeal. The game stands out for its innovative balance of mechanics and graphics, guaranteeing an enjoyable session every time. Copies of the original SPI edition are quite scarce — much more so than copies of 1981's *The Sword and the Stars*, a galaxy-spanning science-fiction game based upon the same system mechanics. The revised edition of *Empires*, available from Decision Games, maintains the flavor of the original, though it abandons the 1980 edition's graphics-driven recordkeeping for a more cumbersome counter system. Still, it's worth owning to make this important milestone of board-game innovation a permanent part of your collection.

TIMOTHY BROWN is a longtime veteran of the gaming industry, working at different times for Game Designers' Workshop, TSR, and FASA. His most notable designs are the *2300AD* roleplaying game, including the Gamer's Choice Award-winning *Star Cruiser* board game, and the *Dark Sun* campaign setting for *Advanced Dungeons & Dragons*. As director of product development for TSR from 1991 to 1995, Tim oversaw the creation of their Ravenloft and Planescape game lines, among many other titles. Tim served as editor of GDW's *Challenge* magazine; contributed to the designs of the *Spellfire*, *Wheel of Time*, and *DragonBall Z* collectible card games; and has designed, edited, or developed more than 100 roleplaying and board games.

Allen Varney on

The Extraordinary Adventures of Baron Munchausen

KEY DESIGNER: JAMES WALLIS

HOGSHEAD PUBLISHING (1998)

IN THIS STRIKINGLY ORIGINAL exercise in competitive storytelling, players take on the roles of nobles sitting around a tavern table in 18th-century Europe. They drink wine and recount self-aggrandizing tall tales in the manner of Rudolph Erich Raspe's *The Surprising Adventures of Baron Munchausen* (1785). After each player has told a tale, they all vote on the best one. The winner buys the next round.

Expanded and embroidered over the centuries by diverse hands, the charming Munchausen whoppers have inspired nearly 2,000 books and comics, the naming of a psychological condition (Munchausen's Syndrome), and film director Terry Gilliam's 1988 extravaganza *The Adventures of Baron Munchausen.*

Not least among the Baron's inspired followers is James Wallis, English gentleman. He started out writing Palladium roleplaying supplements, and later codesigned the innovative Atlas Games storytelling card game *Once Upon a Time.* In 1994, Wallis started Hogshead Publishing. After several years of publishing licensed *Warhammer Fantasy Roleplay* supplements, he finally had the breakthrough that led to Hogshead's first original game.

As Wallis told the gaming website OgreCave in 2000:

> I'd been trying to design a Baron Munchausen RPG for years, a conventional game where the players play either the Baron or his companions, and it had never come together. Then one morning I was in the shower, thinking about the game, and realized that the Munchausen stories never actually happen; instead, they're narrated over a drink . . . and by the time I got out of the shower, I had the entire game, the rules, the system, everything.

A traditional roleplaying design, if it could even grapple with the outlandish Munchausen premise, would serve up detailed character creation and lots of conflict resolution rules, together with one or maybe two scenarios, all in a big rulebook. Wallis transcended convention: His *Munchausen* rulebook runs 24 pages, about as long as the original 1785 edition of the tales, yet includes over 200 story topics. The rules proper fit on one page; most of the text simply elaborates these rules in a note-perfect recreation, as graceful and exuberant as a Strauss waltz, of the good Baron's forthright, unimpeachable sincerity.

Munchausen is rare among RPGs in that you can play it — nay, it demands to be played! — in a bar. Each noble has a supply of coins or tokens. To begin, one noble asks the noble on his right for a story — for instance, "Tell us, Baron, about the time you accidentally impregnated the pope." Saying, "Ah! Yes," the other improvises a fantastic tale up to five minutes long. Other players may spend coins to add a complicating detail to the narrative ("I'll wager, Baron, the sultan must have required you to give him your weight in diamonds") or to question a detail ("Surely, Baron, the king of the moon would be far too large to fit in your coat pocket?"). The tale-teller may accept the spent coin and revise his story accordingly, or may pay one of his own coins to ignore the interjection and insult the interrupter. Sustained objections prompt conflicts, resolved either by rock-paper-scissors or the Baron's preferred method — a duel, fought with sabers or pistols, either to first blood or to the death.

After the teller concludes his tale, he turns to the next noble and names the topic for a new story. "In telling a story," the rules advise, "each player should try to outdo the previous storyteller, with a story that is bigger, wilder, and brings more glory upon themselves." After all nobles have told a tale or passed (which necessitates buying a round of drinks), each player gives all his coins to the teller of his favorite teller as a "bounty." The one with the largest bounty wins.

Though the game is competitive in a sense, it neatly circumvents conventional gamesmanship: At game's end, you abandon all your winnings as another player's bounty. Besides, the winner must then quench the thirst of his parched companions. In this sense the design is truly — how to put it? — *gentlemanly*.

Unfortunately, it can be beastly in play. The game requires improvisation worthy of its namesake, and thus you need a particular kind of player and a particular mood for a session to proceed smoothly. Even more than most RPGs, it is acutely dependent on chemistry.

Yet it is, make no mistake, a roleplaying game. Over repeated plays, you'll notice that the last speaker tends to earn most of the bounties. An earlier player's best defense is to remain in character throughout, interjecting comments that subtly recall his own completed tale. So good roleplaying is key to success.

A surprise hit for Hogshead, *The Extraordinary Adventures of Baron Munchausen* prompted Wallis to start a "New Style" roleplaying line that eventually saw the release of *Puppetland* and *Power Kill* by John Scott Tynes, *Pantheon* by Robin D. Laws, *Violence* by "Designer X" (Greg Costikyan), and an English translation of the Polish game *De Profundis* by Michel Oracz. These inventive games, together with groundbreaking titles from other houses, such as Jonathan Tweet's *Everway*, helped inspire RPG designers to chart exciting new waters.

Along with the New Style line and many fine *Warhammer* supplements, Hogshead published a superb edition of Rebecca Borgstrom's *Nobilis*. Wallis was also instrumental in starting the field's annual Diana Jones Award for innovation in gaming. After eight years running Hogshead, he sold the business in early 2003; in interviews at the time, he claimed what a *Munchausen* noble might call "passing fatigue." The Hogshead edition of *The Extraordinary Adventures of Baron Munchausen* is out of print. However, the game has been reprinted in its entirety as an appendix to *Second Person: Role-Playing and Story in Games and Playable Media*, edited by Pat Harrigan and Noah Wardrip-Fruin (MIT Press, 2007).

Should you encounter him in his native London or on one of his globetrotting adventures, you might ask Baron Wallis to recount how he single-handedly defeated an emir's army with only a tangerine and a butter knife, or the means by which he temporarily stole Saturn's rings. And don't hesitate to ask how he revolutionized the entire roleplaying hobby with just one page of rules and inestimable ingenuity. "Ah! Yes," he will begin. "There's an interesting tale behind that. . . ."

ALLEN VARNEY (www.allenvarney.com) designed the 2004 edition of the classic RPG *Paranoia*, as well as three published board games and two dozen roleplaying supplements. He has written seven books and nearly 300 articles, columns, and reviews, and has contributed to many computer games. His business ethics simulation *Executive Challenge* — found now at www.enspire.com — was covered in *The Wall Street Journal*.

Phil Yates on

FIRE AND FURY

KEY DESIGNER: RICHARD W. HASENAUER
DAVE WAXTEL AND QUANTUM PUBLISHING (1990)

FOR ME, AT LEAST, *Fire and Fury* is one of the best miniature wargames to appear in the last 20 years. It has all of the elements that make a great tabletop game: flavor, simplicity, speed of play, and, most important of all, it feels right for its subject matter — in this case, the American Civil War.

The Civil War is not a period I had ever considered playing before being introduced to *Fire and Fury* a decade ago by a new wargaming acquaintance. I'd moved cities and met Dallas, who had a huge collection of 28-mm Civil War figures. Despite my lack of knowledge of the Civil War, I was immediately struck by how this game gave exactly the feel I had expected. Playing it was like being a general of the period, just commanding tabletop armies rather than the real thing. At the start of the battle the possibilities seemed endless. Both sides maneuvered for advantage, with the battle flaring up as the first units clashed. The fighting quickly spread down the line as units on the flanks were thrown into the maelstrom. At this point, things got really sticky and a slow, bloody brawl ensued. Eventually, after a little bit of clever generalship, lots of tin-soldier heroism, and a modicum of luck, one side would break through and defeat the other — usually with losses so high that victory looked perilously close to defeat.

While this may sound pretty much what you'd expect from such a game, the sad truth is that many tabletop wargames simply don't deliver. The clean, elegant design of *Fire and Fury* works because Rich Hasenauer recognized that it is impossible to create a game that covers all aspects of a historical event. Instead, he picked the features that stand out in battles of the period and brought them into focus, pushing extraneous detail aside.

The core of *Fire and Fury*, and its simple genius, is its handling of the command cycle — the general issuing orders, the troops acting on them, and the general seeing the outcome and issuing more orders. This process is always a problem for tabletop games where you — the "1,500-foot general" standing high over the battlefield and seeing everything — can react instantly to the moves made by the other side. *Fire and Fury* uses a very simple but very nicely done Maneuver Table to determine how the player's troops respond to his orders and the resulting situations in which they find themselves.

Depending on their circumstances and a die roll, your troops may do everything you ask of them, or simply hang back doing nothing while they try to figure out what you really wanted of them. Many times my clever plans were foiled when a poor die roll and bad positioning of my general meant that my second brigade sat back and watched the first brigade charge to their doom, unsupported. Other times my reserves let the front line get blasted in a firefight while they hesitated, instead of marching forward to join their fellows. The uncertainty of your little soldiers' reactions in *Fire and Fury* makes planning ahead essential to cope with unexpected developments.

The very well-balanced and elegant Maneuver Table alone would not be enough to elevate *Fire and Fury* to greatness. Many other games have excellent and innovative command and control systems. (Two really innovative and outstanding games, *Piquet* and *Crossfire*, immediately come to mind.) However, unlike these other titles, *Fire and Fury* keeps the conventional turn structure in which each player alternates moving all of their units, then fighting with all of their units. This method of gameplay is intuitive. In a war, everyone fights at the same time. By the same token, in a conventional wargame, all of your troops fight each turn. It is how we expect such games to go and usually results in faster action than more innovative turn structures, since players spend less time pondering their moves.

While the way turns are structured and the clever handling of the command cycle may make a game flow well, it is the handling of combat that determines how well it captures the essence of the period. *Fire and Fury* uses a tidy system for shooting that imparts the flavor of the Civil War extremely well. It's very hard to actually kill anything by shooting at it in *Fire and Fury*. This conjures images of ragged lines of blue- and gray-clad soldiers wreathed in gunsmoke, blazing away at each other, hiding behind fences, slowly taking casualties. Your firepower is just enough to make a firefight a good option, but not enough to achieve a decisive result. Most of the time, your fire will only result in disordering the enemy or perhaps removing a single stand.

This indecisiveness lends the game the feeling of a long and brutal slugfest. Your troops sit there, turn after turn, hour after hour, shooting and slowly dying. Their numbers are being whittled away, but they fight on, making the enemy pay just a little bit more blood before they can take this miserable piece of land. The indecisiveness of combat also facilitates strategy in the game. Since even a small body of troops can pin down a larger number of opposing troops, part of your force can hold the line while the rest attempt to outmaneuver the enemy; because of the slow casualty rate, they have a good chance of completing the maneuver before your pinning force is shot to bits. Yet, just like the Civil War, the end result is, often as not, a longer battleline blasting away at each other, as the enemy counter-marches their reserves to the flanks in response to your gambit.

Once the line of battle forms, the only real alternative to a long, slow killing match is to charge. There is but one problem — how to get past the enemy firepower. Once again the balance of *Fire and Fury* here is excellent. Your shooting may not destroy the enemy outright, but it is still fairly easy to disorder their ranks with a final volley as they charge, giving you a better than even chance of repelling their assault. A successful assault requires careful preparation with plenty of supporting fire to disorder the enemy, ruining their carefully aimed volley, just as you launch your fateful, all-or-nothing press.

I will always have a soft spot for *Fire and Fury*, both for the fun it has given me and its excellent design. Perhaps the greatest accolades *Fire and Fury* has gathered come in the form of the numerous variants it has spawned, as players use the system to cover a wide variety of European conflicts, from *The Age of Eagles* (for the Napoleonic wars) to *Fire and Furia Francese* (for the Franco-Prussian War). Whichever variant you try — and you really should try at least one of them — you will be in for a challenging game and a rewarding wargaming experience.

PHIL YATES is a New Zealander. He has been wargaming since the early 1970s and designing games since the mid-1980s. The Great War was his first passion, but his current interest is mostly WWII. Phil is the lead games designer for Battlefront Miniatures, the smallish New Zealand company where he designed the *Flames of War* miniatures game. Phil has also written or co-authored more than a dozen Intelligence Handbooks and Battle and Campaign books for *Flames of War*. When Phil is not writing games, he spends his time with his wife Fiona trying to save a regional park, fixing up a house, and kayaking.

William Jones on

FLAMES OF WAR

KEY DESIGNER: PHIL YATES

BATTLEFRONT MINIATURES (SECOND EDITION, 2006)

BEING AN ENTHUSIAST OF historical miniatures games, I share with others the eternal quest for the Holy Grail of rule systems. This means that I'm always looking to the horizon, but skeptical about new games.

When I first encountered *Flames of War*, my initial reaction was colored by two concerns common to all "lead collectors" — longevity and popularity. In other words, before I bought in, I wanted to know how long the game was likely to be supported and how many other players there were out there playing it. These worries exist for other hobbyists, but when dealing with World War II games — particularly miniatures games — these issues are paramount. Changing rule systems can be a time-consuming affair, and without other players, a case full of miniatures is an expensive and lonely proposition. Anyone who has switched from one historical miniatures game to another understands, too, the heartaches associated with "re-basing." Since different rules require different-sized bases — the wooden, plastic, or metal strips that hold the miniatures for play — changing rules can mean shifting hundreds of painted figures from one type of base to another. The thought of this process alone keeps many people from exploring new games. But after only a few minutes skimming through the *Flames of War* rulebook, I set all these concerns aside, at least for a while. I couldn't resist giving the game a try.

Flames of War is a World War II, company-scale miniatures game that follows in the tradition of such classics as Frank Chadwick's *Command Decision*. What is wonderful about the system is its design philosophy. Phil Yates describes some of the design objectives as being fast play, no record keeping or lookup tables, and one-to-one figure scale. These are difficult goals to achieve, given the complexity and nature of WWII battles. But *Flames* achieves them all, even while maintaining a strong level of simulated action.

Perhaps the game's most striking feature is its limited playing time. As someone who is used to multi-week sessions with other games, I found it possible to finish a *Flames of War* scenario in one night (and still be alert the next day). The

Flames mechanics paradigm is similar to many contemporary, non-historical miniatures games on the market. It uses the familiar "I go/you go" turn-based system, with a variety of steps that comprise a player's full turn. This helps the game simulate company-level action while preserving many of the quirks associated with WWII-era equipment. For example, two popular weapons known for their "personalities" on the battlefield are the MG42 German heavy machine gun and the U.S. M1 Garand rifle. In play, the underlying mechanics allow for the MG42's deadly rate of fire and the M1's distinctive semi-automatic capabilities. Such distinctions can bog down historical systems with endless pages of special rules. That isn't the case here. The rules substrata supports a vast array of weapons, creating very few exceptions.

For novices and veteran wargamers alike, finding the right level of historical detail is always difficult. Establishing a game's accuracy level is the burden of its designer — too much detail and novice wargamers shy away, too little detail and grizzled gamers scoff. Reflecting the myriad variations present on the historical WWII battlefield is a daunting task, even without these concerns. *Flames of War* successfully navigates these perilous waters by providing "doctrines" for the various nations — general guides to their military tactics — and a limited number of standardized rules for soldiers, weapons, and vehicles. Adding to this are additional *Intelligence* books that aid players in constructing armies. These source-books provide information about the available forces and their capabilities, so that British Commandos have a different feel from U.S. Rangers or German Fallschirmjägers. The end result is army personality and accuracy without over-burdening details that slow down play.

What is remarkable about *Flames of War* is its tendency to focus upon the salient features of battle while not losing itself in a bewildering fog of rules. Undoubtedly, anyone unfamiliar with WWII miniatures gaming is likely to find the richness of rules intimidating at first. A system where one figure represents one soldier or vehicle (one-to-one scale) makes fielding companies and squadrons somewhat sublime — or outright terrifying at first glance. Heavy and light machine guns and mortars, flamethrowers, rocket launchers, light and heavy armored vehicles, artillery, transports, and air support rules are typically the stuff of tables, charts, and voluminous texts. However, *Flames of War* manages all of this and much more without the need for a heap of handouts referencing special rules and exceptions. The hard work and research required for a quality historical game are built into the rules, shifting the labor from the player to the designer. "Rather than turn our players into human computers, we pre-calculate the outcomes for them and give them a simple mechanism to choose between," is how Phil Yates describes the approach. The overall effect is less pre-game work and more time to engage in strategy and play. Hobbyists know a good thing when they see it, too, so *Flames* has gathered a legion of fans and benefits from continuing publisher support that does not look to be slowing any time soon.

What remains is the issue of basing. Depending upon the size of the battle, players might field hundreds of miniatures for a *Flames of War* scenario. Yet another pleasant surprise awaits veteran hobbyists thinking of giving the game a try. *Flames of War* uses broad base sizes. I found it very easy to convert my *Rapid Fire, Battleground*, and *Command Decision* collections. In many instances, I was able to either use the existing base or glue it onto one of the larger sizes required. Battlefront Miniatures also manufactures convenient plastic bases, available in various assortments without miniatures, and included with their pre-packaged figures. This allows for new players to quickly join the fray, and experienced players to convert their armies with relative ease.

Historical miniature gamers will certainly continue the quest for the perfect new rules systems — the same quest that, in part, brought Phil Yates to create *Flames of War*. But his marvelous design offers quite a lot, especially to those tabletop tacticians who long for a game where strategy is dominant, who want to dedicate more time to plotting a battleplan and less to worrying about the rules. *Flames of War* boasts a wonderful balance between speed of play, detail, and flavor. These are qualities that even an old-school lead collector like myself can enjoy.

WILLIAM JONES is a writer and editor who journeys frequently through the fiction and hobby industries. His efforts in the world of gaming include articles, RPG supplements, and RPG design for Chaosium and other publishers. His fiction spans genres, covering mystery, horror, science fiction, dark fiction, historical, and young adult. He has edited several fiction anthologies and magazines. Presently, William is the editor of *Dark Wisdom* magazine. When not writing and editing, he teaches English at a university in Michigan. Visit him at www.williamjoneswriter.com.

Rick Loomis on

FLUXX

KEY DESIGNER: ANDREW LOONEY

LOONEY LABS (1997)

FLUXX IS A SIMPLE card game that has only two fixed rules: Draw a card and play a card. At the beginning, there isn't even a way to win. Not only can the players change the rules with each play, they get to determine the victory conditions as the game progresses. Each card is either a *rule change* (which goes into effect immediately), a *goal* (which replaces the previous goal), an *action* (which you then perform immediately), or a *keeper* (which you keep, and provides the basis of goals). Rule changes might be something like "Draw two cards," which goes into effect immediately, and now everyone is drawing two cards and playing one. Actions might be something like "Draw three cards and play two of them" (after which you must discard the third one) or "Draw a random card from an opponent and play it" (you must play it, no matter what it is). A goal would be something like "Chocolate Cookies: the player who has both 'Chocolate' and 'Cookies' as keepers in front of him, has won."

As you can imagine, this makes for quite a chaotic game.

A game that claims to be for ages eight and up usually means it is for ages eight to 12, but that's not the case here. There's enough luck involved that my eight-year-old cousin can beat me (and I can console myself with the thought that he "just got lucky"), but enough strategy to allow me to be proud when my choices result in a well-deserved win! You can play *Fluxx* with a group of relatives at a holiday gathering, and even the youngest nephew has a reasonable chance to win against the very competitive 25-year-old cousin. The game can be frustrating to those super-competitive types, as there are chaos-inducing cards such as "Trade hands with another player" or "Hand limit zero" (which means everyone throws away all cards, and until the rule changes everyone merely draws a card, and plays the card he or she just drew). To some, this sort of strategy-foiling zaniness just makes the winner totally random, but it's actually the thing that keeps everyone interested during a game of *Fluxx*, as everything can change in an instant. There is no point at which you might as well give up, because someone is obviously going to win. Final victory is always in doubt, right up until the last card is played.

Despite the undercurrent of chaos, strategy can still matter, because the *order* in which you play your cards is (usually) determined by you and can often impact the game significantly. There are many choices to be made, and many interesting possible combo-plays, since the cards you play don't apply to you until you finish your current turn. My all-time favorite combo-play is to use "Hand limit one," forcing the other players to throw away all their cards but one — at which point they will presumably be saving their best card — and then hit them with the "Tax" card, requiring them each to give me one card of their choice. Another good multi-card combo is "Hand limit zero" and then "Trash a rule," which cancels the "Hand limit zero" for you and allows you to keep all your cards, even after the turn is over. Now, until something changes, everyone else is forced to draw one card and play it, while *you* still have a hand to choose from.

Fluxx makes a good game for a group that has one of those annoying "I-must-win-every-game" types. The rest of you can enjoy yourselves as the game spins out of his control (as it surely will) and perhaps he'll eventually learn to lose gracefully. Meanwhile, *Fluxx* will be busily exercising everyone's logic synapses as you attempt to deal with the chaotic situations that occur because of the cheerful clash of rules. Unusual combinations of cards produce unexpected results, and the players often need to sort the gameplay impact of these oddities out for themselves. In that way, *Fluxx* invites everyone to be a designer, at least for the game currently under way. And if they don't like the way a decision comes out, it won't matter for long. *Fluxx* plays quickly enough that you can easily get in a half-dozen games in an evening.

In a small way, *Fluxx* reminds me of *Cosmic Encounter*, one of the earliest games that included mechanics by which players could twist the rules, but in *Cosmic Encounter* your own personal power lets you break one or more rules. In *Fluxx*, each new rule applies to everyone, pending the impact of other cards. So the limited instability built into *Cosmic Encounter* is the very basis of *Fluxx*.

The spirit of *Fluxx* also sets it apart from other, similar games. There is no combat in *Fluxx*, no aggression or gain of territory. (In this, it reminds me of many German-style resource-management games, where there isn't really any direct conflict, as such.) A *Fluxx* player might occasionally borrow an opponent's keeper card, but, as a general rule, you're trying to change the rules so that you have the best chance to win. The lack of conflict in *Fluxx* is a purposeful and clear manifestation of the philosophies held by the game's designer, Andrew Looney, who proudly describes himself as a hippie. The publishers have already created several variations on *Fluxx*, including *Christian Fluxx*, *Jewish Fluxx*, *Family Fluxx*, *EcoFluxx*, and even (true to their hippie roots) *Stoner Fluxx*.

They're all fun, but the basic edition is still the one to try first. By design, though, your experience won't be typical. *Fluxx* is one game of which it can truly be said that no two sessions are alike!

RICK LOOMIS is the founder and president of Flying Buffalo, Inc, the industry pioneer for commercially moderated/refereed multi-player play-by-mail games (the precursor to today's massively multi-player online games). Rick claims to have been the first person ever to buy a computer (a Raytheon 704, in 1972) solely to play games on it! He designed a half-dozen of Flying Buffalo's play-by-mail games, including the Origins Award-winning *Starweb*; all the expansion sets for the *Nuclear War* card game (also published by Flying Buffalo); and the first solitaire adventure for a roleplaying game — *Buffalo Castle*, for *Tunnels & Trolls*. Rick is one of the founders, the first president, and the current president of GAMA, the game industry trade association, which owns and operates the Origins game convention. Rick resides in Scottsdale, Arizona.

John Kovalic on

FORMULA DÉ

Key Designers: Laurent Lavaur, Eric Randall

Asmodée Editions (English edition, 1991)

I've never been a big fan of pure dice games, and I've never been a big fan of racing games.

So how is it that *Formula Dé*, a dice-based racing game, is, to me, hotter than the Indianapolis 500 or the French Grand Prix?

Like Formula One racing itself, the game is sleek and exciting, but the excitement is built around an engine that's elegant, subtle, and compelling.

Aerodynamic as a Lamborghini, the mechanics behind *Formula Dé* are what let it break away from the pack of so-so speedway games. More than just another racing simulation, the game has become a hobby-market marvel in its own right. Indeed, after a decade and a half in the stores, it's remained as captivating as when it was first introduced.

Few games seem able to satisfy both hardcore gamers and their non-gaming friends, which is another reason to love *Formula Dé*. Crack open the box and, within minutes, almost anyone can get into the cockpit of their race car and take to the streets of Monte Carlo. Or Elkhart Lake. Or Watkins Glen. With dozens of race tracks to choose from in multiple expansion sets, finding a speedway near you can keep the game as local as you'd like. Though there are plenty of exotic and famous tracks available, too.

Yet, if it weren't for the elegance of its design, *Formula Dé* could have stalled before completing a single lap.

Each player gets one or two cars, depending on the number of participants (from two to 10 can play). Races can last one, two, or more laps, over a race track broken up into three lanes, each lane being a couple hundred or so spaces long. Roll the dice, and move your car the number of spaces indicated.

That's all there is to it.

Simplistic? No. *Elegant*, because six colored dice are employed, each representing a different gear available to the racers. From first gear (a lowly yellow four-sided die — a d4) to sixth (a zippy blue 30-sider — a d30), you can find yourself limping along or burning up the track, eating someone's dust or cleaning up the competition, depending on how skillfully you shift gears.

The dice, though, aren't simply numbered from 1 to x. The sides of the d4, for example, are only numbered 1 and 2. The practical result is that, in first gear, you'll either drive one or two squares, with an equal shot at each. Similarly, a roll of second gear's d6 will yield results of two, three, or four squares, with a single 2, two 3s, and three 4s as possible rolls. Knowing that the numbers' distribution is often weighted toward the high end is vital.

Now, any goon can shift *up* as soon as he hits the straightaway. But it's in shifting *down* for the corners where the true greatness of a *Formula Dé* strategist can be found. Victory seldom comes to the first schlub able to push his Maserati furiously into sixth gear, slinging his d30 with the reckless abandon of a NASCAR fan fighting for the last Buffalo wing. Nope. At that point, buddy, you're just Spam in a very, very fast can, and the next corner'll probably be your last. But coax your car nimbly around the bends, playing a tiny bit of chicken with the track you're hurtling down, shifting at *juuussssst* the right moments, and the laurels could be yours.

Approach a curve in a high gear at your own risk. Each corner consists of a number of marked squares. If the curve is flagged *1*, players must end one turn somewhere on the curve. If it's flagged *2*, you have to end two turns within its confines. Should a car move through a corner too quickly, tire points are removed or brake points sacrificed. If a driver doesn't end any turns on a curve requiring two, they're automatically eliminated. Wipe out, and you begin your next turn back in first gear, watching the tail wings of your rivals roar out of view.

As in most games that rely on the roll of the dice, there's a large element of luck in *Formula Dé*. In a one-lap race, this luck factor may be difficult to overcome, and a few fortunate (or unfortunate) rolls will make or break a driver. But in two- or three-lap races, skill and judgment can temper the fates, rewarding the canny driver. There's more time for you to overcome one or two missteps, or for one-time leaders of the pack to falter on one of those hair-pin turns. As in many of the best games, a slow start won't necessarily doom you in the long run.

A seventh die, a black 20-sider with regular number distribution, covers collisions (rare) and over-taxing your car (more common). This "Die of Doom" adds just enough risk to make you think twice about following someone too closely, or gunning your engine for too long.

Oh, sure, there are other nifty little rules governing braking, engine burn-outs, and the like. There are also advanced rules, for those who want a little more meat on their game engine. Still, it all comes down to those six little brightly colored dice and the gears. In fact, the *Dé* in the game's title is simply French for *die*.

As well-written and intuitive as the rules are, it usually takes just a lap or two for novices to get into the swing of things. Indeed, *Formula Dé* becomes that rarest of beasts: a true "gamer's game" that can be enjoyed just as fully by non-gamers. Many's the race where a first-timer can overtake a veteran driver with one or two fortunate curves falling their way.

The mechanics of *Formula Dé* make for a direct, palpable sense of handling a powerful race car through treacherous bends and looming straightaways. The game may neither be the most complex nor the most accurate simulation on the market, but darn it, you can't help but feel you're right there, soaking up the smell of burning tires and motor oil as you fight with your Ferrari to make that last, loathsome curve, with a rival hot on your tail.

Formula Dé provides this kind of experience in spades, easily making it a classic game of the modern era. Ladies and gentlemen, start your engines!

JOHN KOVALIC's multi-Origins Award-winning cartoons have been nominated for two prestigious Harvies, one of the comic book world's premier awards — for best cartoonist and the special award for humor in comics. His comic book *Dork Tower* has sold nearly 500,000 copies, and is celebrating the 10th anniversary of the comic strip's first appearance. *USA Today* called Kovalic a "Hot Pick," and he's a co-owner and co-founder of Out of the Box Games, whose *Apples to Apples* has sold nearly 3,000,000 copies. He's also a bestselling and prolific freelance game illustrator (*Munchkin, Chez Geek, Creatures and Cultists, Mag*Blast*), and his editorial cartoons have appeared in the *New York Times* and the *Washington Post*, while he continues to freelance for Milwaukee's *Daily Reporter* and his hometown *Wisconsin State Journal* (Madison, Wisconsin). In 2003, John became the first cartoonist inducted into the Academy of Adventure Gaming's Hall of Fame. In John's free time, he searches for free time.

THE FURY OF DRACULA

KEY DESIGNER: STEPHEN HAND
GAMES WORKSHOP (FIRST EDITION, 1987)

BASED ON BRAM STOKER'S famous novel, *The Fury of Dracula* is a break-through title that introduced cooperative and deductive elements to the adventure board game subgenre, while managing to retain the feeling of breathless excitement that players seek in an adventure game.

In the 21st century, Games Workshop is known primarily as a superior miniatures hobby company. They have not always been so specialized. The company used to publish board and roleplaying games. Among their better titles were *Chaos Marauders* and *Chainsaw Warrior* (both 1987), *Talisman* (1983), and *Warhammer Fantasy Roleplay* (1986). Standing out as superior, even amongst those great games, was *The Fury of Dracula*.

Fury is for two to four players. One player takes on the role of Count Dracula and the other players take on the roles of the vampire-hunting characters from the novel: Lord Godalming, Professor Van Helsing, and Doctor Seward. All three of these characters are involved in every game, in a communal fashion, regardless of the number of players. (If you're looking for Jonathan Harker, he does make an appearance in some game sessions as a "non-player hunter" who often becomes a vampire.) The hunter players search for Dracula across a nicely detailed map of Victorian-era Europe. Dracula's movement is hidden from the hunters by use of a smaller board behind a screen.

There is not just one way to win in *The Fury of Dracula* — there are degrees of winning. These different degrees mean that strategies and priorities in the game can change, depending on how each side is doing. To win, the Dracula player looks to plant vampires in his wake and to kill the hunters or convert them to undead. The hunters win as a group by either destroying a number of Dracula's vampires or by destroying Dracula himself. Hunters can also keep track of their individual actions, to determine which of them contributed more to their side's victory. The idea that there are degrees of winning rather than one condition or set of conditions is groundbreaking in itself, but combined with the other unique aspects of the game, it's all the more striking.

The game borrows enough elements from solid category leaders to be recognizable to fans of the adventure subgenre; both Greg Costikyan's *DeathMaze* (1979) and John Califf III and William A. Walker's *Riddle of the Ring* (1982) can be identified as the game's forebearers. But *Fury* delivers excitement and duel-natured play in ways that neither of those games does. Instead of a player-versus-player free-for-all, or a more purely cooperative structure where everyone teams up against the board and the rules, *Fury* utilizes its deductive search mechanic and all-against-one structure to capture the best of both arrangements. And with no real treasure in the game, *Fury* flat-out smashes the traditional adventure game mold of "kill the monster, collect the treasure." And its notable cousins that emphasize deduction — such as *Scotland Yard* (1983) — lack the adventure game trappings it maintains. So *The Fury of Dracula* stands alone in its gameplay, and does so with great flair.

Fury also conveys the tension from Stoker's novel in very subtle ways. The hunters travel through Europe looking for clues of Dracula's presence. Meanwhile, the Count scurries about the map, avoiding the hunters, but also leaving hazards for them. Each time the player controlling Dracula moves the vampire into a town or city, he may deposit a token on his hidden map — or he may choose not to; it's up to him. The players won't know which it is until they step into harm's way.

On the surface, this mechanic seems like either a game master placing hazards for players in a roleplaying game or an abstract and strategic game of deduction. It's actually both. The tension of Stoker's novel is felt by the hunter players, who want to find something in a city so that they'll know they're closing in on the monster, yet dread the discovery, too, since it will likely hurt their characters. Conversely, the Dracula player wants the hunters to find the hazards, since it could spell their doom, but fears that the locations of his traps could help the hunters find him. In this the game successfully convey the novel's tone of almost overwhelming dread.

The game also recalls Stoker's story in more predictable ways, by including many of the characters, props, and occurrences from the book. But *Fury*'s narrative isn't constrained by the novel; the players have so much control over how they proceed in the game that they are adding chapters to the book, not recreating it.

They are telling a story themselves through their actions and decisions — even when using the most mechanical parts of the game, such as the combat system.

The combat table — used when hunters encounter Dracula or one of his monstrous followers — is a typical adventure game-style system, with a result chart, weapons choices, and the like. This feature places *The Fury of Dracula* firmly in the adventure game tradition. Combat in the game is enjoyable (though it can, admittedly, take a little too long in some instances). Each player has individual attacks and defenses he uses against an adversary. The weapons options for Dracula and his agents are set, but the hunters can have any combination of tools and weapons — and only that hunter knows what he has in his arsenal before combat starts. In a game where Dracula usually has all of the hidden information, it's a fun turn for the hunter to be the one holding something close to the vest.

To be successful in *The Fury of Dracula*, players must both suss out the plans of their opponent (or opponents) *and* work the mechanics of the game. Using psychology alone to figure out what the hunter players are likely to do next, as in a game of poker, will not earn the Dracula player a win; neither will coldly calculating a likely position for the Count based on the hazards' locations earn the hunters a victory. A winning strategy requires both psychological and mechanical considerations. This necessary combination of approaches sometimes gives new players pause. They are so used to playing games that reward one strategy style or the other that they get hung up on trying to find the single correct approach to *Fury*.

The Fury of Dracula combines its horror-adventure theme and cooperative play in a way that was unique when it was published in 1987, and has still not been rivaled (though adventure game fans can give Fantasy Flight's 2006 revised edition of *Fury* a spin to see how they've tackled the classic). The game encourages deeper interaction by requiring players to consider both the mechanics and the play patterns of the other people around the table, all while interjecting just the right balance of luck and skill into the mix. It conjures Bram Stoker's famous book, but doesn't require players to slavishly follow the novel's plot over and over, as sometimes happens with games derived from other media. The subtlety of its delivery of an adventure gaming experience is the key ingredient that makes *The Fury of Dracula* the best board game ever released by Games Workshop — and quite possibly any other publisher.

★　　★　　★

ANTHONY J. GALLELA is the executive director of the Game Manufacturers Association, the game industry's main trade organization for over 30 years. Before signing on at GAMA, Gallela was a co-producer for the famed ManaFest and KublaCon game conventions; a freelance writer for several industry publications; a game store manager; a consultant and broker for several award-winning games; a co-developer of the *Theatrix* roleplaying game (published by Backstage Press); and the co-designer (with Japji Khalsa) of another adventure game category-breaking title, *Dwarven Dig!* (from Kenzer & Co.), which earned him an Origins Award nomination.

Jesse Scoble on

A GAME OF THRONES

KEY DESIGNER: CHRISTIAN T. PETERSEN

FANTASY FLIGHT GAMES (2003)

"When you play the game of thrones, you win or you die. There is no middle ground."

— Cersei Lannister, *A Game of Thrones*

IN THE BRILLIANT TACTICAL wargame that is *A Game of Thrones*, players take control of one of the great noble families from George R.R. Martin's world of Westeros (depicted in the bestselling A Song of Ice and Fire series) and battle for domination of the Iron Throne. Players must use clever planning and carefully allocate their resources in order to withstand their opponents, but true victory in the "game of thrones" also requires skillful diplomacy.

Although the game is designed for three to five players, it is most balanced — and thrilling — when all five noble houses are utilized, since this allows for the largest and most dynamic web of potential alliances and betrayals. The game is set right after the death of King Robert Baratheon, and the realm trembles with anticipation of war. Players randomly draw a great house to play: the Lannisters, family of King Robert's wife and children; the Baratheons, house of the dead king's older brother and the land's rightful ruler; the Greyjoys, island pirates planning their own rebellion; the Tyrells, southerners who have long aspired to hold the throne; and the Starks, northmen determined to do what is right. While the fictional ambitions of each house color the game's backstory and add to its ambiance, ultimately each player is tasked with the same goals — capture the most cities and strongholds before 10 turns takes place and the game ends.

The game's board does an excellent job of capturing the feel of Martin's fictional world and of the Machiavellian noble houses vying for political and military dominance. The entire continent of Westeros is lavishly depicted, from Castle Black in the north to the Arbor and the Summer Sea in the south, and from the Iron Islands in the west to Dragonstone Island in the east. The houses' starting positions are scattered relatively evenly across the map, and the entire board is divided up into sea and land areas. Sea areas are used to move navies and transport troops, while land areas can be used for troop movement, but are also marked with resource icons. The board includes various tracks that help chart important game elements, such as turns, supplies, and influence.

Each turn is divided into three phases — the draw phase, which involves random Westeros cards that often cause major upheavals; the planning phase, where players simultaneously assign hidden orders (move or attack, defend, support, raid, or consolidate power); and the action phase, where orders are resolved in order. Combat, which is inevitable as armies maneuver to control prize territories, is resolved simply by adding up the value of the pieces, plus the value of supporting units, plus the value of a hidden house noble card (such as Tyrion Lannister or Robb Stark), who may have a significant special ability or military prowess.

One of the most intriguing mechanics is the draw phase at the start of each turn. The Westeros decks contain several balance-shifting cards. The random nature of the events these cards trigger means that players must hope for the appropriate card to fall when it is most beneficial to them, and pray that a particular card won't come up when they can't take advantage of it. For example, the Clash of Kings card represents a dynamic change of the noble houses' power. To determine how the rankings change, players secretly bid power tokens to determine their strength in three areas: rulership (the Iron Throne), feudal military power (the Fiefdoms), and courtly influence (the King's Court). Each position gains a special ability at first rank, such as a combat bonus provided by the Fiefdoms. As players' ranks in these areas change, so, too, do their tactical and strategic choices. A player who seems weak may be saving up his power tokens to win first place of Fiefdoms the next time the Clash of Kings card shows up. A player who finds himself outbid on the King's Court may suddenly find he can't issue enough orders to maintain his control of a region.

The game uses some familiar elements. Its orders and movement mechanic are similar to the ones used in *Diplomacy*, its secret army leaders like those in *Dune*, and the outside barbarian forces like those in *The Cities & Knights of Catan*. But the intersection of all of these aspects is what makes *A Game of Thrones* such a compelling and replayable game. The simultaneous placement of orders (and the limited amount of each type of order anyone can issue) forces players to factor both the rules and their opponents' play style into their strategies; diplomatic truces can hang dangerously in the balance until the orders are revealed and each house's intentions are made clear. Similarly, although the orders are all revealed at once, they are executed one by one, in turn, and a player can gain a tactical edge by having more moves than his opponent, forcing the disadvantaged player into showing his hand or limiting his opportunities.

Like many of the best games, *A Game of Thrones* is fairly easy to learn, but has more than enough complexity and depth that it is challenging to master. Although there are a lot of components, both in pieces and in specific rules, playing through a few turns is all that most casual players will need in order to pick it up. The rulebook is short and well-illustrated with examples that cover most situations, and Fantasy Flight's website is updated with a current FAQ for more rare occurrences. The randomizing factors — from house selection to the Clash of Kings bidding event — ensure that the game has a lot of variety, and calls for players to think quickly to react to new and unexpected situations as they arise.

The randomization of the Westeros decks, by its very nature, allows for flukey situations, such as a game where armies aren't mustered until a very late turn or a player finds he can't draw on the resources of the territories he's worked so hard to secure. Additionally, the three- and four-player options have certain balance issues. But the five-player game (with a slight rules adjustment available on the official website and integrated into later editions) is a great, nail-biting game of ferociously fought territory control and twisted diplomacy. No one can normally win the day entirely by himself, but as the game only allows for one house to be victorious, alliances will often shift and dissolve as the endgame draws near.

Fantasy Flight has even improved significantly on this stellar game by publishing two expansions, named after later novels in the series, *A Clash of Kings* and *A Storm of Swords*. The first expansion, *A Clash of Kings*, added siege engines (amazing for attacking cities or strongholds, as their name suggests, but terrible as defensive units), fortifications, and ports. It also expands the game by adding a house for a sixth player — that of Martell, the Dornish princes of the far south — and board overlays to alter the map. In addition to the map's new face, which significantly rebalances the houses and makes each game more fraught with uncertainty, special one-use order tokens add tremendous flavor to each house.

The second expansion, *A Storm of Swords*, features a self-contained game of four houses set in the Riverlands (on a new board that focuses on the middle of Westeros). It also offers a number of interesting additions, including new house cards, new tactics cards, and rules for weather, allies (which are derived from the lesser noble houses of Westeros), and leader units (who can be captured and, as in the novels, ransomed). Most of these new rules — with the exception of those dealing with weather and allies — can be utilized with the basic game, adding even more options and possibilities. These expansions help the game capture the rich atmosphere of the novels. Combined, they make *A Game of Thrones* into an incredible wargame — certainly one of the best out there.

JESSE SCOBLE is a writer, story editor, and game designer, in no particular order. He was creative director on the award-winning *A Game of Thrones RPG*, and doesn't hide the fact that he's a huge fan of George Martin and the world of Westeros. He also wrote the world bible for the *Silver Age Sentinels* superhero game line. He has contributed to more than two dozen books, including two short-story anthologies (based on *Silver Age Sentinels*), and several books for White Wolf. He has also worked as a web content writer for NCsoft, crafting Web and event fiction for a series of massively multi-player online games, including *City of Heroes*, *Dungeon Runners*, and *Exteel*. After a year in Texas, he has returned to the cold of Canada as a freelance gun-for-hire, to spend time with his dog (a malamute much like a dire wolf) and work on writing screenplays.

Lou Zocchi on

GETTYSBURG

KEY DESIGNER: CHARLES S. ROBERTS

AVALON HILL (FIRST EDITION, 1958)

IT WAS 1959 AND I was stationed in Japan when I first noticed *Gettysburg*, offered for sale by Sears & Roebuck, a sign of the mass-market penetration Avalon Hill's games were beginning to achieve at the time. The many wargames I had played up until then were more like traditional board and strategy games. The player rolled a die and moved the indicated number of squares, hoping to be, in essence, the first to cross the finish line and win the war. The games were also limited in their vision and lacking in any sort of historical accuracy.

Not so with *Gettysburg*.

Gettysburg gives players the opportunity to fight the famous Civil War battle, providing tabletop generals with almost everything their real-life counterparts commanded. Cardboard counters represent every combat unit that fought in and around that Pennsylvania town in July 1863. They carry strength numbers related to each unit's historical muster. That is, a unit with 2,687 men at Gettysburg has a strength of 3 indicated on its game counter. If the unit had 3,972 men at the battle, its unit counter strength is 4. The game marked the first time strength numbers were used to reflect historical battlefield power. That was only one of its important innovations.

Where other wargames of the era typically had you roll a die or spin a spinner or flip over a chance card to bring on more forces, the units in *Gettysburg* enter the game on the road they used in history, timed to coincide with their actual moment of arrival. Their part in the battle's resolution remains more open. The outcome of the day is entirely up to the players' skill and luck, thanks to some clever design.

Back in 1863, the Union army outnumbered the Confederates. In the game, Confederate brigades arrive on the battlefield faster than Union forces. Thus, an aggressive Confederate commander can use his temporary numerical superiority to defeat smaller Union forces as they arrive. This denies the northerners the ability to merge with other units and get the full benefit of their overall superior strength. So even as it was adopting important aspects of historical simulation, designer Charles S. Roberts did so in a context that made it possible for either side of the conflict to win.

It's hard now to fathom just how radical a design concept *Gettysburg* boasted. Charles S. Roberts was founder of Avalon Hill and had previously designed and published a wargame called *Tactics*. But *Tactics* was not an attempt to create a simulation. It provided neither a solid historical tie nor much of a theme at all. *Tactics* — and its successor, *Tactics II* — were more like abstract military exercises in strategy and, well, tactics.

With *Gettysburg*, Roberts created a game that evoked memories of brilliant commanders such as Lee and Jackson, even as players grew to understand the intricacies of their commands. The game is played on a 22" by 28" map depicting the battlefield. The map is overlaid with one-inch squares, with each square covering a quarter-mile of terrain. Infantry units move two squares per turn, while cavalry and artillery units move four squares per turn. Furthermore, a player can move all of his units on the board up to the maximum rate, if he wants to. A move of the entire Confederate force on the board and the countermove by all of the Union forces equals one hour of time passing.

Before this game appeared, playing pieces in most other wargames were moved as in chess and checkers — that is, you move one man, then I move one man. Because *Gettysburg* allows each player to move all of the units he commands during the same turn, a player can assemble a numerically superior force and use it to attack one enemy unit. This was another important design innovation. So, too, the rules allowing units defending from the high ground an advantage when fighting off an attack launched from lower terrain.

Not that the initial release was perfect. Because splash contour lines were used to show where hills began and ended, I had lots of arguments with opponents over which squares were hills and which were not. I solved this problem by coloring all elevated hill squares purple. Exceptionally high terrain squares, like Round Top and Little Round Top, were colored with red highlighter.

After the initial 1958 release, *Gettysburg* underwent revisions for a 1961 second edition. The most important change in the game was the result of an invitation Roberts received from the Rand Corporation.

In 1960, Rand had a fat contract to design military simulations for the Pentagon. They were so impressed by *Gettysburg* that they tracked down Charles

Roberts and asked him to visit. When they asked Roberts which of his employees at Avalon Hill had created the combat results tables used in his games, he told them that he had figured out the results table by himself. They subsequently offered him a job, which he declined. But while visiting Rand, Roberts noticed that they were using a hex-pattern overlay on their maps, which diminished diagonal movement distortion.

Roberts adopted the hex-map overlays for his new wargames, *D-Day* and *Chancellorville*. He also used it for the 1961 *Gettysburg* map board, which had light brown hexes to show higher ground and dark brown hexes to show the highest ground. Each hex depicted only one historical terrain feature. No hex had more than a single such feature.

The changes serve as a fine example of the trial and error way in which games are often updated and revised, how design improvements can often uncover or even create other problems. The hex grid eliminated terrain arguments, but generated complaint mail from purists who wanted the battlefield map board to look like the actual terrain. Worse, Roberts had failed to realize that the new hex map had two hexes where only one square had existed before. Because the units' movement rates had not been bumped up to compensate for the increased number of hexes, players of the 1961 edition spent the first three days of the battle marching toward each other because they were too far from each other to fight!

In July 1964, Avalon Hill announced that the hex grid was being replaced. The 1964 release of *Gettysburg* would have the original, square-grid map. But other innovations would be included in the new edition, such as hidden movement rules and rules allowing artillery units to support infantry actions by shooting out from the same square occupied by the friendly infantry.

By the time the 1964 edition of *Gettysburg* hit store shelves, Charles S. Roberts had left Avalon Hill, the company he had founded a half-dozen years earlier. Under the leadership of Tom Shaw and others, Avalon Hill would grow and thrive for many years, before falling on hard times and being sold off in pieces in the late 1990s. The impact of Roberts' work on *Gettysburg*, his innovative design and fresh ideas, continue to ripple through the hobby game industry. To this day, the awards for excellence in the historical wargaming field are named in his honor.

COLONEL LOUIS ZOCCHI, AL.S.D.F., was one of the first editors for Avalon Hill's magazine, *The General*, and a regular contributor during its first 11 years of publication. He also playtested such important early wargames as *Bismark*, *Afrika Korps*, *Jutland*, *Stalingrad*, and a number of titles Avalon Hill didn't publish. Lou was the first U.S. distributor to sell nothing but adventure games. As a designer, his credits include *Luftwaffe*, *The Battle of Britain*, *Star Fleet Battle Manual*, *Alien Space*, and *Flying Tigers*, as well as the 3-, 5-, 14-, 24-, and 100-sided die. In 1987, he was inducted into the Academy of Adventure Gaming's Hall of Fame.

James Wallis on

GHOSTBUSTERS

KEY DESIGNERS: SANDY PETERSEN, LYNN WILLIS,
GREG STAFFORD, GREG COSTIKYAN

WEST END GAMES (1986)

IT'S A TRUISM THAT games based on movie and TV licenses are not often good. Licensed board games and video games are almost universally worthless and while the roleplaying field has fared a little better, the number of outstanding RPGs based on media properties is still small. And in the mid-1980s, not long after FASA had made a disappointing job of both *Doctor Who* and *Star Trek*, and TSR's *Indiana Jones* and *Conan* had been slammed and cancelled in short order, nobody held much hope that West End's *Ghostbusters* roleplaying game would be anything different.

But the game that emerged from behind that overfamiliar logo was accessible, innovative, exciting, genuinely funny, and had an impact on RPG design that's still felt today. What's more, it pushed some ideas which, had they been picked up by other companies and other designers, might have prevented the RPG industry's slide into obscurity.

Ghostbusters: A Frightfully Cheerful Roleplaying Game was created by a dream team of top-name designers. Though West End was the publisher, the design work was done by Chaosium staff — specifically Sandy Petersen (*Call of Cthulhu*), Greg Stafford (*Pendragon, RuneQuest*), and Lynn Willis (*Godsfire*) — and then edited by Greg Costikyan (*Paranoia, Toon*). It won the H.G. Wells Award for best RPG rules in 1986, directly inspired the mechanics of the *Star Wars Roleplaying Game* (1987) and West End's *d6 System*, as well as many of the notable RPGs of the 1990s.

Ghostbusters was designed to be a pick-up-and-play RPG; a new GM (or "ghostmaster") could begin running his first session of the game in minutes. This required a radically different approach to the whole area of RPG design, which in the 10 years since *D&D* had settled into something of a rut. Open the game's box and you're met by a two-page introduction to the rules, a two-page example of play (and if you've never heard me extol the importance of an example of play, then you've never got me properly drunk), a two-page guide to ghosts, and loads of Ghostbusters paperwork: franchise contracts, EPA permits, last wills and testaments, and the like.

There are also cards. On closer examination, half of these turn out to be pre-generated characters — the movie characters who you already know, since you've bought a game called *Ghostbusters* — and the other half represent equipment that a typical Ghostbuster might carry: proton packs, PKE meters, ghost traps, copies of *Tobin's Spirit Guide*, a bullhorn ("allows user to make more noise than anyone else," but there are two of them), and a beach kit ("triples fun at beach"). So, each player grabs a character card and three equipment cards, the GM reads the first adventure ("30th and Lexington," four pages of pure introductory roleplaying goodness), and you are ready to go. Really, you are.

There's more in the box: the 24-page *Training Manual*, which contains all the game's rules, and the 64-page *Operations Manual*, which is mostly GM advice, adventures, and instructions on how to run a Ghostbusters franchise and a campaign. All of this is laid out in a friendly, accessible way, and decorated with movie stills, caricatures of the principal characters, pull-quotes, and jokes. It makes you feel that this roleplaying stuff is really quite simple. It might even be fun.

And it is fun. Humor is a notoriously difficult thing to capture in a roleplaying game, but *Ghostbusters* gets it right, both to read and to play. A large part of this is down to the game's mechanics which are blisteringly simple, easy to grasp, and perfectly capture the anarchic atmosphere of the original movie. The game does not try to make the movie's story conform to the real world or the needs of a conventional RPG system; instead, what rules there are fit to the atmosphere of a Ghostbusters story, and anything not necessary (hit points, weapons tables) is simply omitted.

A Ghostbusters character has four attributes (called "traits"): *brains, muscle, moves,* and *cool,* all rated between 1 and 7. This represents the number of dice that the player rolls against a difficulty number set by the ghostmaster for any given task. According to the rules picking up someone in a singles bar would be a difficulty 5 (easy) moves task, while eating a telephone would be difficulty 30 (impossible) on muscles. It was the '80s: telephones were larger. This system is generally recognized as the first "dice pool" mechanic in a roleplaying game.

On top of this, each character has one "talent" per trait, a specialization of his or her own choice — and it's often a wild choice, like "shoot .44 so that blood and guts splatters everywhere" or "grab heroine in untoward manner." Talents give a bonus of three additional dice on a difficulty roll. Characters also have "brownie points," a catch-all that encompasses stamina, luck, hero points, experience points, and whatever the GM needs them to be. Brownie points can be used to buy new points in traits, and players can also trade in a trait point to buy more brownie points in an emergency.

That's pretty much it for mechanics, but *Ghostbusters* has one last brilliant trick up its sleeve: the ghost dice. This is a regular six-sider, except the 6 has been replaced by the Ghostbusters logo. The ghost dice must be rolled as one of the dice every time someone makes a trait check. If it comes up ghostly then Something Bad Has Happened, and the worse the roll, the worse the surprise.

All this works together to create an intensely playable and fast-paced game that's spontaneous, exciting, and funny. The broad strokes used to draw the characters and the simplicity of the system keep things on the right side of serious, while never letting play lapse over the edge into slapstick or stupidity. The game can work equally well for one-off adventures or campaign play. In particular, it has an amazing power to remind GMs and players what's great about roleplaying, to refresh the spirit and reinvigorate the palate with a blast of delightful fun.

Sadly, the printed adventures for the game never measured up to its original brilliance, despite a list of top-notch creators including John M Ford, Dan Greenberg, Scott Haring, and an uncredited Allen Varney. *Ghostbusters, International*, released in 1989 to coincide with the second Ghostbusters movie, was not developed by any members of the original creative team and gave the system the one thing it didn't need: more rules. West End's *Men In Black* RPG (1997) tried to recapture the same magic. Despite some interesting ideas, it ended up as no more than a shadow of its inspiration.

Imagine if there had been more pick-up-and-play RPGs back when computer games were making their first serious incursion on to RPGs' traditional turf (and besides *Ghostbusters*, there's only one of any note: 1985's ambitious but flawed *Sandman: The Map of Halaal*). Imagine if other designers had understood the importance of making RPGs accessible and played to their strengths — inspiration, imagination, spontaneity, and social humor — instead of those aspects done better on screen or online. Perhaps the roleplaying game field might have made more inroads into the mass market and would not now be in such decline.

Alas, there weren't, they didn't, it hasn't, and we can only speculate.

Ghostbusters: A Frightfully Cheerful Roleplaying Game remains a unique and audacious oddity, the brilliant forerunner of an entire genre that should have been and never was.

JAMES WALLIS is the former director of Hogshead Publishing, Ltd., and the designer of *Once Upon a Time* and *The Extraordinary Adventures of Baron Munchausen*. He is a narrative media consultant, creating online games for clients including the BBC, the U.K. Home Office, and Endemol Television. He lives in London with his wife and 1d4-1 children.

James M. Ward on

THE GREAT KHAN GAME

KEY DESIGNERS: TOM WHAM, RICHARD HAMBLEN

TSR, INC. (1989)

MY FAVORITE STORY ABOUT *The Great Khan Game* begins in the fall of 1988. I was driving to a little convention in Kentucky with Mark Acres and Tom Moldvay, designers at TSR; I was in the educational department. We were going to fly the company banner at the show and present some of the latest product. At that time, TSR was the hobby industry leader and sales were good. We brought along the prototype for *The Great Khan Game*.

I had already played the game several times, but Mark and Tom hadn't seen it yet. The convention wasn't a good one and there were many problems, including the company vehicle dying on us and forcing us to fly home. The one recurring bright spot during this grim adventure was playing *The Great Khan Game*. We all loved it. No matter how depressed we got, it was fun to play and we laughed doing it. When we got to the airport for our trip home, we couldn't help wondering if, in our run of bad luck, the plane might end up crashing. Because we loved Tom's game so much, we each bought a $100,000 life insurance policy for the plane ride home and signed them over to Tom, just in case. Since I'm writing this now, you can tell that we made it back safe and sound.

The Great Khan Game is a card game about acquiring countries, but not solely through military might. Countries are acquired by gathering the various lands' rulers and important people. The box top recommends it for two or more players, ages 10 to whatever, but the game plays well with any number of players; I've played with eight and nine with no problems.

The game's colorful little board shows a tiny world of 14 countries, more islands than anything else. Each country has its own set of people, represented by individual cards. There are numbered leaders and numbered followers. For the country of Penbroc, for example, card 1 is King Finerb, while card 2 is King Tmosic III, King Ralph MCVI is 3, and so on, down through Queen Sweetsia, the Palace Guard, Prince Ralph MCVII, the Wealthy Nobleman, the Missing Nobles, the Poorer Nobles, the Castle Tmos, and, last, the People.

Cards can be melded to create a set, but only in certain combinations. Queen Sweetsia will only follow — or meld with — cards 1, 2, or 3. But the orders aren't always simple or sequential. Prince Ralph will follow King Ralph or Queen Sweetsia, but the defiant little twerp will not follow Penbroc's other two monarchs, even though their numbers are greater than his. To determine who the Missing Nobles will follow, you need to roll a die. The People, of course, follow almost anyone. The card relationships suggest a backstory for the game world, an amusing web of alliances and grudges that permit or prevent specific characters from pairing up.

Certain cards in each country set display a flag, and the player with the most successfully melded flags owns the country they represent.

If that isn't enough to make your head spin, you can also take over a country with military force. To this end there are mercenary cards and artifact cards, such as the Great Sword of Vandmeer or the Nebelshield. They can be very expensive to own, but have all sorts of fun fantasy powers to help in battle.

Of course, the craziness really begins when event cards turn up. You are constantly drawing cards on your turn, but when a yellow event card appears, the turn stops and everyone must deal with the event. Sometimes assassins kill melded player cards. Plagues have a chance to wipe out every card on the table. Peasant revolts strip away leaders. But not all the events are bad. If the Benevolent Old Fat Wise Man shows up, he gives 10 gold to the weakest player. Event caravans move through the islands, dispensing gold to players with the proper cards. Eventually the Historian event card freezes history and ends the game.

My favorite country is Isle Broddick. It's filled with wizard leaders, but there are also giants, the Faire Fleet, magical towers, crystal balls, and lots of magical spells to toss around. The island is unusually difficult to hold on to, since other players invade it almost every turn. I guess they don't like to see those gold-making spells being used by the wizards there. Imagine that.

While playing the game, you have almost as much fun with Tom Wham's art as you do the clever design mechanics. The art is cartoony, with impossible-looking airships, sword-wielding warriors, bespectacled monkeys at typewriters, and finned sea dragons that look amusing and deadly at the same time. Mixed in with the fantastic stuff are people with World War I-era helmets and an array of historical ships from medieval carracks to the USS *Maine*. This mixture of fantasy and reality, coupled with Tom's whimsical art style, lends *The Great Khan Game* a terrific sense of fun.

When I look at games, I'm searching for certain features that, to my mind, guarantee a great time. *The Great Khan Game* has all of these features.

An easy-to-read rulebook is important for several reasons. If you have to hunt through a book to find a rule, or the mechanics are described in too complex a fashion, the game grinds to a halt. Although the rules for *The Great Khan Game* run for a somewhat daunting 32 pages, the rules themselves take up only about half that space and are nicely organized. They contain lots of great examples of play, lots of clear diagrams, and perfect explanations for all the most difficult cards.

The better games also play a little differently every time you take them up. If you're doing the exact same things in a game all the time, that can become boring. I've probably played *The Great Khan Game* over a thousand times and it's been never been the same experience twice. In fact, I've often played four or more games in a row — an entire day of the *Great Khan* experience. This makes for less of a marathon than you might think; each game can take from 20 minutes to an hour, depending on when the game-ending Historian card is randomly drawn.

I especially like games with what I call a "wahoo!" feature to them, an excitement and unpredictability that makes them fun for everyone at the table. No one likes to get behind in a game, with no chance of catching up. But when the turn of a card can devalue gold for every player but the poorest or a rare disease claim the life of any leader, trailing players can almost always catch up to the leaders and possibly overtake them. This spices up gameplay, though this also means you can be winning for most of a game, only to have an event card wipe you out at the finish. Now, that might sound extremely "unfun," but the game is not meant to be taken that seriously. (Look at the artwork again, if you forget that.) Besides, you can't help but laugh when the calamity that struck your kingdoms comes around to visit the other players, as well.

The Great Khan Game was released by TSR with the Forgotten Realms logo displayed prominently on the box, though that was just a marketing ploy to earn it more sales and get it more attention. At that time, the Realms were red hot and anything with the logo sold well. Come to think of it, that's true today, as well. But *Great Khan* bears no real connection to that expansive fantasy world. It's the creation of Tom Wham, through and through (though Richard Hamblen receives a designer co-credit, as the inspiration for the card meld mechanic).

In my years of gaming, I've never encountered a game as fun or interesting as *The Great Khan Game*, but many of Tom Wham's other creations come close. Many of Tom's games are still in print or are at least available on his website. *Snit Smashing* and *Snit's Revenge* are quick, easy-to-play romps about strange little creatures that are mostly noses, eyes, and legs. *The Awful Green Things From Outer Space* is a wonderful game about alien creatures invading a spaceship. Tom's whimsical art and his cheerful design style fill every one of his games, making them highly enjoyable experiences. When you have time, you should go to his website — www.tomwham.com — and check out the handmade games he has for sale. And if you can manage to track down a copy of *The Great Khan Game*, snap it up. It's truly one of the best hobby games ever.

JAMES M. WARD was born, has lived a pleasantly long time, and has been married since the early 1970s (the latter thanks to the patience of his wife, Janean). He has three unusually charming sons: Breck, James, and Theon. They in turn have given him five startlingly charming grandchildren: Keely, Miriam, Sophia, James Preston, and Teagan. He wrote the very first science-fiction roleplaying game, *Metamorphosis Alpha*, and had the pleasure of working for many years at TSR, Inc., where he wrote lots of *D&D* and *AD&D* things. He also designed the bestselling *Spellfire* and *Dragon Ball Z* collectible card games. He counts his latest Halcyon Blithe novel *Dragonfrigate Wizard* (Tor, 2006) as one of his better and prouder creations.

Gav Thorpe on

HAMMER OF THE SCOTS

KEY DESIGNERS: JERRY TAYLOR, TOM DALGLIESH
COLUMBIA GAMES (2002)

HAMMER OF THE SCOTS is one of the earliest wargames I ever played with my now-regular gaming buddy Max. Many years later, Max's copy is looking a little worn around the edges, but the game itself is as fresh as the first time we played it (to the point of us calling it "the Old Wound"). Such longevity should be praised. *Hammer* has simple rules and therefore its strength lies in the complex strategies and tactics that arise from these basic foundations.

Hammer of the Scots recreates the struggle between the English and the Scots in the late 13th and early 14th century. We usually play the "Braveheart" campaign, which is the more distinctive of the two presented. This starts with Edward I of England in almost total control, and sets him against William Wallace, who has only a couple of nobles and clans to aid him. These one-sided starting forces mean that each army has a very different dynamic right from the first turn, imbuing the game with the character of the historical campaign it represents. The Scots must be wily and avoid too many stand-up fights, while the English must attempt to bring the Scots to decisive battle with their knights and large infantry formations.

The pieces are wooden blocks, giving a nice aesthetic and tactile quality that is sometimes lacking in counter-based games. The blocks are positioned with a blank side toward the opponent during normal play, and their identity and strength is only revealed once battle commences. This simple "fog of war" mechanic is the great appeal that runs through all of Columbia's block games, allowing for no end of dastardly bluff, counter-bluff, and chicanery. The blocks show the unit type, its movement value, and its combat abilities. They also have a current strength. The block's uppermost edge shows its current strength — or "step" — so if the unit takes damage or regains strength, you simply rotate the block accordingly, to reflect its new value.

The board consists of a map of Scotland broken down into irregular territories, with England bordering to the south. Most of the territories are the lands of the various nobles ruling Scotland at the time. The game itself revolves around gaining control of the nobles, so their blocks serve as both fighting units and a way to measure victory. If one side can gain all of the nobles, they've won. This means that a player must constantly balance the risk of losing these blocks in battle against the benefit of capturing others.

During each turn, representing a year, gameplay is driven by a card deck. These cards dictate movement and introduce a few special events — a herald arrives to to turn a noble to your side, a truce prevents your opponent attacking, and so on. Most of the cards are valued between one and three, and each point allows you to move one group of units. The players each secretly pick a card and then simultaneously reveal their choices, with the highest-valued card moving first. Sometimes this is an advantage, sometimes it isn't, depending on the current game situation. For example, moving first allows you to choose the order in which battles are resolved, which can be vital in terms of positioning attacks and retreats. On the other hand, going first allows your opponent to respond and turn a promising situation into a compromising one. This creates one of the many levels of strategy — a high-value hand means you have to be pro-active for the year; a low-value hand means you'll be more reactive. The English always go first in the case of a tie, lending them a much more aggressive style of play. The nature of the game's card play emphasizes emergent strategy and means that you must constantly weigh long-term goals against short-term necessity.

Combat is simple yet elegant. Each block has a speed and a combat value. Blocks in battle activate in descending order, according to their speed ranking. But defenders go first when blocks have the same speed, which often makes staging an attack a trying endeavor. For each strength step the block possesses, you roll a die. If the resulting number is equal to or lower than the block's combat value, an enemy block is reduced by a step. Importantly, nobles blocks are better when defending their own territory, so there's an even greater difficulty in attacking one on its home turf. If you reduce a block to zero steps, it is eliminated. Nobles that are reduced to zero strength immediately switch sides and join the enemy!

Blocks can also retreat instead of attack — believe me, you'll be glad of it on many occasions. Choosing when to stay and fight, and when to cut your losses and run, is vital for success. Retreats don't always have to take a unit back to its starting point, so fast blocks (such as Wallace or the English Hobelars) can skip through enemy armies without fighting, if there's space beyond the fray in which they might end their retreat. Such a ploy can allow blocks to escape a trap or isolate the enemy.

Nobles can also be captured during wintering, which occurs at the end of each year. This phase is where victory is often decided. The majority of nobles must return to their home territory, but if the land is occupied by the enemy, the noble is captured and swaps sides. The sequencing of this allows a Scottish noble to capture an English noble, but not the other way around, giving the Scots a distinct advantage in this phase. Replacements are also made in wintering. Again, the Scots have the home ground advantage here, as they can bring in random new blocks from a replacement pool, while only English infantry may spend the winter in Scotland. Their knights and other units must return to England. The English raise a levy each year, taking blocks randomly and starting them in England in the next year. This mechanic gives the game an ebb and flow, as units cross the border and the English armies build up strength, and then are slowly whittled away if not properly reinforced.

One of the blocks in play may be Edward I himself, probably the most important figure in the game. As well as being impressive in battle, the Longshanks has the ability to winter an army in Scotland rather than have them return home. This creates a formidable fighting force poised in the heart of Scotland, ready to strike in the next year. Whether or not to use the king in this way forms a crucial part of any English strategy. For the Scottish player, the key is divining from your opponent's moves whether the king has come back from France, and if so, what you can do about it. The English player, for his part, can use his blocks to give the impression of not having the king (or act boldly and pretend that he has). These sorts of mind games help make *Hammer of the Scots* so enjoyable.

The cleverly designed blocks, the solid and effective card-based system, and the unique character imbued into the competing armies by the game's mechanics have allowed Max and me to employ endless gambits and counter-strategies over the years. It may be a cliche to say that *Hammer* has never played the same way twice, but that's pretty much true. The diverse turns of fortunes that occur in every game present opportunities or obstacles that can change your entire strategy in an instant. I'm certain we'll enjoy *Hammer of the Scots* for many years to come, and I commend it to anyone interested in a challenging and exciting wargame.

GAV THORPE lives in Nottingham, England, and has been designing and developing products for Games Workshop since 1994. Prominent credits include the *Inquisitor* skirmish game, as well as work on several editions of *Warhammer* and *Warhammer 40,000*, and a long stream of supplements for both game systems. He also designed the board game *Gobbo's Banquet*, and has written more than half a dozen novels for the Black Library. He recently wrote the script for the *Mark of Chaos* computer game. None of this essay was written by a mechanical hamster called Dennis. Honest.

Uli Blennemann on

HERE I STAND

KEY DESIGNERS: ED BEACH, MATTHEW BEACH, ANANDA GUPTA, DAVE CROSS
GMT GAMES (2006)

A *CHALLENGE HAS BEEN* issued. Melanchthon, German professor, theologian, and leading Lutheran reformer, has called upon Johann Tetzel, the famous doctor of Sacred Theology and seller of indulgences ("As soon a coin in coffer rings, the soul from purgatory springs") to participate in a theologian disputation. Melanchthon eloquently "wins" the debate and Tetzel is disgraced. Nuremberg and Regensburg both become Protestant. . . .

At the same time, a mighty Ottoman army, led by Sultan Suleiman the Magnificent, is besieging Vienna, capital of the Habsburg empire. Emperor Charles V personally inspires the defenders of the city. This time, the Western world is lucky. The besieged city holds and the Ottoman army suffers high losses. Winter is near, so the Ottoman army has to retire. . . .

In Rome, Pope Leo X furthers the building of the Basilica of Saint Peter. His plan is to make the basilica the largest church in Christianity. . . .

Meanwhile, in London, Henry VIII is finally convinced that his wife Catherine of Aragon will not give birth to a male heir. The young Anne Boleyn has caught Henry's attention. However, there is one big problem: the pope has to grant Henry a divorce. . . .

Under Francis I, the renaissance has arrived in Paris. He is a man of letters and encourages the greatest artists of the time to come to France. As a "Patron of the Arts" Francis is leading the building of grand estates and showplaces. . . .

Having survived a furious storm, explorer Francisco de Orellana has reached the coast of present day Ecuador with a tiny number of vessels. He is searching, without success, for the golden city of El Dorado. . . .

In the Ionian Sea, a large Ottoman pirate fleet led by Barbarossa Hayreddin Pasha is looking for booty. Although the Habsburgs have a naval squadron at Taranto and are supported by the Knights of St. John at Malta, the Ottoman *pirates are successful and transport a large amount of goods to their pirate haven at Algiers. . . .*

Peter Apian, famous for his works in mathematics, astronomy, and cartography, sees Halley's Comet and observes that the comet's tail is always oriented into the direction away from the sun. . . .

ALL THE ABOVE EVENTS may happen in a game of *Here I Stand*, published by GMT Games. They may even happen during a single game turn.

Here I Stand: Wars of the Reformation 1517-1555 is a three- to six-player game exploring the military, political, and religious conflicts at the start of the Protestant Reformation in 16th-century Europe. A player represents one of the leading powers of the time: the Habsburgs, England, France, the Papacy, the Ottoman Empire, and the forming Protestant states. Games looking at this fascinating period of history are a rarity. The only other notable title simulating this era is *A Mighty Fortress*, released by SPI in 1977, though to only mixed success.

Here I Stand is a so-called "card-driven wargame," a game whose engine is a deck of 110 cards used by all players. In addition to these cards, the game includes two large and nicely detailed map sheets depicting Europe, the North African Coast, and the soon-to-be-explored New World, plus various tracks and tables. There are also several hundred cardboard playing pieces (leaders, military forces, naval squadrons, theological debaters, conquerors, and explorers, plus markers), six power cards (one each for the above mentioned powers), a rules booklet, a scenario booklet, two reference cards, and 10 dice.

In his designer's notes, Ed Beach, who has been fascinated by the period for a long time, admits that *The Napoleonic Wars* (GMT, 2002) was the point of origin for *Here I Stand*. The card-driven game genre allowed Beach to represent the asymmetric configurations of the six powers (with their completely different aims) in a sound way. The Protestant player has to convert as many spaces of the game map to his faith, the Ottoman player is mainly interested in grabbing territory away from Habsburg rule and pirating the Mediterranean Sea, the Papal player intends to build Saint Peter's and starts the Counter Reformation, and so on. The Habsburg player is the most powerful force in the game, but he has the most difficult position: In Germany, the Reformation is under way; the Ottomans are advancing through Hungary to Vienna; France is already at war with him; and the New World, waiting to be explored, needs his attention, too.

Here I Stand comes with three scenarios: the 1517 "campaign" scenario, encompassing 39 years of history, or nine game turns; the 1532 scenario, which lasts six turns; and the tournament scenario, which takes three. It is a quite complex game. However, the rules are extremely well written and not all players need to have read the complete booklet before the start of their first game. The Ottoman player does not need to know the intricacies of the Reformation rules nor the mechanics used for the New World; the latter are uninteresting for the Papal and Protestant player, as well. The Protestant player is involved in military conflict only late in the game, so he may skip these passages initially.

In addition to possessing the determination to read a longer set of rules, the players should also enjoy games that have a long playing time. The full campaign scenario will take at least 10 hours, if played to completion — though there are "sudden death" victory conditions. The game also works best with a full contingent around the table. There are rules for playing with fewer than six players, but I believe the game should be played only with a full group.

Despite the long game length, however, players of *Here I Stand* will face a surprisingly small amount of downtime. They'll find no need to break out a copy of Tolstoy's *War and Peace* while the other players are moving their pieces and conducting battles. Instead, when it is a player's turn, he normally only plays a single card from his hand. In most cases, he either uses the card's command points (between one and five) to conduct actions, *or* he plays the card for the listed event. Afterward, the next player plays a card for either the command points or an event.

By spending command points, a player can move a formation to an adjacent spot, stage a naval move, raise new troops (either regular or mercenary), attack, explore, colonize, call a theological debate, burn books, and an array of other actions. The events determined by the card conjure both specific historical events and the spirit of the era. The event card "Tercios" allows the Habsburg player to use extra dice in a battle. "Philip of Hessen's Bigamy" means the Protestant player must either remove this leader from the game or discard a card from his hand. "War in Persia" draws the Ottoman forces away from the game map, while "Machiavelli: *The Prince*" makes the declaration of war on another player free.

What do I like most about the game? *Here I Stand* offers a ton of period flavor, and it is a game that *tells you a story*. What's more, it's better than a book or a movie. With just a little bit of imagination, you write a part of that story.

Does the game have shortcomings? Yes, it has a few. First, the electorate spaces for Germany are wrong. In the game, you only get six instead of seven electorates, and some are in incorrect locations. And the game's length can be a serious concern for some players. However, such programs as *Aide de Camp II* or *CyberBoard* allow you to move the game mechanics to the computer, so you can either speed things up or even play via the Internet. It's a lot easier to run and complete a full campaign that way — though there's nothing quite like playing a classic design such as *Here I Stand* in person.

THE PAPAL PLAYER USES *the "Halley's Comet" card as an en event and forces the French player to skip his next impulse. The card is discarded after use.*

Why did he choose this action? Well, with a French army in striking distance of Florence, he felt that he needed to move his main army north from Rome before the French troops would be able to reach the city.

But the French player has other plans in mind. He reaches for a card. . . .

ULI BLENNEMANN is brand manager for Phalanx Games b.v., a leading Dutch publisher of board- and card games since 2001. A historian by profession, he founded Moments in History in 1993, selling it in early 1999. Besides testing and a little bit of design work, he has developed more than 40 different games. Uli was born in 1965 and lives in Duelmen, Germany. Besides gaming he likes sports (especially soccer) and reading.

S. Craig Taylor, Jr. on
A HOUSE DIVIDED

KEY DESIGNER: FRANK CHADWICK
GAME DESIGNERS' WORKSHOP (FIRST EDITION, 1981)

IT WAS THE SPRING of 1982. I was working in the Yaquinto Games booth at a perfectly dreadful little gaming convention on the Texas A&M campus — really nothing more than an excuse for the con's organizers to run large roleplaying games all day — and the dealer area was pretty much deserted. Another bored dealer was seeking a way to pass the time. We were both familiar with *A House Divided*, an accessible Civil War game designed by Frank Chadwick, and started to play. When the convention ended before we finished the game, we recorded the locations on the map board. Sure enough, at the next little local convention we both attended, the game was eagerly set back up and finished.

Let's face it: *A House Divided* is not that much to look at, even when brand new — serviceable, easy to read and use, but no "gee whiz" graphics. Still, my battered old copy has survived over 400 plays. Well, actually, in the interest of complete honesty, I must admit that it did not really survive in the physical sense. My current copy is my second one, purchased when the original mapfolds contained more cellophane tape than cardboard creases and so much ink had rubbed off the original counters that they strained these rheumy old eyes. (Even in this second copy, the Union militia cavalry unit shows more white than blue, as some recent and cranky opponents have complained.) But the underlying game has survived for me, quite separate from its functional bits and pieces.

That interrupted session between dealers was a rarity; few games hold your interest over months-long gaps in time. Fewer still survive 400 plays. *A House Divided* has managed to do both. (And at minimal expense; if you think about it, I spent maybe $40 on two copies of the original edition and one copy of the revised edition, so the game has cost me a thrifty 10¢ per play!)

It seems that some wargames are intended to be admired and some wargames are intended to be played. *A House Divided* falls squarely into the latter category. This is not one of those games that you set aside until an entire frosty winter evening or rain-soaked Saturday is available for you to laboriously work through the rulebook, while carefully marking the text with a highlighter. This is a game where you skim the rules, then sit down and blunder through half a game with a friend. Actual play clarifies the rules enough that, by the second session, almost everything in the game is understood and properly employed.

With a point-to-point map board, the number of marches is determined by six-sided die rolls. A minimal number of mostly straightforward rules cover movement (by road, rail, river, and ocean for the Union; more restricted movement for the Confederacy), combat, entrenchment (including coastal defenses), unit promotions, reinforcements, retreats, and cavalry withdrawals. There are also some not-too-onerous options concerning matters such as supply and breaking rail lines. The elemental game system *forces* players to view their strategies through a Civil War prism. The routes of advance correspond to the historical ones. Players must see to rear area security around the main armies to prevent cavalry raids, and operations that start with promising advances often break down when faced with hastily dug entrenchments filled with crack infantry.

From the standpoint of 400 games played, I feel eminently qualified to comment on the game's balance. The key to its equilibrium is player experience. As every designer knows, it is impossible to balance a game for players who do *not* play optimally. Football would not work if points were provided as incentives for sloppy play — that is, for your own team's fumbles, interceptions, and failures to make first downs. *A House Divided*, despite an undemanding game system, requires players to know what they're doing to have any hope of winning.

For example, many novices playing the South focus on cavalry "jump moves" in their early contests, but this mechanic — which allows cavalry units to position themselves for optimal attacks by moving through an enemy without combat — is actually quite easy to block and avoid. Once he outgrows staging these endless diversions by crazed Rebel raiders, a more experienced Confederate player can often take advantage of the game's victory conditions to cling to at least one of the six big Southern port cities through the last turn. I estimate that a Confederate player using that strategy can win some 80 to 85 percent of the time, unless an equally experienced Union player is aware of the necessary tempo of advance and how to achieve it. Then the win ratio falls quite close to the desired 50:50.

Whoa, Craig, you may enjoy *A House Divided*, but this is a small, simple game that is over a quarter-century old. Is this *really* realistic, a claim made by virtually every wargame ever published and the *ne plus ultra* of the whole genre?

If by *realistic* you mean *detailed*, *A House Divided* certainly is not realistic. Apparently, enough people felt details were important that the game's second edition added many more of them. If you ask me, details can sometimes add decision-making that is less important than it is fiddly or even irritating — more stuff to remember, stuff that can distract you from the key decisions you should be focused on. Still, the second edition certainly not a *bad* game and, if details are your cup of tea, by all means flavor to taste and enjoy. (The third edition, from Phalanx Games, wisely separates the original rules from the additional ones, so it can happily serve both masters.) But *realistic* can also mean decision-making processes and game flow that roughly mimics actual events, and if this is your definition, the original, 1981 version of *A House Divided* is realistic — at least as realistic as the later editions, even if less detailed.

For my money, a great game is one that allows the player to make a series of *important* or *key* decisions that directly and understandably reflect on victory or defeat. Games that imitate reality on the game's own selected level without bogging down in details are often referred to as *elegant*, and that, in one word, sums up the appeal of *A House Divided*, the little game that could, and places it unmistakably onto any list of the very best wargames.

Starting with a playtest credit on the 1962 version of Avalon Hill's version of *Bismarck*, S. CRAIG TAYLOR, JR. has been a playtester, designer, developer, researcher, rules writer, and/or producer for well over 100 board, miniature, card, and computer games for such publishers Battleline, Yaquinto, Avalon Hill, Microprose, Imagic, Southpeak, Talonsoft, Lost Battalion Games, and, currently, Breakaway Games. These include such designs as *Wooden Ships & Iron Men*, *Air Force*, *Flattop*, *Battle*, *Wings*, *Gettysburg: Smithsonian Edition*, *Sergeants*, and *Battlegroup*. In his spare time, he enjoys playing games and, occasionally, spearfishing and bloody sprees as an ax murderer.

Scott Haring on

ILLUMINATI

KEY DESIGNER: STEVE JACKSON

STEVE JACKSON GAMES (FIRST EDITION, 1982)

FROM: AGENT L-23
TO: Central Command
RE: *Illuminati* game threat assessment

Our Censorship and Misinformation branch has done an excellent job keeping the masses blissfully unaware of our activities over the past centuries. As we get closer and closer to our goal of Total Global Domination™, secrecy becomes even more important. At this critical juncture, my brothers, we cannot let our plans slip out to an unknowing public.

Which is why we should be very, very concerned about the game called *Illuminati*, designed by Steve Jackson. While masquerading as an innocent card game promising an hour or two's fun for a table full of players, Jackson has come perilously close to describing the inner workings of our Secret Conspiracies™ and Fiendishly Diabolical Plans®!

Of course, Jackson's game is simpler than actually taking over the world. Each player is a competing Illuminatus, a powerful conspiracy bent on world domination. The group is represented by a card with an outgoing arrow along each edge, laid on the table in front of him. Over the course of the game, other cards (with arrows of their own) representing other organizations, places, and people are brought in to join the core group's power structure. The cards range from those representing real-life entities, such as the Democrats and Republicans, Big Media, and the South American Nazis; to the thinly disguised, such as the Society for Creative Anarchism, the Boy Sprouts, and the Semiconscious Liberation Army; to the downright fictional, such as the Iranian Moderates, the Robot Sea Monsters, the Orbital Mind Control Lasers, and the Evil Geniuses for a Better Tomorrow.

Each group has three (sometimes two) stats and a few alignments. (The Mafia and the Cycle Gangs are both identified as "violent," while the Cycle Gangs and the Trekkies are both "weird.") Some of the cards also have bonuses or penalties in special circumstances, most get money as income (which can be spent to influence events), and there are special cards that also affect play. But the heart and soul of the game is acquiring group cards into a power structure. As the structure grows, many cards can join together to make more powerful attacks, and the silly humor of the game masks the serious secrets Jackson is spilling. When a player announces, "The FBI, with help from the UFOs, the Fast Food Chains, and the Underground Newspapers, is attacking to control the Phone Company," he has no idea how close he has come to describing Operation Reach Out and Smack Someone™. At every game I have witnessed, players will frequently hear an attack announced, or look at a power-structure arrangement, and remark, "That explains a lot." This is something we cannot abide, my brothers.

Players can attack available cards in the middle of the table, or try to take cards from other players' structures. Cards can also be destroyed (removed from play) or neutralized (taken from a player's structure and put back in the middle, free for anyone to go after). This is where Jackson's design takes the leap from silly fun to gaming classic, thus making it all the more dangerous to our cause — the other players at the table may join in on any attack, on either side.

Don't want to see another player get that powerful group out of the middle? Spend some of your money to stop him. But do that too many times, and 1) you won't have any money left to boost your own attacks, and 2) a table full of opponents will target you for revenge. The isolation the latter situation causes — as you know from our work, brothers — makes victory nearly impossible. In the game, players usually let each other do what they want until they get close to winning; then the heavy guns come out, and try after try for the brass ring is beaten back, until somebody finally becomes just too strong to stop or the other players run out of things to stop him with.

This player interaction is what brings them back to *Illuminati* time and time again. The rules are not hard to master. Like the best Texas hold 'em players, you're not playing the cards, you're playing the other people around the table. Can you convince your fellows that someone else is closer to winning than you are, that *he* is the biggest threat and more deserving of their attacks? Can you look non-threatening as you capture the Robot Sea Monsters, a relatively weak group, but one that gives you the bonus you need to take the Mafia *next turn* and wrap up the victory? Can you rally the table to attack your chief rival, knowing it will leave them without money when it comes time to stop you from winning?

Interaction like this leads to a certain amount of — well, how to put this . . . friendly animosity. No, that's not it. Backstabbing is more like it. Treachery and betrayal are key elements of *Illuminati*. Experienced players expect it, though it's considered bad form to cheat a new player. (Especially rotten — but particularly Illuminated — is for an experienced player to teach an entire table of newbies the game, and then cheat his way to victory.) Brothers, we can ill afford the sheeplike masses to become more expert at tactics like these. The rules even include a section detailing an officially sanctioned "Cheating Game," in which nearly anything goes (including stealing from the bank, if you can get away with it), but it notes this variation should be played "only with *very* good friends, or with people you will never see again."

In summary, my official threat assessment of the *Illuminati* card game is Condition Magenta. The game strays too close to official Global Conspiracy™ operations to be allowed to continue, and is too much fun and has too much replay value to fade away on its own. Indeed, 25 years after its initial release, *Illuminati* is still immensely popular, having spawned multiple editions, three expansion sets, Steve Jackson Games' corporate logo, a spinoff collectible card game that is still the single biggest-selling product line in SJ Games history, and — my favorite — a complete set of color-coded pins that identified Illuminati members and their specialty. They got every color right except for, ironically enough, Misinformation.

I leave it to Central Command to formulate a response.

CENTRAL COMMAND ACTION REPORT
FILING AGENT: Z-35

Agent L-23 stumbled across a deep-cover operation and reported it to elements of Central Command with insufficient clearance. L-23, along with Agents Q-5 and Q-6, were successfully reprogrammed and returned to duty. Agent Q-7 could not be reprogrammed and had to be liquidated. L-23's report has been taken out of circulation and is now only available to those of Z-level clearance.

Scott (Agent L-23) Haring has been part of the adventure gaming industry since 1982. He spent time on the staffs of TSR, Inc. and Steve Jackson Games, and has written and edited for *Ghostbusters*, *GURPS*, *Car Wars*, *Dungeons & Dragons*, *Top Secret/S.I.*, and *Marvel Super Heroes*. He's served as editor for the publications *Autoduel Quarterly*, *Pyramid*, and *The Gamer*, and been a columnist for *Comics & Games Retailer* since 1987. He lives in central Texas with his wife, a stepson, and several animals. He sings in his church choir and waits for the day his Houston Astros will win the World Series, an event that may very well take an Illuminati-level conspiracy to actually occur.

Dana Lombardy on

JOHNNY REB

KEY DESIGNERS: JOHN HILL, STEVE ST. CLAIR, BERNIE KEMPINSKI

THE JOHNNY REB GAME COMPANY (THIRD EDITION, 1996)

I FELL IN LOVE with the first armies of miniature soldiers that I saw, painted and arrayed for battle on tabletop, back in the mid-1960s. But I did not fall in love with miniatures gaming.

The first miniatures games were very different from the visually powerful fantasy and science fiction products many people associate with the hobby now. There was no *Warhammer* (or a Games Workshop, for that matter) and WizKids' pre-painted *Mage Knight* game, with its built-in "combat dial" bases, was many years off. No, the first miniatures games were historical, set in ancient Greece and Rome, the Napoleonic era, and the like. I really enjoyed the history, but somehow the games themselves could not capture my interest. In fact, they were frustrating to me.

Why? Well, the players all seemed obsessed — then, as now — with uniform details. They spent weeks painting their lead or tin soldiers, intent on getting the minutiae just right. It seemed miniatures gaming meant painting for hours on end and then standing around a table admiring each other's armies. They were nice and all, but wasn't the idea to use them playing a game?

Perhaps the problem was the limited variety of rules available. The first miniatures rules were imports from England, where there was a tradition of fighting battles with toy soldiers. This stretched all the way back to the groundbreaking books *Floor Games* (1911) and *Little Wars* (1913), both by H.G. Wells, and for ship models, to *The Naval War Game* (1898), by naval historian Fred T. Jane. The first U.S. set of miniatures rules was written by Murray Fletcher Pratt, a science fiction and fantasy writer; his *Naval War Game* saw print in 1940. Finally, in 1955, Jack Scruby started manufacturing affordable toy soldiers for American gamers, along with a newsletter that shared sets of rules.

To me, however, these miniatures rules were not as compelling as the then new type of board wargames being published in the 1960s by the Avalon Hill Game Company. Avalon Hill spawned Simulations Publications, Inc. (SPI), Game

Designers' Workshop (GDW), and many other publishers in the 1970s and 1980s that released really creative designs. I was happy playing their board wargames and forgot all about miniatures.

Then I met John Hill.

Like many other wargamers, I'd been very impressed by John's *Squad Leader*, published in 1977 by Avalon Hill. You could start playing that World War II tactical combat game after reading a minimum of rules, and the game boasted what seemed to be unlimited potential for growth, with scenarios that added various armies, more combat units, and the like. But when I met John in 1981, he told me something completely shocking: He had originally designed *Squad Leader* as a miniatures game.

John went on to explain that he preferred miniatures games over all other types. In fact, he was working on a set of miniatures rules for his favorite period of history — the American Civil War. Would I be interested in playtesting?

My first reaction, and what I told John, was "No, thanks. I don't play miniatures games."

John persisted. Reluctantly, I gave in.

Unbelievable.

Amazing.

I had more fun playing John's work-in-progress, titled *Johnny Reb*, than I'd had playing any other historical game, with or without a board.

The game instantly and thoroughly captured my imagination. I became so obsessed with *Johnny Reb* that I insisted we play every weekend possible.

I even bought and painted my own toy soldiers. . . .

I was hooked. I was in love with miniatures gaming. I still am.

And I have *Johnny Reb* to thank for that.

Compared to the miniatures rules that I had played, *Johnny Reb* was packed with innovative elements designed to add depth of gameplay. Most striking of all these is the order system. Instead of writing out orders on a separate sheet of paper, players place one of six types of order markers next to each of their units, be it infantry, cavalry, or artillery.

The order options are simple. For its action, a unit may first fire, charge, hold, move (with direction determined by an arrow on the marker), change formation (move from line to column), or disengage — otherwise known as "run away!" Units move, fire, or charge based upon the pre-determined value of the order. Use first fire and, well, you get to fire before anything else happens. Charging units go second, and so on. This variation from the traditional I go/you go turn sequence helps capture the immediacy of battle by giving the more emotionally packed actions precedence over others.

To avoid the problem of too much mechanical restraint on movement, which could help dispel the realistic chaos of the battlefield, orders are placed face-down. Your opponent has no idea what your units are going to do until everyone's order markers are revealed. This leads to classic rock-paper-scissors dilemmas every turn.

For example, you suspect that your enemy is going to issue a first-fire order this turn, just as he did last turn, inflicting casualties on your regiment before your troops (under a hold order) can fire at him. So you change your own order to first fire for the coming turn. However, when the orders are revealed, your opponent has called for a charge. You shoot first, at long range, and inflict only a few casualties. Then his regiment swarms down on you. In the ensuing "dice down" between these two regiments, not only does your regiment rout (run away because it failed a morale check), a nearby friendly unit is forced to check its morale. The second unit also fails and withdraws. You now have a hole in your line and a crisis to deal with, all because you guessed wrong on that first-fire order.

These command challenges are frequent in *Johnny Reb* and keep players in a high state of tension every turn. Nothing is ever certain, because your soldiers behave like real troops. Instead of fighting to the last man, like robots, more often than not they "skedaddle" under withering fire and force you to adjust your plans.

The first version of *Johnny Reb* was published in 1983 by Adventure Games, a company started by David Arneson, co-designer of *Dungeons & Dragons*. A reprint was done in 1988 by Game Designers' Workshop, with extra player aids and a simplified artillery system. The latest iteration, *Johnny Reb III*, was published in 1996. While the basic rules remain the same, the scale has been modified slightly so that regiments and artillery batteries occupy more historically accurate frontages. A fanzine, *Charge*, has been published since 2003 by Civil War historian and author Scott Mingus. *Charge* offers new scenarios and other support material for the game.

For experienced gamers, it's easy to start playing *Johnny Reb* using the two-page reference chart provided with the rules. I've seen novice gamers learn how to play effectively after being helped through only a few turns.

In 2008, *Johnny Reb* will celebrate its 25th anniversary. John Hill's Civil War miniatures rules remain innovative, challenging, and lots of fun, a claim supported by the game's loyal fan support. Clubs still stage *Johnny Reb* sessions at conventions around the world, more than 20 years after the rules were introduced.

For all these reasons, *Johnny Reb* deserves to be considered one of the best games ever designed.

DANA LOMBARDY is best known for his award-winning *Streets of Stalingrad* board wargame, published in three separate editions since its first release in 1979. He's also known for his appearances on various television shows, including multiple episodes of the History Channel's *Tales of the Gun*. Lombardy has contributed as an editor, cartographer, graphic artist, and designer to many books, games, and magazines. He served as publisher of *Napoleon Journal* from 1996 to 2000.

JUNTA

KEY DESIGNERS: VINCENT TSAO, ERIC GOLDBERG, BEN GROSSMAN
WEST END GAMES (SECOND EDITION, 1985)

JUNTA NEVER QUITE GETS the respect it deserves. If you spend a lot of time hanging out with board game cognoscenti, bringing it up will almost invariably spark a discussion of its various minor flaws — it doesn't adapt well to smaller groups, coups take too long, there's too many fiddly bits and not enough different kinds of cards, and so on. Everybody's got a suggestion for improving it. In the end, though, even these jaded experts have to admit that for sheer, goofy fun, *Junta* fights way out of its weight class.

The game's premise simply drips with politically incorrect atmosphere. Players each represent an entire family, part of the governmental power structure of La República de los Bananas. (La República is a stereotypical Central American nation, a battleground of corruption and villainy.) Turns represent entire years, in which one family manages to get its representative elected president and therefore controls the purse strings on the randomly determined amount of foreign aid coming in from an unnamed superpower. The president also gets to assign other players their roles in the ruling cabinet, from the tremendously powerful minister of internal security, through the various generals controlling individual armies, to the disrespected admiral of the navy. The president uses these powers, along with bribes and promises, to curry favor and set his opponents against each other. Then, all players must select a secret location for themselves, choosing from the bank (the only place money can be safely deposited), headquarters (from where coups can be launched), or the somewhat safer home, nightclub, or paramour (because what's the fun in ruling a tiny, corrupt, war-torn country if you can't let your hair down once in a while?). Opposing players can use cards to summon assassins to pursue you; if they've correctly guessed your location, they can send you to your undoubtedly well-deserved final resting place. Of course, this also allows them to pocket your undeposited cash and take whatever cards you're holding.

If members of the cabinet are unhappy with their lowly positions, they can always declare a coup against the current president. If — or, rather, *when* — this happens, the game suddenly becomes a small tactical wargame, as players maneuver their assembled forces around the small city map, trying to seize the major buildings as they avoid shelling from the air force and gunboats. During the coup, the rebels must also sort out a new government by promising exciting jobs to potential allies in exchange for their support with both bullet and ballot. Since the rebellion is often led by the admiral, holder of the weakest role in the cabinet, the coup traditionally begins with what's known as "the ceremonial shelling of the presidential palace" by the gunboats. Once the chaos is over, and the president has either fought off the rebels or fallen to their torch-wielding hordes, a new cabinet is convened and the process begins again. Eventually the foreign aid runs out, at which point the winner is determined by the amount of money each players has socked away in a secret Swiss bank account.

The basics for *Junta* in many ways resemble a faster-paced, tongue-in-cheek version of *Diplomacy*, with a hot-blooded looseness more appropriate to the warmer climes. Players lie through their teeth in order to form temporary alliances, most of which fall apart as soon as the money gets tight. Fortunately, the mechanics of *Junta* don't encourage vendettas. After all, once a player has been assassinated or executed for treason (and thus missed the rest of the turn), his family sends out a new leading candidate, who will no doubt loudly proclaim his personal disgust at the actions of his cousin last round and his great loyalty to whichever of his compatriots has most recently seized power.

And there's a big part of *Junta*'s appeal — the incidental roleplaying opportunities afforded by the game, and its emphasis on atmosphere and personal interaction. Most every game I've played has involved *El Presidente* sadly clucking over the pile of foreign aid cash (which only he can count), bemoaning the sad twists of fate that have left him unable to offer his beloved associates anything more than the smallest of budgets for the year — while, of course, he secretly lines his own pockets with far more than his fair share. Usually this is done in an approximation of a Central American accent that would make Ricardo Montalban cry.

Also, just when you're coming to appreciate the elegant mechanics of the money and assassinations, you find the coup portion of the game tucked inside, like the candy in a piñata, a whole separate mini-wargame used as a resolution mechanic. For some this is actually a negative, as the jump from negotiation and backstabbing to a relatively unsophisticated tile-based skirmish can be jarring and can slow down the game. On the other hand, how the coup plays out is determined by, and interwoven with, the game's negotiation mechanics. Cabinet assignments greatly affect the coup's outcome, since the positions that are weakest in the negotiation phase — the generals and the admiral — control the majority of the units and firepower on the board. So the president must factor this into his decision-making process in the assignment and budget phases. After all, if he angers the military by shorting their pay, he can't exactly count on their support when the bullets begin to fly, as they inevitably will.

Junta was re-released in a new, updated version by the latest iteration of West End Games in 2005, after many years of being out of print and hard to find. Changes to the most recent edition are minor — for example, the president's brother-in-law has been renamed the president's cousin. for some reason— but the game board itself has been materially improved. The old one was fairly notorious for falling apart almost immediately. Of course, the primary pieces are still tiny cardboard chits of various colors; none of that Eurogames-style heavy bits to be found here. The card set in the new edition has, unfortunately, lost my personal favorite illustration: the "amateur assassin," a drunken killer throwing a grenade pin into a window instead of the grenade. Nevertheless, the game's overall fun quotient remains remarkably high.

Junta isn't one of the 100 greatest hobby games because of its rules and mechanics — they're good, each of them, but not brilliant. It's a great hobby game because it creates a mood and captures a theme brilliantly, and integrates every single design element to that cause. With its wonderful sense of comical menace, political instability, and institutionalized corruption, _Junta_ is a hoot and a half to play. Badly rolling your _r_'s as you argue over the annual budget just adds to the fun.

DARREN WATTS is the president and co-owner of Hero Games, publishers of _Champions_ and other games using the Hero System. He wrote or co-wrote (among others) _Champions Universe_, _Millennium City_, _UNTIL: Defenders Of Freedom_, _Champions Worldwide_, and _Lucha Hero_, the RPG of Mexican wrestling and monster movies.

Greg Stafford on

KINGMAKER

KEY DESIGNERS: ANDREW MCNEIL, MICK (MIKE) UHL, DON TURNBULL

AVALON HILL (REVISED EDITION, 1975)

A GAME'S QUALITY IS measured by two things: fun and replayability. *Kingmaker* ranks *way* high in both. It is not perfect, but its strengths more than make up for its weaknesses. The game is fun because it's a multi-player political wargame that is largely abstract, thus lacking a lot of the fussy detail required of a true historical simulation. It distills out the politics and the personalities to a manageable level, giving players a fast-moving experience, while maintaining a feel for the ever-shifting politics, tangled diplomacy, and dangerous battles of 15th-century England. It also possesses extremely high replay value because of the near-infinite variety of starting positions inherent in its design.

Kingmaker is based on the events of England's War of the Roses (1455 – 1487). The two claimants for the crown of England were rival branches of the old Plantagenet family, called the Yorkists and Lancanstrians. Both had roses as household badges — York, white; Lancaster, red — hence the flowery name for a long and brutal war.

The game takes its title from the nickname of one of the leading figures of the period, Richard Neville, the earl of Warwick. He was the richest and most powerful man in England, and his support in the war meant certain victory for his chosen candidate — well, at least until the earl was killed in battle. In the game, each player vies to become a kingmaker in his own right. To this end, players gather armies and resources, then give their support to one of the royal heirs and work to eliminate all rivals, until just one survives to ascend to the throne.

With any tabletop game a lot of pleasure comes from the face-to-face interpersonal activity it inspires. *Kingmaker* rates high on this diplomacy factor, because fortunes shift quickly and it's usually necessary for players to team up to defeat the current leader. The game can support as much negotiation as players desire. But don't be too trusting! Old alliances are dropped and new ones forged many times throughout a typical session.

Final victory goes to whomever has the last potential king or queen left on the field, but the heirs of each house are ranked, setting up midgame rivalries not only between the houses, but within them. If your faction includes only the heir ranked second or third within the House of York, then you need to destroy the faction or factions with the heirs senior to yours.

Game components are universally colorful. The board is a stylized map of Medieval Britain, divided into irregularly shaped rectangles that look weird, but manage to capture both the difficulties and ease of travel in different parts of England and Wales. The game's tokens are marked with the nobles' coats of arms. Finally, there's an 80-card crown deck and a 90-card event deck.

The crown cards are the foundation for a faction's power. These include the great barons of the realm, who make up the army, and thus are the most important cards to get. These nobles can command mercenaries, bishops, cities, and ships, all of which give them certain powers and advantages in battle. The crown cards also include royal offices, like marshal of England or chancellor, and titles, such as duke of Essex and earl of Richmond. These can also be assigned to nobles, giving them even more power.

Starting resources are randomly determined. Thirty-six cards from the crown deck are dealt, evenly divided among the three to seven people at the table. The random distribution of the crown deck is a key to the game's replayability. No two games ever have the same forces arrayed against each other at the start.

In the game's early stages, players must unite their scattered forces and grab up the royal heirs, meanwhile slowly accumulating more resources.

Kingmaker is turn-based. Factions go in order of the importance of their office, so the chancellor's faction is first. Each turn begins with a player drawing an event card. These cards are based on actual events and lend historical veracity to the game. Rebellions break out in Wales or the Southeast, the Scots invade, ambassadors visit England and cause the current king to travel to places he might not wish to go, and so on.

Each event *requires* the presence of various nobles, so that the marshal of England, for instance, is often called away to perform his duties, suppressing rebels or driving off would-be invaders. Thus a player's plans are upset when his army is abruptly pulled apart by these emergencies, which take key nobles far from the theater of action. Worse, events often take nobles into enemy territory, where an opposing army, too small to attack them while they're part of a player's main force, can destroy the now-isolated official.

Other events conspire to whittle down a large force. Plagues destroy armies hiding within the otherwise safe walls of a city. Storms at sea force inconvenient landings. Parliament is summoned, bringing enemies much too close together for comfort. A few event cards give a free move or allow refuge in foreign lands, but many undermine the leading players' hold on power.

Kingmaker was the first game to prove the effectiveness of a card mechanic to insert random events in a board game, and these event cards — like the initial, random assignment of crown cards — provide a near-infinite variety to each game.

Each turn ends when the player chooses one of the remaining crown cards and thus increases the strength of his faction. The growing admixture of resources is another random factor that enhances replayability. Additional mercenaries and other forces can be held hidden, as a surprise reserve, but if the supplemental event cards are used (which I recommend) then they might be lost due to treachery.

Thus the second phase of play consists of consolidating strength and position, forging of alliances, and a great increase in combat, particularly the ambushing of weak forces.

In combat the event cards serve their secondary purpose: to resolve battles. Opposing armies are counted up and their ratio calculated (a handy table is provided to speed this along). Then an event card is turned. In addition to an event, each card lists a value telling what battle ratio denotes a victory. Sometimes the attacking army can win with only a 5:4 superiority, while at other times it requires a 4:1 or more. Sometimes bad weather simply cancels the attack. And if a noble's name is listed on the event card used to resolve a battle in which he participates, he's killed outright.

The use of these cards for battle also impacts the events that occur during the game. Some game-changing events might never take place — the plague may never hit London, or the French king may never come to Rye — if those cards are turned and used for combat.

The last phase of *Kingmaker* consists of maneuvering toward a final great battle. At this stage, most of the heirs have been killed and the leading players are massing their armies for the ultimate conflict. The slow growth of hostilities in the game — from the scramble of lots of small factions to the slow, rumbling advance of massive armies — effectively imitates the sequence of this war. Some players criticize *Kingmaker*'s endgame, which can be dragged out, especially by conservative play. But I have found that an alliance of minor players adopting a baronial attitude of bold action is likely to win against a cautious leading player, even one with a wildly superior force.

Kingmaker was first published by Philmar, Ltd. in the United Kingdom in 1974. Its immediate popularity prompted Avalon Hill to publish its own version a year later. The revised edition made the game better. It boasts a number of improvements: a corrected map, a more complicated Parliament system, more powerful bishops, writs used to summon lords to parliament or send a different lord on official business, a chance for a simple majority to win a battle, the addition of Irish and French forces, royal bodyguards for the two heirs, and several new event cards. Even the game designer has agreed that the Avalon Hill edition is an improvement over the original.

Kingmaker won the Charles S. Roberts Award for Best Professional Game of 1975. The game has been going strong ever since and has lost none of its play, nor replay, value.

GREG STAFFORD is one of the founders of the adventure game industry, working as a publisher and author since his first professional game, *White Bear & Red Moon,* was released in 1975. He founded Chaosium and led it when it was a dynamic creative force, publishing *Thieves World, Call of Cthulhu,* and many other notable and successful games. Greg is the designer or co-designer of five RPGs (*RuneQuest, King Arthur Pendragon, Prince Valiant, Ghostbusters,* and *HeroQuest*), four board games (*White Bear & Red Moon/Dragon Pass, Nomad Gods, Elric,* and *King Arthur's Knights*), one miniature game (*Merlin*), and one computer game (*King of Dragon Pass*), plus numerous campaigns, scenarios, and game aids. He is currently president of Issaries, Inc. which has licensed *HeroQuest* and *Questworlds* to Moon Design and *RuneQuest* to Mongoose, and is busy writing Gloranthan novels. Greg is a practicing mythologist, high priest of the First Reformed Church of Elvis, and great supreme gronk of Saurintology.

Lester Smith on

KREMLIN

KEY DESIGNERS: URS HOSTETTLER, STEFAN HOSLI

AVALON HILL (ENGLISH EDITION, 1988)

THERE WAS A TIME — when my kids were little and I lived in Illinois, working for Game Designers' Workshop — that I had a "study" all to myself, with shelves full of books and games, and a small table at which to play. Since moving to Wisconsin in 1991, originally to work for TSR, I've had to keep most of my game collection in storage. Recently, our family moved again, with the help of some old TSR buddies, who chided me about having to carry so many boxes of games, boxes that clearly hadn't been opened since they were packed in Illinois.

Part of the fun of having a collection, however, is the occasional reminder of just how good a particular item is. For example, one of those boxes is marked, *Dad's Games: Kremlin, Outdoor Survival, and Arkham Horror*. While other games also reside in that box, these three got top billing. You'll note that *Kremlin* comes first in the list. Recently, I had a chance to introduce the game to some of those old TSR buddies, who had never had the chance to wrestle one another for power over Politburo seats in the last days of the old Soviet Union.

Reviewing the rules proved pretty simple, even after 16 years: The basic game takes up just three 8 ½" by 11" pages of a four-page rules folder, with the back occupied by a "health table." The advanced rules fill just a page and a half of another four-page folder, with a page of history and credits, and a second copy of the health table. The turn sequence is conveniently repeated on the game board itself, with a detailed summary of each step. And the basic concept is easy to grasp: You win by controlling the chief of the Communist Party three years (turns) out of 10 during the October Parade, assuming he's not too ill to wave — and that's no certain thing. (There is a reason the game includes two copies of that health table, as you'll soon see.)

Gaining control of the party chief, and maintaining that control, is not easy. Before the game begins, players secretly assign their influence points to some of the 26 different candidates vying for the job, and you can't be certain which player really controls each candidate until all influence points are revealed. Typically, players reveal only as many assigned points as they have to — and just enough to take control of a candidate at a crucial time. In any given turn, eight of those 26 characters occupy the Politburo offices depicted on the board. The offices all have different powers and responsibilities — from the head of the KGB, who can "purge" other members; to the defense minister, who can open spy investigations and trials; to the foreign minister, who can nominate a new party chief when the old one is purged, dies, or retires upon reaching the age of 96. The last is rather unlikely.

Age and health play critical roles in the game. Each year includes a health phase, in which players must check the fitness of every Politburo member on the aforementioned health table. The older the member, the more likely is is that he or she will take sick, become dangerously ill, or even die. Most political actions in the game age the character undertaking them, due to the stress and peril the actions entail. Promoting or demoting a subordinate "costs" one year; purging someone costs one, though a failed purge costs three; condemning a Politburo candidate to Siberia costs two; and so on — so the more active a Politburo member, the quicker he ages, which makes this health roll increasingly hazardous.

During the cure phase, each member has an opportunity to spend the next year in a sanatorium, to rest up and gain better odds on the health table. However, being away from the office makes that member more susceptible to political machinations by the rest of his comrades. It also means some other Politburo member gets to exercise that character's power. For example, if the head of the KGB is taking the cure, the ideology chief gets to fill in during the ever-perilous purge phase — perhaps even purging the absent head of the KGB, for whom he is acting!

One thing about gaming with industry pros is that discussion of the game design is a natural part of most sessions. At our recent *Kremlin* game, the garishness of the board colors was mentioned (something I hadn't really noticed in the late '80s), as was the number of counters required to keep track of age, illness, spy investigations, and so on (something more likely to be assigned to a computer nowadays). Also, as I gave an overview of the rules, someone remarked that the game is basically just an extended joke.

But it's a good joke! And it never seems to wear thin. By the end of the evening, finishing our second game, we were all laughing so hard we could barely breathe. In part, it's the character names: Alexej Goferbrok, Karel Krakemheds, Boris

Badenuff, Natasha Nogoodnik, and so on. In part, it's the sudden surprises. You work hard to elevate Comrade Krakemheds to party chief, and then another player reveals more influence points and takes control of him away from you. Then poor Karel tries to wave during the October Parade, only to succumb to illness and die. Before you can fully savor the irony there, the member you spent the most points on is sent to Siberia as part of a general purge, before you've even revealed your control of him.

But it's more than just satiric names and sudden surprises that give the game its punch; it's also the general theme. The Politburo members all struggle and scheme, age and sicken, to gain control of an empire that was — even when the game was originally released in 1988 — creaking with age and staggering to its demise. (The game itself was originally published in Europe as *Kreml*, and won the German Game of the Year award.)

The game design is masterful, with just enough luck of the die to force players to hedge their bets, and fully enough strategy to keep them involved from start to finish. The board and cards make learning easy, and the graduated rules (including one expansion set, with historical figures) add new wrinkles to keep even experienced players intrigued. And the fact that players are working behind the scenes, as factions controlling Politburo members, instead of directly involved, provides enough distance to keep you laughing, even when your own complicated plans crumble into ruin.

There is a tragic grandeur to much of Russian history, and more than its share of ridiculousness, too. *Kremlin* invites us to look back on the Soviet era and put it in perspective through laughter. The humor in *Kremlin* is gallows humor, of course, as anyone who lived through the 1980s would attest. But the satire isn't constrained by its ties to the past, or to one political superpower; with the minimum of imagination, *Kremlin* can easily be seen as a pointed jab at any corrupt and treacherous bureaucracy populated by ambitious old men.

LESTER SMITH began his game-design career in 1984 with *Mind Duel*, a science-fiction board game submission to *Space Gamer* magazine. In 1985, he joined the staff at GDW, where he converted *Traveller: 2300* to *2300 AD*, wrote the *Dark Conspiracy* roleplaying game, and designed the

Minion Hunter and *Temple of the Beastmen* board games, among other duties. In 1991, he was hired by TSR and contributed to the *AD&D* and *Amazing Engine* roleplaying game lines, eventually designing the Origins Award-winning *Dragon Dice*. Les has also done work for FASA, Flying Buffalo, West End Games, Imperium Games, Sovereign Press, and others, acquiring two other Origins Awards in the process. Nowadays, he works as an educational writer and technologist for a Houghton Mifflin design house and is president of the Wisconsin Fellowship of Poets. Les argues that poetry, game design, and computer coding are all different sides of the same multi-dimensional coin, each using ritual structure to create wondrously magical effects — if you get the "spelling" right.

Wolfgang Baur on

LEGEND OF THE FIVE RINGS

KEY DESIGNERS: DAVID WILLIAMS, JOHN WICK, MATT STAROSCIK, JOHN ZINSER, RYAN S. DANCEY, DAVID SEAY, MATT WILSON

ALDERAC ENTERTAINMENT GROUP (1995)

SOMETIMES IT'S NOT THE pioneers that get it right; sometimes it's the second generation. In the case of collectible card games, the outstanding title after *Magic: The Gathering* is *Legend of the Five Rings* (known to its fans as *L5R*). It inspires loyalty and devotion in those fans unlike any other CCG, and for good reason.

In terms of pure design, the basic rules set for *L5R* is good, especially given its publication date of 1995. It is a combat game for two or more players; each player controls a clan of samurai warriors in the mythical land of Rokugan and seeks to destroy his enemy's "provinces." These provinces are represented by spaces on the table where new resources enter the game, such as cards depicting samurai, silver mines, and demons.

David Williams, the game's lead designer, split *Magic*'s single deck into two to address issues with resources, in this case the land cards that you use to pay for putting other cards into play. In a clever twist, these get their own deck in *L5R*, making them more predictable. The game uses three main victory conditions, one military, one political, and one abstract "enlightenment" condition. Over time, these rules have been refined and the basic card mix has been updated to favor various elements of the game. In that respect, it's similar to most other CCGs.

The game's underlying play balance is finely tuned; beginners have a fair chance to compete with anyone, but for advanced players, a single mistake is enough to swing a session's momentum. The level of concentration required of the game's masters mimics that of a high stakes duel with katanas. The broad range of approaches and countermeasures in casual play quickly grows less forgiving in tournament play.

While the deep gameplay supports a variety of strategies and play styles, *L5R*'s mechanics are not the reason that players travel around the country to compete at major game conventions and special tournaments (and yell "Banzai!" at the start of each round). The game's real brilliance lies in the way it invented and perfected the feedback loop between a game and its audience.

Legend of the Five Rings is a game designed to be modified by its players, like *Fluxx* or *Cosmic Encounter*, but on a larger scale and with the additional facet of international competitive play. Each year during the "Kotei Season," Alderac Entertainment organizes and stages important *L5R* tournaments around the world. Players gather at these events with particular decks to support their clan and hope to win, not just for personal glory, but to advance their clan's place in the wider story built up around the game. Tournament winners decide various story points, such as which clan finds a famous sword or who succeeds to the throne in a given year. The results are then added into the game as cards printed in a later expansion set. For instance, the winners in the 2006 Kotei Season chose personalities who became enlightened — that is, gained a true understanding of the elements, which in turn grants great power — and a special series of cards was printed to reflect this. In this sense, the game is a saga, with each new edition building on the one before, retaining characters and also creating updated, older versions of those characters over time. Half the fun is in cheering on your favorites.

Choosing to play a deck built to feature one of roughly a dozen clans is a game element — but the loyalty that these clans can inspire in some players surprises even the designers and publisher. The genius of *L5R* lies in the harnessing of this tribalism for game purposes.

The clans themselves are quite distinct, and each is built to emphasize certain game mechanics. The members of the Crane Clan are duelists, the Mantis are pirates, and so on. The stories developed around these general tropes help to further differentiate the clans — by play style, by the particular virtues that the clan can claim, and by their mechanical strengths and weaknesses. Knowing an opponent's clan affiliation also tells you something interesting about him before you play a single card. A Phoenix deck is likely to contain magic effects. A Unicorn deck will probably use cavalry cards.

The graphic design and artwork used for the various cards further develops and refines each clan's identity. Aligning the graphic look, the mechanics, and the character backdrops this way makes the game even more compelling. It also helps keep the game accessible, since distinct clans are easy to summarize to a new player and help let the uninitiated quickly identify what groups in the game might most appeal to their own ideals of heroism. Love raw strength and guts? Crab Clan is for you, my boy. Love magic and sorcery most? The Phoenix is your path.

This heavy reliance on group identification is not without its downside, especially for those who side with certain clans: the Crane are mocked as courtiers, the Scorpion are derided as untrustworthy ninjas, and the players of the evil Shadowlands catch a lot of grief from everyone. (The Shadowlands Clan functions in the game to provide a source of evil and corruption against which all other clans can side.) At the same time, choosing sides and defending them also strengthens a player's loyalty to the clan ideals — and to the game. It's a lot of fun to proclaim "I am a Dragon!" with your fellow clan members at a major tournament. These public shows of enthusiasm are often the publisher's best recruitment tools for new players, too.

The stories behind *L5R*'s clans have grown and evolved in a narrative arc developed by John Wick, Ree Soesbee, and others over the many editions of the game, as well as in related novels and a roleplaying game. At its most interesting junctures, though, the *Legend of the Five Rings* metaplot has been driven by its players, through collaborative storytelling and the tournament structure. Winning clans are rewarded not only with a say in the evolving plot, but additional time in the limelight through official short stories published on the company website and so forth. This is clearly what keeps the core fans coming back for more. In fact, some of the expansion sets that have been criticized by casual players for their weak rules have still found acceptance with the core *L5R* community because they provide fan-favorite story elements, art, or characters. This allows each expansion to succeed or fail in several ways, based on more factors than its power-gaming appeal.

That's a quite a trick, and it's just part of what inspires otherwise sane card gamers to stand up and shout "Banzai!" at the top of their lungs, or to share their enthusiasm for *Legend of the Five Rings* with perfect strangers.

Speaking of which, if you'd like to join the fun, I just happen to have a Crane deck here you could borrow. . . .

WOLFGANG BAUR is an RPG designer, columnist, and short story author for Wizards of the Coast, Paizo, Malhavoc, Chaosium, Privateer Press, and his own imprint, Open Design. He is the publisher of *Kobold Quarterly* magazine, and previously served as an editor for both *Dragon* and *Dungeon*. His roleplaying game titles include *Dark*Matter*, *Expedition to the Demonweb Pits*, *Book of Roguish Luck*, *Frostburn*, *Castle Shadowcrag*, and *Empire of the Ghouls*. Wolfgang writes games for small groups of patrons as experiments in collaboration, and he comments on game design at wolfgangbaur.com. If you visit, he will give you a cookie.

Marc W. Miller on

LENSMAN

KEY DESIGNER: PHILIP N. PRITCHARD

SPARTAN INTERNATIONAL (SECOND EDITION, 1969)

WE SEEK OUT GAMES because there is something in their subjects, or their mechanics, or even in their social interaction that appeals to us, that resonates with some part of us. In the early days of wargaming — that would have been the early 1970s — gamers could play a few standard Avalon Hill games on fairly mainstream (for wargaming) subjects, or a growing number of SPI games on increasingly esoteric subjects, but there were virtually no science-fiction games. It was a tiny ad buried in a limited-circulation fanzine that first told me about Phil Pritchard's *Lensman*.

Today we have a plethora of science-fiction storylines, but in 1972 the galaxy-spanning space opera had been in decline for quite a while, and its revival through *Star Wars* was still some five years away. But we were science-fiction readers: we — that is my few gamer friends and I — already knew what a Lensman was. I had read the whole series. Twice. Lensman, E.E. "Doc" Smith's science-fiction series, chronicled the fight between good and evil across two billion years and the entire galaxy. The books defined space opera. I was a brand-new gamer and I wanted to play a science-fiction game. So when I saw that ad, I ordered my very own copy by mail. I could hardly wait for it to arrive.

The Lensman novels, beginning with *Triplanetary*, are filled with powerful heroes and villains, inertialess-drive starships, aliens, and complex plot twists. Phil Pritchard's *Lensman* took the only approach to the topic possible for a wargame of the era, by focusing on interstellar strategy. The game itself includes a hex map filled with stars, a sheet of counters for starships and other things, and a nice little rules booklet that explains the mechanics clearly enough that an experienced gamer will have no trouble getting started. The graphics, by the standard of the day, are dazzling — a black deep-space map with white hex-grid lines and colored-in stars echoing their "true" spectral types. Typical of a '70s game from a small publisher, *Lensman* requires its owners to paste the counters to cardboard and cut them out; for this game, I was willing to make that effort. And you have to find an additional blank hex grid for use as a battle board, so just getting ready to play this game is work. But it's worth it.

Lensman is a true strategic interstellar wargame. The short game can be played in a few hours, but the expanded version pulls out all the stops. There's exploration into unknown space, colonization of star systems, industrialization, allocation of resources to build new and better starships. . . . In the long game, *Lensman* includes tactical combat on battle boards in deep space or in star systems. Interstellar maneuvers bring ships together, but then you have to change hats from strategic admiral to tactical captain and fight out ship-to-ship combat at a much-reduced tactical scale.

When our copy arrived back in 1972, we carefully found a safe place to set up the game and then spent some three days and nights playing and playing and playing. True to the type of game, there never was a formal victory or ending; exhaustion set in and after the third day, my group and I went on to other things.

But the game stuck with me, for a number of reasons.

First, *Lensman* remained true to its inspiration, detailing interstellar battleships like the dreadnaught and the mauler, and showing us a space map with familiar star names strewn about. But on a deeper level, Phil Pritchard offered up an exhaustive treatment of the strategic economic wargame that had dominated the form for the 20 years prior to its publication. His was not only the first of the science-fiction wargames, it also laid the foundation for several distinct evolutionary lines of wargame design. *Lensman* pioneered the battle board concept, wherein players pull strategic components from the main game map to a detailed smaller board for tactical resolution. *Lensman* also showed gamers how to build economic strategy games with a rich decision-making environment that makes replaying the game rewarding time after time.

So, how do we count the games that *Lensman* spawned? I know firsthand that one late-night session of blank hex-grid battle board combat for *Lensman* inspired the design for *Triplanetary*, with its image of our solar system and use of vector movement. Playing Phil Pritchard's creation well into many late nights inspired the Game Designers' Workshop staff to come up with a similarly star-spanning strategic interstellar wargame titled *Imperium*; that *Imperium* was never published, but was ultimately transformed into a simpler game with the same name: *Imperium, Empires in Conflict/Worlds in the Balance*. And when *Lensman* and its progeny were crossed with the revolutionary *Dungeons & Dragons*, the result was my role-playing game *Traveller*. And the influences move on from there.

Phil Pritchard's *Lensman* sold several thousand copies over its lifetime in the early 1970s, but is now nearly impossible to find. A small start-up publisher, Tsunami Press, plans a new boxed edition for release in 2007. It faithfully reproduces the original game, but also includes updated rules and charts.

I've played a lot of games; I've scanned even more, just to see what they do and how they do it. But *Lensman* stands out as one I enjoyed playing once-upon-a-time, and one that I look forward to once again having on my game shelf.

In 1973 **Marc W. Miller** co-founded Game Designers' Workshop with three other designers: Frank Chadwick, Rich Banner, and Loren Wiseman. He has designed and published titles in every field within adventure gaming: obscure wargames such as *Chaco* (covering the war between Paraguay and Bolivia in the 1930s) and *The Russo-Japanese War*, card games such as *SuperDeck!*, and computer games such as *Challenge of the Five Realms*. His specialty is science-fiction games, of which his credits include *Imperium*, *Double Star*, and the *Traveller* role-playing game. He was the seventh game designer inducted into the Academy of Adventure Gaming's Hall of Fame, and his *Traveller* was inducted in 1996.

Ted S. Raicer on

LONDON'S BURNING

KEY DESIGNERS: BEN KNIGHT, MARK SIMONITCH

AVALON HILL (1995)

THE 1940 GERMAN AIR assault on England — the famed Battle of Britain —
is the focus of *London's Burning.* The subject is inherently dramatic, with the fate
of Britain, and perhaps the world, hanging in the balance. But *London's Burning*
has a lot more going for it as a wargame than just its subject matter — it is one of
the most multifaceted and imaginative game designs in the 50-year history of commercial wargaming. It provides real insight into the historical events it portrays.
And, oh yes, it's also a great deal of fun to play.

Air campaigns are notoriously complex affairs, fought in three dimensions,
over extended periods of time. A game on the Battle of Britain also has to deal
with many different airplane types (*London's Burning*'s counter mix includes four
different German bombers and two German fighters, in addition to the British
Hurricanes and Spitfires), heavy and light anti-aircraft guns, the effects of weather,
and Radar, which gave the RAF its main advantage over the Luftwaffe. Even in its
most basic outline, that's a lot of ground — or air — for a game to cover.

Designer Ben Knight apparently wasn't satisfied with simply conquering all
those challenges. He decided to design *London's Burning* as a solitaire game, with
the player taking the role of the RAF, thus requiring the game itself to simulate an
effective German opponent. (Ben may have been inspired by West End Games'
earlier *RAF*, a fine solitaire game about the Battle of Britain, which has, however,
very little in common with *London's Burning* in terms of game mechanics.) He
then added not one, but a pair of two-player options — one cooperative, where
both players take the side of the Brits, and the other adversarial, where they command opposing German and British forces. And he wanted to give gamers not just
an operational view of the campaign, but the flavor of individual pilots engaged
in desperate dogfights.

At this point, one can be forgiven for thinking that the designer was biting off
more than he could chew.

What was required to keep this all from collapsing into an unplayable heap was the sort of imaginative leap that marks the best wargame designs. Fortunately Ben, inspired no doubt by those RAF pilots of long ago, rose to the challenge. The breakthrough was the decision to have the actions of just two RAF planes, as they fly to intercept a single German raiding force, act as representative of the air battles being fought by scores of other fighters against other German raiders, all across southeast England. In doing so, he allows gamers to simultaneously step into the shoes of individual pilots and to model the overall course of the campaign.

In the solo version of *London's Burning* (which is the heart of the design) you begin by randomly drawing two pilots from a pool of eight, five trained on Hurricanes and three on the more effective Spits. One pilot starts the game as an ace. Other pilots can become aces after they shoot down five enemies. As you would expect, aces are better in combat, but beyond that you develop a real attachment to a pilot you have guided to ace status. The half-inch pilot counters are also named, and include a photograph of the pilot. Though the names are fictional, this adds a strong roleplaying element that makes sending your "few" into danger such a tense gaming experience.

A game turn covers a single day, from August 13 to September 15, 1940. Each raid is divided into a variable number of five-minute impulses. A player may have to face as many as four German raids in a single day. The size of each German raiding force is randomly determined, and its exact composition and altitude is unknown until you intercept. It moves across the map by rolling for its "flight path" and bombs the first undamaged target it reaches (or London, regardless of the bomb damage the city has suffered). As was the case historically, targets that have been only lightly bombed are taken by the German High Command to be destroyed, causing the German "player" to pass over one set of potential targets for another.

Enemy raids, damage from bombing, and the location of your two RAF planes are tracked on an attractive, mounted 16" by 22" large-hex map of southeast England. The status of British and German planes, your two pilots, and the current altitude of both your planes and the German raiding force (important for resolving both bombing and dogfights) are tracked on a separate 16" by 22" mounted board, using displays that are both efficient and aesthetically pleasing.

At the start of each turn, you have to decide whether to have your pilots stand by at an airbase or begin the turn on patrol in the skies. The latter allows you to respond more quickly to an enemy raid but continuous patrolling will rapidly exhaust your pilots. If your Chain Home radar stations on the coast are damaged by German bombs, your response time to enemy raids is delayed, increasing the need to patrol.

Balancing the need to intercept German raids with the need to rest your pilots is a major element of play. If you try and intercept every raid, your pilots will soon be asleep in their cockpits. But if enemy raids get through and damage your radar stations and coastal air bases, the Luftwaffe will become harder to intercept. You can rapidly find yourself in a downward spiral, praying for a stretch of bad weather to allow your pilots to get some sleep.

When you intercept a German raid a simple system is used to resolve the resulting dogfights. Simple — but flavorful (a combination designers and critics usually refer to as "elegant"). Combat resolution takes into account the quality of the planes and pilots, relative altitudes, whether you are diving out of the sun or approaching the enemy head-on, and even the limited number of ammo bursts your plane has available. Combat can result in downed or damaged planes, as well as killed or wounded pilots. You can be forced to bail-out, or crash-land, and a wounded pilot will face a period of recovery before returning to the fray.

I'll just briefly touch on the two-player versions of the design, where players either team up against the Luftwaffe or take the opposing British and German sides in the Battle of Britain. Both versions are enjoyable challenges for two players. They certainly don't feel like mere afterthoughts to the solitaire design. Most importantly, they work without major changes to the game system, so you don't have to learn the game three times over.

The brilliance of the decision to focus play on the actions of two pilots is that you share their exhaustion as they return to the skies again and again, feel pain when they are wounded or lost, and cheer when they shoot down their fifth kill and become an ace. This makes *London's Burning* a challenging game, an effective history lesson, and an experience in historical roleplaying that puts you in the cockpit of a Spitfire or Hurricane as you go up against "the Hun." Tally-ho!

TED S. RAICER became a board wargamer in 1970 at the age of 12, when his father, who was born in 1914, bought him the game *1914*, designed by James F. Dunnigan and published by Avalon Hill. So he was perhaps fated to make his biggest mark as a wargame designer doing games on the Great War, to the extent that he is sometimes jokingly referred to as "Mr. World War I." His most famous design is *Paths of Glory*, available from GMT Games, but he has published 10 other games on WWI, as well as games on WWII and the Russian Civil War. He has nine Charles S. Roberts awards, a *Games* magazine Historical Game of the Year Award (for *Paths of Glory*), and is a member of the wargame designers Hall of Fame, which he intends to visit if someone ever actually builds it. Until then, you can find him online at Consimworld.com or in person by hanging out in the Bronx.

Teeuwynn Woodruff on
LORD OF THE RINGS

KEY DESIGNER: REINER KNIZIA

FANTASY FLIGHT GAMES (2000)

J.R.R. TOLKIEN'S EPIC SAGA, *The Lord of the Rings*, is a sweeping tale of good triumphing over evil. It is also a story that teaches the lesson that even the smallest of us can make a tremendous difference in the world if we persevere and work together. Reiner Knizia's *Lord of the Rings* takes on the immense task of reducing the epic world of Middle Earth into the relatively sparse confines of a board game. Unlike roleplaying games, such as Iron Crown Enterprises' *Middle Earth Role Playing*, a board game doesn't allow its designer to spend pages and pages elaborating on the world and the characters who make their home in it. The recent film adaptations also can take advantage of their cinematic scope to paint a picture of Middle Earth by spending millions of dollars creating ents, trolls, and oliphants for us. So, how does a board game without hundreds of pages of text or millions of dollars worth of special-effects images convey the rich depth of fellowship and epic adventure that is at the heart of this beloved high fantasy work?

Reiner Knizia is no novice when it comes to game design. Having published more than 400 games and won approximately umpteen zillion awards, this doctor of mathematics still had to come up with a game to satisfy both hardcore board-gaming fans and the legions who venerate J.R.R. Tolkien's masterpiece. Instead of making the *Lord of the Rings* board game a straightforward experience, in which players compete directly against each other to win, Knizia created an almost entirely cooperative game. This decision kept the game true to Tolkien's world while emphasizing the trilogy's spirit and theme. In *Lord of the Rings*, each player takes on the role of a Hobbit bent on getting the One Ring to the top of Mount Doom and destroying it in the dread volcano's depths. In the game, as in the novels, Frodo and his companions must make their way from Bag End to Mordor, gaining help from the elves and other friends and facing increasingly more deadly attacks from Sauron and his minions.

The game itself has either an entire board or a single location for each of the main lands through which the Hobbits journey on their way to Mount Doom.

Places such as Bag End and Rivendell are innocuous oases of rest, where the players can receive cards or other types of advantages. Menacing places as Moria, Helm's Deep, Shelob's Lair, and Mordor are detailed on separate boards that contain multiple paths. The party must face the perils on each of these boards.

The main board also displays a path of corruption — from purest good to blackest evil. Sauron and the Hobbits begin the game at opposite ends of this board, Sauron in the dark, the Hobbits in the light. Different events move the sides closer together. Carrying the powerful One Ring, for example, causes a Hobbit to move down the path toward the dark. If one of the Hobbits ever meets up with the Dark Lord, it's curtains for said Hobbit. Should the current Ring-bearer meet this fate, the game is over and everyone has lost. You can scale a session's difficulty by placing Sauron closer to, or farther from, the Hobbits at the start of the game. This is a nice means of maintaining the game's challenge. As you and your fellow players get better at making the trek to Mount Doom, you can challenge yourselves by decreasing the starting distance between you and your adversary.

The path of corruption mechanic might seem like it would push players to take individual actions to save their own hairy Hobbit feet from Sauron, but it actually binds the group together strategically. When a Hobbit grows too burdened — that is, corrupt — from carrying the Ring, it behooves the entire party to make sure that another Hobbit shares that burden for a time. The One Ring is not without its benefits; it is dangerous, but it is also powerful. Any time in the game, the Hobbit carrying the Ring can put it on, so that the party can progress, invisible, along one of the multiple game tracks, avoiding its greatest perils. The temporary safety comes at a price, though, as the Hobbit wearing the Ring almost inevitably journeys closer to the Dark Lord.

In playing the game, on every player's turn, one or more tiles are turned over to see if time advances. When it does, bad things tend to happen — such as drawing the notice of the Watcher in the Water, on the Moria board. In that encounter, the players must either discard a certain type of card or roll a die that will move them down the path of corruption. If the group hasn't prepared for these sort of confrontations, the Hobbits will slide quickly into the dark, lose important cards, or face an advancing Sauron. In the case of the Watcher, a savvy group will work together to make certain it has the proper card and resources in place before moving into Moria and facing this threat. This is a radical departure from most board games, where hoarding information is one of the strategic keys to victory. Here, a player who hides information will damage the party, thus increasing the likelihood that the Hobbits will fail in their quest to destroy the Ring . . . in which case, everyone loses.

In fact, the design's underpinning of cooperation is so strong that players sometimes find that they must make the choice to sacrifice themselves to allow the Ring-bearer to get to Mount Doom. Unlike so many other strategic board games, *Lord of the Rings* rewards community and self-sacrifice as a necessary components for victory. It should be noted that the game does include a way to determine an ultimate winner among the individual players, but we've never even bothered to use it, since it runs counter to the game's primary victory condition and theme.

The *Lord of the Rings* board game has proven quite successful, spawning several expansions. The first of these, *Friends & Foes*, was released in 2001 by Fantasy Flight Games. *Friends & Foes* introduces a new potential military victory to the game. Players can win by defeating all of the foes, in place of destroying the Ring. This is an easier victory condition — perhaps too easy — for players to accomplish.

The second *Lord of the Rings* expansion, *Sauron*, was released by Fantasy Flight Games in 2002. It significantly changes the game's dynamics by allowing one person to direct the Dark Lord. In a somewhat more traditional form of competitive gaming, that person clashes directly with the other players, who still take on the roles of the questing Hobbits. *Sauron* is well done and is a worthy addition to the series, but the adversarial aspect makes *Lord of the Rings* a rather different game from the original, fully cooperative version. Still, it's an interesting variation and the majority of the players continue to work together, even with the odd player out; if you only buy one of the expansions to the core game, buy this one.

The third expansion, *Battlefields*, was released by Fantasy Flight Games in 2006. *Battlefields* introduces more non-Hobbit members of the Fellowship of the Ring. This ties the overall game more strongly to Tolkien's narrative. However, the quality of the art in this expansion falls flat when compared to the brilliant work by John Howe found in the original game and previous expansions.

Two other recent hobby games based upon Tolkien's high fantasy epic deserve brief mention — one by the designer of the *Lord of the Rings* board game, both from its publisher.

Lord of the Rings: The Confrontation, released in 2002, is also designed by

Reiner Knizia. This clever two-player game has a *Stratego*-like feel. One player controls a force of good guys, the other Sauron's minions, with all the characters' identities hidden at the game's start. It's a well-made, straightforward design, but due to its competitive nature, it does not convey a sense of the world of Middle Earth anywhere near as well as Knizia's more ambitious board game.

War of the Ring is Fantasy Flight Games' other major offering based upon *The Lord of the Rings*. Published in 2004 and designed by Marco Maggi, Fransesco Nepitello, and Roberto Di Meglio, *War of the Ring* is a somewhat standard, but very well-reviewed wargame. In it, the dark forces loyal to Sauron are countered by the allied Free Peoples — once they can be convinced of the growing threat and mustered to the cause. Again, though, the game fails to capture the core spirit of Tolkien's novels, since it focuses almost exclusively on battles. There are certainly many clashes of steel in the trilogy, but they are tangential to the central story — that of a small group of friends working together diligently, almost invisibly, to save their world.

Where Reiner Knizia's *Lord of the Rings* board game delivers brilliantly is in conveying this all-important feeling of fellowship through every aspect of its design. In order to beat the game, players must talk to each other, work together, and one or more Hobbits may have to sacrifice themselves so that the Ring-bearer can get to Mount Doom and destroy his dangerous burden. When your group manages to achieve this lofty goal, it's a victory for all. In this, players get to realize, to some degree, the same sense of community that Frodo, Sam, and rest of the Fellowship feels in Middle Earth as they struggle against an overwhelming force, one far more powerful than any of the individuals opposing it. Their incredible strength comes from their unity, and Reiner Knizia's *Lord of the Rings* board game reflects that truth beautifully.

TEEUWYNN WOODRUFF is an award-winning game designer, author, puzzle- and immersive events designer based in Sammamish, Washington. She has written dozens of roleplaying game products for companies such as TSR, White Wolf, FASA, and Wizards of the Coast. Teeuwynn has also worked on a number of successful trading card, miniatures, online, and board games, including *Pokémon*, *Magic: The Gathering*, *Duelmasters*,

Dreamblade, *AngelQuest*, and *Betrayal at House on the Hill*. She has co-created and run immersive events for companies such as Microsoft; Gen Con, LLC; and Lucasfilm. Teeuwynn was a game designer at Wizards of the Coast for over a decade before becoming the creative director of Lone Shark Games.

Mike Breault on

MACHIAVELLI

KEY DESIGNERS: JAMES G. WOODS, S. CRAIG TAYLOR, JR.
BATTLELINE PUBLICATIONS (FIRST EDITION, 1977)

> *"When I was a child, I played* Risk. *As a youth, I played* Diplomacy.
> *Now that I am an adult, I play* Machiavelli.*"
>
> — Ancient strategy gamer's proverb

OKAY, SO IT'S NOT really an ancient proverb, but feel free to use it when the opportunity arises. The saying does sum up my feelings about the game of *Machiavelli*, however. Building upon mechanics familiar from simpler games, *Machiavelli* greatly expands upon them to set forth a veritable banquet of gameplay.

Machiavelli is a high-level strategy game set in Renaissance Italy. Two to eight players contest for control of the Italian peninsula in historical scenarios that collectively cover the years from 1385 through 1530. Those were interesting times on the old boot, as major Italian city-states and nearby foreign powers waxed and waned in influence over the years. The modern state of Italy arose from these struggles, and one of the game's greatest thrills is re-enacting them. In the middle of sessions I've sometimes found myself wondering, *What did Florence really do in this situation?* or, *Would the pope really have been quite as gleeful about stabbing his allies like that?* Games resound with famous and influential names such as Medici, Hapsburg, and Domino's (the last not actually a historical power but still a vital part of every *Machiavelli* game).

The game's paper map is an appealingly simple, four-color representation of Italy and surrounding regions, all divided into provinces and sea areas. Slivers of French, Austrian, and Turkish territory lurk around the edges of the map board, leering with barely hidden avarice at the smorgasbord of Italian delicacies glistening in the map's center.

The players are thrust onto this historical stage. Each randomly picks one of up to eight major regional powers: Florence, Milan, Venice, Naples, the Papacy, France, Austria, and Turkey. The different scenarios presented in the rulebook can accommodate varying numbers of players, from two to eight, generally giving you the choice of two or more scenarios for your group's size.

Those who've played *Diplomacy* are already familiar with a portion of *Machiavelli*'s core gameplay. The comforting mechanics of intense negotiations, hidden order writing, simultaneous order resolution, and the inevitability of sweet, sweet backstabbing are all here. As in *Diplomacy*, the number of military units a player possesses depends upon the number of cities he controls. Some provinces contain cities, some don't; you want to grab the ones that have them. And the familiar phases of unit adjustment, negotiation, order writing, and order execution/conflict resolution regulate the progress of a game of *Machiavelli*. But to these well-established mechanics, the designers add multiple layers of intriguing complexity.

In addition to the standard armies and fleets, *Machiavelli* players enjoy the innovation of garrison units, forces that exist solely to man the walls of cities, making them entities separate from the provinces in which they reside. With a garrison in their city, denizens can waggle their private parts at besieging units sitting, frustrated, out in the useless provincial countryside. To the standard suite of *Diplomacy* orders — move, hold, support, and convoy — the presence of garrison units adds besiege, lift siege, and convert to *Machiavelli*'s list. The conquest of a city often involves besieging the local garrison for a season or two, a fact that adds a level of historical accuracy to the mechanics. Another twist is the addition of autonomous garrison units in certain neutral cities. It requires a determined siege to conquer these key sites.

The advanced and optional rules are what really set *Machiavelli* on a higher plane. Just a glance at the complete set of phases in an advanced/optional season of play should make your gameplay taste buds tingle: famine, unit adjustment and income, famine unit removal, plague, negotiation, ducat borrowing, order writing, ducat expenditure, assassination(!), and order execution/conflict resolution.

That list brings up another bonus — the complete rules add an economic system to the game, granting players ducats of income from every province and city they control. This largess is typically spent on military units you want to keep. It can also be spent in much more amusing ways, such as bribing other player's units to disband or convert to your side, fomenting rebellion in the enemy's provinces, or, best of all, paying for the chance to assassinate another player's ruler and immobilize his units for a season. You can also use ducats to counteract others' expenditures against you. A counter-bribe of three ducats to ensure the loyalty of your garrison in Rome can negate an opponent's attempted bribery — unless the treacherous dog suspects that you'll counter-bribe and ups his bribe amount to compensate. Fun! The economic system alone adds a complex (yet fast-playing) dimension of calculation and interaction to *Machiavelli* that its rivals lack.

And who can resist the appeal of randomly generated plague and famine in a game? Not me! As in olden times, these natural disasters strike with little warning, foiling the best-laid plans of flea-infested mice and men. Cheer when your foes' military units succumb to the plague and groan when yours occasionally suffer the same fate. Famine wipes out garrisons in affected provinces and chases off other military units, creating power vacuums that opportunistic players swiftly fill. The random nature of *Machiavelli*'s natural disasters means there's no sure route to victory; flexibility is key to survival.

With all this depth, richness, and historical context, *Machiavelli*'s gameplay still flows smoothly and swiftly along. It's a tribute to its outstanding design and development that *Machiavelli* works so well on so many levels. From a basic rule set that itself surpasses any other game of its type, multiple gameplay-enhancing layers can be added as desired, to weave a tapestry of intrigue and interaction unrivaled in hobby games.

I've always played with the original Battleline edition of the game from 1977, but Avalon Hill later purchased the publishing rights to *Machiavelli* and put out editions in 1980, 1983, and 1995. If you can find the original version, I'd urge you to buy that one, but the later editions will do as well.

Machiavelli is the stuff of legend in my household. Long ago, I rudely cut short a first date so I could go play a game of it with some friends. Twenty-five years later, my now-wife has mostly forgiven me, but I still sometimes catch the random glare and mutters of "that damn game," which remind me that some rare titles leave indelible marks on gamers and non-gamers alike. *Machiavelli* will always have a place of pride on my game shelves, and I hope it finds one on yours, as well.

MIKE BREAULT has worked in the games industry since 1984. He began with TSR, writing, editing, and developing over 100 games, modules, and hardback books in five years. In 1988, he co-designed the original *Pool*

of Radiance computer game, which started him on a different path. For the next 10 years, he designed and wrote for numerous computer and video games, and various platforms, from the NES and Genesis to the PS2. In 1999, he was offered a job writing and designing computer/video games for Volition, Inc. in Champaign, Illinois, where he's been ever since. Mike lives there with his wife Mary, son Chris (now at Washington University in St. Louis), daughter Amelia (going to Haverford College), and dog Rags (home-schooled).

MAGIC: THE GATHERING

KEY DESIGNER: RICHARD GARFIELD

WIZARDS OF THE COAST (1993)

I LOVE GAMES THAT challenge and change our definition of adventure gaming, and *Magic: The Gathering* is definitely one of a very short list of titles that has accomplished that elusive goal. By combining the collecting and trading elements of baseball cards with the fantasy play dynamics of roleplaying games, *Magic* created a whole new genre of product that changed our industry forever.

Magic: The Gathering was brought to life by the collaboration of two talented individuals. Mathematics professor Richard Garfield had been an aspiring game designer for many years by the time I saw his first design. Richard brought *RoboRally* to Ross Babcock and me at FASA. As you might know, *RoboRally* is a fantastically fun and simple game featuring an "animated" board that propels the pieces in different directions, to often satisfyingly funny demises. We really wanted to produce the game at FASA, but could not find a way to merge it into our existing lines. So Richard presented *RoboRally* to Peter Adkison, founder of Wizards of the Coast.

Peter loved the game, too, and while working with Richard on *RoboRally* came to learn of Richard's pet project — an expandable card game. Knowing Peter, I am certain he immediately recognized the potential for a game that was endlessly expandable and could be produced in various rarity levels, thus encouraging players to collect and trade the cards. I think Richard's accomplishment would not have seen the light of day without the vision and business acumen of Peter Adkison, who believed so deeply in Richard's invention that he recast the company's primary mission from publishing roleplaying game modules to publishing *Magic: The Gathering*.

The core concepts of *Magic* seem obvious in retrospect, as do all great ideas, but they represent some really significant creative leaps from what had come before. In short, Richard completely reconceived how cards and decks are used within a game structure.

He did this by establishing a simple premise as the base mechanic of the game:

Two wizards with their spellbooks (decks of cards) face off in a duel to the death. Each spell (card played) interacts with every other spell that remains face-up on the table.

Each class of spells has its own function, and each card has rules that dictate how that card can be used in play, which allows the game to be infinitely expandable. Some cards serve as resources to allow the use of other cards. Other cards are completely straightforward, simple to use and understand. Still others may need combinations of cards on the table in order to be played, creating complex interactions that require strategies to be planned out in advance. Some cards can be played instantly out of your hand.

The concept of each player constructing his or her own deck, deciding such basic elements as how many cards it will contain (with some restrictions), was something that had never been done before. Deck construction was the key to *Magic*'s success, as it allowed players to create a unique play strategy, reducing the usual randomness of a card game to a level that would reward solid strategy over blind luck more often then not. The mathematical genius of *Magic* is the diversity of viable deck construction tactics, which revolutionized how people learn, play, and enjoy games.

The basic play of *Magic: The Gathering* is as follows:

You shuffle your deck, cut your opponent's deck, and draw seven cards. At the beginning of your turn, you play resource cards — land cards that provide you with mana, or magical energy. You may then rotate (tap) those land cards to generate mana, which is used to "purchase" a spell — anything from a creature to an instant effect to an artifact that produces a global effect for the rest of the game.

Each spell card requires you to tap one or more specific types of mana, in specific quantities, to put it into play. For example, a spell such as Llanowar Elves might require only the presence of green mana (one land card), while other, more powerful cards, such as Force of Nature, might require multiple green mana (tapped from multiple lands) or even a mix of green *and* black mana (again tapped from different lands). On the turn after a card is placed on the table, and all turns afterward, you can use it to attack the opposing player's defenses — the creatures, spells, or artifacts he has put into play — and, after they are defeated, directly attack the player's life points. Instant spells can be used right out of a player's hand at certain points during play, most commonly during combat. For example, a Giant Growth card can be used this way to make a creature more powerful.

The game ends when one player's life points reach zero.

One of *Magic*'s brilliant elements is that its core play structure is very simple and accessible, but the game becomes very sophisticated when all the special card-specific rules are taken into account. Cards interact with each other, and the rules in general, in various ways. (The creature that benefitted from that Giant Growth card earlier may do nothing in combat if an opponent uses an Unsummon card to send the spell back to its player's hand at just the right time.) Many pundits have commented that not only is the game infinitely expandable, but so are its rules clarification documents and FAQ; *Magic* currently offers over 137 pages of rules for the devoted player to digest.

The audience response to the release of *Magic* was immediate and immense: the game instantly sold out. Starting as a casual game that people played in between their roleplaying or board game sessions, it quickly grew to be an obsession all its own.

Wizards of the Coast upped the ante once again by quickly introducing organized competitive play, eventually offering significant cash prizes. The Pro Tour became an aspirational goal for many *Magic* players and drove attendance at local and regional competitions to the highest volume this industry has ever seen. These events achieved such broad appeal that the top-level competitions even appeared on ESPN.

The differing rarity of the cards and the additional strategies that become available to a player as they collect those rare cards means that someone with a larger and more complete collection has an inherent advantage over someone with smaller collection. This is not to say that a great player cannot overcome a disparity in collection size, but when equally matched players meet, the size of their collection will often be a dominant factor in who wins. To offset this potential imbalance in sponsored events, Wizards introduced Booster Draft and Booster Draw tournament formats, which require players to construct their decks at the tournament from the cards they receive in boosters they purchase there.

The legacy of *Magic: The Gathering* is a totally altered adventure-game and toy industry. Without *Magic*, there would have been no *Pokémon*, no *Yu-Gi-Oh!*, not even the collectible miniatures games *Mage Knight* or *HeroClix*. These games all dramatically expanded the industry, attracting new product outlets and new players. While organized play and a vibrant fan community had been a key element to the success of many roleplaying game publishers, *Magic* really woke up the game industry as a whole to the importance of those things. *Magic*, and many of the collectible games that followed it, have been supported by large, dynamic, publisher-sponsored communities that players will enjoy for many years to come.

The sales success of collectible games is directly related to the willingness of players to spend hundreds or even thousands of dollars each year on their hobbies. In the 1990s, incredible sales for all sorts of collectible games were fueled by the robust economy. It will be interesting to see how the typical high-cost, blind-collectible format will fare in the tougher economic times we currently face, and are likely to see continue for the near future.

Magic: The Gathering already has evolved to adapt to the demands of the 21st-century consumer, through innovative release structures merging ground-breaking technology with compelling storylines and products. But whatever form it takes in the future, the flexible and elegant design of *Magic: The Gathering* will surely guarantee continued success.

JORDAN WEISMAN has been the creative and motivating force behind the founding and success of a number of entertainment companies, including FASA Corporation, Virtual World Entertainment (the world's first public networked virtual reality entertainment centers; acquired by Disney in 1992), FASA Interactive (PC games, including the *MechWarrior* franchise; acquired by Microsoft in 1999), and WizKids (acquired by Topps Inc. in 2003). At Microsoft, Jordan was the creative director for the entire entertainment business unit, which included all PC and Xbox titles. During his tenure, the unit created a new genre of interactive entertainment called alternate reality games, for Steven Spielberg's movie *A.I.* Jordan and the 42Entertainment team have remained in the forefront of ARGs with such experiences as *I Love Bees*. During his career, Jordan has created some of the largest and longest-lasting franchises in the gaming industry, including *BattleTech/MechWarrior*, *Shadowrun*, and *Crimson Skies*. He has won more than 100 awards, including election to the Hall of Fame by the Academy of Adventure Gaming Arts & Design. In 2003 he was selected as the Pacific Northwest Entrepreneur of the Year by Ernst & Young.

Steve Kenson on

MARVEL SUPER HEROES

KEY DESIGNER: JEFF GRUBB

TSR, INC. (BASIC SET, 1984)

I LOVE COMIC BOOKS, and I love superhero games. As a game designer, I think Jeff Grubb's work on *Marvel Super Heroes* is still the gold standard when it comes to superhero roleplaying. So it's rather funny that when I first bought the game, I disliked it so much I returned it to the store for a refund the next day!

The reason for my discontent was simple: I was weaned on the likes of *Champions* and *Villains & Vigilantes*, the thunder lizards of superhero gaming. So this quick, bright-eyed mammal called *Marvel Super Heroes* confused the heck out of me. "Super-strength" wasn't listed as a power, when everybody knew that it was! The Thing had "body armor" when everyone *knew* he was "invulnerable" or "really tough" or something like that — but he didn't wear armor! "Fighting" was an ability score! Ranks? FEATs? Areas? Karma? In short, the whole package blew my 15-year-old mind, and I would have none of it.

Of course, I later relented due to reading Jeff Grubb's *Marvel-Phile* column in *Dragon* magazine and checking out the first releases for the new game, products like *Breeder Bombs* (featuring the X-Men) and *Avengers Assembled!* I cautiously ventured back to the hobby store, bought another copy of the bright yellow boxed set, and tried to read it without any preconceptions this time. I'm glad I did, since *Marvel Super Heroes* became the foundation for the longest campaign I ever ran.

The game was innovative in a number of ways. First, it uses descriptive terms along with numerical values for character traits. So rather than having "an agility score of 50" Spider-Man has "Amazing Agility." The same for the Hulk's Unearthly Strength or Iron Man's Incredible Reason. These terms — right down to their emphatic capitalization — help capture the flavor of the Marvel comic books, both in game stats and during play; there's nothing like answering the game master's question of "What's your Fighting?" with a confident "Incredible!"

Second, *Marvel Super Heroes* has a single "Universal Table" for resolving all actions, called FEATs (for Function of Exceptional Ability or Talent). The table itself is graded with levels of success, color coded green, yellow, and red. So a

Fighting FEAT in combat could result in a miss, a hit, a slam (sending the opponent flying), or a stun (potentially knocking them out): variety and simplicity, all in one. This, too, helps the game encompass the fast-paced action of a comic book story. The whole Universal Table thing even became a brief fad for TSR, which used the same approach in their *Indiana Jones* game and, later, in new editions of *Star Frontiers* and *Gamma World*.

Then there is the application of karma points. Their use to enhance die rolls and get heroes out of tight spots is similar to luck mechanics in other RPGs, but the way they are awarded *or taken away* based on how well characters live up to their heroic ideals — that's all new. Spider-Man gets karma for stopping crimes without harming bystanders or criminals *and* for making his dinner date with Mary Jane Watson. Thus the game provides a rules reason for players to stick to their heroic codes rather than dispatch their foes (and other problems) as brutally and efficiently as possible. They have reason to encourage their fellow heroes to do the same, since penalties can be shared. (If Wolverine kills someone, *all* the X-Men lose karma.) It even does the same for villains: a bad guy who offs some nameless minion in a fit of pique gets a quick karma recharge, but villains *lose* karma for casually killing their heroic foes rather than taking the time to place them in cunning deathtraps and gloat.

There are some kinks in the rules, to be sure. The average housecat has more health points than the average human — owing to its higher agility — and the limited number of ability ranks for defining characters means two foes with the same rank in damage and armor literally can't hurt each other. Still, the flaws are comparatively minor, and the game really captures the spirit of the four-color comics.

Maybe the greatest innovation of *Marvel Super Heroes* isn't the system *per se*, but the fact that it was the first superhero roleplaying game to abandon the idea of game balance, as it applied to creating and playing superheroes. Marvel characters are all over the map, in terms of power levels, and always have been; the Avengers had Thor, a literal Norse god, fighting alongside the Wasp, who could shrink, fly, and deliver a "sting" powerful enough to stun but not much more. The X-Men had Cyclops, with a powerful optic blast, but no special invulnerability or the like, alongside Phoenix, a cosmic-level telepath and telekinetic. *Marvel Super Heroes* embraced this situation rather than trying to force characters into cookie-cutter balance through cost accounting, wherein every character has a set and equal budget for powers and abilities, forcing players to stay within a narrow range of character types and concepts. The only options for character creation in the *Marvel Basic Set* were play one of the existing Marvel characters provided or roll up a new character randomly, with the same wide variations in possible powers. The *Advanced Set* added the idea of character modeling, which allowed players to assign a new character (presumably modeled on an existing comic book hero) whatever traits seem appropriate.

The thing is, this balance-free approach works! For the most part, Thor can fight alongside the "perfect fighting machine" Captain America; Iron Man, with his advanced power armor; and the aforementioned Wasp, yet players still come away with a satisfying game experience. The combination of the compressed range of traits (characters tend to operate in a range of seven or eight ranks) and karma points help to make it possible, although some good game mastering, aided by villains with karma points of their own, certainly helps. Superhero RPGs such as *Marvel* are also more forgiving than most, since characters rarely die and there's always a chance to come back for a win (or for a vanquished villain to come back with another sinister plot).

For an RPG with all the earmarks of a pickup game, *Marvel Super Heroes* is remarkably — or is that Amazingly? Monstrously? — robust. As I mentioned, my longest-running campaign ever was a *Marvel* game, largely because game preparation was so easy and gameplay was so much fun.

I understand TSR came very close to completing a hardcover edition of *Marvel Super Heroes* before they lost the Marvel Comics license and the project was permanently shelved. It's a pity such a magnum opus was never published, but it's a testament to the game's longevity that it still has enthusiastic fan support on the Internet and an active play community more than a decade after its last product was published. Even more so that it continues to set a standard by which new superhero roleplaying games are measured. Like modern comic book writers and artists following the greats of the Silver Age, modern RPG designers have a tough act to follow. When it comes to setting the bar high for a superhero game, in the words of Stan "the Man" Lee, "Make Mine Marvel!"

STEVE KENSON is the designer and line developer of the *Mutants & Masterminds* superhero RPG for Green Ronin Publishing. He has worked

as an author and game designer since 1995, and is particularly known for his writing on such superhero games as *Champions*, *Aberrant*, and *Silver Age Sentinels*, in addition to *M&M*. He also designed the award-winning Freedom City campaign setting for *Mutants & Masterminds*. Steve lives in Merrimack, New Hampshire, with his partner, Christopher Penczak, and a tremendous shared comic book collection.

METAMORPHOSIS ALPHA

KEY DESIGNER: JAMES M. WARD

MUDPUPPY GAMES (FOURTH EDITION, 2006)

EARLY IN 1976 I was privileged to be one of the playtesters for the initial draft of the *Metamorphosis Alpha* roleplaying game. It captivated me then, and its fourth edition continues to do so now, 30 years later. *Metamorphosis Alpha* was the first published RPG that was based in the genre of science fiction, albeit leaning heavily toward science fantasy.

If asked to describe the game in a few words, I would say this: It is the most surreal of all RPGs. The design of *Metamorphosis Alpha* combines the best elements of fantasy and science fiction to create a nonesuch. Thus there are bizarre mutations of humans and all manner of other creatures, some totally alien, scattered about a gigantic space vessel with multiple levels, each measuring many square kilometers in area. Because of the disaster that struck this colony starship, many of the levels that were once re-creations of natural human or animal habitats are now entirely changed. Some so changed, in fact, that explorers hardly recognize the original design of the place. Of course, erratic computers have much to do with the state of things, with some of these machines actually being controlled by deadly mutant species bent on exterminating the humans aboard the ship. Combined with unpredictable and dangerous androids and mad robots — mad in both senses of the word: crazed and angry — each *MA* game adventure is absolutely unpredictable and filled with startling new discoveries, continual conundrums, and ever-present danger of the most dire sort.

Metamorphosis Alpha proves a departure from the *Dungeons & Dragons* roleplaying game model because it has no archetypical characters or character classes, and is not level-based. The character with which one begins is pretty much unaltered through the course of play. Although there is no level progression in the game, though, the rewards for characters are considerable. First and foremost is the discovery of the bewildering array of creatures, places, and things to be found aboard the lost *Starship Warden* — or whatever similar vessel the game master might create for his campaign environment. There are the technological devices, too, along with discovered skills and possible new mutations to be gained. A plethora of technological items, in fact — some wonderfully helpful, some of little value, and not a few highly dangerous to the character attempting to discover how the strange device functions.

The initial edition of *Metamorphosis Alpha* did not provide a ready-to-play campaign base. The game master was required to make up his own based on a few initial suggestions, the backstory and general information found in the rulebook, and his own imagination. My own colony starship concept for a campaign was a massive sort. A vast central sphere had radiating from it many arms terminating in disk-shaped environmental pods, each a great plate of around two miles depth and 20 miles diameter duplicating a region of earth. The central globe for this incredible vessel was likewise 20 miles in equatorial diameter, this location being that from which the tubular connecting arms of one mile diameter radiated out to the dozen distinct environmental disks. Super science indeed. It goes without saying that mutations occurred in all of these areas, and the clever mutated species migrated to the central sphere and on into some of the other pods.

The latest, fourth edition of the game provides the GM with a schematic of the *Starship Warden*, as well as notes for the many large levels of the colony vessel. Thus, unless the game master is ambitious and decides to create his own campaign world, the rulebook provides everything needed to develop specific ship-level maps and begin playing. Although it might seem whimsical to the uninitiated, the underlying assumption of *Metamorphosis Alpha* is that precise details are not necessary to providing an exciting adventure. What is needed in the way of such particulars can be devised by the GM on the spot, then recorded in the form of a few notes so as to keep things consistent in later play sessions.

As play requires thinking, all of the game's character choices assume intelligence. There are mutations to heighten character intellect and other brain powers, as well as programs for mechanical adventurers to do the same. This brings us to the selection of player character types.

In the original version of *Metamorphosis Alpha*, the player character choices were pure-strain human, mutant human, or mutant animal of virtually any sort. Because of the fascinating array of mutations possible, most characters were mutated humans or animals. With such personae there was also the chance of radiation exposure generating another, useful, mutation. While such an array was ample, designer James M. Ward outdid himself when creating the game's fourth edition, for Mudpuppy Games. Players have greatly expanded character choices. In addition to the original human and mutant selections, one can now opt to play as any one of a vast multitude of robots, the great variety made possible by a robotic component selection mechanic. Add to that the possibility of choosing an android character, with a considerable number of options in regards to type and skills, and the variety of PC choices in the latest version is astonishingly broad.

As I noted in the beginning of this essay, *Metamorphosis Alpha* was the first science fiction/science fantasy RPG. From the initial edition of the game sprang the more elaborate *Gamma World*, which was based on the *MA* game system, but for a variety of reasons *Gamma World* proved somewhat inferior. (I say that even though I had the honor of adding the mutant riding animals to the game.) Perhaps its worse failing was that it did not link in any formal way to the superior *Metamorphosis Alpha*.

It has remained a mystery to me why, after both *Metamorphosis Alpha* and *Gamma World* were out of print, no other RPG publisher offered another fantasy-leaning science fiction game. Until *Metamorphosis Alpha* was released in a new edition in the 1990s, the genre was basically ignored. There were hard science fiction and post-apocalyptic designs in print, but no games mixing the science fantasy and science fiction genres. Fortunately, though, *MA* is available once more.

To sum up, *Metamorphosis Alpha* is a game that breaks the typical level-progression reward mold but nevertheless offers a rich, if sometimes difficult to gain, array of player rewards — from the knowledge of the environment to beneficial character mutations, learned skills to the acquisition of tech items and other equipment. Furthermore it blends fantasy with weird and super science in a unique manner that is captivating to players with imaginations suited to such a startling mixture. *Metamorphosis Alpha* — in any edition — stimulates the imagination, encourages keen thinking, and breaks the mold of typical fantasy and science fiction roleplaying games. If that doesn't make it one of the best hobby games ever, I don't know what would.

GARY GYGAX has written or co-authored and had published over 80 games, game products, and books since he began creating in the 1960s, when he founded the world-renowned Gen Con gaming convention. His first professional gaming work was published in 1971. He co-founded the game publishing company Tactical Studies Rules (later TSR, Inc.) in 1973 with his longtime friend from Lake Geneva, Don Kaye. He is best known for co-creating and authoring the original *Dungeons & Dragons* roleplaying game; creating the *AD&D* game and the World of Greyhawk fantasy setting; and writing the Gord the Rogue novels, as well as a trio of fantasy-mystery novels featuring the Aegyptian wizard-priest Magister Setne Inhetep. Gary is often referred to (by others) as the "Father of Roleplaying." He is currently living in Lake Geneva, Wisconsin, his childhood home. Gary is not as active in creating material as he was when he wrote his first major game in 1972-3 because of a bout of ill health in 2004, but he continues to serve as editor-in-chief for Troll Lord Games' series of fantasy reference books, Gygaxian Fantasy Worlds. In their "30 Most Influential People in Gaming" article series, released in March of 2002, *GameSpy* magazine placed Gary at # 18, tied with J.R.R. Tolkien and just after George Lucas. In 2005, *Sync* magazine placed him at the top of their list of "The 50 Biggest Nerds of All Time." The same year, a new strain of bacteria was named after Gary — *Arthronema gygaxiana*. RPG fans are everywhere these days. . . .

Greg Costikyan on

MY LIFE WITH MASTER

KEY DESIGNER: PAUL CZEGE

HALF-MEME PRESS (2003)

"The life of a minion is not an easy one. They are shunned for their fright-ening visages and disfigured bodies, for their mental and physical scars and their horrific afflictions, and for their bizarre, asocial behaviors."
— *My Life with Master*, p. 19.

FOR MANY OF TODAY'S game designers, the tension between story and game is central to their creative efforts, and the relationship between the two has become a point of contention in both the digital and tabletop game industries, as well as among game studies academics (in the continuing "narratology versus ludology" debate). The tension is particularly important in tabletop roleplaying, partly due to its origins in tabletop miniatures: the original *Dungeons & Dragons* was an elaboration of the *Chainmail* fantasy miniatures game, and contained scant reference either to plot or to playing a role — the focus was on combat.

Despite this, the success of *Dungeons & Dragons*, in both the artistic and com-mercial senses, was due precisely to its connection to story: it bound players to individual characters in an imaginary world. The other elements of story — plot, character growth, and the evocation of a rich world — were missing, but this was still a far different experience from the abstracted strategy prevalent in board games of a prior era.

The next and logical step from classic *D&D* was to elaborate setting and back-ground; while most immediate imitators simply took the *D&D* paradigm to other genres, others began (as with *RuneQuest* and *Empire of the Petal Throne*) to develop fantasy worlds with the kind of detail and richness seen previously only in the work of Tolkien.

In short, tabletop roleplaying, which began as an outgrowth of wargaming, rapidly became, at least for some players, a form of rules-guided improvisational theater. And yet the rules of most games were inherently unsuited to this: they required extensive table look-ups, rote memorization of minor die-roll modifiers, and the like, so that the action was often interrupted to research and apply some minor rule, with a consequent break in both the narrative and the spontaneity of the actors.

Understandably, RPGs of the late '80s began to adopt simpler rules — *Paranoia* and *Vampire: The Masquerade*, being two good examples. But even this didn't address the central problem: the inherent conflict between the demands of simulation (the central focus of the wargame) and the requirements of plot and character development.

"Success results in an increase in the minion's Self-loathing."
— *My Life with Master*, p. 31.

AT THE SAME TIME, digital games have struggled with the same issue, in a different context: Stories are by nature linear, but games must provide the players a sense of freedom. That is, the writer or teller of a story does his or her best to have events follow in a sequence that makes for the most compelling possible story; but if a player is confined to a single linear path, he feels as if he is hardly playing at all, but simply wading through a story imposed from above. Not surprisingly, most digital games that are dependent on story take a "beads on a string" approach, granting a player a fair degree of freedom of action within a bead (or level, if you prefer), but with beads following one another in a constrained linear progression. (For a more detailed exploration of these issues, c.f. "Games, Storytelling, and Breaking the String," Greg Costikyan, in *Second Person: Role-Playing and Story in Games and Playable Media*, ed. Harrigan & Waldrip-Fruin, 2007, MIT University Press, pp. 5-13.)

In the late '90s, a group of experimental roleplaying game designers coalesced around the The Forge (http://www.indie-rpgs.com/forum/), an online community for independently developed tabletop RPGs, and began experimenting with ways to better enable what might call "true roleplaying," that is, the sort of rules-guided improvisation of character and story that commercial RPGs point to but rarely sustain. Many adopted Ron Edward's conception of "gamist/narrativist/simula-tions theory" (http://www.indie-rpgs.com/articles/1/) as a structure, and a variety of interesting works emerged — of which *My Life with Master* is among the most important.

My Life with Master is a serious attempt to grapple with, and solve, the central conflict between story and game: that plots are inherently linear (that is, that any deviation from the plot is likely to produce a less compelling story) while games that do not provide players with the sense of freedom of action are inherently unsatisfying.

> *"And so the mechanics consciously empower the gamemaster's use of an aggressive scene framing technique to deliver pacing and dramatic tension across a series of game sessions comprised of individual scenes with these characters."*
>
> — *My Life with Master*, p. 44.

BECAUSE OF THE SIMULATIONIST origin of the tabletop RPG, the usual paradigm is to constrain a character's action from moment to moment through a set of rules that simulate actions and their consequences. Thus, when you pick a lock, you roll dice (or apply some other system) to determine whether or not you succeed. However, the usual RPG provides no functional constraint on the evolution of the story; instead, the story is supposed to magically emerge from the decisions and actions of the player-characters, coupled with the game master's desperate improvisation. In other words, actions are rules-bound, the story is freeform. And because it is freeform, there's no guarantee that a particularly satisfying story will emerge from play — and indeed, quite often it does not. (Note that "telling a satisfying story" is only one of the possible pleasures to be gained through roleplaying; it's quite possible for all to have an enjoyable experience without doing so.)

My Life with Master turns this basic paradigm on its head. The rules dictate a fixed and immovable story, and outcomes for individual characters within that story are mutable only within strict limits. Conversely, in order to preserve a feeling of player freedom of action within the constraints of the system, the game utterly throws open action on a moment-to-moment basis.

The game is played in a sequence of "scenes," and after an initial description of the set-up from the game master, the game system is used to determine whether the outcome of the scene is "favorable" or "unfavorable" for the main characters involved. They are then utterly free to improvise and roleplay the scene and its outcome — and never, say, roll to see whether they can pick a lock. They can pick the lock or not, depending on the demands of the story as they choose to tell it.

In part, *My Life with Master* works because Czege has chosen as the theme for his game a story genre (Gothic horror) that has a defined narrative arc: hubris and terror, followed by a fall. Of course, many narrative genres also follow a conventional arc. You could see the same approach working for, say, the romance story, or for the by-now stereotyped adventure quest fantasy. Because each is a class of stories that are variations on a theme, *My Life with Master*'s predefined narrative arc is adaptable to many types of stories — not all, to be sure, but a good many.

Work it does, and extremely well; the rules are few and the system tightly constrained, but they suffice both to shape the plot and to evoke a real sense of drama, pity, and horror among the players. A game of *My Life with Master* (in the hands of a good game master—always a caveat with tabletop roleplaying) can be, in fact, a harrowing, and chastening, emotional experience. In a commercial medium where most players ask nothing more of a game than it be "fun," *My Life with Master* instead strives to provide a game that not merely recreates a story of the piteousness and beauty of *Frankenstein* or *Castle of Otranto,* but by placing the players within it and making them complicit in the uncomfortable actions demanded of them by "the Master," provides an experience that can be even more powerful for the players than that provided by traditional narrative.

Unlike conventional RPGs, *My Life with Master* comes to an end — a conclusion. Of course, it must do so; it strives to tell a story, and stories have endings. Consequently, it is not a game you are likely to play more than once or a handful of times. But what of it? That's the kind of game it is — *sui generis,* to be sure.

My Life with Master is, in conclusion, an important game: It solves, within its limited sphere, the most intractable problem faced by narrative games, that of reconciling plot with player freedom. It evokes emotions and feelings rare in games. And it stands as one of a very few games we can show the skeptics when we claim that games can be art.

> *"He has demonstrated his humanity, regardless of the outcome."*
> — *My Life with Master,* p. 28.

GREG COSTIKYAN is CEO of Manifesto Games, a start-up devoted to providing a viable path to market for independently developed computer games. He has designed more than 30 commercially published board, roleplaying, computer, online, and mobile games since the 1970s, is the winner of five Origins Awards, the Maverick Award for untiring promotion of independently published games, and is an inductee into the Academy of Adventure Gaming's Hall of Fame. He has written on games, game design, and game industry business issues for publications including the *New York Times*, *Wall Street Journal Interactive*, *Salon*, and *The Escapist*, and is the author of four published science fiction novels.

John D. Rateliff on

MYTHOS

KEY DESIGNER: CHARLIE KRANK

CHAOSIUM (1996)

IN THE BEGINNING, THERE was *Magic: The Gathering*. Then came a flood of collectible card games that sought to capitalize on the market *Magic*'s enormous success had created. One of the last games in that first wave, *Mythos*, marked old-school publisher Chaosium's belated entry into an already crowded field. It was worth the wait. Even now, a decade since the last new cards were released for *Mythos*, it remains the high water mark for capturing roleplaying sensibilities within a trading card game, and also stands as the best translation of a RPG into a card game, conveying the flavor of the original roleplaying game while also succeeding as a card game in its own right.

That roleplaying game was, of course, Sandy Petersen's *Call of Cthulhu*, widely recognized as one of the most elegant pairings of a rules system with its subject matter (in this case, the horror stories of H.P. Lovecraft). Continuously in print now for more than a quarter-century with only minor modifications to the original rules — a record unmatched by any other major RPG — *Call of Cthulhu* is obviously a hard act to follow. It's thus a tribute to *Mythos* that its designer managed to create a suitable analogue within the card game for *Call of Cthulhu*'s signature mechanic: the sanity roll. In both games, you play an occult investigator, searching out the ululating horrors that haunt the world's dark places (some of which turn out to be uncomfortably near at hand). Within the RPG, the more characters learn about the threats facing them, the less capable they become of dealing with them. They become more powerful yet more fragile at the same time, losing sanity every time they challenge another unearthly horror, with such encounters eventually scouring away the last remnants of their grasp on reality. Similarly, instead of the standard life points of most CCGs, *Mythos* players start out with a variable number of sanity points, and practically everything they do within the game impacts that number.

Therein lies the rub: Lose all your sanity points, and you've lost the game. Not only will your opponent(s) in a game of *Mythos* constantly throw things against you that cost your investigator sanity, but most of the actions you take yourself also affect your sanity points. A quick trip to a nearby asylum will restore some sanity or eliminate a crippling phobia (like the Dendrophobia you picked up after narrowly escaping from that Dark Young of Shub-Niggurath), but only at the cost of skipping a turn or two — and watching while your opponents get that much closer to victory. Play thus becomes a balancing act between trying to achieve your own goals while simultaneously frustrating the goals of all the other players and struggling to protect your character's sanity. Because of this, while *Mythos* works just fine as a straight-up duel between two players (and, in fact, the excellent *Standard Game Set* is organized with two well-tuned pregenerated decks for just such a style of play), it is even better with an ensemble of three or more players. (I've played at tables of up to eight players at a time, but this is pushing it; three to five is optimum for the game's dynamic.)

Perhaps the key to *Mythos*'s success in bringing a roleplaying sensibility to the card table lies in two unusual card types not seen in collectible card games before (nor, so far as I know, since): investigator and adventure cards. At the start of a game, each player has to choose which Investigator he or she will play; these over-sized cards range from such archetypical *Call of Cthulhu* protagonists as the Capable Graduate Student, Staid University Professor, Grizzled Boston Detective, and Brilliant Egyptian Archaeologist to more unusual choices, such as the Inquisitive Chinese Intellectual or Diabolical Cultist. Each investigator has different characteristics (starting sanity points, maximum and minimum number of cards that can be held in hand, languages known, etc.), so the investigator you choose has to be carefully selected to match the deck you're playing. More importantly, having an investigator puts a face on what would otherwise be an abstraction and gives gameplay a focus, the impression that all the events represented by the cards are happening to a specific person, who thus becomes very much like a roleplaying character.

The second unusual card type, the adventure card, outlines the story populated by the investigators. Each adventure card lists several cards or card types you must either have played or have in play: together these make up a scenario that, once completed, gains you victory points. It takes a total of 20 points to win, and hence comes the basic strategy of the game. A simple, easy-to-complete adventure might grant five points and a point or two of sanity as well; a fiendishly difficult adventure, like The Dunwich Horror or Summon Great Cthulhu, will grant as many as

15 or 13 points, respectively, and five of sanity. The longer an adventure, the more specific unique cards it requires, the more difficult these are to bring into play, and the easier it is to be derailed by an opponent, who might force a vital card out of the game — for example, by summoning a faceless nightgaunt to carry Randolph Carter off to the discard pile. Shorter adventures are much less challenging but require resetting your goal multiple times within a single game, which presents challenges of its own.

Actual gameplay centers around the remaining card types, which therefore make up the bulk of most decks. For example, your investigator might use a Dirigible (an event) to escape from the Silver Twilight Lodge (a location), entrust Herbert West (an ally) with a Mi-Go Braincase (an artifact), summon a Shoggoth or Formless Spawn (a monster) to drive an opponent mad, or cast Elder Sign (a spell) from *The Necronomicon* (a tome) to banish a Great Old One. One of the game's strengths is that it draws locations and characters not just from Lovecraft's stories but from Chaosium's impressive back catalogue of *Call of Cthulhu* adventures, as well as actual real-world people and places: Asenath Waite Derby, Carl Stanford, and Harry Houdini can all be encountered in the same deck, along with Lovecraft himself.

Perhaps most importantly, Chaosium included blank adventure cards in the deck, along with rules for creating your own adventures. This led to an outpouring of creativity, as the game's faithful circulated adventures they had created, many of them excellent. One fan even designed a *Scooby-Doo* theme set that was not just true to the spirit of the old TV show but completely playable in *Mythos* terms; others adopted classic *Call of Cthulhu* campaigns or horror stories by authors other than Lovecraft, such as Roger Zelazny's *A Night in Lonesome October*.

Unfortunately, like most collectible card games, *Mythos* eventually ran its course; there came a day when the profits from a successful release were ploughed into the next, unsuccessful release, causing an abrupt cash-flow problem. By all accounts the original set and the first three sets of boosters — *Expeditions of Miskatonic University*, *Cthulhu Rising*, and *Legends of the Necronomicon* (all 1996) — did very well, a tribute to the excellence of the design. The non-collectible *Mythos Standard Game Set* (1997) that followed is a model of how to create a tutorial that also appeals to veteran players, since its cards were fully compatible with the existing sets and nicely expanded the overall pool. Unfortunately, the next set was not only a stand-alone setting not fully compatible with all that had gone before, but it focused on a part of Lovecraft's work that, while including perhaps his best stories, has never been particularly popular with gamers: the Dreamlands. (A much better choice would have been Chaosium's 1890s *Cthulhu by Gaslight* setting.) *Dreamlands* (1997) sold poorly compared to the original releases, and while the next and final set, *New Aeon* (also 1997), did a much better job by both covering the modern era and providing plenty of cards usable in any setting, it was too late to undo the damage. No more new releases were forthcoming. Despite an active fanbase that lasted for several years thereafter, *Mythos* faded from view.

It somehow seems appropriate that a game set primarily in the 1920s should ultimately vanish because of a sudden financial crash; that it should stand valiantly for a brief time, only to succumb to the dark forces of the cosmos, like one of its own doomed investigators. Perhaps, though, the fate of *Mythos* is a little more cheerful, since the world has not quite forgotten its glory. Or perhaps the game is like Cthulhu himself, in his house at R'yleh — dead, but dreaming.

JOHN D. RATELIFF is an independent scholar whose most recent publication is *The History of The Hobbit* (HarperCollins, 2007), an edition of the original manuscript draft of J.R.R. Tolkien's *The Hobbit* with extensive commentary. He's helped organize several major Tolkien conferences and contributed essays to Christopher Tolkien's festschrift (*Tolkien's Legendarium*) and a volume marking the fiftieth anniversary of *The Lord of the Rings*. Having written his dissertation on Lord Dunsany, he likes to describe his degree as "a Ph.D. in fantasy." Co-editor of the third edition *D&D Player's Handbook* and *Dungeon Master's Guide* (the original d20 System game rules), he is also proud to have worked on such titles as *Mark of Amber*, *Night Below*, *Return to the Tomb of Horrors*, the Eberron core rulebook, and Decipher's *Lord of the Rings Roleplaying Game*. He is the author of the adventures *Standing Stone* and *Return to the Keep on the Borderlands*, as well as co-editor of (and contributor to) *d20 Cthulhu*.

Chris "Gerry" Klug on

NAPOLEON'S LAST BATTLES

KEY DESIGNERS: KEVIN ZUCKER, J.A. NELSON

SIMULATIONS PUBLICATIONS, INC. (FIRST EDITION, 1976)

NAPOLEON'S LAST BATTLES IS one of the best pencil-and-paper military simulations ever because it's a gloriously wonderful blend of solid, no-frills design, intelligent packaging, and a synergistic combination of the two that delivers a game that is (perhaps unintentionally) more than intended and results in a very happy consumer.

Napoleon's Last Battles (hereafter *NLB*) is not a single game but instead a related series of small, individual battle simulations that, when put together, allow you to play out the entire Waterloo campaign. The individual games were dubbed "folios" by the publisher, SPI, and could be purchased separately back in the 1970s. By putting the four folio games together and linking them into a campaign, the whole indeed became greater than the sum of the parts. When packaged together the group was called a "quadrigame" — meaning four games in one, I suppose.

The quadrigame was an interesting concept in the first place. The wargame industry in the '70s was facing a fascinating, and longstanding, conundrum: many of its core customers clamored for large, complex games, but because those games were — well, *huge* — they tended to sit on the shelf and not get played very much. Finding opponents for any wargame was always tough, particularly in the days before the Internet, and while many hardcore players lusted to sit down and really dig into monsters like *War in the East* or *Highway to the Reich*, practicality and common sense won out more often than not. The monster game was set aside for another day, as what players could be gathered together settled for something that could be understood and played to a reasonable conclusion in a single sitting.

SPI's quadrigame concept addressed that need very nicely. The idea, in short, was to design four small games linked thematically (say, four World War II battles or four Civil War battles), prepare a common set of rules for all the games (though some unique rules serving each separate battle were allowed), and then sell each battle individually, wrapped in a folio, while also boxing the set together. Once you learned the rules for one of the games, you knew the rules for all the games, and could play them all. Almost all of the smaller battles were played on one map, could be completed in a single evening, and most of them used rules concepts that almost every wargamer already knew — zones of control, combat results tables, and so on. As tasty as these individual folio games were, there was a downside: Even as the customer was playing these compact simulations, they were probably longing for something with a little more meat.

NLB gives players some of that meat in the form of its campaign game. This is possible because the four battles are not only linked thematically, but literally. The grand three-day battle that culminated at Waterloo involving the British, Prussian, and French forces can easily be viewed as four battles — Quatre Bras, Ligny, Waterloo, and Wavre. Divide the battleground into four maps and place one crucial engagement on each map. Allow each battle to be played by itself. Then, deliver a set of campaign rules where the maps could be placed side by side and allow the whole battle to played out, with each engagement flowing into the other, as they did historically, culminating with the Imperial Guard's fatal charge and defeat at Waterloo. Now you have the best of both worlds — battles with small, manageable chunks which, when combined, build something eminently greater and more enjoyable.

The design challenge was both simple and difficult at the same time. It's Waterloo, after all, arguably the most well-known battle to occur in the Western world for the last thousand years. In addition, one that has been wargamed to death in all levels of detail since the dawn of the wargame industry. However, in the end, Waterloo is a set-piece battle that is well served by even the simplest of simulation systems.

I have always felt that good design in any medium is best served by the general approach that the more you throw away, the better you are. That is to say, to keep a design properly focused, what you take away is more important than what you leave in. There are many, many games in all genres and media that suffer from the problem of "six pounds of material in a five-pound bag." Not only are many of those games not very enjoyable to play or easy to understand, they don't help the player get a feel for what he should be concentrating on when he sits down to play. The original *SimCity* is an example of the best of this kind of focused design. I never once worried whether every last element of running a city was included in the simulation because the design so elegantly captured the *essence* of running and creating a metropolis.

Tonight, as I skimmed through the rules of *NLB* looking for reminders of the things that made the game so special for me, I came across this bit of commentary in the Campaign Notes (written either by Kevin Zucker or Jay Nelson, it's not clear which):

> It is important that the simulation of an event take a relatively limited point of view in its interpretation of that event. A game which presents more than a few interrelating points of view is a *very* complex game. In designing a campaign game, we first tried to gain an all-important under- standing of the terrain as the battles and battlefields were studied individ- ually. Then one major point of view was chosen — the Command and Control Structures . . . and the relative competence of the individuals. . . .

The addition of the elegant command rules makes the campaign game not only play differently from the folio games, but it adds an exquisite layer of complexity to it. The campaign game is not just bigger, it's better. An *NLB* campaign requires you to focus on the abilities of the individual commanders in a way that makes you conscious of who they were and what their abilities were, but does so with- out undercutting the other important gameplay elements.

And for me, there you have it. Take a well-known battle (with all of its built- in romance and drama), simulate it simply so that the game system becomes almost invisible to the players, and layer in one set of (slightly) more complex rules (command and control). Give the player some flexibility on how much of the game he wants to consume at one time, and you've got a product that appeals to a broad set of customers while self-scaling to their needs and capacity.

I certainly didn't analyze these features at the time I bought this little gem. I only knew then that *Napoleon's Last Battles* delivered Napoleonic conflict at a level that was engrossing but not too taxing, and allowed me to enjoy it either by myself or gather three other friends, divide up the commands, and play the whole campaign comfortably over the course of a day or two.

Brilliantly simple. Brilliantly effective. Brilliantly fun.

CHRIS KLUG (some might know him as Gerry Klug; it's Gerard Christopher, for those of you who desire full disclosure) is currently the creative director for Cheyenne Mountain Entertainment's *Stargate Worlds* massively multi-player online game, but since the 1970s he's had an interesting and varied career in the entertainment industry, doing one thing or another. Trained as a theatrical lighting designer, Chris worked on Broadway, Off-Broadway, regional theater, opera, and toured with various '70s rock 'n' roll bands. He won two New Jersey Critic's Circle Awards for lighting designs at the New Jersey Theater Forum. Then he began writing adventures for Simulations Publications, Incorporated's line of roleplaying games. He assisted with the design of *Universe*, *Horror Hotel*, *Damocles Mission*, and the second edition of *DragonQuest*. When TSR bought SPI in 1982, Chris and the rest of the SPI design staff moved on to form Victory Games. There, Chris designed the *James Bond 007* roleplaying game, designed a half-dozen more titles, and was, for a time, design director. In the computer game field, his credits include *Star Trek DS9: Dominion Wars*, *Europa Universalis*, *Diamond Dreams Baseball*, and *Aidyn Chronicles: First Mage*. From 2001 through 2004, Chris served as creative director for EA's MMORPG, *Earth & Beyond*.

John Scott Tynes on

NAVAL WAR

KEY DESIGNERS: S. CRAIG TAYLOR, JR., NEIL ZIMMERER

BATTLELINE PUBLICATIONS (FIRST EDITION, 1979)

THERE ARE A LOT of reasons to love the *Naval War* card game, and I'll get to most of them in a minute. But I have a unique one that demands telling.

When I was about nine years old, my father played wargames with a friend of his whose college roommate had been S. Craig Taylor, Jr. Craig was the designer of *Wooden Ships & Iron Men,* among many other games, and by the good grace of this friendship, my father and his friend were offered the chance to work as "booth weasels" for Yaquinto, the wargame company, at a Philadelphia convention, circa 1980. (Booth weasels are a hobby gaming tradition — fans who work the convention booth for a company while the game designers are off gaming and carousing.) They spent a couple of days selling product for Yaquinto and then, to their dismay, learned they would have to pay all their own expenses for the show. Yaquinto erred in telling them this at the beginning of their last shift because my father and his friend, thusly disgruntled, took the opportunity to loot the Yaquinto cash register of the money needed to cover their costs.

They enjoyed one other bonus: the time-honored booth weasel tradition of trading your company's games for those of other companies. So it was that my father came home from his adventure none the poorer and with a giant stack of wargames in his arms. One of these was S. Craig Taylor's *Naval War,* in its first edition from Battleline, and when I look back now it seems as if my parents and I did nothing for the next couple of years but play *Naval War* morning, noon, and night. Most of our games lived in the closet, where you could find *Monopoly* and *Sorry!* and *Clue.* But *Naval War* lived in the kitchen drawer, alongside other things we used every single day, and we wore those little cards to pieces.

Naval War is an early example of a casual wargame. It's a fast-paced card game that causes some wargamers to sniff because of its ahistorical abstractions: you assemble a hodgepodge fleet of ships from the navies of World War II, so that one player might have the American *Missouri,* the Japanese *Yamato,* and the British *Nelson,* while another player has the British *King George V* and the

German *Bismarck*. It's as if you've entered some naval afterlife where all the great warships rise rusting from the depths and join together in a nationless battle that never ends, a Valhalla of clashing steel.

The game cheerfully accepts three to nine players. And while gameplay involves a lot of luck, it's also fast and brutal enough to encourage temporary alliances and smirking revenge. I remember all too well the look of triumph on my loving mother's face as she slapped down a destroyer squadron and dared my father and I to sink it before she unleashed flaming death on whichever of us most deserved it that week.

Play is pleasingly simple. You draw a card and if it's red, you have to play it immediately. If it's black, you add it to your hand and then can play or discard any one card. There are no exceptions, no playing out of turn. Combat is conducted by playing a salvo card. Each salvo card is rated for a shell size, as is each ship. A ship with 14" guns cannot fire a 15" salvo and so on. (The presence of a 12.6" gun is a charmingly quirky bit of historical fidelity in an abstract game, the decimal place a knowing wink to military buffs.) Each salvo inflicts damage points on the ship and when a ship loses all its damage, it sinks, earning points for the player who delivered the killing blow.

The interesting bits are how the cards drive the interaction of the players. A minefield card applies one or two hits to every ship in the targeted fleet; the player who plays it is something of a *picador,* spearing the bull to wound it and make it an attractive target while deflecting attention from himself, but you get no points for such wounds. The destroyer squadron sits ominously for an entire round and then, on the player's next turn, destroys one to six ships of a targeted enemy — a devastating attack, but one whose target is undeclared until the die is rolled, meaning that for the tense round before it goes off the other players must decide whether to work together to destroy it or hide behind smoke cards that shield them from the attack since none of them know who it will strike. Should the first player inflict damage on the destroyer squadron and the second player play a smoke card and hide, cries of betrayal are commonplace and the looming doom awaiting the un-smoked player makes him an object of merriment for everyone else.

Naval War spoiled me for most other beer-and-pretzels games because of its speed. A four-player game of the more complicated *Wiz-War* (Jolly Games, 1985) could easily consume four hours; in that same time you could play a dozen or more sessions of *Naval War*. I knew two roommates in college who played hundreds of sessions and kept a running score. Much like potato chips, it's hard to stop at one. The game is so fast, fun, and simple that as soon as one player wins, somebody starts shuffling the cards to play again.

Naval War's swift, abstracted gameplay influenced other games. *Enemy in Sight* (Avalon Hill, 1988) and *Modern Naval Battles* (3W, 1989) use the age of sail and modern warships as their respective themes, but share the core gameplay of *Naval War*. My own card game, *Creatures & Cultists* (Pagan Publishing, 1993), was inspired by it as well.

There hasn't been an edition of *Naval War* since Avalon Hill's in 1983 and the game is long out of print. Yet the World Boardgaming Championships have crowned a *Naval War* champion every single year since 1992, a testament to the vitality and irresistible appeal of this superb game. *Naval War* lives on!

JOHN SCOTT TYNES is an award-winning game designer and writer who has worked in the hobby games field since 1990. His games include *Unknown Armies, Puppetland, Creatures & Cultists*, and *The Hills Rise Wild!* He also co-authored the critically acclaimed *Delta Green* series of roleplaying game sourcebooks and founded Pagan Publishing and *The Unspeakable Oath* magazine. He was the first content lead on the *Magic: The Gathering* trading card game and was the original line editor for Robin Laws' *Feng Shui* RPG. Today he is the producer for *Pirates of the Burning Sea,* a massively multi-player online computer game from Flying Lab Software. He has written about games for *Salon, The Escapist, Pyramid, X360 UK*, and *The Stranger*.

Erick Wujcik on

OGRE

KEY DESIGNER: STEVE JACKSON

METAGAMING (FIRST EDITION, 1977)

I'M DATING MYSELF HERE, but I played a lot of games, for a lot of years, before Steve Jackson's *Ogre* came along.

My first complex board game was Avalon Hill's *Midway*, back in the mid-1960s. (How could I not play *Midway*? My own father had served as the chief electrical engineer on the USS *Pensacola* during that battle.) This was followed by a bunch of other Avalon Hill, and then SPI, hex-based, rules-heavy, out-and-out military board games. None of them were games I really absorbed, really loved, or really wanted to own. Looking back, none of them seemed to offer sufficient reward for the time I needed to invest in playing. Instead, when players were available, I'd want to break out *Risk* or *Acquire* or even *Diplomacy*, but not military games.

Then came *Ogre*, an incredibly affordable little bundle of tank warfare goodness, and suddenly I was playing, I was pestering other players to play with me, and my mind was spinning out of control with all the terrific possibilities. *Ogre* was, for me, the be all and end all of board gaming. In fact, it was my last great fling with board games, before my life was completely consumed by roleplaying games.

From my current perspective as a seasoned game designer, 30 years later, looking back at my fanatic appreciation of *Ogre*, I think its success really boils down to four essentials:

OGRE IS FAST: I'm a huge fan of fast. If we've got multiple hours, I'd rather play multiple sessions. I'm a social guy, but I also like to win. My idea of a perfect evening of game playing is for me to win the majority of the games we play, but for everyone else to win at least one. With *Ogre*, playing a good game takes less than an hour. Heck, I've had *great* games that were over in less than 25 minutes. That's fast!

OGRE IS ASYMMETRICAL: Much as I love fast, I love the asymmetry of *Ogre* even more. In the case of *Ogre*, one player gets to be the behemoth, the giant, the armored killing machine — the Ogre. Meanwhile, the other guy gets to play everybody else, which includes all the vulnerable infantry (and oh, they are so, so fragile flesh, those infantry units in *Ogre*); the light-, missile-, and heavy tanks; the G.E.V.s (swift-moving Ground Effect Vehicles); and the immobile, place-'em-and-hope howitzers.

A lesser designer would have loaded down the game with what had been traditional, hidebound, locked-in, never-to-be-questioned symmetry, following the path heavily trod these past thousands of years. Like chess, like go, like everything, *Ogre* in the hands of someone other than Steve Jackson would have had each player field identical forces. One Ogre for blue, another for red; two heavy tanks for blue, two heavy tanks for red; and so forth, sinking the game right into the great ocean of the mundane, the dull, and the unremarkable.

Instead, we have something completely different, and something completely wonderful. *Ogre* is a lopsided game, where two players have very different experiences, with remarkably even odds of success.

OGRE IS OPEN-ENDED: Yes, I love it quick, and, yes, I'm tickled by the asymmetry, but give me a chance to be creative and you steal my soul. By including different possible missions, with different potential force mixes, as well as different Ogres (both the Mark III and the Mark V were in the original version), Steve Jackson encourages players to come up with their own creative versions of the game. The first thing I did was rummage around for different hex boards, and for a few weeks I played exclusively using some old fantasy game board, complete with rivers and forests, gradually adding new units and rules. The multi-player modifications came next, making it possible for several players to get into the action simultaneous. Eventually, in my case, I ended up running an *Ogre* roleplaying campaign at my university game club, complete with homebrew rules for salvaging dead units and operating tank factories, and formulas for designing completely new units (I recall the heavy missile tank was a personal favorite).

OGRE IS A TEACHING TOOL: Speed, uneven match-ups, and the chance to burn new neural pathways already make for a killer combination, but these days there's a crying need for tools that teach game design. *Ogre* had restructured my mind pretty completely, but it wasn't until 2002, when I took up a gig as a game design instructor in Hong Kong, that I realized how effective *Ogre* is at getting across so many important component mechanisms of play and design. Steve Jackson's elegant creation deserves a place on the short list of games as laboratory exercises; *Ogre* teaches game assembly, game systems, and, in particular, does a brilliant job of teaching game components. Each piece tells us about itself, but also about every other piece. With an incredible economy of description, both the functionality and the virtual image of Ogres and tanks, infantry and howitzers, not to mention the transcendental G.E.V. (a unit that moves, fires, and moves again), is branded into every player's brain.

So, THEORY ASIDE, HOW does it work? One player fields a single unit, the Ogre. It's a unit powerful enough to justify its own character sheet, which itemizes main and secondary guns, as well as AP (anti-personnel weapons; for use against infantry only) and missiles (the expendable kind; cross 'em off after firing). It also holds check-off boxes for the all-important units of tread, the loss of which gradually slow down the Ogre's movement.

It's the other guy's job — the non-Ogre player's job — to figure out combinations of a dozen or so much lesser units, and attempt to stop the Ogre.

Physically, the Ogre player moves a single tiny square of cardboard (and believe me, the original Metagaming game pieces defined *flimsy*), then runs a finger down the list of the Ogre's weapons, using, or not using, each in turn. The non-Ogre player counters with movements and fire for all the remaining pieces.

All this action is conveyed somehow by a paper sheet printed with a hexagonal pattern, covered with scattered chits of black and white cardboard. And yet gameplay summons to mind a futuristic nightmare of desperation and exhilaration, where rumbling machines unleash barrage after barrage of titanic weaponry and the inexorable advance of a soulless giant can only be stopped by zinging swarms of self-sacrificing martyrs. An ebb and flow of vivid battle, conjured not by processors and graphic boards, but by force of game design alone.

Genius! Put aside everything else the man has done — from *Car Wars* to *Illuminati* to *GURPS* — and with *Ogre* alone Steve Jackson earns a place in the pantheon of game design immortals.

As a roleplaying game designer, ERICK WUJCIK is best known for his *Teenage Mutant Ninja Turtles & Other Strangeness,* as well as *Revised RECON, Ninjas & Superspies, Rifts China 1* and *2,* and a whole slew of other games and supplements from Palladium Books, plus *Amber Diceless Role-Playing* (soon to be re-released by a new company, Diceless by Design). Since the mid-1990s, he has toiled away in the electronic game biz, on titles from Sierra, THQ, and Ubisoft. As of early 2007, Erick became the senior game designer/writer for Totally Games, located just north of San Francisco's Golden Gate Bridge, though he also continues to write the occasional paper RPG. His handmade HTML homepage can be found at www.47rpg.com.

Marc Gascoigne on

ONCE UPON A TIME

KEY DESIGNERS: RICHARD LAMBERT, ANDREW RILSTONE, JAMES WALLIS

ATLAS GAMES (SECOND EDITION, 1995)

THE IRISH GAMING CONVENTION scene is one of the world's most vibrant and Dublin's annual Gaelcon is perhaps its crowning glory. Famous — indeed, Diana Jones Award-winning — for its massive charity auctions, it also delivers year after year on a far quieter but equally laudable aim of promoting new games and the sheer joy of gaming to the wider Irish public. Some years back I helped them run some board game events over a few cons, and it was always a privilege to help a young, or not-so-young, gamer discover a new favorite game. The organizers had cunningly timed the con to fall just after the massive Essen Game Fair, so they always had the very latest titles to test, hot off the plane from Germany. More importantly, Gaelcon has always placed a massive premium on introducing newcomers. How many game cons have you been to where the organizers have gotten every single person in the hall sat down and playing something — that's *every single person?*

So what does this have to do with *Once Upon a Time*? Well, this innocent little card game of telling fairy stories is one of the best ways I've ever found to grab a non-gamer by their imagination and fling them into our world, and it came into its own for me at Gaelcon. I almost hesitate to suggest it, but perhaps it was a touch of the good old Irish blarney that helped make the game work from the moment we cracked the shrinkwrap. Even the shyest youngsters, inexperienced gamers though they may be, were soon relating the most fabulous stories. But, in truth, I've found players the world over who have had tremendous fun creating stories and frustrating their fellow storytellers with this unusual but enthralling card game.

Crucially for any introductory game, gameplay is simplicity itself. From a shuffled deck, every player is dealt a hand of cards, five to 10 depending on the number of players, each bearing a word or phrase instantly familiar to anyone who's ever heard a traditional folk tale. For example, you may have a hand that includes a crown, time passing, an old man, a dark night, and a bridge. Everyone also gets a card bearing their own particular Happy Ever After ending, which they must keep secret until they reach it. For the object of the game is to tell a tale incorporating as many of your own cards' words, each laid down as you include it, no more than one per sentence, until the very last card you play is your own particular ending, whether it be "True love had broken the enchantment" or "So the evil-doers were thrown down a well." Three mechanics are there to hinder you: if you mention something that another player has on one of his cards, he can lay it down to trump you and pick up your story, inevitably twisting it to his own ends. If you run out of inspiration, you pick up a card and the story passes to your neighbor. The only other rule — the story has to make a certain amount of narrative sense, as voted by the group. Games may take as little as 15 minutes, but you try playing just once.

This simplicity, coupled with a near-universal theme, makes *Once Upon a Time* an ideal introductory game, especially for young players new to the sometimes complicated rules of hobby games, but very much at home with this game's central task. It's a game of telling fairy stories, and everyone, whether thanks to a rich European cultural heritage or merely a childhood enthralled by Disney animation, knows all about princesses, forests, dwarfs, and treasure. Its only real mechanic is trumping another storyteller, again familiar to even the youngest card player. The one challenge the game does present is to one's own self-consciousness or coolness — players sometimes start their first game unsure whether relating a tale about a princess getting a kiss from a prince is for them. Younger players rarely have such qualms, and parents similarly need little persuasion to charge headlong into what can prove to be not much more stretching than your typical bedtime story session. (Incidentally, the game also doubles as a great tool for when one's own imagination is running dry.)

After you've played a few times, and become familiar with all the possible Happy Ever Afters, gameplay actually creeps back in, in the form of red herrings. Deliberately mention a particular enchantment or that magical well early enough in your tale and you can guarantee that the other players will expend a great deal of energy trying to divert you from any path toward that ending, allowing your real ending to take them unawares.

This storytelling element was not new to *Once Upon a Time*, of course. The game *Dark Cults* (1983) had already allowed players to use card play to create newly minted ghost stories, but used a turn-based system that stopped particularly gifted storytellers from running away with the game — which for me is one of the extra joys *Once Upon a Time* sometimes brings. The game doesn't allow rules to get in the way, either, which means the storytelling always wins. My own private theory holds that an occasional but always riotous round in the venerable BBC Radio comedy panel game *I'm Sorry I Haven't a Clue*, in which opposing teams have to force a shared story to their own particular punchline, was far more of an influence.

James Wallis later took the storytelling approach to more rarefied climes, with his deceptively brief but critically applauded *The Extraordinary Adventures of Baron Munchausen*. That game centers even more upon the group having a shared goal of telling a great story, rather than winning by the act of laying the best cards. (In passing I'm of two minds about mentioning James's similarly inspired but tragically unpublished crime story game, *Cop Show* — working title: *Get Your Trousers On, Love, You're Nicked*.) Meanwhile, *Once Upon a Time* was expanded with both a new set of cards bearing darker words and phrases for spookier *Dark Tales* (2004) and a spare set for creating your own, should you need them.

Whether expanded or not, *Once Upon a Time* remains a great way to bring the very young into the rarefied world of gaming, and is just as good for breaking the ice with any clutch of strangers who sit down at a table for the first time, having been persuaded to check out the wonderful world of hobby games for the first time.

When he's had a few, MARC GASCOIGNE has been known to claim to have co-written two of the three bestselling British roleplaying games of all time — Games Workshop's original *Judge Dredd Roleplaying Game* and Puffin's mass-market Advanced Fighting Fantasy trilogy — and published the very top selling, *Warhammer Fantasy Roleplay*. He's also written and edited for Chaosium, West End, and FASA in his day, and had his name on more than 70 books, gaming supplements, and board games. He now spends his days roleplaying at being general manager of Games Workshop's BL Publishing division, making books, board games, and RPGs. He lives in Nottingham with his wife and two small children.

Mike Bennighof on
PANZERBLITZ

KEY DESIGNER: JAMES F. DUNNIGAN

AVALON HILL (FIRST EDITION, 1970)

I MUST HAVE BEEN 12 years old, which would put it in the mid-1970s, when I first ran across *PanzerBlitz*. Kevin Davidson from my Scout troop sold me the game in its garish black-and-orange box for two dollars. I wasn't that sure about spending two whole dollars on this thing, and had not the slightest idea that I'd just started something that would last for the next 30 years.

The game had not been played, but over the next few years I would take care of that, playing it endlessly solo and hundreds of times against other teenagers. The brown and gray counters became very worn. It was different from every other game released to that point — it had ranged fire. For the first time in a wargame, you "shot" at the other guy's units. At a time when video games consisted of *Pong* and *Space Invaders* (arcade version only), this was pretty cool.

A lot of people apparently thought so; *PanzerBlitz* became one of the best-selling games of all time and is sometimes considered the bestselling traditional wargame ever. Somewhere north of a quarter-million copies were produced and sold during its heyday (just how many of them were actually played is an open question). These days a very good wargame release can sell 10,000 copies — way better than roleplaying games, but a pale shadow of the golden era.

So what is this game all about?

PanzerBlitz comes with 176 pieces each for the Germans and Soviets, portraying platoons (for the Germans) or companies (for the Soviets) of tanks, infantry, and artillery. It has a dozen scenarios, or separate game situations, each supposedly based on a battle that took place on the Eastern Front in 1943 or 1944. Instead of individual battle maps, there are three hexagon-covered geomorphic playing boards that you configure for each scenario based on the little diagram on the scenario card. Each side has objectives to meet to win the game, usually capturing towns or eliminating enemy units.

The tank pieces have silhouettes of the actual tanks on them, something I'd never seen before back when I was 12. The pieces don't represent specific units, but rather generic platoons and companies that you combine to make up the regiments and brigades in the game. And it comes with a chart showing just how many of each go into a higher-level unit, plus another one describing how many men and weapons make up each playing piece. Back in the '70s, this made it all seem a very accurate re-creation.

After a while, I began to want to play with other pieces and create other battles. Struck by variant articles in the old Avalon Hill *General* magazine, I began to make up my own. It was the start of a game design career that's lasted now for over 25 years. I added Finnish troops and scenarios, even though the three boards had the wrong terrain for Finland. And Italians and Romanians and helicopters and stuff I can't even remember, and then I began to get them published in various magazines.

"Painted wings and giant rings make way for other toys," Peter Yarrow wrote not long before I was born, and he had the cycle down pretty well. By the time I entered college, I began to understand more of what *PanzerBlitz* was trying to depict. And the more I understood, the more I saw that it did not depict it very well. Much like little Jackie leaving Puff behind, it was a sad transition.

PanzerBlitz relies solely on odds-based combat results. Given the number of radical new concepts it contains compared to other wargames of the time, it probably had to stick to tried-and-true convention in at least some areas. *PanzerBlitz* is also an artifact of the Cold War. All sophisticated games tell a story, either openly, in the case of roleplaying games, or more subtly, in the case of board games. The story in *PanzerBlitz* is one of heroic Germans holding off hordes of "Russians," drawing on the lies defeated German generals told in their memoirs.

History is not about the past, any more than science fiction is about the future. In each case, they tell a story about the present — and if they're to gain an audience, they tell the story that the present wants to hear. In the mid-1970s, with defeat in Vietnam weighting the American psyche and the Red Army of Workers and Peasants looming across the Iron Curtain, the thought that outnumbered Germans had performed so heroically proved a comfort. After all, the U.S. Army had beaten the living hell out of the Nazis. So by simple math, A > B > C, maybe we didn't have to fear defeat in the coming war we all believed inevitable.

And *PanzerBlitz* accomplishes something that few other wargames have managed, though I try to re-create the effect in every game I design: It uses very simple mechanics to put across a complex historical narrative. Just the differences in values between the various pieces tells a story of tank design and employment, for example. And with generic pieces, the game is infinitely re-playable — another startling concept for its era.

When *PanzerBlitz* was new, there was no Internet. Were it released today, it would quickly attract a hail of hate mail declaring the game "broken" (the favorite epithet of today's angry gamer). Balancing that, the play experience of thousands of gamers would identify its flaws and probably fix them fairly easily.

PanzerBlitz also pre-dates the widespread popularity of *Dungeons & Dragons* and the raft of roleplaying imitators that followed. That helps explain its sales figures, but also meant it was never marketed on the "core/supplement" model that *D&D* brought to the hobby games industry. *PanzerBlitz* stood alone, with no modules or expansion sets, just a pair of very loosely related sequels that were never labeled as "PanzerBlitz Series Games." That kept its rules static, and gave its fans little reason to keep playing once they tired of its dozen scenarios.

Still, *PanzerBlitz* has to stand as one of the most influential games in our industry's brief history. Board games like *Panzer Grenadier*, *Advanced Squad Leader*, and *Memoir '44* are its direct descendants; so are computer games like *Panzer General*, *Steel Panthers*, or *Close Combat*.

PanzerBlitz may be a flawed foundation, but it's one that's supported the play of millions of gamers and has allowed me to make a living. So while I haven't broken out my copy of *PanzerBlitz* in over 20 years and probably never will again, I look at the box every day and smile.

MIKE BENNIGHOF, Ph.D., has been designing games since the early 1980s, working on over 100 titles as designer or developer. A Fulbright Scholar, he holds a doctorate in History from Emory University, has played and coached semi-pro football, taught college, worked as a newspaper reporter, shoveled gravel professionally, and currently is president of Avalanche Press, Ltd., the largest publisher of traditional board wargames in the known universe. He's won Origins Awards both for wargame design (*U.S. Navy Plan Orange*) and roleplaying game design (*Celtic Age*). He has never set foot in a Taco Bell. He scripted the acclaimed *Panzer General II* and *Destroyer Commander* computer games, among others; designed such games as *Survival of the Witless*, *Panzer Grenadier*, and *Great War at Sea*; and was the author of the infamous "naked lady pirate book," *Black Flags*. He speaks four languages and can still run the 40-yard dash in 4.6 seconds.

PARANOIA

KEY DESIGNERS: GREG COSTIKYAN, DAN GELBER,
ERIC GOLDBERG, KEN ROLSTON
WEST END GAMES (FIRST EDITION, 1984)

TRUST THE COMPUTER! THE COMPUTER IS YOUR FRIEND!

PARANOIA IS A DEEPLY subversive game that distorts, subverts, and mocks all
the classic tropes of roleplaying. It was released in 1984; the current edition, from
Mongoose Publishing, could be called the sixth, since it follows the fifth, even
though the fifth followed the second. . . . But we digress. For me, the first edition
remains the purest *Paranoia*, with the best supplements, though beyond a doubt
the second edition rules are faster and smoother.

STAY ALERT! TRUST NO ONE! KEEP YOUR LASER HANDY!

In *Paranoia*, players take on the roles of Troubleshooters — very low-level
enforcers of law and order in a world that already has far too much of both. The
citizens of Alpha Complex are interchangeable cogs in The Computer's badly broken utopia. They eat vat-brewed algae and wash it down with Bouncy Bubble
Beverage. They never see daylight. They have gender, but no sex. Their lives hang
on the whims of dozens of competing groups and a mad Artificial Intelligence.
And they are told that they live in the best of all possible worlds.

THE COMPUTER WANTS YOU TO BE HAPPY. UNHAPPINESS IS TREASON.
ARE YOU HAPPY, CITIZEN?

I admire *Paranoia* intensely. Not just because it's fun to play — though it is!
Not just because it so effectively evoked the fears of the early 1980s. But because
it was the first sophisticated parody of the basic tropes of roleplaying. *Paranoia*
didn't offer dungeons full of monsters with sillier names than those in *D&D*. It
introduced something scarier . . . the futuristic tunnels of Alpha Complex, in

which all the monsters were human and nobody ever got out. *Paranoia* held all of roleplaying, as it was then practiced, to a dark and twisted mirror. Then it threw cream pies.

Jim Holloway's brilliant drawings for the original edition (accept no substitutes, Citizen!) show the Troubleshooters not as heroes, but as earnest, out-of-shape, and often terrified Everymen. The two iconic *Paranoia* images are the video monitor showing the latest treacly homily or incomprehensible directive from The Computer . . . and the smoking boot that is all that remains of a Troubleshooter just trying to do his job. (Or, as the case may be, of a commie mutant traitor, righteously terminated by the loyal servants of Alpha Complex. Take your pick.)

So what makes *Paranoia* such an effective send-up of the dungeon crawl subgenre? At first look it has nothing to do with dungeons at all; it's a science fiction game. But, ah, when you look more closely, it's all about the power-mad dungeon master, the trite plots, the murderous players. . . .

The deck is utterly and totally stacked against the characters. If a *D&D* dungeon master is God, the game master of a *Paranoia* game is the mother of all uber-Gods. The life of every player character is in the GM's hands from the moment the game starts, and the proper *Paranoia* atmosphere requires no mercy:

★ Each PC must take a mutation at character generation. But being a mutant is treason.

★ Each PC must be a member of a secret society. Being a member of a secret society is treason.

★ Any knowledge of "outside," or of the days before the establishment of Alpha Complex, is treason. Just try to go a couple of hours without any treasonous table talk.

★ Questioning The Computer, or the instructions of anyone who outranks you, is treason.

★ However, following the orders of a traitor, even if he is your direct supervisor, is also treason.

★ The GM's book is classified at a level higher than that given to the characters. Showing knowledge of the rules or other information in the GM's book is treason.

★ Treason is punishable by death.

Just as the stereotypical roleplayer reacts to character death by creating another, very similar character, the *Paranoia* player returns instantly to play when his character is killed . . . with a literal clone of that character. Every citizen of Alpha Complex exists as a set of six numbered clones, and when one is killed, he is immediately replaced by the next one. Problems of logic are ignored; if Citizen Ted-Y-BER-1 is discovered to have a traitorous mutation, shouldn't Ted-Y-BER-2 through -6 be terminated immediately? Evidently not! Problems of logistics are waved off as the trivia they are; if Ted-Y-BER-3 is killed in a remote part of the complex while the party is out of communications range, how does Ted-Y-BER-4 show up instantly? Don't ask! After all, Citizen, this is how The Computer says it should work. Surely you are not questioning The Computer!

RUMORS ARE TREASON. WHAT RUMORS HAVE YOU HEARD TODAY?

The typical dungeon-crawl RPG starts with the party as nominal allies, but often descends to backstabbing. *Paranoia* often gets to the backstabbing within the first two minutes of play. If you can trick a fellow Troubleshooter into saying something treasonous during the initial briefing, your duty to The Computer is to terminate him instantly. You might do this because your secret society has given you a covert mission, and he might threaten that mission. You might want the equipment he's been issued. Or you might do it just for fun.

FUN IS MANDATORY, CITIZEN.

The classic dungeon-crawl RPG starts in a tavern, where a Little Old Man gives the characters a map and sends them on a quest to find riches and right wrongs. The standard *Paranoia* game starts in a briefing room — or, for variety, with the PCs being awakened in their dormitory and asked why they are not already in the briefing room. During the briefing, one or more non-player characters, with their own axes to grind, will give the Troubleshooters a rough idea of what they are expected to accomplish for the glory of The Computer, and the terrible consequences of failure.

Attempts to get actual, useful information will be met by stonewalling, suspicion, or laser fire, depending on whether the briefer is genuinely ignorant or the Troubleshooters are already being set up as patsies. An experienced player group will get into the spirit of things by seizing on each others' words to launch accusations of treason, which are inevitably followed by laser fire. It's not unusual for every character to lose at least one clone before the briefing is over.

TRAITORS ARE EVERYWHERE!

And just as the traditional dungeon-crawl RPG then leads its characters through the armory and the magic shop to gear up, *Paranoia* takes the hapless Troubleshooters to R&D. There they will be issued complex equipment of the sort that our favorite Coyote orders from Acme. But the Acme stuff is far more reliable. If the gadgets come with instructions, they'll be wrong. If there are no instructions, a wise Troubleshooter won't ask. It's treason to request documents above your clearance level! Nevertheless, the Troubleshooters will be held responsible for any malfunction and required to fill out many, many forms . . . unless they can hang the blame on an enemy of The Computer. Traitors are everywhere!

THE COMPUTER IS HAPPY. THE COMPUTER IS CRAZY.
THE COMPUTER WANTS YOU TO BE HAPPY. THIS WILL DRIVE YOU CRAZY.

Key tropes of *Paranoia* include:

VIOLENCE: Characters should shoot first and ask questions later, if ever. After all, everyone superior to you will claim to speak for The Computer, and questioning The Computer is treason.

BUREAUCRACY: Alpha Complex is strictly hierarchical, with many competing hierarchies. Everything is pigeonholed. (Where did you hear about pigeons, Citizen? Pigeons are an Outside thing. Keep your hands high in the air and think carefully about your answer. . . .)

CONTRADICTION AND SKEWED LOGIC: It's possible to play *Paranoia* without irony, but why bother?

THE NAME GAME: Character names in *Paranoia* follow a specific pattern — a genuine first name, one of the spectrum letters ROYGBIVU, and any three-letter sequence. Part of the fun is to create evocative (or just stupid) names that fit the pattern and match the character's secret society or Alpha Complex job. Low-level ones for characters, like Sid-R-THA (a member of the Mystics) or Bob-O-LNK (who reports to the Sierra Club). High-level ones for non-player characters, like the cyborg Mark-V-OGR and the mad food chemist Sam-I-AMM.

STAY ALERT! TRUST NO ONE! KEEP YOUR LASER HANDY!

You've made it through R&D. You have your equipment. You probably have at least three clones left. Your directive, then: Find a GM with a sense of humor. Find a copy of this classic — first edition for style, second for clean rules, or the current Mongoose edition, which was formerly tagged *XP* and is now called just *Paranoia*. (Most *Paranoia* fans would advise you to avoid the fifth edition; publishing it was treason.) And play. If you can get your hands on John M. Ford's brilliant adventure, *The Yellow Clearance Black Box Blues*, so much the better. No one knows what's in the Black Box, but everyone wants it; the situation becomes one "where ignorant armies clash by night," with the players directing the lowest and most ignorant recruits.

"Night? No, I didn't say 'night.' Night is an Outside thing. I meant, uh, 'nightcycle,' of course. No! Don't shoot. . . !"

STEVE JACKSON has been designing games since 1976. His first professional work was for Metagaming, which published his *Ogre, G.E.V., Melee, Wizard,* and other titles. In 1980, he went independent. *Raid on Iran* was an immediate success. The next year, Steve Jackson Games released *Car Wars* , followed shortly by *Illuminati*, and later by *GURPS*, the "Generic Universal Roleplaying System." In 1990 the Secret Service invaded his office, confiscating equipment and manuscripts in a misguided "hacker hunt." With the help of the Electronic Frontier Foundation, SJ Games took the government to court and won. His current big hit is *Munchkin*, a very silly card game about killing monsters and taking their stuff.

PENDRAGON

KEY DESIGNER: GREG STAFFORD

WHITE WOLF (FIFTH EDITION, 2006)

IN THE MID-1980S two divergent design philosophies appeared in the roleplaying industry. On the one hand you had universal systems meant to apply to all possible genres. *GURPS* (1986) is the best-known example of this type of game. On the other hand you had systems that were increasingly specialized for precise settings. *King Arthur Pendragon* (1985), by Greg Stafford, is not only one of the finest examples of the latter sort of game, but is often held up by designers to show how powerful creating a game for an individual setting can be.

The background of *Pendragon* is, of course, the tale of Arthur and his Round Table, particularly as described in Sir Thomas Malory's *Le Morte D'Arthur*. *Pendragon*'s game system is a distant cousin to Chaosium's *Basic Role-Playing* that offers simpler gameplay. Characters are defined by statistics and skills, and the skills can be individually increased through usage.

Part of the beauty of *Pendragon* lies in the fact that the whole game is designed to simulate Arthurian stories. Players play knights — not thieves, men-at-arms, clerics, or magicians (except in the out-of-print fourth edition, which did introduce Celtic magic). They duel in tournaments, feast in great halls, and quest for the glory of their lord. This knightly milieu is further highlighted by an innovative system of "personality traits" and "passions."

Legendary Arthurian Britain was a place of strong emotions. Christianity and Paganism clashed, just as Rome sought to chain the independent British spirit. Each of these cultures had different moral ideals, and it is those ideals that come to the forefront in *Pendragon*'s personality traits. To use the game's terms, a pagan is energetic, generous, honest, lustful, and proud, while a Roman Christian is chaste, forgiving, merciful, modest, and temperate.

Each of these traits is embodied through an opposing pair of mental characteristics such as just/arbitrary and modest/proud. A character starts out with values in each pair of traits that add up to 20. These values will then change during play: when a knight acts in a way appropriate to a trait — by, say, demanding a defeated foe be treated justly by the local lord — the game master awards increases to that trait (just), and the opposed trait (arbitrary) decreases, as well.

Through continued change a character can eventually qualify for magical rewards appropriate to his culture and religion, such as improved constitution or mystical armor. These rewards encourage players to act in knightly ways appropriate to the setting, while at the same time setting up the pivotal cultural conflicts that defined Arthurian Britain.

Pendragon's passions are similar to personality traits, but they reflect the more tragic and uncontrollable emotions depicted in Malory's *Le Morte D'Arthur*. Just as Lancelot slept with his king's wife, and later slew Sir Gareth and many other knights to save her from burning, so the players might also be possessed by destructive and irrational fervors. *Pendragon*'s passions include fears, loyalties, loves, and hatreds. They help make the player knights into fully realized characters who sometimes act tragically — just like King Arthur, Sir Lancelot, Queen Guinevere, and the rest of the Round Table.

Together these personality traits and passions add a new, moral dimension to *Pendragon*, one that appeals to parents, educators, and others concerned with the content of roleplaying games. Characters are required to face difficult ethical and emotional challenges, but always have guides at hand. The "Twelve Rules of the Round Table," featured in the supplement *Book of Knights* (2000), includes such dictates as "to injure no one needlessly" and "to practice religion most diligently."

Another way in which *Pendragon* reflects the thematic content of *Le Morte D'Arthur* is through the genealogical and generational components of its character design rules. Malory's story is very much about families. Uther Pendragon becomes king of Britain to avenge his brother, Aurelius Ambrosius. The feud between Lot of Orkney and Pellinore of Listenoise, and their families, motivates the actions of several important figures throughout the tale, and contributes to Camelot's doom.

During character creation, a *Pendragon* player learns not just about his character's immediate past, but also about the adventures had by his father and grandfather. This emphasizes the character's place within a larger web of relationships. Then, after each adventure, characters are assumed to "winter," and a year passes. Over months of play, this mechanic ages characters rapidly. And when a knight character becomes too old to adventure, a player creates his successor, an heir who shares some of his sire's characteristics, but is unique in other ways.

238 ★ Hobby Games: The 100 Best

Each characters's family tree grows from the fertile soil of Arthurian legend. The core *Pendragon* rulebook outlines the Matter of Britain in broad strokes, from the reign of King Uther to the death of Arthur at the disastrous battle of Camlann. The Matter is handled in much greater detail in *The Great Pendragon Campaign* (2006), an impressive 429-page tome that describes the whole story, chronicling every year from 485 to 566, with lists of court events and battles for each summer. It also includes about 100 short adventures scattered across this history. Still, game masters are not required to tie their own campaigns to any specific events; it's up to each gaming group to determine where and how its shared story intertwines with the complicated tale of Camelot's rise and fall.

Many roleplaying games have attempted to construct a compelling metaplot, a controlling storyline that defines the direction of the entire game line. However, such storylines very often suffer from the lack of a unified vision. Not so with *Pendragon*. From the start, the game has developed against a clear and consistent narrative, one with a beginning, middle, and end well known to its players. How they interact with that familiar story and strive, through their characters, to face the moral challenges it depicts and embody the noble ideals it promotes — that is the heart of the *Pendragon* gaming experience.

King Arthur Pendragon could be lauded as a top RPG solely based upon the innovation it brought to the industry. Its concentration on epic storytelling and its traits mechanic were both notable and original when the game was released in 1985. However, even today, *Pendragon* remains vital. It provides a picture-perfect model of literary knighthood and, through its well-crafted and well-considered design, effortlessly conjures its theme — so successfully, in fact, that few other publishers in the last 20 years have even tried to bring another Arthurian roleplaying game to market. You just can't improve on perfection.

Although originally produced by Chaosium, and later Green Knight Publishing, *Pendragon* is now published by ArtHaus, an imprint of White Wolf. Their line currently consists of the fifth edition of the core rules and *The Great Pendragon Campaign*. Older editions of the game were supported by numerous regional and cultural supplements, as well as several adventures, all of which can enhance a *Pendragon* campaign. However it is the White Wolf edition of the core rulebook that stands as the most perfect embodiment of this brilliant game.

★   ★   ★

SHANNON APPELCLINE has been involved in the roleplaying industry since
he sold a Dragon magazine index to TSR in 1990. He served on the staff
at Chaosium for a two-and-a-half-year stint and has freelanced as a writer
for such games as *Ars Magica*, *HeroQuest*, *Nephilim*, *Pendragon*, and
RuneQuest. He now works for the online game company Skotos Tech,
oversees the hobby game-related website RPGnet, and writes board game
articles for *Knucklebones* magazine. His current all-consuming project is
a history of the RPG industry, with particular focus on the companies and
games that make it so interesting. The series is being previewed at
www.rpg.net as "A Brief History of Game." The story of *Pendragon*
appears in the third, fifth, and twelfth columns in the series.

PIRATE'S COVE

KEY DESIGNERS: PAUL RANDLES, DANIEL STAHL

DAYS OF WONDER (ENGLISH EDITION, 2003)

I FIRST BECAME ACQUAINTED with *Pirate's Cove*, sadly, at the wake of Paul Randles — one of the game's designers, and one of the nicest men I'd ever had the privilege of knowing. I knew Paul from working at Wizards of the Coast, where he was known as "Papa Christmas" for his practice of keeping a Christmas stocking full of candy at his desk, for everyone to enjoy, free of charge. (All you had to do to get the free candy was say, "Every day is Christmas!")

About a year after he left Wizards, Paul discovered he had pancreatic cancer. He and his wife quickly exhausted their savings paying for treatments and medication — but, as pancreatic cancer is invariably terminal, it was just a matter of time.

While at Wizards, I never had a chance to give *Pirate's Cove* a try. I was mostly into roleplaying, and on those rare occasions when my friends wanted to play something else, another game always took precedence. So, after Paul's death, I really just wanted to pick up a copy as a memento, but, after I'd tried it just once, I was hooked. And I wasted no time getting my friends hooked, as well.

Pirate's Cove isn't exactly a simulation of historical events, despite the inclusion of legendary pirates such as Edward "Blackbeard" Teach, Ann Bonny, and Mary Read. It's more of a simulation of the pirate life — at least, a glamorized and sanitized interpretation of it. The players take on the roles of buccaneers struggling against the Royal Navy, those legendary pirates, and most commonly, each other, while trying to collect as much treasure as possible to bury on Treasure Island, thus gaining fame points and becoming "Most Famous Pirate." In other words, the player with the most gold wins — which, for my Hollywood-colored vision of piracy, is a pretty accurate simulation.

The gameplay of *Pirate's Cove* combines strategy, resource management, hidden information (and bluffing), random events, and straightforward, easily grasped rules into an extraordinarily fun and engaging game. But, like many other award-winning board games, it's "complexity-ready." That means that the further you get into any given game of *Pirate's Cove*, the more complex the rules become.

For my money, that last bit is the crucial part. If *any* game is too complex for the basics to be summed up in less than a couple thousand words, it's probably too complex for the average novice player; the lighthearted treatment *Pirate's Cove* gives its subject matter and the simplicity of its core rules make it just too charming to exclude those casual players. To succeed in holding those players after a few sessions, though, it needs to offer more.

So *Pirate's Cove* has its complexities, as well — and it handles them rather elegantly. The treasure cards to be found on the five outer islands (Tavern Island, Hull Island, Sail Island, Cannon Island, and Crew Island) are randomly assigned and revealed one per location per turn, giving the players a major decision point: the choice of destinations. This also entails a significant temptation to risk each others' cannons for a chance at the best loot.

Out of this opening step grows a nice combination of game elements including hidden information, strategy, and bluffing. As each player secretly sets his course with his cleverly designed captain's wheel, he's not only betting on where his opponents are likely to go (and, therefore, whether or not he's likely to have to fight for his treasure), he's establishing an overall strategy for the eventual endgame.

The beauty of the fame-focused victory condition is that there are three viable routes to collect fame, each appealing to a different play style. A cautious player might avoid the other players as much as possible and go for the *second*-best treasure every turn, racking up treasure without risking a confrontation with one or more opponents. On the other hand, a bolder player might keep his ship reasonably well outfitted — upgrading his speed and combat readiness — and fight the other players for the best treasures on the board every turn. And an aggressive player might upgrade his ship at every opportunity and spend the game hunting legendary pirates for their fame points — after getting in some combat practice for the big matches by beating up on the other players.

Once hostilities commence, combat between players is hardly gentle. The best strategy is the most obvious: Shoot at the weakest section of your opponent's ship (hull, cannon, crew, or sail) until there's nothing left and your opponent loses the fight. He then has to return to Pirate's Cove — the game's "safe" port, usually known among our group as "Crybaby Island." He gets to keep his ship, though at the cost of repairs to get it seaworthy again. Bad luck in a fight can steer a player's strategy completely off course, so only the best-prepared ship can reasonably expect to come out ahead — and only the luckiest player can expect to come out of a fight unscathed.

Fortunately, things need not get mired in combat at every turn, which brings up another of the game's decision points: A player can choose to flee, rather than fight. Of course, that's not necessarily a wise move. Despite the obvious advantage of avoiding grievous damage by running from a battle, turning tail can cause the crew to mutiny, which takes all of the player's gold and treasure and damages his reputation. The latter translates to a fame point penalty, too. In this way, the mechanics help establish the game's mood and subtly reward play that honors it.

Combat with a legendary pirate is considerably more deadly than a skirmish with another player's buccaneer, and it takes either a well-prepared or lucky player to win the fight — or a group of players working together. Of course, such a coalition might not last any longer than the alliances of real pirates ever did. Once the legendary pirate is off the map, the players still have to deal with each other — at which point they can fight it out to the bitter end, or quietly go their separate ways (perhaps to face the disappointment of their potentially mutinous crews).

On the other hand, a few trips to Tavern Island can garner a decent array of rewards, in the form of tavern cards. These can be purchased at the island for two gold and offer a variety of interesting possibilities, from wise old parrots to mastercraft ship upgrades, secret maps to such battle tricks as smoke screens and augmented grapple attacks. But the cards are purchased blindly, so spending the time and money at the island is a risk that may not be rewarded the way a player hopes.

It is entirely within the scope of the game for a player to get by without ever participating in a single battle, and sometimes even to win with that strategy. (My girlfriend's mother — a casual board game player — has won some 12 out of 14 games of *Pirate's Cove* taking that tack.) It is also within the game's scope for a player to come from behind at the last moment, so there's no reason to despair at what might, in another game, seem an insurmountable gap.

As a roleplayer from way back, *Pirate's Cove* also amuses me in that it seems to lend itself to campy pirate characterizations, just by virtue of play styles and situations. Attacking another player's ship frequently produces a hearty "Avast ye!" Take a bit of hull damage and it's "Shiver me timbers!" And a trip to Crybaby Island for repairs is often the occasion for a disconsolate "Yarr." On one hand, it's just getting into the spirit of the game — but it's also a rather nice introduction to roleplaying for the neophyte.

All in all, *Pirate's Cove* is a fun game for casual and hardcore gamers alike, and the constantly changing environment means that there's no single, perfect strategy. More to the point, it's an easy game to pick up, and only gets complicated if a player wants to dabble in the subsystems. It's earned a permanent place of honor on my shelf — and that much more admiration for my late friend Paul Randles.

JD WIKER originally hails from Indianapolis, where he began his lifelong love of gaming, starting with his family's collection of board games and the weekly "game night" (usually consisting of *Life*, *Monopoly*, or *Clue*). He designed his first game — a mash-up of *Stratego* and *Tank Battle* (but with a fantasy theme, so it wasn't that much of a ripoff) — in 1977, and discovered *Dungeons & Dragons* while buying miniatures to use as playing pieces. JD is best known for his work on Wizards of the Coast's version of the *Star Wars Roleplaying Game*, including *The Dark Side Sourcebook*, *The Hero's Guide*, and *The Galactic Campaign Guide*. After leaving Wizards in 2002, he founded The Game Mechanics, and is the company's president and lead roleplaying game designer, with credits including *Artifacts of the Ages: Swords & Staves* and the City Quarters series: *Thieves' Quarter*, *Temple Quarter*, and *Arcane Quarter*. JD currently lives and works in the San Diego area.

Richard H. Berg on

PLAGUE!

KEY DESIGNER: STEVEN BARSKY

B&B PRODUCTIONS (1991)

I DON'T REALLY PLAY many games these days. I spend far too much time designing them, and I have the unfortunate burden, when I do play, of watching the game "work" (or not), rather than just sitting back and enjoying it (or not). Then there is the problem of actually coming up with something to write about, in the context of this project. Asking someone for their favorite game is like asking a father which of his children is the favorite, or which book he liked best, which food he likes best, and so on, *ad infinitum*. There really is no cogent answer, as one tends to like a lot of things without ranking or rating them . . . unless you're one of those compulsive list-makers.

However, I promised the editor of this Gaddis-like tome to come up with something, so, after some extended rumination, a large dose of caffeine, and an ersatz visit with a Spiritualist medium, I decided to write about a game that I have had marvelous fun playing, as opposed to one that stands at the pinnacle of game design work. Fun, after all, is the main purpose of this hobby.

The game I've chosen is *Plague!*, a privately published effort from a young British couple — well, they were young when they brought it out — that not only has a nice sense of time and place but contains something almost unheard of in this hobby: Wit and Humor.

Plague! is a theme game, but, unlike far too many "Euros," the game is actually about the theme. (The perfect example of anti-theme might be the immensely popular *Carcassonne*, which is not only dominos with better visuals, but has zippo to do with that magnificent, if touristy, medieval city in the Languedoc region of France.) The theme of *Plague!* is the arrival of the Black Plague in Weymouth, England, in 1348. Handsomely and solidly boxed (especially for a privately published game), with an evocative, witty, albeit sepia-toned cover, the game includes a large, mounted board showing a glaringly pastel, but relatively accurate map of 18th-century Weymouth and Melcombe Regis (that's just one of the humorous time warps the game has, along with vacuum cleaners); a deck of utilitarian cards (no visuals); a sheet of circular cardboard markers of various types that you place, for selection, into a very nice cloth container labeled "The Rat Bag"; a pad of "In Remembrance" sheets for keeping track of all the bodies you are carrying and/or have buried; and a set of rules, four pages, which are mostly clear and written with a nice sense of style and humor.

Basically, each player is trying to become the first to pick up 99 plague victim bodies with his wagon and get them dumped into the burial sites. Sounds like *Chutes and Ladders* for the demented, but it is far from that. The map is a series of streets, down which you move, surrounding blocks of buildings. The player throws two dice: the large one (a 12-sider) is for his wagon; the small one (a d6) is for the nasties — the rats and the fleas, along with an occasional rat-eating cat. With these numbers in mind, that player then picks a card. The cards serve to not only inject some offbeat — and occasionally, rather spurious — information into the game, but they keep the players "honest" by shuffling the situation. Public orders close off streets, strikes by the grave diggers close the burial sites, and a series of cards for the Pied Piper shift the rats all over the board. And then there are the cards that politely — and not so politely — inform you that you are dead. (Our particular favorite is the "Allo, Allo, Allo . . . what have we 'ere" bobby card. Best Lionel Jeffries imitation gets an extra body — house rule.)

Now the player gets a chance to load his wagon. He uses his d12 die roll to move into buildings and pick up the dead — one point spent per box moved, one point per body loaded. Some buildings allow you to load up with the wagon limit of 12 the instant you enter, others double what you already have. However, once entered by a player, that building is off limits for the rest of the game. In the beginning, pickings are fairly easy, as all buildings are open and there are few obstructions. On the other hand, only one of the burial sites is open, the rest being available only from the cards. The burial sites also close down by time limit (literally), so obstructionist players quickly learn how to play slowly or rapidly, as the situation demands.

After a while, wagon movement becomes rather difficult for one other reason: the board becomes littered with rats and fleas, both of which may be moved by the players in their Rat Bag phase (after the wagon moves). Rats block movement, which they do quite effectively because the streets are all one lane. Fleas kill, and players help them do just that by moving them into their opponents' wagons.

Again, all is not in vain, as the worst that can happen when you die is you lose your wagonload of corpses and get resurrected in the stables.

What you eventually get, after a fast and wild opening section, is quite a bit of "what do I move, and where to?" strategizing by all players, as each tries to block off an opponent (or drop a flea on 'im) while keeping his own options open. That's all scrambled not so infrequently by the cards, which move a player clear across the board, close down a burial site, open the sewers for rapid rat movement, or simply give you a touch of the old bubonic while you've got a cart full of a couple dozen rotting corpses that'll put you over the limit to win, if only you could get them over to Clarks Hill.

Plague! is a clever design by the rather dryly witty Mr. Barsky, a chiropodist by trade. Just as you perceive what you think is a maximum strategy, along comes the game to throw that one into the harbor. The system is so random, and the situation changes so quickly, that whatever you were doing at one point has little application 10 minutes later.

Plague! is not a game to play to see who wins, mostly because it is so chaotic and random at times. It is a game that delightfully highlights the fact that, as with many trips, it's not where you're going but how you get there.

Aside from his present stint as a game designer with a production rate efficiency better than that of the alien queen in *Aliens*, RICHARD H. BERG has had more careers than Madonna (with somewhat less financial success). These include, in no particular order, criminal defense trial attorney, media communications consultant, actor, director, author, lyricist, composer, as well as a horrifying stint of six weeks with the IRS. Those interested in his game design work can check out an almost-complete list online at en.wikipedia.org/wiki/Richard_Berg.

Martin Wallace on

POWER GRID

KEY DESIGNER: FRIEDEMANN FRIESE

RIO GRANDE GAMES (ENGLISH EDITION, 2004)

FOR THOSE WHO MIGHT not be familiar with the designer Friedemann Friese, he's the one with the green hair who is responsible for some decidedly odd games. I think the hair helped in the early days, when he used to sell games from a suitcase at the Essen Game Fair — people could recognize him from a distance. The majority of his games have titles beginning with the letter *F*, which must present an upper limit to the total number of games he can put out. And before you say, "Hold on, *Power Grid* does not begin with an *F*," please remember the original game was called *Funkenschlag* when it was released in Germany in 2001.

I did actually play the first version, which used crayons to mark links in the competing power grids. I was impressed with it the one time I played it, but never got the chance to do so again. The new version came out in 2004 with the assistance of Jay Tummelson, of Rio Grande fame. *Power Grid* now had fixed connections, all-new artwork, a proper box, plus lots of wooden dobbers.

I cannot say the game is definitively a classic. What I do know is that it still gets played regularly around the U.K. games scene. The vast majority of board games get dragged out once or twice and are then chucked to one side to collect dust until either auctioned or hidden in the loft by the better half. *Power Grid* has hung around because it has that certain something about it that makes you happy to sit down and play a game, a bit like *Puerto Rico*.

Just in case you have never heard of the game before, let me attempt a quick description. It's all about building power stations and linking them to cities. The power stations are powered by different fuels: coal, oil, waste, wind, and nuclear. The size of a power station determines how many cities it can light up. The power stations come on cards and a clever mechanism ensures that the smaller ones will come up earlier in play than the bigger ones. Power stations only produce electricity if you feed them the right fuel, which you have to purchase. To reach a city you pay to build the connection from a city in your existing grid, which has prompted some people to call *Power Grid* a train game in disguise. The money you get at the end of the turn depends on the number of cities you are lighting up. The first player to connect to a certain number of cities ends the game, with the winner being the person who has lit up the most cities.

When you design a game, the same problems keep cropping up. How you deal with them is the tough part of the art of design.

Order of play in a game can be absolutely crucial. In many well-known games, the mechanism for dealing with the order of play is central, relegating the rest of the design to mere window dressing. Think of *El Grande*, where you bid for turn order, or *Puerto Rico*, where turn order changes for different actions. Imagine those games without the order of play mechanisms they utilize. And there are other options. For my own designs, such as *Age of Steam* and *Struggle of Empires*, I've very often adopted an auction system.

The reason the order of play is so vital for many games is because they are built around resources, and you cannot have the same players getting first choice of whatever good stuff you have on offer every turn. You also want to allow players to position themselves so that they can get the good stuff before other players, or play later in the turn to react to other players' actions.

Power Grid deals with the problem in a simple, but very effective manner. The order is determined by how many cities each player is connected to, from highest to lowest. However, as the game is broken into different phases, the order of play switches between first to last and last to first, usually giving an advantage to the player connected to the fewest cities. This gives *Power Grid* the feel of a 1,500-meter race, where you don't want to break into a lead too early, but at the same time you don't want to lag too far behind the pack. Timing when to break for the lead is a key part of the game, something I usually get horribly wrong.

How to set the price of stuff is another major design quandary. If you simply assign fixed prices to things, you'd better make sure you've got the prices right. You don't want to skew a game by making some things so cheap they become an automatic purchase, while other items so expensive they never get bought.

Power Grid adopts an auction system to determine who gets to buy which power stations, but with some nice twists. Only a small selection of power stations are on display and they have a minimum price — always a good idea to stop the good stuff from going for almost nothing. In addition, you can only buy one station during a turn — but if you fail to bid on a station, you cannot take part in any further auctions during that turn. This leads to some rather nasty choices. Do you start an auction for a power station you might not want and run the risk of being forced to take it, or do you drop out and miss out on the chance to bid on something juicy coming up later in the turn? The price of fuel is also set in a simple manner. As players buy a particular type of fuel the price automatically goes up. Since fuel is purchased in reverse turn order, it's good to be lagging a bit, as you can grab the cheap fuel first. At times, leading players end up not being able to buy any fuel at all — resulting in much merriment all around.

Positive feedback — that is, how one useful action impacts all subsequent actions — is another design beast that has to be driven off with pointed sticks. Any game where the rich get steadily and inexorably richer is potentially broken and the winner could well be determined after the first few turns. Ways to rein in early leaders are not always easy to apply in a simple and effective manner. *Power Grid* deals with this problem through the order of play and also by reducing the returns on cities as you connect to more and more of them. This is a much more effective system of balancing the game then leaving it to other players to gang up on the perceived leader.

Geography can be another important factor in a good design. Many German games lack geography, by which I mean a map on which players mark control of locations. *Princes of Florence* has no geography; neither does *Puerto Rico*. Each player exists in his own world and only interacts in the struggle to get stuff. Geography introduces direct conflict for positions, but contains the seed of a problem. If a player can be hemmed in too easily and his choices limited, then geography becomes a problem. Such a situation can kill a game for a player very early on, leaving him to wait for the session to end or perhaps whine about the unfairness of the other players. *Power Grid* has some of these issues, but ameliorates the effect of geography by allowing players to build in the same locations, but only later on in the game. It is also possible for a player to light up cities unconnected to his current grid, although this is expensive.

Finally, we come to luck. Very often complaints thrown at a game will focus on its luck element. (I know that this happens with my designs — usually with the criticisms of my combat systems.) Personally, I like a little luck in a game; it adds a sparkle of uncertainty. Luck-free games can be rather plodding affairs, prone to analysis paralysis and lacking in the entertainment value of the unexpected and unusual. *Power Grid* has a smattering of luck in the order in which the power station cards are drawn. Once again, this leads to some tough decision making. Do you take one of the power stations on offer or do you chance drawing a better one from the deck? The way the power stations come out in different orders also has a subtle effect on each game, one of the factors contributing to its replay value.

I can see *Power Grid* being played for many years to come, a mark of its emerging classic status. It certainly gets regular outings at my local club. My only gripe would be that I hardly ever win. I've only ever won one game, and that was on the Italian map. Even when I teach the game to newbies I get my rear end handed to me on a platter.

When you design a game, you cannot simply say to yourself, "Hey, today I'm going to design a classic." There's hard work involved, of course, and no small amount of skill. But there's also a spark of *something* that enters into it — call it inspiration or luck or whatever. Sometimes, for reasons you can't entirely explain, the various elements you juxtapose hang together in a natural, pleasing manner. It's nice when that happens, and I'm certain Friedemann is quietly pleased that he produced such a design with *Power Grid*.

MARTIN WALLACE was born and raised in the U.K., and has been resident in Manchester for most of those years. He began gaming in his teens, starting with titles from SPI and Avalon Hill. Like a lot of students of that era, he got into *D&D* — but escaped relatively undamaged. He worked for a while at Games Workshop, then started designing games in earnest in the early '90s, his first DTP game being *Lords of Creation*. Eventually German companies picked up a few of his games, such as *Und Tschüss*, *Volldampf*, and *Tempus*. He has also published a number of games through his own company, Warfrog. These include such titles as *Struggle of Empires*, *Princes of the Renaissance*, and *Age of Steam*. Martin is now a full-time game designer and lives with his partner, Julia, and her two children, Robert and Hannah, in one of the less expensive suburbs of Manchester. As well as designing games Martin enjoys walking, reading, squash, and lazing about.

Tom Wham on

PUERTO RICO

KEY DESIGNER: ANDREAS SEYFARTH

RIO GRANDE GAMES (ENGLISH EDITION, 2002)

I FIRST DISCOVERED THE wonderful board game *Puerto Rico* when I attended the last Milwaukee Gen Con game fair in 2002. (The convention has since moved to Indianapolis.) This was a sad occasion for an old gamer who used to work for TSR and has been to all but two Gen Cons. But enough about that. . . . At this particular Gen Con, some of my best friends were involved in a tournament at the Rio Grande Games area, so I went to watch — and immediately fell in love with Andreas Seyfarth's masterpiece. I played it a couple times that year, then bought a copy and took it home to foist upon the rest of my gaming buddies.

The game casts you in the role of a Spanish grandee, sent to Puerto Rico during colonial times. Your goal is to develop and colonize the island and make the king of Spain rich. In game terms, this means you must ship goods to the mother country (and in the process score victory points). You accumulate plantations in the hinterlands and build production facilities in the city, where you process the goods produced in the plantations. You must acquire colonists to work your plantations or in the factories. The game inherits and improves upon mechanics I love from Francis Tresham's classic *Civilization* and James Hlavaty's *Outpost*. (The latter's core mechanics can also be seen in Jens Drögemüller's more recent creation, *The Scepter of Zavandor*.) However *Puerto Rico* does what these other games do in much less time and in a more balanced fashion.

The heart of the game is the development of an economic structure, which you create by constructing those aforementioned plantations and factories, then producing goods from them, which are in turn sold or shipped. How you develop this economy, the order in which you handle the various tasks and the importance you put on each during any given round, is up to you. And if you balance your efforts and manage the greed factor well, you build an economy that feeds and grows itself. There are many different paths a player may take to get to that happy place, but eventually all of them help you score victory points.

Even with a full complement of five at the table, *Puerto Rico* keeps everyone involved in the action. At the start of each turn, a player must choose one of seven roles: settler, mayor, builder, craftsman, trader, prospector, or captain. Each comes with a special ability that helps the player with specific aspects of the economy he's trying to develop. The trader gets an extra doubloon of income when he sells goods to the trading house. The craftsman produces an extra good when he works. Taking the role does not exclude the other players from trading or producing goods; for this turn, though, you do the job you've chosen a little better than everyone else. There are some roles — like the prospector — that carry exclusive benefits, but, really, the mechanic is set so that everyone stays involved in all the game's phases. As a player, you're just not going to have time to read a paperback book while waiting to do something.

Resources on the island are not unlimited, so you have to make your choices carefully. Once a resource has been exhausted, you're not going to be able to force any more of it from the ground. And when the colonists or the victory point chips run out, the game comes to an end. The player who has amassed the most victory points is declared the winner.

I was overjoyed in 2004 when I was invited to the Origins game convention. There I met the designer of *Puerto Rico*, Andreas Seyfarth. I got him to autograph my copy of the game, and he taught me how to play *San Juan*, a card game based on *Puerto Rico*. (It has the feel of *Puerto Rico*, but plays with up to eight players, if you put two sets together, and takes less time than its parent.) We played lots of both, and I hope someday to work on a game with Andreas. He's designed or co-designed a number of terrific titles, including such award winners as *Manhattan* and *Thurn and Taxis*. If his name is on a game's box, it's well worth a look.

Not too long ago, the German website Brett Spiel Welt brought *Puerto Rico* to the Internet. It's a nice enough adaptation and you can usually play a game in less time that it takes with real people on a tabletop. It wasn't the first time this classic had been digitized, either. A couple years back, Eagle Games released a smart computer version of *Puerto Rico* that could be played solo, on the Internet, or with up to five friends on a local network. The graphics are much better that those available on Brett Spiel, and I enjoy the music. Sadly, Eagle Games filed for bankruptcy, but if you like *Puerto Rico*, you must have this version of the game!

Much as I like them, however, I find the computer versions of *Puerto Rico* pale beside the original. There's just something about the nice little counters and the social interaction that occurs (not to mention the complaints from those who are losing) when friends gather around an actual table to play with them.

If you haven't had the pleasure of experiencing *Puerto Rico* yet, get yourself to a convention, where you can give the game a try, or, better still, stop by your local hobby shop and pick up a copy to foist on your friends the next time you get together. They'll surely thank you for it.

TOM WHAM became a game designer around age seven, when he got his first *Monopoly* set and immediately began modifying the rules. In 1972, he landed a job with Don Lowry at Guidon Games, in the shipping/lay-out/whatever department of *Campaign* magazine. There he co-authored a set of Civil War naval miniature rules, *Ironclad*. May 1977 found him in Lake Geneva, as employee number 13 of TSR, Inc. After running the Dungeon Hobby Shop for a summer, he was bumped upstairs (literally) to the art department, where he worked with Dave Sutherland and Dave Trampier on the original *Monster Manual*. Then came a deal with Tim Kask, editor of *The Dragon*, to do a game in the centerfold — *Snit Smashing*. This led to other games in *Dragon*, including *The Awful Green Things From Outer Space* (which is still in print today). After TSR, he collaborated on books with Rose Estes, and did his own novelette in Christopher Stasheff's *The Exotic Enchanter*. More games followed, including *Kings & Things* (with Rob Kuntz), the *SimCity* card game, and *Iron Dragon* (the latter two by Mayfair Games). More recent efforts include a reprint of *Snits* from Steve Jackson Games, *Planet Busters* by Troll Lords, and a soon-to-appear game with James M. Ward through Margaret Weis Productions.

Joseph Miranda on

RENAISSANCE OF INFANTRY

KEY DESIGNERS: ALBERT A. NOFI, REDMOND A. SIMONSEN
SIMULATIONS PUBLICATIONS, INC. (*S&T* #22, JULY/AUG. 1970)

THE FIRST WARGAME I played from *Strategy & Tactics* was *Renaissance of Infantry*, published back in 1970. Now, several decades later, I'm editor of that magazine and have over 100 published wargames to my credit. In part, I give credit for both those accomplishments to *Renaissance of Infantry*. While I'd been a wargamer for a couple of years prior, the moment I played this game I realized that I was on to something new.

What made *Renaissance of Infantry* so inspirational? For one thing, it had a theme, and used that theme to demonstrate the course of European battles from the late Middle Ages through the Renaissance. Designer Al Nofi seems to have been influenced by Charles Oman's epic work, *Art of Warfare in the Middle Ages* (both volumes), and his follow-up, *Art of Warfare in the Sixteenth Century*. Oman's work was groundbreaking since he did much to reconstruct actual orders of battle. But he also looked at tactics from what would be today called the combined arms perspective. Heavy cavalry was effective against infantry until infantry took up the pike phalanx or the longbow. The pike phalanxes were in turn broken by different varieties of "weapons systems," usually a combination of missile, sword, and cavalry which, when working together, proved greater than the sum of their parts. Later, as gunpowder came to the forefront, the battlefield was again revolutionized.

All this is in the game. Different troop types have different effects against other types. Heavy cavalry reduce the defense strength of swordsmen by 50 percent; pikes are doubled in defense against cavalry, but halved when attacked by swordsmen; and so forth. The combat results table is constructed in such a manner that no one troop type can cause a decisive outcome. Players have to use their units in the right combination to gain victory — troops with ranged attacks disrupt enemy stacks so melee troops can finish them off. It's all there without a lot of special rules to force the situation. You learn by applying the correct combination of tactics in order to win the battle.

Renaissance of Infantry uses a systems approach to simulation. This goes beyond trying to recreate an individual battle or campaign. Rather, it shows that these individual battles are part of a "universe" of conflict and can be understood more thoroughly by looking at the big picture. Each major system has an algorithm to model its peculiar effects. The combat unit capability chart shows the interaction of different weapons systems in a convenient manner so players can analyze potential outcomes.

Renaissance of Infantry was one of the first wargames to make morale a critical element. As armies in the game take losses they accumulate panic points, and when they reach their panic level they break and head for the hills. You don't have to wipe out an enemy army to win, just inflict sufficient casualties to panic it. Morale rules had been used in miniatures wargaming before *Renaissance*, usually with a lot of extra complications, but this was one of the first attempts to put them into a playable board game format. There was also a rudimentary attempt at command control, with leaders on the field providing die roll modifiers to various actions. This all sounds very mundane today, but back in 1970 it was quite extraordinary.

The game has numerous optional rules: Swiss and Spanish troops can be ferocious, armies are subject to treachery, gunpowder weapons improve as the decades march on, and you can grant a stricken foe the Honors of War in order to reduce casualties on both sides. Even if the orders of battle sometimes appear to be similar, armies have different characteristics. For example, the feudal rule requires heavy cavalry to move and attack an enemy force within a certain range of hexes. This is supposed to show the over-enthusiasm of heavy cavalry for closing with the enemy, although one suspects an element of democratic propaganda on the part of the designers. (The lowly foot troops have much better tactical sense than the high and mighty feudal lords). Ferocious troops create the possibility of enemy forces becoming demoralized when in proximity, thereby allowing a small (ferocious) force to take on a larger (but non-ferocious) force. Instead of playing the numbers game, you can win by exploiting the non-material aspects of battle.

Renaissance of Infantry includes 20 scenarios. The scenario chart is presented in a columnar format which allows you to see how armies literally evolved over several centuries. Battles include Legnano (where the Italian militia trounced Emperor Barbarossa's knights); Crécy and Agincourt (English longbows versus the cream of French chivalry); Scots, Flemish, and Swiss pikemen versus everyone; and various battles of the Italian Wars between the Spanish and French. There are also some hypothetical scenarios, including Renaissance mastermind Niccolo Machiavelli's plan to recreate the Roman legion.

Players can construct new scenarios by using the unit types provided in the counter mix. These include commanders; heavy and light cavalry; professional and militia pikes; swordsmen; various types of missile troops (longbow, crossbow, arquebus); and heavy and light artillery. There are also some optional artillery crews. The rules state that each unit represents about 500 soldiers, though a subsequent article from *Moves* magazine (#3, June 1972) indicates that the proportions are actually 500 for cavalry and 1,000 for infantry (since horsemen take up more space than foot troops). Each unit is rated for its melee attack, defense, and movement factors, and its flank/rear defense. Missile troops additionally have a fire combat factor and range.

The counters use quasi-abstract icons, based on the unit's primary weapon. This is a fairly solid approach, somewhere between the abstract NATO standard symbol system, and what I consider to be the rather overdone picture-of-a-soldier-crammed-onto-a-counter iconography that is all the rage today. *Renaissance of Infantry* gives just the right amount of information so you can figure out which troop type a unit represents.

A typical scenario showing the system's strength is Biococca, 27 April 1522. Biococca was one of those great turning points of warfare, taking place during the seemingly endless Italian Wars. A French army confronted a Spanish-Italian force dug in at the park of Biococca. The French commander, quite sensibly, wanted to maneuver the Spaniards out of their position. But the Swiss contingent in French employ, having their pay in arrears, insisted on immediate battle. So the French attacked and were shot to pieces by the dug-in Spanish arquebusiers, the surviving Swiss being hacked up by mercenary Landsknechts. In the scenario, the Spaniards have improved arquebusiers, pikemen, some sword-and-shield men, cannon, and a few cavalry. The French have pikes, cavalry, crossbows, and also some cannon. The Spaniards start deployed inside of a trench line. As the French commander, you have to figure the best way to dig them out. As the Spanish commander, you have to figure the best way to hold your position with an outnumbered but, for the era, high-tech force. Both sides have different problems they need to solve to win the day.

The game system is expandable. You can create your own scenarios by doing some research and then choosing units and options. The map represents sufficient types of terrain to recreate just about any battle of the era in Western Europe. Map scale is around 100 meters per hex. Interestingly enough, *Renaissance of Infantry* was alternatively titled *Tactical Game 14*, part of a series which gave rise to *Tactical Game 3*, also known as *PanzerBlitz*.

Renaissance of Infantry became the basis for an entire series of SPI tactical games. The first sequel was *Centurion*, covering battles during the era of the Roman Empire. Later games in the series refined various elements, notably command control. SPI eventually published the PRESTAGS series, which provided a unified tactical system from ancient times to the 16th century, and *Renaissance of Infantry* was redesigned as *Yeoman*, dropping some of the optional rules in the process.

Renaissance of Infantry's rules freely state that if players do not like something in the game, they should change it. This was a revolutionary concept back in 1970, and it remains so today. Over the years, I've updated some of the scenarios and added several more, which appear now and then in print and online. There's still a lively discussion about this game. After all these decades, *Renaissance of Infantry* is still marching to battle.

JOSEPH MIRANDA is the editor of *Strategy & Tactics* magazine and has designed over 100 published wargames. Mr. Miranda has also worked for various computer game design firms including HPS Simulations and Hexagon Interactive. He is currently designing a simulation of the struggle for Baghdad for Modern Conflict Studies Group. He is a former U.S. Army officer who has taught unconventional warfare topics at the JFK Special Warfare Center, and more recently has developed courses in terrorism and Middle Eastern conflict for Chapman University. He's been a featured speaker at the USAF Connections simulations conference, the Military Operations Research Society, and the Origins national wargaming convention. He has a complete set of *Strategy & Tactics* magazines, likes off-the-wall wargame topics such as *Plot to Assassinate Hitler*, and has side hobbies in cyberpunk and film noir.

ROBORALLY

BEFORE EVERY GAMER KNEW his name, Richard Garfield was a struggling doctor of mathematics who hoped one day to become a rich and famous game designer like me. He spent several years shopping around a clever little board game called *RoboRally*, and brought the game in 1991 to Seattle roleplaying game publisher Wizards of the Coast. *RoboRally* struck the fancy of CEO Peter Adkison, whose main concern was that the game would be very expensive to print. To help raise the cash needed to produce *RoboRally*, Adkison suggested that Garfield turn his focus to a quick little money maker, a project that eventually became the collectible card game called *Magic: The Gathering*. As a source of start-up cash, *Magic* was a colossal success.

Wizards released *RoboRally* in 1994, with art and character designs by comic book legend Phil Foglio. The game is basically a robot racing game, featuring crazed and suicidal robots, speeding to hit all the flags on a deadly factory floor.

Basic gameplay is simple: players choose from a hand of program cards such as move ahead, turn left, or back up. On every round, each player gives his robot five instructions, and then all the robots execute their programs together. After the fifth instruction, players draw new cards and play another round. This continues until one player's robot has touched every flag.

While following their programs, robots must also deal with board elements such as conveyor belts, walls, pits, and lasers. These elements make it quite a bit more challenging to get around the factory floor. In addition, robots can push and shoot each other, meaning that even a perfect plan can be foiled when an enemy robot interferes. And, since the programmers are only human, not every plan is perfect to begin with.

Programming five turns of movement in advance can be somewhat hairy, even if you aren't required to guess what nearby robots will do. If you misjudge the effect of a board element — a conveyor belt that turns as it moves, for example, or a right-turning gear that you thought was turning left — you will find your robot heading off in a whole new direction. Of course, once you're pushed off course by forces beyond your control, all bets are off.

It's possible for robots to take damage, usually from the lasers on the board or those sported by opposing robots. Damage basically hurts a robot by giving it fewer program cards to choose from. A severely damaged robot might even have some of its registers locked, meaning that it is forced to repeat the same instructions every round.

It's quite easy to die in this game (that's probably not surprising), either from taking a lot of damage, or from stumbling into an instantly fatal trap, like a pit or a crusher. But dying doesn't knock you out of the game. If you take the time to have your robot touch repair spaces along the way, you can retrieve an archive copy (slightly damaged) from the last one you hit.

RoboRally is a great game: strategic, accessible, and well thought-out. It's got plenty of details that don't get in the way of a first-time player, which is hard to achieve. For example, board layouts can be customized for infinite variety, with six boards and hundreds of flag configurations to choose from (as well as multiple expansion boards). Players can improve their robots with upgrade cards like lasers and shields. There is a system of timing rules that covers the interactions of all the program cards, board elements, and option cards. At times, this can feel like too much detail. The first edition rulebook recommends that only one player really needs to know all the hard stuff; everybody else can just get by knowing the easy rules. And they can.

Why is *RoboRally* one of the best hobby games ever? Besides being a completely solid game at heart, *RoboRally* succeeds at one of the hardest tricks in game design: it is genuinely funny. I don't just mean that it has funny jokes in the rules or funny robot characters. It has those things, but putting jokes in a rulebook is relatively easy. The richest humor in this game comes from the play of the game itself.

There's just something funny about a robot that's too badly damaged to receive new commands. Or a robot that's forced (by one of the optional weapons) to copy the program of the robot that shot it. And, of course, there's nothing funnier than a robot falling into a pit. Especially when it's done it twice before, and especially when it did it on purpose, so it might blink back to a better starting point.

While playing their program cards, players unconsciously "do the robot dance," squirming in their seats as they try to predict what their robot will actually do. Several times per game, robots will career off course, either by mistake or thanks to another robot. That's comedy. It's even funny when your own robot dies, because death in this game is so temporary. Just pull a (slightly damaged) archive copy, and get back into the race.

The reason that funny mechanics always trump jokes in the rules is that they will never get old. Okay, saying "Twonky" never gets old either, but in general, once you've heard a joke it gets tired pretty fast. Not so the play of *RoboRally*, which keeps you on your toes throughout the game, and always gives you something fresh to enjoy.

JAMES ERNEST is best known as the founder and head honcho of Cheapass Games, a quirky little game company with more than 100 titles to its credit, including *Kill Doctor Lucky*, *Button Men*, and *Give Me the Brain*. In addition, James has created games for several less-cheap publishers including Rio Grande Games, WizKids, and Wizards of the Coast. He's also an avid poker player and retired professional juggler (no kidding), and currently makes his living in the computer gaming business.

RUNEQUEST

KEY DESIGNERS: STEVE PERRIN, RAY TURNEY, STEVE HENDERSON,
WARREN JAMES, GREG STAFFORD

CHAOSIUM (FIRST EDITION, 1978)

DURING THE SUMMER OF 1978, the hobby gaming world was ready to embrace new ideas that would change the way we roleplayed. A set of game rules housed in a red and brown cover debuted at the Origins game convention in Ann Arbor, Michigan, and heralded the coming of a true second generation of roleplaying designs. The first generation of popular fantasy games — including *Dungeons & Dragons*, *Tunnels & Trolls*, and *Chivalry & Sorcery* — all stayed close to home, as far as the type of experience that they offered. Most took place in an ambiguously generic westernized fantasy world drawn from a host of literary sources, such as *The Lord of the Rings*, Howard's Conan cycle, Fritz Leiber's tales of Fafhrd and the Gray Mouser, and Arthurian lore, with a sprinkling of Greek and Norse mythology to provide fantastic beasties. They restricted the player to a narrowly defined role as a wizard, warrior, thief, or martial cleric. Few, if any, had a unified structure for handling both gameplay and character advancement.

From these foundational sources, roleplayers created their worlds of fantasy and adventure — worlds that would invariably resemble one another as subtle variations on the same pseudo-medieval melange. Wizards cast spells and ran around in robes. Warriors bashed monsters and got to wear all the cool hardware. Thieves snuck about and stole things. Clerics hit things less effectively than warriors, but did so with the blessings of their ambiguous, spell-granting deities. Everyone had a defined role and stuck to it. Player advancement was defined by accumulating experience to advance upward through arbitrary levels of power.

RuneQuest changed all that.

Breaking away from generic fantasy, the game transported players to the vibrant setting of Dragon Pass in Greg Stafford's Glorantha, an archaic world grown from the myths and legends of Bronze Age peoples. Inside the amateurish single rules volume was a well-defined mythology of gods and heroes whose influence is tightly woven into the fabric of the people's lives. *RuneQuest* was not the first RPG to spring out of an established fictional world. M.A.R. Barker's *Empires of the Petal Throne* (*EPT*), based in his deeply detailed world of Tékumel, had broken that ground in 1975. Yet *RuneQuest* made the premise work, made it popular, and drew players into the world of Glorantha in a way that the original *EPT*, based on simplified early *Dungeons & Dragons* rules, never would.

For those of us discovering it for the first time that summer, Dragon Pass and its inhabitants were like nothing seen before. Instead of unrelated groups of monsters lurking amidst ambiguous hex-shaped geography or dwelling in convenient 10' by 10' rooms beneath the ground, we discovered a living environment populated by real-seeming peoples of many cultures and races, not all of them human. Monsters had as much reason for existing as the humans who shared their world.

While new to roleplayers, the world of Glorantha had previously appeared in *White Bear & Red Moon* and *Nomad Gods*, a pair of board games designed by Greg Stafford and produced by Chaosium. In those games, the wars between a powerful empire and the barbarian tribes they sought to subjugate defined the peoples, places, and creatures of the world. It was a rich resource upon which to build a roleplaying game setting.

Glorantha brings to mind what life might have been like in ancient Greece or Mesopotamia, where every event had supernatural significance. It is a world where divine beings need the worship of followers as much or even more than those followers need the abilities gained from their gods. It is a world permeated with magic on all levels. One's place and influence are defined not by arbitrary power levels, but by choices of allegiance and service. To succeed in the world of Glorantha, a player's character has to become enmeshed within the world's complex society and structure.

In the world of *RuneQuest*, heroic adventurers battle frightening foes to preserve their Bronze Age way of life and bring glory and honor upon clan, tribe, or temple. Heroes fight nasty (and I mean *vile*) goat-headed broos, whose diseased touch poisons the world; run in fear from pumpkin-headed jack-o-bears; avoid the gloppy advances of amorphic gorps; dodge the lunges of spring-tailed stake snakes; and bash zombies to flinders to defeat them.

RuneQuest has no player classes (such as wizard, fighter, thief, and the like). No mages who can't fight or wear armor. No warriors limited to just hitting things and absorbing damage. Everyone can try their hands at picking a pocket or a lock. And priests are something you study to become, not a career you choose at the outset of a campaign. Player choices regarding weapons, armor, skills, and magic seem more meaningful because they define who your character is and, more importantly, who he or she will become.

The arms and armor Gloranthan heroes use have more to do with Homer's *Odyssey* than they do with medieval romances. Bronze is the metal of choice, for those rich enough to afford metal. Iron can only be used by powerful Rune Lords and Rune Priests, who gain it through service to their deities. Everyone has access to spirit, or battle magics, but powerful Rune magic is gained only by permanently sacrificing personal power to one's deity.

The *RuneQuest* rules seek to simulate a more realistic type of combat within a simple structure. All player abilities use a unified, skill-based system. Success with a weapon attack or a skill can be determined by a single percentile die roll. Weapon choice matters. Stabbing with a two-handed spear means you have a chance to hit a sword-wielding foe long before he hits you. Armor choice matters, because the hit location mechanic actually makes wearing a helmet relevant to gameplay, not just a fashion choice. Whether one is fighting a foe with a sword, jumping a chasm, or trying to talk a monster out of eating a pal, the same mechanics applies to every action. And if a character succeeds at something, she gets a chance to improve that skill.

In time, *RuneQuest* would be updated to a second and third edition (moving away from its strictly Gloranthan roots). Yet the game had already left its stamp. Its unified combat and skill system would become the foundation for Chaosium's generic *Basic Role-Playing* rules, upon which Sandy Petersen would build his immensely popular *Call of Cthulhu* game, among others. The idea of generic rules would later become the motivation for enduring systems like Steve Jackson Games' *GURPS* and Wizards of the Coast's pervasive d20 System rules.

After *RuneQuest* and Glorantha, detailed fantasy worlds would become the norm, not the exception. Dragon Pass paved the way for TSR's Faerûn, better known as the Forgotten Realms, and Krynn, setting for the Dragonlance saga. But few would ever achieve the elegant but approachable rules complexity of the original *RuneQuest* or instill a fervent loyalty in fans that would span decades.

In the muggy heat of that Michigan summer, *RuneQuest* changed the way we gamed.

★ ★ ★

Paul Jaquays pioneered pre-made RPG scenarios in his *D&D* fanzine *The Dungeoneer* in 1976 and was well known for his enduring game adventures *Dark Tower* and *Griffin Mountain*. He assembled one of the first art and design studios for video game development at Coleco to make ColecoVision games. After working as an illustrator, designer, author, and editor, he returned to computer games in 1997 as a level designer for id Software and currently works as an artist for Microsoft/Ensemble Studios. He helped set up The Guildhall at SMU (Southern Methodist University), one of the foremost schools for digital game development, and continues as an advisor to the program.

Richard Dansky on

THE SETTLERS OF CATAN

KEY DESIGNER: KLAUS TEUBER

MAYFAIR GAMES (ENGLISH EDITION, 1995)

IT IS REASONABLY SAFE to say that if it were not for *The Settlers of Catan*, you might not be reading this book right now.

Seriously. It's that important.

Designed by Klaus Teuber, *Settlers* was originally released in 1995 in Germany by Kosmos, but the game rapidly went global. Thus far it's been translated into 25 languages, won an Origins Award for best science fiction/fantasy board game (1996), and been named to *Games* magazine's Hall of Fame. It's also generated innumerable spinoffs, expansions, and online interpretations, but that's not important. What matters is that despite an unprepossessing appearance — DUPLO-sized hexagonal tiles? Little wooden pieces that look like escapees from the 1960s edition of *Risk*? — *The Settlers of Catan* is one of the most engrossing, enjoyable board games to come down the pike in years.

Settlers is, at heart, a resource-management game. The board is made up of randomly placed hexagonal tiles, all of which (save one) represent one of five raw materials: wood, sheep, wheat, brick, or ore. Each tile is also assigned a number. When the number corresponding to a hex is rolled, then any players who have built a settlement — or a city, if they've gotten greedy — on the corner of that tile collects the appropriate resource. Resources can in turn be traded in for structures (settlements, roads, and cities) to be placed on the board, or for development cards that can provide a boost of one sort or another. Players can also swap resource cards, leading to sudden bursts of construction, changes of fortune, and bouts of horsetrading the likes of which would stand out at a used car dealers' convention for their savagery.

The ultimate goal is to achieve 10 victory points, which can be acquired through a combination of construction and card play. Settlements and cities provide victory points, as do singular achievements, such as building the longest contiguous road on the board, amassing the largest army of soldier development cards, and the like. Half the process is transparent — cities are hard to hide, after all — while half is hidden, which allows players to think they know who's in the lead. Often, they're wrong, which is where things really start to get interesting.

But even with the knowledge of who's winning — or who's about to win, which isn't the same thing — you can't go after the current leader in the way you'd think you might. There's absolutely no direct conflict in the game, no combat whatsoever. Cities cannot be destroyed, roads cannot be demolished, and the "soldiers" you acquire through card purchase can't march off into battle.

And yet, *Settlers* is one of the most cutthroat games imaginable. There may not be direct conflict, but from the moment the board is laid out, there is desperate, bloodthirsty competition for resources. Moreover, the gameplay is as much about preventing opponents from obtaining resources as it is about gathering them yourself. Throwing a road across an enemy's line of advance creates an impenetrable barrier between them and the precious goods toward which they were moving. Or, since settlements can't be built on contiguous corners of a hex, laying one down in just the right spot can often block an opponent from building one of their own, freezing them out from a particular hex and all of the goodies it will generate in the turns to come.

Layered beneath the basic resource acquisition dynamic are a number of elegant secondary mechanics that provide alternate means for players to remain in the game long after primary avenues for advancement have been exhausted. Blocked from a resource? Trade with another player, or build to one of the ports that line the board, which will allow you to transmogrify one resource into another. A certain hex is providing too much loot to a particular opponent? Use a die roll or development cards to maneuver the resource-sapping robber unit onto that hex and, by doing so, cut off its production. No one is ever that far out of the lead, and no player is so far down that they cannot have a tremendous impact on the proceedings.

But that's merely a summary of how you play, more or less. The rules, by themselves, don't convey why this game matters so very much. And yes, it does matter, on a level that is still playing out, a decade after its introduction.

Bearing in mind that, as a game, *The Settlers of Catan* is sheer, unadulterated brilliance, its real importance rests in the fact that it kicked open the door for the current board game revolution in America. In the dark days before *Settlers*, say "board game" and most people figured you meant *Risk* or *Monopoly*, games you played on rainy days at grandma's if you hadn't lost too many of the pieces the last time around. For all the fine work that was being done in the field at the fringes, the general public's perception of the form was both painfully limited and completely outdated.

Then came *Settlers*, and suddenly board games were cool. People played it, and liked it, and told others about it — nay, dragged their friends bodily over to the gaming table and created new converts in great, cheerful mobs. The cult of *Settlers* fans grew astronomically, and as it did, its members realized that there might be other games out there worth playing, too. From that came a renaissance, a flood of creativity that has given us access to new choices such as *Grave Robbers From Outer Space* and *Hey! That's My Fish!* Hobby board games were rediscovered, as with *Arkham Horror*, or imported, or created to meet the new demand. Suddenly, the range of great board game on offer was huge and vital and ever-expanding.

I must confess that I came late to the *Settlers* craze. Friends and professional peers had raved about it at length, but at that time, I was off board games. I was into roleplaying games, after all. A few card games. You know, *sophisticated* stuff.

You may commence laughing, if you wish. I'll wait for you to finish.

There. Feeling better now? Right.

In fact, it wasn't until nearly five years after the game came out that I actually played, frog-marched into a round at a friend's game night. It took about three minutes to pick up the rules, another couple to squint hard enough to be able to differentiate the various resource icons on the reference card, and that was it. I was hooked. Gaffed, even. Hopelessly addicted.

Why? Because for all of its elemental simplicity, it has breathtaking depth and breadth of experience. It's a resource-management game, defined by position and strategizing. It's a social game, defined by horsetrading of resource cards and "Siccing the Fritz" (as my friends call the robber) with bloodthirsty bonhomie. It's a game of chance, ruled by die rolls and card draws. It's a hardcore game and a light social pastime and everything in between, a laboratory where I can test a hundred different play styles and a genuine reason to invite friends over.

And isn't that, really, what board games are for — to provide a structured activity that allows players to compete and socialize simultaneously? I'd like to think so. And if there's a game out there from the past couple of decades that does it better than *Settlers*, I — and a whole lot of other people — haven't found it yet.

★ ★ ★

The manager of design at Red Storm Entertainment and central Clancy writer for Ubisoft, **RICHARD DANSKY** has worked on numerous video games, including *Splinter Cell: Double* Agent and *Rainbow Six: Black Arrow*. Prior to his involvement in the video game industry, he spent four years as a developer for White Wolf on games such as *Wraith: The Oblivion* and *Vampire: The Dark Ages*. He has written, designed, or otherwise contributed to over 100 RPG books. Richard's next novel, *Firefly Rain*, will be published in January of 2008. He lives in North Carolina with his wife and their two inevitable cats, who make it a point not to tell him about their characters.

Ken St. Andre on

SHADOWFIST

KEY DESIGNERS: ROBIN D. LAWS, JOSE GARCIA
DAEDALUS ENTERTAINMENT (1995)

OF ALL THE COLLECTIBLE card games, *Shadowfist* is, in my opinion, the most pure fun. I've played all the big ones — *Magic, Legend of the Five Rings, Pokémon, Yu-Gi-Oh!, Star Wars* — and I'll take *Shadowfist* over the others any time. This is not to say that *Yu-Gi-Oh!* and the rest aren't fun. They're great games, but . . .

Shadowfist made its debut in 1995, two years after *Magic* established a new genre of gaming. Designed by Robin Laws and Jose Garcia, *Shadowfist* borrows heavily from that earlier game. The similarities in mechanics and presentation are considerable. Both games require players to turn cards to indicate that they have been played. *Magic*'s land cards equate to feng shui sites for producing power. Characters and monsters have costs, strengths, and special abilities. Spells equate to events, and artifacts are the same as states. Both games feature exceptionally good art on all the cards, from a wide variety of America's best fantasy artists — that is, they are delightful to look at. Both have rare cards that are harder to get and often deliver more powerful effects within the game.

But *Shadowfist* had something going for it when it was first released, something that *Magic* lacked in its earliest incarnations. It was linked to a full-blown roleplaying game — the *Feng Shui* RPG, also designed by Laws and Garcia — which meant that a coherent world underlay its design. That world was not the standard, pseudo-medieval fantasy setting associated with so many other games of the day. No, *Shadowfist*'s setting was inspired by the look and feel of Hong Kong action movies, the classic exploits of Bruce Lee, Jackie Chan, and Chow Yun-Fat. The game is even framed in cinematic terms — establishing shot, main shot, locations, and so on — so much so that it inspires a kind of filmmaker quality in the best players. Like movie directors, they develop their own styles of staging action and constructing stories.

The framing device for *Shadowfist* is especially nice — a secret war ranging through time and space for control of the world by various factions. Time travel utilizes an alternate dimension called the Netherworld. The Netherworld is only open at certain time junctures — currently A.D. 81, 1862, 1938, 2007, and 2068. One of the open junctions will always be the current year. The other open junctions advance in time as the current date changes, but maintain the same basic interval between the dates. Factions that may have dominated in the past, but have lost their dominance, live on in the Netherworld, and plot their return.

Although *Shadowfist* can be played as a two-player duel, it is really more fun in a multi-player environment. Each match is a race to accumulate magical feng shui power by controlling a pre-set number of feng shui sites. Each site generates one point of power per turn, which is then used to summon characters and monsters, play spells, buy special equipment, and so on. Special non-feng shui sites may generate less or more power, but do not count toward victory. Power can be accumulated, and it can be spent at any time for certain actions. The magic number of feng shui sites needed to win is five, and the last one must be taken from an opponent. Two-player duels require six sites to win. This is arbitrary and could be changed by the players if they felt like it, without affecting the way the game plays. Five produces a game that is usually short enough to remain interesting, and long enough to get complicated.

As the game progresses, an action film full of heroes and villains and monsters begins to play in your head. Try saying things like "Ting-Ting attacks your Bomb Factory" without grinning at the images conjured. "I also give her a Really Big Gun and Explosives and a Big Rig." Then the other player counters with something like "I defend the site with two Butterfly Knights using Claws of Fury." Sly references to pop culture and history add yet another sort of resonance; for example, the Jammers faction includes a number of ape cards with names such as Battlechimp Potempkin and Furious George. If you know about the battleship *Potemkin* or R.A. Rey's beloved character Curious George, then you get that extra frisson of amusement when those cards are played.

To inspire player loyalty, and conflict within the game itself, the designers who have worked on *Shadowfist* over the years — first for Daedalus, then Z-Man Games, and now Shadowfist Games — have created and developed a wide variety of factions. Each embodies a philosophy and possesses a history that make it easy to identify and appealing to many different types of gamers.

The only really "good" faction is the Dragons. They are a mismatched gaggle of heroes who may be as commonplace as Average Joe (picture a mean old biker or trucker for this guy) or as exceptional as the Nemesis (looks like a cross between the Green Hornet and the Shadow). One of the Dragons' very best is Ting-Ting, a Chinese mistress of the martial arts who would have won Bruce Lee's heart in a second. (I was invincible in my last *Shadowfist* tournament, as long as I had Ting-Ting on the field. I lost when she failed to come out of the deck for me in the last game.)

The game's other nine factions embody varying degrees of evil and amorality. They include:

THE ASCENDED: Animals that evolved into human form. They gain their power from various forms of coercion and mind control.

THE GUIDING HAND: A secret society of Shaolin masters and martial artists who use their *chi* to achieve magical effects, in hopes of returning the world to the stability of dynastic China. This faction is directly inspired by kung fu films.

THE EATERS OF THE LOTUS: The flip side of the Guiding Hand, these evil sorcerers from ancient China gain their powers through necromancy, demon control, and corruption of every form.

THE SEVEN MASTERS: Another Chinese faction akin to the Guiding Hand, but more isolationist in practice. They don't want to control the world, nor do they wish to be subject to some other group that controls the world. In contrast to the Guiding Hand, Seven Masters was inspired by Chinese *wuxia* films.

THE FOUR MONARCHS: Two brothers and two sisters who ruled an alternate Earth, before they were exiled to the Netherworld. Each monarch represents a separate type of power — thunder, darkness, ice, or fire.

THE ARCHITECTS OF THE FLESH: Scientists from the future who utilize genetic engineering and totalitarian technology. They combine magic and science to form Arcano-technology.

THE JAMMERS: A very loose collection of rebels and cyborg simians from the future. They are devoted to destroying feng shui sites in order to free humanity.

The Purists: Future wizards who use quantum paradox magic that sounds an awful lot like modern physics.

The Syndicate: A secret criminal organization that rules the world of 2066. They came into power when the timeline controlled by the Architects was erased.

As in most multi-player games, diplomacy plays an important role in *Shadowfist*. No matter how good a player is, he can't win if all the other players band against him. The game allows players to join in on someone else's attacks, and also to help defend against them. One very tricky rule requires that players do all they can to prevent someone from winning, even if doing so will strip their own forces down to nothing. Manipulating your foes into harming each other, while quietly helping you, is quite an art. A game of *Shadowfist* is more than card against card. It's guile against guile. And don't we all want to be the mastermind who controls both Time and Fortune?

Shadowfist has never had the marketing power of a corporation behind it, and thus never gained the prominence of *Yu-Gi-Oh!* or *Magic*. None of the "big box" retailers have even heard of it, and far too few specialty stores stock it in depth. *Shadowfist* is a game for the cognoscenti — those True Gamers who appreciate its high quality and the infinite variability of its design. If you want to join that happy band, though, a special order through your local hobby shop or, barring that, an Internet search are all that's required to get you right up to the front lines of the Secret War. Welcome to the fight!

Ken St. Andre is a librarian and game designer who lives in Phoenix, Arizona. Best known for *Tunnels & Trolls*, a fast-playing and humorous alternative to *Dungeons & Dragons*, Ken has also helped co-author the award-winning RPG *Stormbringer*, based on the Elric stories of Michael Moorcock, and *Wasteland*, the first post-nuclear computer RPG, back in 1985. Although he has freelanced for various companies, Ken is chiefly associated with Flying Buffalo, Inc., publishers of the *Tunnels & Trolls* line, which has now been in print for over 30 years. He maintains a web-based fanclub for *T&T* aficionados at www.trollhalla.com.

Steven S. Long on

SHADOWRUN

KEY DESIGNERS: JORDAN WEISMAN, BOB CHARRETTE, PAUL HUME, TOM DOWD, L. ROSS BABCOCK III, SAM LEWIS, DAVE WYLIE

FASA CORPORATION (SECOND EDITION, 1992)

WAY BACK WHEN, IN the misty depths of time — 1989, to be precise — I was in law school and gaming primarily with a group of friends at my alma mater, Duke University. My games of choice at the time were *Champions* and *D&D*, but I was an avid reader of *Dragon* magazine and always willing to consider something new. I'd gotten interested in cyberpunk science fiction and was considering the gaming possibilities when I began to see ads for a new game called *Shadowrun*.

The advertisements described it as a cyberpunk game . . . but with magic, elves, dragons — all the usual *D&D* elements. That struck me as kind of odd. The ad also promised that the game was going to be well supported, with plenty of supplements and adventures planned. I'd heard that sort of thing before, so I scoffed. *This game isn't going to last six months*, I thought. Cyberpunk with magic? That just didn't make sense.

Except that it did. A few months later one of my gamer friends got a copy and we tried it out. I was immediately taken with the world of *Shadowrun* and soon ran out to buy my own copy of the rulebook and a couple of early supplements. Unfortunately, "real life" intruded and we never really got a campaign going.

Fast-forward a few years, to the mid-1990s. I was in a different gaming group then, one with some *Shadowrun* experience, and someone raised the idea of starting a campaign. Remembering my initial interest in the game, I was all in favor. Once again I went to the gaming store to get the latest version of the rulebook — the second edition — and a few key supplements my friends had recommended.

I've bought a lot of blah games and supplements over the years, but I've never regretted buying those *Shadowrun* books, or any of dozens that followed them onto my shelves. The game has never failed to reach out and grab me with its fascinating setting. And it's that element — the setting and how it's worked into the game as a whole — that makes me think of *Shadowrun* second edition as one of the best hobby games ever.

In modern game design, there's a lot of emphasis on setting. Game designers often seem as intent on developing an intellectual property as they do creating a game. In other words, they want to establish an entire world that might exist independently of the game in which it first appears, characters and concepts that they can exploit in other media — novels, films, video games, and so on. One can certainly criticize that approach, since it often leads to games that are no fun to play, but when it's done right — when the IP development enhances the game rather than detracts from it — it's a thing of beauty to behold. And I don't think anyone has done quite as good a job at walking that creative tightrope as the people behind *Shadowrun* second edition. The cyberpunk-with-magic world that its authors and artists developed flows through the books, making them enjoyable reads all on their own, even if you don't play the game. Just as important, though, the game itself rewards you with consistently entertaining play once you are drawn in by the clever ideas and smart writing.

To this day, of the hundreds of RPG books I own, there are only a very, very few that I'll go back and read just for fun — and nearly all of them are *Shadowrun* second edition books. The supplements from the mid-1990s — books such as *Fields of Fire*, *Shadowtech*, *Awakenings*, *Paranormal Animals of North America*, and *Cybertechnology* — stand in my mind as models of how to give gamers great technical rules material wrapped up almost seamlessly in setting material.

For example, in most of the *Shadowrun* books I'm talking about, the setting material is often conveyed in the form of computer bulletin board posts from shadowrunners, who are commenting about whatever a page or paragraph depicts. Not only are these fun reads, but they contain little snippets of rules information that provide the inside scoop on how the weapon, spell, animal, or what have you works. (This approach was not without its perils; on rare occasions, miscommunication meant the designers didn't fully integrate the comments with the rules, so it was left to the game master and players to decide how, or whether, to alter the rules accordingly.) Over the course of many supplements, some of these commentator characters — Hatchetman, Hangfire, and Fastjack, to name just three — became regulars, and readers got to know them and enjoy their interplay without ever having to see a character sheet.

The second-edition *Shadowrun* books also succeed on the "gaming fiction" front. Like many RPG supplements, they include snippets of fiction, ranging from several pages to half a column or so, designed to illustrate the game world. These fiction bits, such as "Becoming Prairie Dog" from *Awakenings,* are not only well-written, they do an excellent job of introducing readers to the new ideas and themes, drawing them into the setting in a way most game fiction does not. After reading "Becoming Prairie Dog," I wanted to try playing a prairie dog shaman, which would never even have occurred to me otherwise. That's *just* the sort of thing fiction in RPG books should do.

But for all its emphasis of the overall intellectual property, *Shadowrun* second edition belongs on the list of best hobby games because it so superbly integrates the gaming-specific material with the setting information. In doing so it satisfies what many gamers see as their twin needs: hard-and-fast rules that make game-play fun; and an immersive setting that enhances the gaming experience, rather than detracting from it. *Shadowrun* serves as an excellent model for game designers who want to combine those two elements in their RPGs (as so many of them seem to do these days), and I hope that it influences as many game designers as profoundly as it has me.

STEVE LONG began working in the RPG industry in 1992 as a freelancer for Hero Games. In 1997 he quit his job practicing law to devote himself full-time to writing and designing games. Since then he's written, co-authored, edited, developed, or otherwise had a significant hand in well over 100 gaming books and supplements. He's held full-time positions with Last Unicorn Games, Wizards of the Coast, and Decipher, and won two Origins Awards for best roleplaying game of the year. In December 2001, he and his partners bought the assets of Hero Games and he took on his industry dream job — *HERO System* line developer, a position he still holds and in which he's overseen the creation and publishing of approximately 70 titles.

SHADOWS OVER CAMELOT

KEY DESIGNERS: SERGE LAGET, BRUNO CATHALA

DAYS OF WONDER (ENGLISH EDITION, 2005)

SHADOWS OVER CAMELOT IS a sumptuous, crafty board game for three to seven players. The players cooperatively try to stem the rise of evil in King Arthur's domain. Together they will face many perils (and ways to lose), but they must be wary of their fellows, too, for there may be treachery afoot!

The Matter of Britain is one of the world's greatest mythic cycles and it is fitting that such a great game covers this seminal Western cultural tradition. *Shadows over Camelot* serves as a wonderful introduction to the Matter, while allowing the well-read Arthurian buff a bit of a smile as he sees how his favorite literary cycle is rendered into a highly playable board game.

Each player selects one of seven great knights of legend: Gawain, Percival, Galahad, Kay, Palamedes, Tristan, or King Arthur himself. The knights each have a special power related to their legendary roles. For instance, King Arthur, known for exchanging gifts, gets to trade a white card (representing good events or characters) with other players. Sir Galahad, known for his miracles, gets to play a special white card for free. Sir Palamedes, who lives for the quest, gets an extra point of life for each victorious mission.

The board represents a stylized Arthurian Britain. Camelot and the legendary Round Table encompass one corner. This is where your knight's playing piece starts, and where you can return to replenish resources — in the form of white cards — to your hand. The Round Table also tracks the collection of up to 12 swords as the game progresses. White swords mark victory for the side of good; black swords mark defeat by evil. The game ends immediately if there are ever seven or more black swords on the Round Table.

The players must win collectively. (There is one possible exception to this rule, but we'll get to that blackguard in a moment.) If your knight loses all life points, you are individually defeated and out of the game. If all the loyal knights are slain, the game is lost.

Camelot is surrounded on all sides by peril: the Saxon War, the Pict War, and the Black Knight. To conquer these threats, and others that arise during the game, knights go on quests. Multiple players can cooperatively undertake some quests, but others can only be faced by a single knight. If the players succeed, they clear the looming peril, gain white swords, draw white cards to replenish their hands, and regain life levels. If they fail, they gain black swords and lose life levels.

Before the castle rages the siege of Camelot. If you suffer defeat at the hands of the Saxons and Picts, besides all other hazards, siege engines are arrayed before the keep. Knights can sally to the siege area in a quest to destroy a few catapults, but once 12 siege engines arrive, Camelot falls. This is the third way for the players to collectively lose.

There are also special one-time quests that bring players closer to victory; they also help the game capture the spirit of the original Arthurian tales. Knights can seek after Lancelot's armor, Excalibur, or even the Holy Grail itself. These relics have substantial powers — the Grail, for example, can restore four life points to a wounded knight. Once the quest for Lancelot's armor has been successfully accomplished, an even more difficult dragon's quest is revealed.

Quests are met by playing sets of white cards like poker hands, with totals that exceed the challenges faced. Defeating the Black Knight requires two pair; the Saxon and Pict Wars a straight. The dragon is toughest of all, requiring three different sets of triples greater than the dragon's formidable hand.

Play begins each turn with the knights hastening the fall of the kingdom, during what the rules call the Progression of Evil phase.

Each turn, a knight must choose between three unpleasant options: draw a black card and play it, add a siege engine to those massed before Camelot, or lose a life point. There are no good options. Players have to decide which of these grim choices will harm the collective cause the least, then follow through with it. The Progression of Evil mechanic brilliantly captures a central theme of the Arthurian legends — the duel nature of humankind. No knight is without sin, no defender of Camelot completely free from blame for its destruction.

Only after harming the cause can a player strive to help it — by directing his knight to undertake or complete a quest, by playing a special white card, or through other, similar actions. For players to achieve a victory, they must coordinate their actions carefully in this phase and implement strategies that will allow them to stave off the myriad threats closing in on Camelot.

Unless, of course, one of those players secretly wants the kingdom to fall.

At the start of the game, each player is given one of eight loyalty cards. All of these cards identify the holder as a loyal knight, except one, which marks the traitor. While all the loyal knights work for the good of Camelot, the traitor secretly (or not-so-secretly) schemes to undermine the success of the realm.

Depending on the variant played, there may be no traitor in the game, a guaranteed traitor, or just the possibility of a traitor — the latter thanks to a random draw that may not assign the traitor card at all. This reflects the different phases of the Arthurian legend, from its youthful innocence, to the days of intrigue and suspicion, to its corruption and downfall. But it's wisely left up to the players to set the game's tone, from cooperative to cutthroat.

Gameplay around the traitor is similar to discovering the murderer in a good game of *Clue*. Unlike *Clue*, though, revealing the traitor's identity is not the point of the game; even if the traitor is exposed, play continues. If he's discovered, the traitor's playing piece is removed from the board, yet, with a nefarious cackle, he can continue to work in the shadows, taunting the other players by discarding random white cards from their hands and advancing the Progression of Evil.

An eighth knight — Sir Bedivere — was added to the game in 2005. Arthur's loyal supporter has the special power to discard and draw a white card during his turn. The figure was originally available through promotions in different gaming-related magazines around the world — *Spielbox* in Germany, *Game Master* in Italy, and *Game Trade Magazine* in the United States. Later that same year Days of Wonder released *A Company of Knights*; the set includes painted versions of all the knights available for the game, including the elusive Sir Bedivere.

Through the presence of the secret traitor and the Progression of Evil mechanics, *Shadows over Camelot* cleverly adapts the Arthurian legends to board game form. As you play, you can feel the tension inherent in the struggle to shore up the doomed glory of Camelot against an ever-pressuring darkness. Playable within an hour to an hour-and-a-half, the game offers players a rousing adventure with incredibly strong replay value. Players quite often want to try their hand at rescuing the kingdom from the forces of evil — and themselves — more than once over the course of a full evening. In all, Bruno Cathala and Serge Laget's design for *Shadows over Camelot* is a worthy representation of the seminal Arthurian legends, and a wonderful addition to any game library.

★   ★   ★

PETER CORLESS has been part of the gaming industry since the 1980s, first employed at West End Games, where he worked on various projects, from *Paranoia* to the *Star Wars Roleplaying Game* and *Star Warriors* board game. His more recent works include adventure supplements for the *Pendragon* roleplaying game, originally published by Chaosium and later by his own company, Green Knight Publishing. He lives in Mountain View, California, along with a collection of far too many books on medieval history and the Arthurian legends.

Dale Donovan on

SILENT DEATH:
THE NEXT MILLENNIUM

KEY DESIGNERS: KEVIN BARRETT, MATT FORBECK

IRON CROWN ENTERPRISES (1995)

FLY 'TIL YOU DIE. I'd been on the editorial staff of *Dragon* magazine for only a few months when ads sporting this catchphrase started showing up on my desk. It was the advertising tagline for the original edition of *Silent Death*, a spaceship combat game from Iron Crown Enterprises. The ads certainly piqued my interest in the game, and I wasn't the only one. Before too long, William Connors, Timothy Brown, and a few others around the TSR offices joined me in becoming deeply addicted to this game. When we weren't playing — or neck-deep in some deadline — we were poring over the ship specs, comparing the strengths and weaknesses of the various craft, looking for an edge in the next game. And we spent many lunch hours sending those fighters screaming through the emptiness of space, intent on dealing out explosive, flaming death to anything we encountered. A ship's destruction was usually met with a chorus of cheers, regardless of who was blowing up. That's how much fun this game was to play.

I still recall that tagline all these years later because it perfectly encapsulates the feel of *Silent Death*, because die you will, and often. But you won't be bothered too much by that; the game is so smooth you'll be having too much fun to care.

Silent Death: The Next Millennium is the outstanding revision of the original *Silent Death,* itself an innovative, fast-paced, easy-to-learn game of starcraft combat: no complex simulation mechanics or vector movement systems here. The game's mechanics, presentation, and high-quality miniatures all come together so well that *Silent Death: The Next Millennium* is simply the best tactical starfighter game ever.

Sharing Iron Crown's *Spacemaster* roleplaying game setting, this board game comes with a huge amount of optional background material. Briefly, the setting detailed in *The Next Millennium* rulebook is one of interstellar adventure, with a chaotic array of successor states struggling for dominance in the aftermath of a galactic war that devastated a monolithic empire. You'll do furious space-battle as members of one of a dozen powerful family houses, each trying to forge its destiny among the stars. This backstory material isn't necessary to play the combat game, but it adds terrific context to all the shooting and exploding.

As in many tactical air- or spacecraft games — such as Task Force Games' *Star Fleet Battles,* West End's *Star Warriors,* or even GDW's *Blue Max* — your turn consists of moving and firing. It's in the inventive execution of these common mechanics, though, where *Silent Death* sets itself apart. Each starfighter has a number of drive points; each point allows the craft to move forward one hex or change its facing by one hex-side.

There's nothing new or innovative there, but this system also contains a terrific twist. The result of a single die roll, modified by the pilot's skill rating, allows a "tight turn." This lets the craft end up facing toward any hex-side, eliminating the tedious plotting and executing of any complex maneuvers. This simple mechanic greatly speeds play, letting you get about the task of blowing each other to atoms that much quicker.

The aspect of the game that gets the most attention is its attack dice system. In his "Designer's Notes" for the original edition, Kevin Barrett explains that the system was developed from another Iron Crown miniatures release — Coleman Charleton's fantasy skirmish game, *Bladestorm.* The modified system works quite well for a science fiction setting and an array of futuristic armaments that includes mass drivers, lasers, blasters, ion cannons, plasma cannons, and energy bolters. The weapon being fired determines the first two dice to be rolled, plus a third die determined by the gunner's skill rating. If the attack is successful, the resulting damage is again determined by the weapon type and the gunner's skill, read from the same three dice used to determine the attack's result. *Silent Death* was the first game I'd ever encountered where you didn't have to stop and roll a second batch of dice to determine how much damage your attack did. With dozens of shots fired over the course of a session, the time saved by this ingenious mechanic adds up quickly.

The game's final success is the starcraft display sheet. Designed by Will Hyde for the original edition, each of these sheets contains all the details of a particular craft needed for play; a quick glance lets you easily track your craft's attacks numbers, weapons, drive, defense, damage, and critical hits in a clean and clear layout. Especially handy is the damage track, which incorporates a ship's decreasing performance as it is slowly hammered to bits. (And *Silent Death* boasts some of the best weapon and vessel names ever. No true gamer can resist smiling when saying, "I'm shooting my splatterguns at your Lance Electra" or "Firing my blatguns at your Hell Bender's Six.")

The gang at TSR had moved on to other games in the five years after the original's release. When *Silent Death: The Next Millennium* saw release in 1995, however, our addictions quickly resurfaced. Designer Matt Forbeck streamlined and clarified the rules and modified some of the ships for better balance. The redesigned plastic miniatures, sculpted by Bob Naismith, looked damn cool with their smooth, flowing lines. You could almost feel them screaming through space after their targets.

It was two additional changes, however, that Forbeck made to take this already great game to its exceptional status. He added a codified ship-design system so players could create their own craft to take into battle. Five years of play also allowed Forbeck to offer up a battalion of flight-tested new optional rules for those who wanted more detail in their battles among the stars. These new options include pilot luck; several advanced attack, defense, and movement options; debris, asteroids, and other space hazards; and (you gotta love it) ramming. Among other things, these options allow you to follow your pilot's career from an untested rookie to a savvy and deadly starfighter ace.

Silent Death was one of the first games I encountered where the elegance of the mechanics impressed me as much as its theme attracted me. I can count on one hand the other titles that so successfully meld their mechanical elements into the overall feel of the game. *Silent Death: The Next Millennium* is an experience every gamer should seek out.

Good luck, warm up those blatguns, and fly 'til you die!

DALE DONOVAN has toiled in the hobby-gaming industry since 1989. A past editor of *Dragon* magazine, he worked for TSR, Inc., Wizards of the Coast, and Hasbro for more than 12 years. His time at TSR/Wizards included four fun-filled years on the Forgotten Realms campaign setting team, a stint as a managing editor, and work as a writer or editor on every roleplaying game line produced by the company during his tenure. Since going freelance in 2002, he's worked for Green Ronin, Upper Deck, White Wolf/Sword & Sorcery, Sovereign Press, Steve Jackson Games, Guardians of Order, and the Valar Project, among others. He loves games, books, games, movies, games, and his wonderful wife and lovely daughter.

Matt Forbeck on

SPACE HULK

KEY DESIGNER: RICHARD HALLIWELL

GAMES WORKSHOP (FIRST EDITION, 1989)

IN THE DARK FUTURE of *Warhammer 40,000*, an immortal Emperor and his genetically engineered soldiers offer humanity's only hope against total annihilation at the hands of their alien foes. Of the Emperor's warriors, the greatest are the Space Marines, and the cream of that crop are the power-armored Terminators, walking tanks that spit death from both fists.

Deep within the darkest reaches of space, a Space Marine vessel encounters an abandoned structure, a hulk comprised of countless pieces of other ships and space junk stitched together in impossible ways. The ship's captain sends his Terminators to investigate. Aboard the hulk, the five-man squads soon determine that something there is horribly wrong. Aliens known as Genestealers course through the ship, at first only appearing as blips on the Terminator's radar, and then swarming forth out of the cold, airless darkness to attack with their savage claws.

In *Space Hulk*, one player maneuvers squads of Terminators trying to make it through various parts of the hulk, while the other player charges forward with his horde of Genestealers. The game comes with a number of scenarios, which all share one common rule — the last survivor wins.

Space Hulk uses plastic miniatures to represent the combatant as they march through the dungeonlike tunnels that riddle the hulk. You play the game on a set of heavy-duty cardboard tiles that represent corridors and rooms, marked off with an inch-square grid. The connector points are jig-cut to snap together, making for a sturdy board that doesn't fall to pieces when you jar the table. Best of all, you can configure the board pieces in an astonishing variety of ways, keeping the game fresh over scores of plays.

On your turn, you move and attack with each of your figures. The Terminators each have six action points, while the Genestealers have nine, representing their ferocious and superior speed. The Terminators have big, bulky guns called bolters that they can fire down the length of the map — if they can find a line of sight to a target — while the Genestealers only have their claws. There are only a handful or two of Terminators at most, while the Genestealers never seem to stop coming.

The biggest difference between the two sides, though, is that the Genestealers have all day to make their move, while the Terminators must work against the clock. (Your own stopwatch or an egg timer works well for this.) As the Terminator player, you literally have only seconds to complete your move. How much time you have is based upon how many of your figures remain on the table, but it's never enough, and those last-second countdowns can be murder. When time's up, your figures are stuck where they stand, whether you wanted them there or not.

To make things for the Terminators even worse, most of the Genestealers start out as blips — cardboard disks that move on the map like figures. The moment a Terminator can spot a blip, though, the Genestealer player flips it over, revealing a number from one to three and then replaces the blip with that many of his figures. The Genestealer player knows what the number is and can toy with the Terminator player, sending a few one-figure blips forward and keeping the big-number blips in reserve. When a blip flips, the Terminator player might breathe a sigh of relief at only seeing a single Genestealer replace it, but that relief is temporary. He knows that the three-figure blip is still out there, waiting for him.

To make up for this imbalance, at least a little, the Terminator player can put any of his figures on "overwatch" at the end of its move by spending two action points. This prepares the soldier to shoot at oncoming Genestealers when they move — even during the Genestealer's turn, although at a substantial penalty. Six-sided dice rule the day, determining each figure's fate.

Think of the game as *Aliens* or *Doom*, but cast in plastic on cardboard. It's a brilliant, elegant design, packed with inherent tension. Unlike most tactical combat games — like *Warhammer 40,000*, from which it draws its setting — *Space Hulk* only features one kind of fight, but it handles it better than anything else.

The first edition of the game saw two boxed supplements: *Deathwing* and *Genestealer*. The first adds all sorts of tactical options and a random scenario generator, while the second layers on a card-based system of psychic powers for both sides. Both hit shops in 1990. A number of articles about the game were published in *White Dwarf* magazine, which later appeared as part of the *Space Hulk Campaigns* book in 1991.

Space Hulk won the Origins Award for the best science fiction or fantasy board game of 1989, while *Genestealer* won the same award for 1990. *Space Hulk* directly inspired a fistful of great games including *Space Crusade*, *Advanced Space Crusade*, and *Ultra Marines*, plus a pair of tactical shooter computer games released in 1993 and 1995, a cell phone game in 2005, and a short-lived second edition in 1996. You can also see its influence in the Gothica games (*Dracula's Revenge* and *Frankenstein's Children*) I designed for Human Head Studios, plus Hasbro's *HeroQuest* and Games Workshop's *Advanced HeroQuest*.

It's hard to overstate the original game's simplicity, focus, and elegance. You can open up the massive box stuffed with boards and figs and — once you finish assembling all the pieces — start playing a game within minutes. It fits the old maxim for great games: "Easy to learn, hard to master."

Space Hulk taught me more about elegance in design than any other game. It's an icon of well-nested mechanics that build a system far greater than its parts. Better yet, every part of the game works to support not only each other but the game's underlying metaphor, giving a united play experience that's unmatched.

The slow and chunky Space Marines look and work like personal tanks stuffed to their helmets with deadly ordnance. The fast and furious Genestealers, with their reaching, razor-sharp claws and hungry maws, seem and act like lethal appetites on feet. Even the design of the boards emphasizes the claustrophobic and labyrinthine feel of a hulk's interior. The blips add an essential element of mystery to the game, not only acting like radar on a map but looking like it too. The timer applies almost unbearable pressure to every moment of the Marine player's turn, and its absence for the Genestealer's illustrates just how fast the creatures are.

It all hangs together like a work of art.

Play it. As a gamer, you owe it to yourself.

MATT FORBECK is a full-time writer and game designer. Since taking the leap in 1989, he's worked with many top companies, including Atari, Ubisoft, Mattel, Playmates Toys, Wizards of the Coast, Games Workshop, TSR, Decipher, White Wolf, Pinnacle, Green Ronin, AEG, Reaper Miniatures, Image Comics, WildStorm Productions, Idea + Design Works, and Human Head. He has designed collectible card games, roleplaying games, miniatures games, and board games, and written interviews, essays, short fiction, comic books, novels, and computer game scripts and stories, including work on *Deathwing* and *Genestealer*. He is a proud member of the Alliterates writers' group and also belongs to the IGDA, the IAMTW, and the AAGAD. Projects he worked on have garnered 12 Origins Awards and five ENnies and been published in nine languages. He lives in Wisconsin with his wife Ann and their children: Marty, Pat, Nick, Ken, and Helen. For more details, visit www.forbeck.com.

Ray Winninger on

SQUAD LEADER

KEY DESIGNERS: JOHN HILL, DON GREENWOOD
AVALON HILL (1977)

AVALON HILL BUILT ITS reputation in the 1960s with elegant wargames that asked players to rout Ney off the Quatre Bras Heights, to encircle Tobruk with Montgomery's 8th Army, or to stave off Army Group Center's advance on Moscow. When it exploded onto the scene in 1977, John Hill's *Squad Leader* presented armchair generals with a new and unusual challenge — crossing a street. It's a lot more exciting than it sounds.

Squad Leader is a game of tactical infantry combat in the Second World War. The game pieces represent single squads (10 to 12 soldiers) and individual leaders, vehicles, and guns. These cardboard troops fight their way across four game boards dotted with hills, streets, factories, and wheat fields. The boards are *geomorphic*, meaning they were designed in a way that allows them to fit together in a wide variety of configurations. A game of *Squad Leader* recreates a single small engagement and calls upon Russian, German, or American soldiers to, say, knock out a bunker, silence an enemy gun, or fight their way into a fortified building. Players sweat over where to place their foxholes and machine guns, how to get a bazooka close enough to pick off a stray tank, and yes, how to get their men safely across a city street under fire.

Squad Leader was the first successful board wargame to recreate modern combat at such a small scale. (*Sniper!*, an earlier effort by Avalon Hill's rival SPI, and AH's own *Tobruk* were commercial and evolutionary dead ends.) Prior to its arrival, tactical wargaming was usually conducted with lead miniatures and model scenery, limiting the appeal to an affluent few. *Squad Leader*, on the other hand, was a huge mainstream hit by wargaming standards; reportedly, 250,000 copies were sold between 1977 and 1984. The new and smaller scale undoubtedly played a significant role in the game's success. Thanks to John Wayne and Lee Marvin, it was relatively easy for gamers to translate the action on the game board into "real" battles in their imaginations, lending the whole experience a lively, escapist quality. (By contrast, try to imagine exactly what a "2-to-1 attack" on Leningrad looks like.) Nor did it hurt that when *Squad Leader* was first published, it set a new high watermark for production values. Glancing down at the beautiful, hand-painted map boards felt like soaring over Stalingrad in a Messerschmitt.

Of course, the real reason why *Squad Leader* was so successful is that it's a virtuoso bit of game design. The classic trade-off in wargame construction is realism versus playability — accurately simulating the conflict in question or optimizing for lively play. The conventional wisdom holds that an improvement in one always comes at the expense of the other. *Risk* is a fun game but in the real world, its tried-and-true stratagem of seizing Australia is hardly the geopolitical key to global domination. On the other hand, SPI's old *Campaign for North Africa* accounted for every imaginable factor that impacted Rommel's drive into Egypt, right down to the rate of evaporation in the panzers' gas tanks, but it's less fun than completing a decade's worth of tax returns. Somehow, against all odds, *Squad Leader* emerged as a paragon of both playability *and* realism.

What makes *Squad Leader* so much fun is its propensity for generating seat-squirming, nail-biting tension. Most sessions require players to beat the clock — take a hill in seven turns, eliminate five enemy squads before they eliminate five of yours, and so on. Whenever the game starts to get predictable, fate inevitably intervenes with a nasty shock — maybe a critical machine gun overheats or one of your squads goes "berserk" and charges into enemy gunfire. All too often, the game is won or lost on the very last roll of the dice after two-and-a-half hours of thrills and spills. *Squad Leader* also deftly avoids many of the pitfalls that plague most other wargames of its era. It's fast-paced (games rarely last more than two or three hours), it uses relatively few pieces, and because it allows players to shoot in the middle of each other's turns, it keeps both parties engaged at all times. Games such as *Third Reich* or *The Russian Campaign,* by way of contrast, might take eight hours or more to finish, they pile so many pieces so close together that the combatants are forced to push around their armored divisions with tweezers, and they give players the luxury of catching a half-hour nap while waiting for an opponent to finish a turn.

The characteristics that make *Squad Leader* "realistic" are even more interesting. Hill's design recreates World War II combat in the same way that a great caricaturist recreates a face — by exaggerating the important bits and abstracting everything else. Many of the game's individual concepts are decidedly "unrealistic." Players possess almost omniscient knowledge of the battlefield, cardboard soldiers are all too eager to fight to the last man, key weapon systems and environmental effects are vastly oversimplified. Yet, added together, these details produce an end result that somehow feels real. By exaggerating, oversimplifying, and abstracting, Hill provides a decent primer on World War II infantry tactics — the importance of covering fire and maneuver, the use of machine guns to prevent movement across open spaces, the key differences between German and Russian combatants, and so forth.

Sadly, as *Squad Leader* was later expanded by various add-ons, the beautiful caricature started to break down in favor of a more simulationist approach. *Cross of Iron* completely reworked the game's treatment of armored vehicles, *Crescendo of Doom* introduced the British and French armies, and *GI: Anvil of Victory* expanded the American forces and reworked many of the game's basic systems. This trend reached its peak in 1985 when *Squad Leader* was essentially replaced with a new game, *Advanced Squad Leader* (*ASL*), which added eye-popping levels of detail. Though many gamers appreciate *ASL* for its encyclopedic authority, there's still much to recommend Hill's original design. Despite the fact that a game of *ASL* often resembles a high-stakes legal battle, with both sides calling for continuances to research the law laid down in the voluminous rulebook, the end result doesn't necessarily feel any more real than the basic game of eight years earlier.

While the original *Squad Leader* is long out-of-print, copies aren't hard to come by on eBay and elsewhere. If you do decide to take the plunge and give the game a try, here's a tip — before you cross that street, you not only want to look both ways; you want to make sure you lay down plenty of covering fire and drop a few smoke grenades.

RAY WINNINGER is the former editorial director of Mayfair Games and a former contributing editor of *Dragon* magazine. He wrote numerous role-playing sourcebooks and supplements for TSR, FASA, Mayfair Games, West End Games, Last Unicorn, White Wolf, Wizards of the Coast, and Pagan Publishing. Although Ray is the designer of the late, lamented RPG *Underground* and the co-designer of *Torg* and *DC Heroes*, board games were his first love. He's currently a senior platform strategist at Microsoft.

Lewis Pulsipher on

STALINGRAD

KEY DESIGNERS: THOMAS SHAW, LINDSLEY SCHUTZ

AVALON HILL (FIRST EDITION, 1963)

THREE GREAT GAMES STRONGLY affected my life, *Stalingrad*, *Diplomacy*, and *Dungeons & Dragons*. My apprenticeship as a commercial game designer came through creating dozens of variants of *Diplomacy*, and then add-ons for *D&D*. I no longer play any of these three classics, because I devote my time now to playtesting prototypes, but I love them all.

To me, a game is great if you want to play it again and again, if you still enjoy it decades after your first session, if you'll travel long distances to play, if you can almost endlessly discuss the intricacies of good strategy, if you mull over past games and remember them fondly, or if you can create many variants that are also fine games in and of themselves. Those are the things I'm looking for in a game, not a pleasant diversion or a way to kill time.

When I was young, I didn't have the experience to know how standards — of dress, of behavior, and many other things — change over time. Now that I'm much older, I understand that opinions change, sometimes drastically. This applies to games just as it does to other fields, disciplines, and hobbies. Louis Spohr (who?) was regarded by contemporaries as a great composer. J.S. Bach was nearly forgotten for many decades. Modern art is junk to me, but many people love it. So why would we only apply contemporary standards to assess the greatness of a game?

What if *Monopoly* or *Scrabble* were issued for the first time today? I asked experienced gamers that question, and many agreed that they would be no more notable than many other games on the market. What they have going for them is timing. They claimed their spot in the marketplace early, which led to longevity and, in the cases of these two titles, a part in popular culture. "Getting there first" is important. Longevity is important. A new game may offer excellent play value and other elements, but can we know the game is great until many years have passed? Perhaps the historian in me makes me think that we cannot.

It is not any particular element of a game, or particular set of elements, that makes a game great. A game must meet a minimum standard, surely, but there are great games that don't have fine physical components, don't have very clear rules sets, don't encourage player interaction, or don't avoid player elimination, and so on. There are so many differences of opinion about what design elements make an outstanding game that we cannot come to a consensus. Hence, I think, we should turn to what effect the game has on people.

At the World Boardgaming Championships not long ago I watched a tournament of a multi-player game several years out of print. The players had families, typically, and jobs that required a lot of energy and mental acumen — they were lawyers, physicians, software development managers, university professors, and so on. I asked one how many times he'd played the game. He calculated a little, then replied, "About five hundred times." (This for a title that took four to five hours to play!) Another player nodded his head to agree. Every year they return for the tournament, and play constantly by e-mail or as regularly as possible face-to-face. A great game ought to engender this kind of devotion.

Stalingrad engendered such devotion in its fans, and people still play it today, 45 years after publication. That devotion comes primarily from the game's strategic character rather than a fascination with its theme — the Eastern Front in World War II. While there have been many games about the largest military campaign in history, few could be called great. Stalingrad benefited from being the first commercial game on the subject, but that isn't the source of its greatness.

On its plain 22" by 28" map board *Stalingrad* represents on a large scale — 1,700 by 1,200 miles — the German attack on the Soviet Union. Action takes place in 24 turns, each representing a month, beginning in June 1941. To win, the Germans must wipe out the "Russians," or at least hold three strategic enemy cities for two months. Otherwise, the Soviets are victorious. Railroads, cities, swamps, and hills are represented on the hex-grid map. The two-player game takes two to five hours to complete.

We're used to thinking of hex wargames as complex, but the rules for *Stalingrad* are only three closely printed pages, and just a hundred half-inch die-cut pieces are used. It is a pretty simple game to play, which surely contributes to its greatness.

Stalingrad's hex-grid was a great advancement over squares for realistic game movement. The diagonal of a square is about 1.41 times as long as the side. Hence, on a square grid, diagonal movement is much "faster" than orthogonal (non-diagonal) movement — that is, with the same number of moves, you go a lot farther with the former than the latter. The distance distortion on a hexagonal grid is much smaller, making for more accurate movement representation.

Moreover, *Stalingrad* uses the Avalon Hill standard "3-to-1" combat table, based on the premise that an attacker needed a 3-to-1 superiority to guarantee reasonable success. With better odds you suffer even fewer casualties. In any strategic game involving dice, many good players want to hold down the number of times they need to trust to luck. (Anyone who has ever played a game of *Risk* and rolled just a single six knows how much the luck of the dice can distort a battle's outcome.) Avalon Hill's combat table makes this a practical goal, though a top-class opponent will force you to take chances. Still, in *Stalingrad* you can actually assure victory in a particular battle if you devote enough force, something unheard of in other games of the time that used dice.

Phrases in the rules such as "your chessmen" and "unlike chess" show how new this kind of game was in the early 1960s. But it was clearly a welcome innovation, one worthy of intense study. *Stalingrad* generated discussions and articles on a variety of Russian defenses and German openings — on all aspects of the game's strategy and tactics, in fact — similar to writings about chess.

Love of games and love of history came together for me in *Stalingrad*. To be sure, the game has been criticized as a poor simulation of the Eastern Front. As the first commercial game model of the Eastern Front, it seemed wonderful at the time of its release, though time has revealed its weaknesses. But I have never played games to learn history — that's what books are for. I play them because they can conjure the spirit of an event, rather than its precise details. In fact, I'd argue that virtually no wargame meant to represent a specific series of events is a good simulation, for no other reason than the distorting effects of hindsight; further, the weight of historical accuracy makes most "good simulations" poor games. In any case, its most devoted fans play *Stalingrad* for its strategic character, not the quality of simulation.

Stalingrad is representative of the entire Charles S. Roberts-led first wave of historical commercial games, a wave that included *Tactics II*, *Gettysburg*, *Africa Corps*, *D-Day*, and *Waterloo*. (*Stalingrad*, oddly enough, was not designed by Roberts, but it embodies the techniques he devised for those other games.) They were our first major commercial examples of games that closely modeled reality, as opposed to abstract games (checkers, go) or games such as *Conflict*, *Risk*, and *Monopoly* that bear little resemblance to reality. Avalon Hill showed us that a game could be strategic but not abstract, that a game could use dice but not be dominated by dice, that a game could be commercially successful without appealing to the entire family.

Practically speaking, Charles Roberts invented hobby board gaming (as opposed to family board gaming), and profoundly influenced the other kinds of hobby games that would later be invented. For example, Gary Gygax was a board wargamer when Dave Arneson devised a miniatures-based fantasy game that Gary perfected as *Advanced Dungeons & Dragons*. Many of the other early designers and publishers of roleplaying games were board gamers, too.

Wargames were the foundation of Avalon Hill's success. They would later branch out into non-wargames — *Facts in Five* and *Outdoor Survival* outsold their military titles. But the wargames were their heart and soul. At one time, these releases sold in all kinds of retail outlets, including mainstream department stores. In the '60s and '70s, gamers anticipated every new Avalon Hill release in a way that would make any publisher's sales staff ecstatic today. SPI and other companies arose to benefit from Avalon Hill's success, but Avalon Hill remained the "big daddy" of hobby gaming, at least until ruined by mismanagement.

While the company name lives on as an imprint at Hasbro, Avalon Hill's legacy is more substantial. It provided the foundation for the entire hobby gaming industry, and of Avalon Hill's many groundbreaking early titles, *Stalingrad* is the best.

DR. LEW PULSIPHER started playing board games 50 years ago. He designed his own games, then discovered strategic "realistic" gaming with early Avalon Hill wargames, and ultimately earned a doctorate in Military and Diplomatic History. Formerly contributing editor to several roleplaying game magazines and author of over 100 game articles, he is the designer of *Britannia* (released in the U.K., U.S., and Germany, in separate editions), *Dragon Rage*, *Valley of the Four Winds*, *Swords & Wizardry*, and *Diplomacy Games & Variants*. *Britannia* (second edition) appeared in 2006. Current projects can be previewed at www.PulsipherGames.com. He teaches college-level computer networking, Web development, and game design in North Carolina.

Bruce Nesmith on

STAR FLEET BATTLES

KEY DESIGNER: STEPHEN V. COLE

TASK FORCE GAMES (DESIGNER'S EDITION, 1979)

THE KLINGON D7 BATTLECRUISER is right behind you and closing fast. Your Federation CA Cruiser is only going at a speed of six and the Klingon will overtake you in five impulses. It's been pounding your number four shield, which won't hold out for much longer. You look at your movement chart and see that you have a high-energy turn plotted. Grinning, you spin your ship 180 degrees and announce that you are firing all forward weapons into the front shield of the Klingon, including the overloaded photon torpedoes. You gather up a fist full of dice to roll for damage. It's a bad night to be a Klingon!

That's *Star Fleet Battles*. No other game in hobby game history so completely captures the feel of ship-to-ship combat in space than *Star Fleet Battles*. The fact that it does so in the Star Trek Universe is icing on the cake.

First released in 1979, *Star Fleet Battles* was the inspiration of Stephen V. Cole, with help from Barry Jacobs. It quickly became a hobby favorite. What started as a pocket game shipped in a ziplock bag soon blossomed into an entire franchise. Over time, Task Force Games would publish over 100 supplements and related titles. The core rules themselves have been revised many times and are now in a fourth edition. Hundreds of suggestions from the fans themselves have found their way into the books. Expansions include everything from miniatures and computer games, to strategy board games such as *Federation & Empire* (1987). The breadth of the line is remarkable. Task Force Games no longer exists, but the franchise is still in the safe hands of Steve Cole, now of the Amarillo Design Bureau. Very few games can boast this type of longevity.

Oh, and did I mention it's Star Trek? Through a convoluted fluke of legalities, little Task Force Games managed to secure the license to the Star Trek universe. That story could fill a small book by itself. By the time Paramount realized what it had given away, it was too late. Tens of thousands of happy gamers had one of the greatest ship-to-ship combat games ever, and it was Star Trek. While the official products can't refer to the specific movie and TV show characters and ships, the rest of us can. I'm not just piloting my Federation CA Cruiser — I am Captain James T. Kirk of the starship *Enterprise*. Or Jean-Luc Picard, or any one of the other famous figures in the Star Trek Universe.

Fans of the game are enthusiastic bordering on rabid. They obsess over rules details and are known to launch heated discussions about such things as fractional energy points. They know dozens of tactics, each custom tailored for particular ships and races. The amazing thing about *Star Fleet Battles* is that a dozen viable tactics actually exist. There are hundreds of hobby games for which there are only one or two winning strategies. And I'm talking about the good games.

New players take heed — *Star Fleet Battles* is not for the faint of heart. The rules are complex and detailed. The 1979 boxed "designer's edition" is printed in the infamously impenetrable case format; in small, dense type; without a single picture. However, beneath this lack of spit and polish lies the heart and soul of a great game. Playing *Star Fleet Battles*, you feel like you are commanding the *Enterprise* — and that, after a few games, you'll be able to fill in for Kirk or Picard in a tight spot. The level of simulation is amazing, and spot-on with the various TV shows and movies.

One of the things that sets *Star Fleet Battles* apart from other games is that fearless pursuit of detail and simulation. It all starts with the energy allocation chart. Every ship in the game system has a unique Ship Systems Display sheet describing its capabilities and available energies. As a starship captain, you decide each turn how to allocate the ship's power. Should you reinforce that number three shield? If you do that, you won't be able to move very quickly this turn. Maybe if you conserve some energy you can overload those photon torpedoes. . . .

The movement system accurately and smoothly models different speeds. If your speed is 15 and your opponent's is 11, you slowly pull away from him over the course of a turn. Most hobby games would have been content to have simultaneous movement and let combat happen after all movement is complete. Not *Star Fleet Battles*. You can choose to fire at any time during the turn. It's not uncommon for a captain to turn off at the last minute so he can bring additional weapons to bear on his opponent's damaged — or, better still, disabled — shield.

There are detailed tables showing how much potential damage you might do, depending on the distance from your target. If you penetrate his shields, its easy to determine the effects of that damage with dice and the slick table that identifies which system is harmed. It takes a while to mark it all off on your record sheet, but the end result feels like your ship really did get hit with phaser fire.

If the detail and complexity are too daunting, never fear. There are numerous rules and supplements to make the game easier and faster. There are battle cards you can use in place of the ship damage chart. Instead of plotted movement, you can use free movement — meaning players can choose which direction to turn without committing in advance. There are even programs you can get to help you manage your energy allocation chart. This kind of flexibility in a set of game rules is rare, and greatly appreciated by its fans.

Playing *Star Fleet Battles* has never failed to leave a grin on my face and a twinkle in my eye. It is a grand game executed on a grand scale. As a game designer, I am humbled by its accomplishments. As a fan and player I am overjoyed by them.

Now, who wants to take a shot at beating my Fed CA Cruiser? Anybody?

In 1981 BRUCE NESMITH was hired by TSR, Inc. to do computer games on the Apple II+. He soon moved on to be a writer of *Dungeons & Dragons* modules. Over a decade later he has dozens of *AD&D* game accessories to his credit, including the popular *Ravenloft* boxed set, and a handful of board games. In 1995 Bruce moved into the computer game field, contributing to the *The Elder Scrolls II: Daggerfall* computer roleplaying game, and *Terminator* computer games. Currently, he's a senior game designer for Bethesda Game Studios, where he worked extensively on the popular *The Elder Scrolls IV: Oblivion* and its expansion, *The Shivering Isles*. He'd tell you what he's working on now, but then he'd have to kill you.

Steve Winter on

THE SWORD AND THE FLAME

KEY DESIGNER: LARRY V. BROM

YAQUINTO PUBLICATIONS (1979)

Walk wide o' the Widow at Windsor,
For 'alf o' creation she owns.
We 'ave bought 'er the same with the Sword an' the Flame,
An' we've salted it down with our bones.

THOSE STIRRING LINES FROM Rudyard Kipling's poem "The Widow at Windsor" are also the opening words in *The Sword and the Flame*, and no more apt introduction is possible.

The Sword and the Flame is a slim, softcover volume of rules for tabletop miniature wargames set in the British Empire of Queen Victoria. These desperate battles at the edges of civilization pit a handful of stalwart, red-coated soldiers against an onrushing tide of fearless Zulus, fanatical Dervishes, wily Pathans, rebellious Egyptian fellahin, and sharpshooting Boers. Whether your sympathy falls with the natives resisting invading imperialism or the doughty redcoats pushing outward the frontiers of commerce and science, your heart will beat faster to the crash of volleys and clash of spears against bayonets.

The Sword and the Flame was published in 1979. At that time, the historical miniatures hobby and industry were both in atrophy. Through the 1970s, most rules for miniature tabletop wargames were still amateur publications. They tended to be formulaic and predictable and to have low production values. The '70s also saw an explosion in the quantity and quality of paper-map-and-counter wargames which drew players away from the more traditional toy-soldier incarnations. The simultaneous explosion of roleplaying games diverted the companies that made miniature figures away from bulk-sale, low-profit historical themes to individually packaged, high-profit fantasy heroes and monsters.

Miniatures players were hungry for something new, even if they themselves didn't realize it.

That's the environment in which *The Sword and the Flame* appeared. To say that it "burst on the scene" would be a gross overstatement. It entered quietly, slipped in amongst the various other, more traditional game offerings from Texas-based Yaquinto Publications.

But the buyer knew immediately that this was something different from the home-typed, amateur publications he was used to. The booklet had a professional-looking cover and real typesetting. Inside were well-drawn illustrations and a clean, logical layout. From the first paragraph, the player was told what to expect, and it wasn't the typical historical game:

> To all those who cherish the poems of Rudyard Kipling, and who think *Gunga Din*, *Four Feathers*, and *Zulu* are among the finest films ever produced, these game rules are respectfully dedicated. With these rules, a light heart, an open mind, and a vivid imagination, we will return to the days of the British Empire with the chatter of the Gatlings, the skirl of bagpipes, the Dervish screams, the crack of the rifles, and the ring of broadsword on bayonet.

What was this talk of *imagination* and *a light heart*? This was not the usual stuff of historical miniatures games. It promised adventure and romance!

The overriding theme of *The Sword and the Flame* is not simulation, not detailed study of organization, maneuver, and firepower, but fun. It's about playing with toy soldiers.

Out of 32 pages in the booklet, only eight are the rules of the game. The other 24 describe the various forces involved, the settings of these wars on the frontier of Victoria's empire, basic directions for painting your first miniatures and building simple, easy-to-use terrain, and a sample game that has become a classic scenario, "The Battle of Chamla Valley."

The rules, too, are innovative and were a departure for their day. *The Sword and the Flame* introduced concepts that have since become standard fare in miniatures and paper-map wargames.

First and foremost is the random turn sequence. Instead of a rigid, alternating sequence or a complex, interlaced sequence, *TS&TF* uses a standard deck of playing cards, flipped one at a time. On a red card, a British unit moves; on a black card, a native unit moves. When all movement is done, the same system determines when units can fire. What's more, movement distances are determined randomly by rolling dice. When a unit dashes toward a hill, there is no telling whether the soldiers will make it. The deck of cards makes a third appearance in determining randomly which figures are hit by gunfire.

No previous game had taken control so far out of the players' hands for the sake of fun. Now, decades later, these innovations in various forms are almost never absent from new sets of rules.

Ultimately, the game is all about close combat. Sooner or later, the Zulus will crash into the British square, the Dervishes or the Pathans will launch their ambush. At that point, *TS&TF* becomes truly cinematic, with desperate, one-on-one duels between the steady redcoats and their savage foes. Real British pluck can even win the Victoria Cross for some lucky, lead soldier.

It all adds up to a game that captures the spirit of wild exploits on the fringe of civilization in an almost boys'-adventure-book style. Where did it come from? The author, Larry Brom, is that rare game designer who knows real war firsthand, from his time as a USMC squad leader in Korea. Such a grueling experience was nothing he wanted to recreate in a game. Instead, his lifelong, exuberant love for Victorian adventure steered him down a different path from the simulation-heavy rules that were the norm of the day. The result was the light-hearted *The Sword and the Flame*.

Since its first publication, *TS&TF* has become a franchise. The rules are so solid and flexible that they have been adapted to nearly every historical period, including even naval combat. The game's current publisher, Larry Brom's own company And That's the Way it Was . . . , offers variant expansions covering the French Foreign Legion, the Spanish-American War, the Boxer Rebellion, the French and Indian War, the Palestinian campaigns of World War I, the Maximilian intervention in Mexico, the U.S. Marines in Nicaragua and other "banana wars" of the 1920s and '30s, and clashes between the U.S. cavalry and Plains Indian tribes. Other companies, game clubs, and individuals have issued their own variants covering periods as far back as Rome's struggles with the Gauls, Spain's conquest of the New World, and the English Civil War; as far forward as the Spanish Civil War and World War II (with the ever-so-clever title, *The Samurai Sword and the Flamethrower*); and as far afield as Victorian-style science fiction set on Venus and Mars. There are official variants for smaller-scale skirmishes (*The Sword in Africa*, involving European explorers, Zanzibari slavers, and African warriors) and full-size, brigade-level battles (*Eight Hundred Fighting Englishmen*).

The Sword and the Flame is the closest thing that any historical period has to a universal set of rules. Even the rare colonial wargamer who doesn't use *The Sword and the Flame* for his own games has certainly played with them at some point. At wargame conventions, the vast majority of colonial-themed games use *TS&TF*, not only because it's fast moving and fun but because everyone knows the rules.

Miniatures rules come and go, enjoying a few years of popularity before being replaced by the next new thing. In 1999, *The Sword and the Flame* celebrated its 20th anniversary with a new, lightly revised edition. The game continues as strong as ever and shows every sign of enjoying a 40th anniversary in 2019.

STEVE WINTER was introduced to hobby games through Avalon Hill wargames in the 1970s. Those led him to a college wargaming club, which led to *Dungeons & Dragons* and other roleplaying games, which led to a job with TSR, Inc. in 1981. From that day on, he has worked and played as a full-time game editor, developer, designer, author, manager, and creative director. Once he discovered tabletop miniatures games and *The Sword and the Flame*, however, toy soldiers in all their variety became his gaming delight. Convention-goers can generally find him presiding over a table filled with onrushing Zulus, Pz III and T-34 tanks, or mobile infantry fending off hordes of alien bugs. Steve currently lives in Seattle and works as a producer for Wizards of the Coast's *D&D* and *D&D Miniatures* websites.

Jeff Grubb on

TALES OF THE
ARABIAN NIGHTS

KEY DESIGNER: ERIC GOLDBERG

WEST END GAMES (1985)

STRANGE CREATIONS FESTER AND grow at the crossroads where storytelling meets board games. Here can be found ruthless clockwork mechanisms that deny free will to the players and rob them of enjoyment in the name of experiencing a pre-determined plot. Here also thrive wild chaotic creations that drag the users out into the deep woods of storytelling and then abandon them, depriving victims of even a trail of breadcrumbs to bring them home.

And then there are the few that succeed — the ones that function both as board game and storytelling device. Among the best of those is West End Games' *Tales of the Arabian Nights*, designed by Eric Goldberg and developed by Doug Kaufman and Ken Rolston.

Tales of the Arabian Nights is set against the folk tales of Arabia and Persia, tales known to West by numerous names, including *The Book of One Thousand and One Nights*. The framing story of these tales is that of Sheherezad, an ingenious young woman who keeps herself alive by telling stories to the Sultan. Each tale leads to another, and so Sheherezad leaves the Sultan wanting more and her head on her shoulders. Sheherezad's tales contribute most of our genre ideas of Arabian fantasy — Rocs, genies, ghouls, and evil red wizards, as well as the stories of Sinbad, Aladdin, and Ali Baba.

In the game version of these tales, you take the part of an adventurer, and travel throughout the world, seeking your destiny and stories worth telling. The board is a map of the Old World, with Arabia and North Africa swollen to represent their greater importance, while Europe and the Far East are cut down accordingly. Paths link cities, sites, and places of power, and your level of wealth determines your movement — the wealthier you are, the farther you may move on land and sea.

There are a number of ways to win the game. In the standard game, you can win by either a balance of story and destiny points, or by becoming Sultan. At the start of the game, you split 20 points between story and destiny, and if you reach those totals in your adventures, you return to Baghdad in glory. Within the story, as well, you have the chance of becoming Sultan, attaining the highest honor and winning the game.

Story and destiny points come from the adventures, and it is here that the game shines, with a densely packed (1,399 entries) *Book of Tales*. Cards and locations lead to a particular entry, and the player in turn sets his or her fate by choice, by appropriate skill, and, on occasion, by random chance.

You begin the game with a handful of skills, and gain more through your adventures. Skills are primarily used within the entries, usually but not always to your benefit. As a result of your adventures, you also gain status markers. Within the standard game, you may only have one status marker at a time, which vary from Beloved to Blessed to Insane to Outlaw (which can quickly lead to the status of Imprisoned). These statuses function to further change your opportunities, and one such status, Sultan, can win the game.

The wide variety of opportunities — through location on the board, cards, paragraphs, reactions, and statuses, all create a gaming environment that holds up over multiple plays, a particular challenge to many storytelling games. While certain motifs recur through the game, each experience is fresh and new.

The standard game is one of four versions. There is a solitaire game that is completely serviceable and good for getting a feeling for the game (though it is a better experience in a group). The adventure game is a collection of optional rules that can be installed and removed at the wish of the players. Here we see alternate play and victory conditions for quests and for merchants. It also contains rules for using skills and cards on other players, and in particular removing the limit on the number of status markers on a character. This last tends to be the first optional rule adopted, as individuals quickly absorb a fistful of statuses. As a house rule, we would eliminate a status only if the same character had an apparently contradictory status — one could not be both Respected and Scorned.

Tales of the Arabian Nights also contains a storytelling game, leading into those murky waters where the players must come up with their own tales. The designers put the concept forward in the most painless fashion possible, marrying it to the rules neatly as an encouraged option, rewarding it liberally, and supporting it strongly with examples. The storytelling process is a challenge, and best played among friends of similar abilities and dispositions, but the end result weds fully the act of storytelling with the experience of a board game.

Tales of the Arabian Nights succeeds because its rules match its subject matter so well. The paragraph system within the *Book of Tales* nicely mirrors the type of original storytelling in content, framework, and descriptive language. The original *One Thousand and One Nights* (translated into English many times, from the bowdlerizing E.W. Lane to the bawdy Sir Richard Francis Burton) were a collection of short adventures, sometimes spun out serially, but just as often nested one within the other like Russian matryoshka dolls. The game experience is similar: your encounter with the friendly hunchback can lead you to a kindly efreet, who in turn gives you the opportunity to enter a place of power in the distant islands to the north (Stonehenge). The tales naturally spin out of each other, each being short and self-contained. The game similarly stresses the episodic nature of these magical tales.

And, as an in-joke, the *Book of Tales* has a 1,400th entry, in which the various miscreants (including the design team) are thrown down a well in punishment for all those paragraphs. It is a sacrifice well made to produce a pearl of a game.

JEFF GRUBB is the designer of *Al-Qadim, Arabian Adventures*, a setting for *Dungeons & Dragons* in the time of the Arabian Nights. He is also one of the co-founders of the Dragonlance setting and the co-creator of the Forgotten Realms setting with Ed Greenwood. He is the author of over a dozen novels and 30 short stories. He is currently building worlds for computer game companies. None of these companies have yet thrown him down a well.

TALISMAN

KEY DESIGNER: ROBERT HARRIS

GAMES WORKSHOP (SECOND EDITION, 1985)

TALISMAN. THE VERY NAME conjures a smile — if not a nerdish giggle — from most thirty-something gamers as they recall countless high school and college days playing this simple and addictive game.

For those who have missed out on this classic, *Talisman* is a board game Games Workshop first published in 1983, back when they did other things besides *Warhammer*, *Warhammer 40K*, and *Lord of the Rings*. Those were the glorious, eclectic days of such board game greats as *Chainsaw Warrior*, *Rogue Trooper*, *The Fury of Dracula*, and *Block Wars* (from the Judge Dredd comics).

But nothing topped *Talisman*.

Oddly enough, *Talisman* wasn't designed as a fantasy homage to Games Workshop's still-forming oeuvre. According to creator Robert Harris on his website (www.harris-authors.com/talisman.html):

We played [*Dungeons & Dragons*] for an entire weekend, hardly pausing for sleep or food. It was an intoxicating experience as character after character was horribly killed to be replaced by another freshly created adventurer. After that we played regularly, but while others worked up new scenarios, I had it in mind to come up with a way we could have all the excitement of a roleplaying adventure without all the hard work of creating characters and drawing maps.

One key to *Talisman*'s success, I believe, lies here. Harris styled his game's heroes after those used in *Dungeons & Dragons*, giving them special abilities and a simple advancement system. With this, he captured the essence of what makes traditional roleplaying games so engaging — personalization and customization. (It's the same trend we see today in electronic games.) More astonishingly, Harris didn't *over*complicate this process either. In fact, he displayed an amazing understanding of streamlined gameplay throughout the project, especially in an age where most board games in the budding adventure games industry were of the SPI and Avalon Hill variety, with very complex rules. *Talisman* bucked the trend with eight short and sweet pages of rules — including art and a turn flowchart.

Actual play proves simple and fast moving. Each player selects a character — at random officially, but most groups I know dice for choice — and sets the matching full-color stand-up on the board in its starting location. Players then roll the dice, moves their heroes, and deal with whatever monsters or treasure they encounter along the way.

Combat is resolved by adding a d6 to either the character's strength (for physical encounters) or craft (for mental or psychic tests). The higher roll wins. Monsters are typically destroyed in a single blow, while heroes have two to four lives, but can sometimes discard certain items or followers to heal a wound or deflect the damage from an attack.

If your character perishes, no problem! Grab another (at random) and start over. You might even get your old loot back, because it's left where your previous adventurer fell. As you might suspect, a fallen warrior with lots of gold and magic can quickly turn his comrades into scrambling vultures.

The game's environment is as engaging as the character mechanics, with a full-color board packed with magic and mystery. Play begins on the lowest of three rings, called the Outer Region. Here, characters move about, flipping over a variable number of adventure cards in each location and dealing with whatever comes up, from traps to treasures, allies and foes. Most draws are mixed blessings, holding both monsters and treasure — and yes, the monsters have to be defeated before an adventurer can take any loot they happen to be guarding. Successfully defeating these threats can also help increase a character's statistics, making him tougher and more likely to survive the challenges ahead.

After traipsing about the wilderness, gathering treasure and improving their stats, characters can move on to the more challenging Middle Region. The obstacles faced here are a bit more difficult, but a wily warrior can hold his own until he discovers a talisman that will open the gateway to the Inner Region.

In the Inner Region, your character will either die or become the ultimate ruler of all creation. At the region's center, after completing several onerous tasks of craft and strength, the hero will find the Crown of Command. Reach the crown and win the game. Unless, of course, you're playing with *Talisman: The Adventure*, which all self-respecting gamers do.

With this expansion, the game's ending — what awaits the adventurer upon the quest's completion — is placed face-down at the center of the table. The prize might be the Crown of Command, but it might also be the Void, which consumes the hapless hero utterly. Or he might open Pandora's Box, giving him a random number of spells and adventure cards each turn, which he can then use to destroy the other adventurers before they destroy him. Or your hero might "meat" the Dragon King, who is just as likely to hand over his horde as he is to eat someone.

The alternate endings add great variety to the game and require a very different strategy. Do you let your enemy conquer the Inner Region first? Maybe he'll gain a quick victory, but he might also fall victim to the Void or reveal the session's true threat, allowing you to better prepare for the eventual *denouement*.

So what makes *Talisman* so much fun? What keeps it so enjoyable for me, even after more than *two decades*?

INTERESTING CHARACTERS: Each character has a unique ability that sets him apart from all the others — from the thief's annoying power to steal your gold and items, to the ghoul's disturbing ability to take one of your lives and add it to his own. This mechanic gives all the players distinct roles and even serves up opportunities for roleplaying.

ADVENTURE: Fighting monsters is always fun, but *Talisman* has obstacles, as well. Your hero has to climb, swim, or jump his way closer to the Inner Region. Sure, these obstacles are overcome with simple strength or craft rolls, but their presence helps maintain the game's breathless tone, its aura of action.

RANDOMNESS: Turning over a new adventure card is always exciting. Will you find a magic sword or an angry, curse-spewing hag, uncover gold or a vampire? I think *Talisman* hit upon one of the key factors in the later success of collectible card games — random card draws are an inherently exciting mechanic. Combine that with imaginative and evocative art, and you've got an easy recipe for success.

THE WEASEL FACTOR: While all of the above are important, the *real* fun in *Talisman* is stabbing your best friends in the back. I mentioned before that most groups I know dice for character choice. The reason why is very simple: While most of the characters have a good chance of winning the game if played properly, some are set up from the beginning to do it at the expense of others! The thief is always an optimum choice here. Can't find a talisman? Just take one from someone else. Need a Holy Lance? The priest might have one — take his!

Another great character — and perhaps the most annoying of all, if someone else plays him — is the samurai, introduced in *Talisman: The Adventure*. If you're low on life and wind up within three spaces of the samurai (and his three-space ranged attack), the odds are pretty good he'll plink an arrow your way, laugh while you die, and take all your stuff just as soon as he can loot the body.

It may sound harsh, but this sort of cutthroat interaction makes *Talisman* the game it is.

Talisman has seen release in three official editions, with the second generally considered the best. It, in turn, spawned six expansions: *Talisman Expansion Set*, *Talisman: The Adventure*, *Talisman Dungeon*, *Talisman Timescape*, *Talisman City*, and finally *Talisman Dragon*. *Talisman Expansion Set* and *The Adventure* are the most solid. *Dungeon* makes the game a little long and *City* isn't challenging enough, but both still present many news monsters to slay and items to find. *Timescape* isn't particularly well-balanced, but who cares — you can come out of there with a chainsaw! Even better, your hero can be a Space Marine or Chainsaw Warrior, both brutes in combat.

The original *Talisman* is long out of print but still a hot-seller on the secondary market. The good news is, a new edition is on the way from Games Workshop. (I'll dice you for the thief!) I'm guessing it'll be a little faster to play, with all-new artwork, but at its heart, it will still be the same great game that has kept us happily at each other's throats for more than two decades.

Shane Lacy Hensley started in the hobby game industry writing and designing for such companies as West End Games, TSR, FASA, and White Wolf. He later moved into computer games with SSI, Cryptic Studios, and now Superstition Studios, where his background has been put to work on massively multi-player online RPGs. He is best known for his own game company, Pinnacle Entertainment Group, and its bestselling *Deadlands* and *Weird Wars* properties.

Douglas Niles on

TERRIBLE SWIFT SWORD

KEY DESIGNER: RICHARD H. BERG

SIMULATIONS PUBLICATIONS, INC. (FIRST EDITION, 1976)

"He hath loosed the fateful lightning of his terrible swift sword. . ."
— "The Battle Hymn of the Republic"

THE BATTLE OF GETTYSBURG is a crucible of American history for a number of important reasons. It was *the* decisive battle of the Civil War, the turning point that has accurately been described as the high water mark of the Confederacy, and the true beginning of the Union's relentless march to Appomattox Court House. It was the largest battle ever fought on either American continent (at least in recorded history), and its three days resulted in more casualties than any other clash of armies in that most bloody of American wars. It would become the subject of what is arguably the greatest speech in U.S. history. For all these reasons, and more, Gettysburg has attracted and continues to attract the attention of historians, novelists (including some notable alternate history tales), and, of course, game designers.

It is only fitting that this closely fought, epic confrontation — a battle that clearly could have been won by either side — should be the subject of a spectacular, compelling, and innovative development in the wargame industry: the grand tactical monster game. With its three maps and more than 2,000 counters, *Terrible Swift Sword* immediately established a new standard for tactical board games when it was released in 1976. It deservedly won the Charles S. Roberts Awards for best wargame (one source calls this award "best pre-20th century board game") and best graphics in its year of release. It was the first huge, multiple-map tactical game, the precursor of many classics to come.

The look of the game is spectacular, with its large sweep of landscape, blue and gray columns and lines taking and holding such fabled positions as Cemetery Ridge and Little Round Top. *Terrible Swift Sword* was originally released in a flat pack plastic box, which was followed a year later by a double-sized cardboard box version. In 1985, it was revised by TSR into a second edition that brought it into line with the whole "Great Battles of the American Civil War" series — a collection of games that owe their existence to the original *Terrible Swift Sword*. (The full-color maps and counters of this later edition allowed for detailed differentiation of terrain levels and easy grouping of unit counters into corps, though purists maintain that it actually got a little *too* colorful.)

Because of the level of detail on the maps (125 yards per hex) and counters (regimental scale, with brigade, division, and corps command represented), the epic scope of conflict is presented with an astonishing level of tactical detail. The weaponry of individual units, including artillery batteries, factors in range and rate of fire. Cannons occupy high ground to strike targets across the battlefield, while infantry utilize terrain for cover and, at face-to-face range, defend or attack at the point of the bayonet. The scope of landscape available for maneuver allows for a wide variety of grand tactical options. And like the real clash, the game presents three distinctly different phases, one on each day of the battle.

It is true that playing a game of *Terrible Swift Sword* can seem like a rather formidable task. It can involve many people — I have played it with as many as eight or nine — and uncountable hours of play. But, like the real battle, it starts small: a mere two brigades of Union cavalry fight a delaying action against a steady stream of Confederate infantry brigades marching down a single road. The northern horsemen fight dismounted, firing carbines (among the most modern weapons on the battlefield, a lethality reflected in the game rules) as they strive to delay the Rebels across a series of ridges to the northwest of the town. Union reinforcements gradually appear on the other edges of the game map, various corps marching to the sound of the guns. Because the units are organized by a clear command hierarchy, it is easy to divide an army between multiple players. Despite its complexity, it is also a good game for incorporating novice players into a veteran group — and a rookie mistake with one brigade or division will likely not result in the collapse of an entire army!

In some ways, *TSS* brought the tactical feel of miniatures gaming onto a wargame map, including a workable system for recording casualties. Berg's rules offer the optional concept of "brigade combat effectiveness." This set of morale rules forces players into a more realistic appraisal of the fatigue and fear that would wear down units subject to long and brutal combat — and the recovery made possible by the two nights both armies spent on the field. Various levels of morale reflect the historical performance of different classes of troops. The

Union's First Brigade of the 1st Division of the I Corps, for example, will stand and fight nearly to the last man, befitting the reputation and the actual performance of the "Iron Brigade" during the crucial first day of the battle.

As befitting a complex portrayal of a complex event, *TSS* will allow for some outcomes that are contrary to the actual history of the battle. Confederate success on the first day, for example, can result in great opportunities for the second and third days. Players seeking an outcome that more accurately reflects the course of the actual battle can decide to play the game as one of its three main scenarios, which will insure a more historical progress of the second and third days of the battle — though even a one-day scenario of *TSS* requires a long weekend to play through.

This game greatly expanded my interest in board gaming. It led me to *Wellington's Victory*, another grand tactical monster, and to the games, small and large, of the Great Battles of the American Civil War System, all of which evolved from the original *TSS* rules. It even motivated me to drive all night, with two friends and fellow wargamers, from southern Wisconsin to Gettysburg. There, Zeb Cook, Steve Winter, and I soaked up the history and walked the landscape where these great events played out. It was a connection between gaming, history, and real life that I have never surpassed — and one I vividly remember whenever I have a chance to play *Terrible Swift Sword*.

Douglas Niles designed dozens of games for TSR, Inc. and SPI, including four Origins Award-winning board games and miniatures rulebooks. He is the designer of 1985's *World War II: European Theatre of Operations*, a grand strategic game currently in its third edition. The author of some 40 novels, best known as a writer of adventure fantasy and science fiction, Niles also co-authored three major World War II alternate history novels: *MacArthur's War*, *Fox on the Rhine*, and *Fox at the Front* (all with Michael Dobson). Writer of the very first Forgotten Realms novel, *Darkwalker on Moonshae*, he continues to contribute extensively to the bestselling Dragonlance series.

Ed Greenwood on

THURN AND TAXIS

KEY DESIGNERS: KAREN SEYFARTH, ANDREAS SEYFARTH
RIO GRANDE GAMES (ENGLISH EDITION, 2006)

SOME BOARD GAMES SEEK to recreate real-world battles as realistically as possible. Others postulate "what if" scenarios or (like chess) make combat abstract. Not everyone likes violent conflict as entertainment, though, so games likely to appeal to the whole family often make the conflict funny, or very abstract, or even emphasize cooperation. Then there are "builder" games, where players compete by personally trying to achieve a goal or build something either first, or better than other players, or to win by reaching a goal whose achievement will block other players from achieving their own winning goal.

Every game design is a compromise. Intense realism may involve frustrating strategic limitations on players ("It's militarily idiotic to charge over that hill. But, historically, that's what the Voldomodavians did, and that's what you must do at the start of the game!") or make playing a game take a l-o-o-o-ng time ("The Gold Rush lasted another three years; that's 36 more turns, folks; hurry up and draw those cards!"). Shifting to the abstract can take away a lot of possible tactics — those black and white squares on a chessboard are all the same; none are forts or bridges or rivers, and you can't hide a playing piece from an opponent behind one. And whereas wargamers may be willing take eight hours to play through an accurate, but hopeless simulation — of, say, Rorke's Drift, where a handful of British are *always* overwhelmed by thousands of Zulus — just to see how things turn out, tired Dad or short-tempered Grandpa wants any game they get persuaded to play to be much more obviously *fun*.

More than that: Only devoted game fans want a hard-thinking, match-wits game like chess every time, and no one likes a game entirely ruled by luck, wherein planning and playing skill don't matter. In a good design, luck must be balanced against utter player control. Rewards must also be balanced against difficulties, what players know (and can plan with) against the unknown. A single strategy that earns a victory every time is deadly, though an overabundance of options invites confusion-spawned paralysis. There are other factors, too — theme and complexity and time and age range. . . . All these things must be considered and dealt with in ways that don't unbalance the design.

Consider, then, creating a game that is fun, can be completed in an hour or less, stands up to repeated play, *and* will appeal to dedicated hobbyists as much as Grandpa. It must be awfully difficult to do, right?

Difficult, but it can be done, as Karen and Andreas Seyfarth have proved with *Thurn and Taxis* — a game about delivering the mail.

Thurn and Taxis is one of those rare games that isn't blood-and-guts, doesn't take forever to play, boasts remarkably effective and simple rules, and can be enjoyed over and over by both novice players aged 10 and up and hardcore strategists of considerably more years. Its somewhat obscure theme is even presented in a way that's appealing to those of us without doctorates in European history.

A beautiful game board transports us back to 17th-century Germany, when the notion of delivering mail by stagecoach has just been introduced. (The game's title is derived from the name of the family that established the first well-organized postal systems in Europe.) Two to four players compete, each striving to build the best postal delivery network. Very briefly explaining the game to Grandpa might go like this: "It's a route-building game — postal routes — no shooting at each other! It's like multi-player solitaire: we all play side-by-side on the same board, and the one who does the best building his route wins!"

Play in *Thurn and Taxis* consists of turns, wherein a player draws a card (an unknown card from the top of a deck, or one of six visible cards on the board), and then plays a card. That card must extend the player's existing postal route at one end, or begin a new route. If the player's route is at least three cities long, the player may choose to close it, which makes possible upgrading carriages used to deliver the mail or placing depots along the route.

Each turn, a player may use one of four privileges: draw two cards instead of one; play two cards instead of one; wipe away all six cards displayed on the board and replace them with new ones; or, if closing a route, earn a higher carriage upgrade than the route would normally allow. Points are earned by completing the most lucrative routes and placing the most depots in cities. Players who achieve these goals first earn more points than players who follow in their wake.

The game ends when a player first places the last of their 20 depots on the board, or upgrades to the highest possible carriage. All players then total their points — route tiles acquired, plus the value of their carriage, minus depots not yet played — and the highest score wins.

Handling your cards effectively throughout the game is crucial, but the building aspect can make play satisfying no matter who wins. The game usually takes a little more than an hour to play — an hour and a half at most, but less than an hour if there are fewer than four players, or everyone's a *Thurn and Taxis* veteran. Like many of the best games, it seems a simple proposition at first glance, yet becomes much more challenging the more you play. The strategy involved in planning routes and managing resources makes it an ideal tool for teaching younger players those skills in a way that won't feel like typical classroom tedium.

Thurn and Taxis deservedly won the 2006 Spiel des Jahres award in Germany, and was nicely expanded in 2007 with the *Power and Glory* supplement, which adds new map boards and potential routes. In all, *Thurn and Taxis* is one of the most visually beautiful board games I own. It's a keeper, to play again and again.

ED GREENWOOD is the creator of the Forgotten Realms campaign ("home world" of the second edition *Dungeons & Dragons* game, and arguably the largest and most detailed fantasy world ever) and the Castlemourn setting, and is co-creator (with fantasy novelist Lynn Abbey) of the Mornmist fantasy setting. Ed is the author or co-author of several hundred game products and fantasy novels, and has written over a thousand gaming magazine and website articles. He has been contributing editor and creative editor of *Dragon* magazine, and is an award-winning gamer (best player, 1984 Gen Con *AD&D* Open tournament) and game designer (several Gamer's Choice Awards and Origins Awards). He was inducted into the Gamer's Choice Hall of Fame in 1992 and the Academy of Adventure Gaming's Hall of Fame in 2003.

Mike Fitzgerald on

TICKET TO RIDE

KEY DESIGNER: ALAN R. MOON

DAYS OF WONDER (ENGLISH EDITION, 2004)

I AM SITTING DOWN at a game table with my friends Mark and Ralph, ready to play my 588th face-to-face game of *Ticket to Ride*. (I've played online thousands more times.) This has been the title I've played the most each year since 2004, when it was first published. I love the basic game, but also *Ticket to Ride: Europe, Ticket to Ride: Märklin*, the online *Ticket to Ride: Switzerland*, and the latest *USA 1910* expansion, which adds a lot to the core game.

The basic *Ticket to Ride* game is played on a board showing a map of the United States. Cities are connected by chains of colored rectangles, like lines of box cars. You build a rail network by collecting and playing train cards that match the specific colors of those blocks, then placing little plastic train markers on the route to claim it. You're also secretly trying to link certain cities, determined by destination tickets you draw at the game's outset; the cities might be close together, they might be on opposite coasts. But the routes between cities are limited, and some harder to complete than others. You get points for linking any two cities, but more points for completing those specific routes on your destination tickets.

When Mark, Ralph, and I sit down together, we need a good three-player game, which is not that easy to find. *Ticket to Ride* plays very well with any number of players from two to five. This is accomplished by a very simple rule tying how many connections between cities are open for use with the number of players. Many adjacent cities, at least those somewhat close together, are connected by two side-by-side routes. When you play with two or three players, only one of those routes can be used. This keeps the game competitive.

Why do I like *Ticket to Ride* so much? Well, it's a bit hard to explain. Perhaps the best way to share my thoughts on the game would be to let you inside my head while I'm playing.

As we set up, I take 45 yellow trains (I am always yellow), Ralph takes 45 green trains (Ralph is always green), and Mark takes 45 red trains (he doesn't care which color he gets because he always wins). We're playing the basic *Ticket to*

Ride game with the U.S. map and the *1910* expansion, which adds new destination tickets and replaces the smaller-sized cards from the original with larger ones. We shuffle all 69 destination tickets and draw five, of which we have to keep at least three.

The five destination tickets I'm dealt are: Dallas-to-New York, Duluth-to-Dallas, Pittsburgh-to-New Orleans, Toronto-to-Charleston, and Salt Lake City-to-Kansas City. All of these are smaller routes that are relatively easy to complete. Since there are two that include Dallas and a lot of connections in the East, I decide to keep them all. *Ticket to Ride* requires long-term strategic planning at the beginning of the game. My plan is to make a continuous route that covers all these cities, though I'm concerned that there are no routes worth a lot of points here. Later in the game, I'll have to draw more destination tickets to try to find a high-value East Coast-to-West Coast destination that will fit with the route I am building. Of course, what Mark and Ralph do during the game could alter this plan quite a bit.

Next, we deal out four train cards to each player. These come in eight different colors, just like the blocks linking the cities on the map. We have a face-down draw pile of train cards, as well as a tableau that is now set up with five face-up train cards. Since I'm going first, I have the option to draw two cards from one of these sources. If I don't want cards, I can either play train cards from my hand to complete a connection from one city to another, or draw four new destination tickets and keep at least one of them. (These rules on drawing destination tickets are from the *1910* expansion. Basic game rules differ slightly.) Since each player can only do one of these three things, the game moves very quickly.

I'm very glad to be going first because I want the single-block connection that links Nashville to Atlanta. In sessions of *Ticket to Ride*, this is the first space taken, since it is key for Eastern routes and helps a lot in some big ticket East-to-West routes. Since it is colored gray — essentially a wild card — I can play any color train card to claim it. I play one black train card and place one of my yellow trains on the space. Ralph instantly groans, so I know he wanted that connection, too. *Ticket to Ride* has a delicious tension throughout, as you hold your breath wondering if someone else will take the connections you want.

As the game moves on, Mark and Ralph spend most of their turns drawing train cards. They end up with massive hands, meaning they are probably looking to build connections in the West, where the links between cities require more train cards. (It is a very good idea to track the train cards that your opponents grab from the face-up tableau. This can help you in figuring out where they want to go, since you can match up the colors they're taking with the available routes on the map.) Better still, once they start claiming routes, it's clear that they're going to fighting each other for connections. I'm left to my own devices in the East, where I easily complete all my destination tickets.

But I'm still missing that big-point East-to-West destination — until my last turn. Earlier, I'd taken a shot and drew new destination tickets. I was lucky enough to draw San Francisco-to-Atlanta, which I had a chance of making. Just barely, as it turns out.

I receive the end-of-the-game bonus for completing the most tickets, while Mark gets the bonus for longest route. *Ticket to Ride* has enough endgame scoring opportunities to keep the outcome in doubt until the final reckoning, when everyone tallies up their points for destinations completed and adds that to amount they've already earned for building each link in their rail networks. In this case, Mark and I are close in the scoring, but Mark wins (as usual). Ralph is close, but fails to complete one destination ticket because Mark and I have taken all four routes into New York, blocking him out of a necessary city. *Ticket to Ride* does not particularly reward cutthroat play; the best strategy is usually to complete your own tickets. This makes it quite suitable for casual family use. However, it involves enough interactive strategy involved that competitive players will find it enjoyable, too.

I've thanked designer Alan Moon many times for creating a game that I never tire of, one that lends itself well to the many expansions that Days of Wonder have released. The design principles it uses are all simple and have been done before, but they have never been put together in a game as compelling as *Ticket to Ride*.

MIKE FITZGERALD started designing games right after *Magic: The Gathering* came out in 1993. His first design was a trading card game called *Wyvern*, which was published by U.S. Games. This resulted in a contract with Wizards of the Coast to do more designs, including the *Nitro* (WCW wrestling) and *X-Men* trading card games. He is currently working for Pokémon USA, helping to put together the pre-constructed decks that are sold with every *Pokémon* expansion. Mike is also the designer of the *Mystery Rummy* series. The fifth *Mystery Rummy* game, based on Bonnie and Clyde, should see release in 2007 from Rio Grande Games. Mike combines game design with a long and successful radio career as an on-air personality. As Mike's kids say, "Dad plays games and plays songs for a living." Most of all Mike has fun.

Thomas Lehmann on

TIGRIS & EUPHRATES

KEY DESIGNER: REINER KNIZIA

MAYFAIR GAMES (ENGLISH EDITION, 1999)

REINER KNIZIA IS AMONG the most prolific and talented game designers working today. Many consider *Tigris & Euphrates* (*T&E*) to be his masterpiece. In addition to being an intense, fluid game of tile placement and conflict, *T&E*, despite its abstract nature, captures the essence of its theme: the rise and fall of kingdoms in the eastern Fertile Crescent, between the Euphrates and Tigris rivers.

The goal is to have the most points at game's end. However, victory cubes are earned in four categories and your score is the number of *complete sets* (all four colors) of victory cubes. Excess cubes are worthless, except as tie-breakers. Balance is everything.

The board is a grid of river and land squares. Ten temple tiles, each with a treasure, begin in pre-set locations, scattered about the map. There are four tile types. One type can be placed on river squares; the other three on land. Land spaces can be occupied by either tiles or leaders.

Each player begins with four leaders (one for each tile type), two disasters, and a random hand of six tiles. A player's turn is two actions, each of four possible choices: place (or shift) a leader, adjacent to any temple tile; place a tile; play a disaster; or replace some or all of your tiles in hand.

The four colors of victory cubes correspond to each tile/leader type. By playing a tile in a chain connected to a leader of that type, the leader's owner receives a victory cube of that color. Since the goal is to have complete sets, you must usually get all four of your leaders in play, to earn victory cubes as you place tiles. However, each kingdom can only have one leader of each type. Do you put your leaders (representing specialized family branches of your dynasty) all in one kingdom or do you scatter them about?

Kingdoms can grow from single temples into large chains of leaders and tiles, or can be torn apart, upon coming into contact with other kingdoms. Hedging your bets by scattering your leaders means the merged kingdoms are effectively shared among several players, with different agendas. This creates tension and contrasts *T&E* with most expansion-mechanic games, where each player typically controls a single entity.

The treasures help motivate kingdom expansion. Whenever two of the original 10 temples are linked by a chain of tiles, the owner of the merchant leader in this kingdom generally takes a treasure. Each treasure is a wild victory cube, of any color, which is *very* useful for filling out complete sets at the end of the game.

When kingdoms meet, they merge, provided no pairs of leaders of the same type exist in the joined kingdoms. Otherwise, conflict takes place. In the color in conflict (chosen by the merging player), the attacker totals the number of those tiles in his or her kingdom, possibly adding matching tiles from his or her hand. The defender, after seeing the attacker's total, does the same. Ties go to the defender. The loser's leader *and* all tiles of that color in the loser's kingdom are removed, with the winner gaining one victory cube for each removed piece. Then, if leaders in conflict still exist, this process is repeated.

This removal rule is pure genius. Kingdoms, depending on how they were built, can be shattered into disconnected fragments by conflicts. Many games portray expansion and conflict; very few games also depict decay and dissolution. Conflicts allow players to potentially earn many cubes with a single play, instead of the usual one cube for playing a tile matching a leader.

A kingdom with mixed ownership often has very different expansion goals, as one player tries to merge where its leader has an advantage while another tries to avoid this, possibly by playing disasters — which permanently destroy a tile and its square — to either block contact, sever a kingdom in two, or remove a vulnerable leader who has only one adjacent temple.

Internal conflicts, or coups, occur when a second leader of the same type is placed in a kingdom. Each owner totals the temple tiles *adjacent* to their leader, plus any temple tiles chosen for play from his or her hand. The losing leader is removed. These rules produce an *extremely* fluid game, as coups can arise at any point and external conflicts will often dramatically rearrange the board.

Monuments are another source of victory cubes. A player placing the fourth tile of the same type in a square formation can choose to flip these tiles over and build one. Each wooden monument has two colors, one matching the tiles used to build it and the other of the builder's choice. Any matching leaders connected to a monument earn one victory cube in that color at the end of their owners' turns. This steady cube income really adds up, often motivating coup attempts.

Thus, if you are short tiles of one color, one approach to score cubes is to oust a leader from a kingdom with lots of the desired tiles and then engineer an external conflict. Another is to acquire enough treasures to make up the deficit. A third is to horn in on an existing monument of the color you need. A fourth is to build a monument of a color you already have, whose second color is the one you need.

It is this variety of options that makes playing *T&E* so creative and satisfying. There's usually a way to accomplish your goals, if you can think of it.

Meanwhile, the "action pressure" is tremendous. Over and over, players really want to take *three* actions in a turn, but have only *two*. Choosing your actions and hoping that the option to complete your plan next turn will still be there (in the face of your opponents' reactions) makes playing *T&E* quite intense.

Each game takes about an hour, ending when either the tile bag is exhausted or two or fewer treasures are left. The game works equally well with two, three, or four players.

Every game tends to develop differently. Some sessions will see lots of monument building; others, none at all. Some are filled with conflict, right from the start; others have mostly well-separated kingdoms, minding their own business.

A final board position often holds two or three large kingdoms, plus a much-disputed area of disaster tiles, kingdom fragments, and even abandoned monuments (from when all the nearby temples have been destroyed). Looking at such positions and considering the ebb and flow of kingdoms in the game, I am reminded of Shelley's poem "Ozymandias," in which a traveler comes across the head of a once-great monument, now broken and half sunk in the desert: "My name is Ozymandias, king of kings: / Look on my works, ye mighty, and despair!"

If you are looking for a tactically rich, intense strategy game with lots of conflict (unusual in a German game), try *Tigris & Euphrates* and see why so many players consider this game Reiner Knizia's masterpiece.

Tom Lehmann is the former publisher and designer of Prism Games. He now designs games for the international market. His works include *Fast Food Franchise*, *Time Agent*, *2038* (with Jim Hlavaty), *1846*, *Magellan/Pizarro & Co.*, *Jericho*, *To Court the King*, and the forthcoming titles *Phoenicia*, *1834*, and *Race for the Galaxy*.

Warren Spector on

TIKAL

KEY DESIGNERS: MICHAEL KIESLING, WOLFGANG KRAMER

RIO GRANDE GAMES (ENGLISH EDITION, 1999)

GAMES WORK THEIR MAGIC on us in a variety of ways.

It may be a title that tells you you'll get to be the hero of that TV show you love. It may be a fiction, a fantasy, you just have to live out — "You're the last space marine standing between Earth and alien invaders." Or it may be gameplay so compelling you *have* to play — "Mate in three."

A game's true appeal may lie in the opportunities it provides for socialization; even mediocre games offer us a tribal togetherness we've all but lost in Western culture. Hence the appeal of everything from "Tag, you're it" to "You didn't know Britney Spears was a Mouseketeer?!"

Well, *Tikal* has a bad title and dull fiction, but it nails the gameplay and socialization aspects of great gaming — and that forgives a lot of sins. . . .

Why is "Tikal" a terrible name? For starters, it's hard to pronounce, hard to remember, and devoid of meaning for most people. (Who knew that, in the real world, Tikal is the largest and most important Mayan archaeological site? If the rulebook hadn't told me, I *still* wouldn't have any idea!)

Fiction and fantasy? How many of us aspire to become intrepid archaeologists, competing with other archaeologists for the privilege of unearthing an ancient city's secrets? (Okay, maybe Indiana Jones made archaeologists sexy, but check out the other games in this book and you'll find a lot more generals, starship pilots, even businessmen, than shovel-wielding scientists. . . .)

Bad name, obscure fiction, and limited fantasy appeal notwithstanding, here's *Tikal* in a book about the all-time best hobby games. And let no man or woman say it doesn't belong. Remember, great gameplay that encourages player interaction is powerful stuff, and *Tikal*'s a corker of a design — easy to learn, perfect balance of luck and strategy, multiple ways to win (which ensures that no two sessions unfold or feel the same). . . . It also offers *plenty* of opportunities to screw your friends — perhaps the single element that unites all great games. On top of that, *Tikal* has an impressive pedigree. Wolfgang Kramer and Michael Kiesling are responsible for a lot of incredible games. Kramer could have retired after *Niki Lauda's Formel 1* or *El Grande* and his place in gaming history would have been secure.

If you need external validation, try this on for size: *Tikal* won the 2000 *Games* magazine award for best family strategy game, the International Gamers Award for best strategy game, a Deutscher Spiele Preis for best family/adult game in 1999, and, of course, the prestigious Spiel Des Jahres (Game of the Year) that same year.

So how does *Tikal* play? What makes it tick?

The game is for two to four players, each taking the role of director of an expedition exploring the Guatemalan jungles to uncover the lost temples and hidden treasures of Mayan civilization. When the game begins, the board, divided into hexagonal areas, consists of a small base camp, two temples, and a clear, passable area.

Each player's turn begins with the random selection of a hex tile (a temple, a treasure, or a cleared jungle area). A fourth type of tile, the volcano, triggers a scoring round. Each hex-side on a tile contains zero to three "stones"; in order to move from one tile to the next, there must be at least one stone on the side the player wishes to cross. If no stones exist on a hex-side, or on the hex-side of the adjacent stone, that path is impassable. The exact number of stones on a side determines the cost to move from one hex to another.

Temple tiles have a starting value and can be made even more valuable by continued excavation, which is accomplished by selecting higher-numbered temple tiles and placing them on the terrain tile. (As the temple tiles are placed one atop the other, they create a nifty 3-D pyramid on the board.) Uncovering higher-value temple levels is a key scoring element.

Treasure tiles contain one to three golden masks; the number of masks determines how many treasure tokens are available when the tile is placed. Collecting sets of identical treasures is another key scoring element. The more of a treasure type you have, the more points you score.

Once a terrain tile has been placed, players can do several things: You can place or move an expedition member; uncover temple levels; recover treasures or exchange them with another player; establish a base camp in a cleared jungle tile; or place a guard on a temple.

Whenever a volcano tile is revealed, a scoring round occurs. There are three volcano tiles and when the last one is played, the game ends. The player with the most temple and treasure points at that point wins.

Simple. Nothing innovative or new here — just solid execution of time-tested ideas. If players could just do everything they wanted, there'd be no game at all. If players got to do an arbitrary number of each action type, you'd have an okay, but not great, design. But *Tikal is* a great game, and that's largely a result of Kramer and Kiesling's action point system.

Players get just 10 action points a turn. Want to bring a new expedition member onto the board? That's one AP. Place as many as you like, up to the maximum of 10. Move an expedition member? One AP per stone you traverse. Annoyed that you placed a tile in such a way that it costs six points to cross from one tile to another? Tough. Pay up. Uncovering a temple level costs two AP. Recovering one treasure costs three points. Exchanging a treasure with another player, three points. Establishing a camp or placing a guard? *Five* points!

This simple idea makes *Tikal* sing. You can *never* do everything you want in a turn. You're always making tough decisions. The game is a teeth-gnashing struggle to find the most efficient way to use a fixed, limited resource.

THE ACTION POINT SYSTEM is the heart of *Tikal*, but there are other game elements worth mentioning:

Tikal has a ton of "toy value" — not the hundreds of plastic soldiers or spaceships we usually think of when we talk about toy value, but dozens of solid components of varying sizes, shapes and textures. There are big hexes; temple level tiles of varying size, so little pyramids actually grow on the board; coinlike cardboard treasure pieces; wood cubes representing expedition members. . . . The variety of pieces makes *Tikal* a tactile joy.

In addition, every turn offers opportunities to screw your friends. You can place tiles in such a way that an opponent's path is blocked, choking off access to rewards. You can steal treasures to increase your own wealth. You can even maneuver so you have more expedition members in a temple hex than an opponent, ensuring they get no points for the temple, even if they did most of the work excavating it. Delicious!

You can win with a temple strategy or a treasure strategy or a combination of both. The variety of rewards allows different strategies.

Scoring rounds are random but predictable — you have an idea when volcano tiles *might* show up but can't *know*. That creates incredible tension, as the inevitable eruption approaches. You can almost see the smoke plume rising. The need to balance action and consolidation prior to scoring is huge.

At the end of the day, *Tikal* offers a near perfect balance of luck and skill. Preplanning is rewarded, but not *too* much preplanning. Set things up a turn or two ahead and you're good to go. Anything more than that and the other players *will* do something to disrupt your plan.

All of this makes *Tikal* a "gamers' game" that, well, *normal* people can play and appreciate. (I once had a girlfriend who'd frustrate the heck out of me by reminding me that she just "played for fun," as I agonized over every nuance of every turn. *Tikal* was *made* for people like her. . . .)

If it sounds like *too* much randomness for you, there's an official variant auction option that eliminates some of the luck. Ignore it — the balance of luck and skill is critical to the game's success.

Once you're hooked on *Tikal*, you can move on to the other games in Kiesling and Kramer's "Mask" trilogy. The games *Mexica* and *Java* share some mechanics, but feature different settings, fiction, and some new gameplay elements. Try them, for sure, but if you're like most people, you'll find yourself coming back to *Tikal*, once the novelty of the newer games wears off. As is so often the case, the first is still the best.

WARREN SPECTOR entered the games business in 1983 when, just shy of his doctorate in Radio-TV-Film, he joined Steve Jackson Games. For SJG he worked on a variety of board games and RPGs, including *Toon: The Cartoon Roleplaying Game*, *GURPS*, and others, while rising to the position of editor-in-chief. Four years later, he moved to TSR, where he worked on *Top Secret/S.I.*, *The Bullwinkle and Rocky Party Roleplaying Game*, and the second edition *AD&D* rules set, as well as board games, choose-your-own-adventure books, and novels. In 1989, Warren joined ORIGIN, a developer/publisher of electronic games. There he co-produced *Ultima VI* and *Wing Commander* and produced *Ultima Underworld 1* and 2, *Ultima VII: Serpent Isle*, *System Shock*, *Wings of Glory*, *Bad*

Blood, *Martian Dreams*, and others. In 1997, after a year as general manager of Looking Glass Austin, Warren started Ion Storm's Austin development studio, where he directed the award-winning action/RPG, *Deus Ex* (2000). As Ion Storm studio director, he oversaw development of *Deus Ex: Invisible War* (2003) and *Thief: Deadly Shadows* (2004) before leaving to found Junction Point Studios in 2004. In July 2007, JPS was acquired by The Walt Disney Company to work on as-yet-unannounced projects.

TOON

KEY DESIGNERS: GREG COSTIKYAN, WARREN SPECTOR

STEVE JACKSON GAMES (1984)

WITH ITS OUTRAGEOUSLY RED cover, *Toon* heralded something different in the roleplaying world upon its publication in 1984. Perhaps it was the title, rendered in bright yellow letters, or the manically cheerful rabbit on the cover poised to hurl a pie, but there was little mistaking the fact that this was anything but an ordinary roleplaying game. *Toon* was shooting for the impossible.

If it wasn't obvious from the title, *Toon* was the first ever cartoon roleplaying game. It was the only game where you got to play anarchic rabbits, neurotic ducks, dim-witted dogs, sociopathic mice, and even over-educated cats. It was the game where you got to defy the laws of physics and reason all in the name of a good gag. In a time when every roleplaying game before it had been serious — full of barbarians and wizards fighting dragons, secret agents battling egotistical villains, or space-suited soldiers exploring the war-torn fringes of the galaxy — *Toon* was anything but. *Toon* was the first comedy roleplaying game.

It was a wedding of two impossible traits — rules and anarchy. Roleplaying games are all about rules. Rules are the thing that creates the logic and order game designers want to impose on fantastic settings. There are rules to say how many spells a wizard can cast or how fast a spaceship can fly. As a player you learn the rules, operate within the rules, and master the rules on your way to greatness. And that order is just what you need to dispatch a dragon or pilot that spaceship — but cartoons live in an entirely different kind of universe. With cartoons, logic and order go out the window. It's all about the improbable, impossible, and silly. To have a roleplaying game, a creature of rules, using the logic of cartoons is a contradiction of terms.

Which is not to say that *Toon* does not have rules. It does; within the rulebook are all the rules you need to play. They are necessarily simple and, even then, still probably too many. Everything is done with a few basic six-sided dice. Characters have abilities (because it is a roleplaying game) that rate how good they are in a few areas — muscle (how brawny your character is), chutzpah (your ability to lie, bluff, and just be cool), smarts (what they teach you in books), and zip (speed, agility, and everything to do with motion). More importantly characters learn shticks, special things they can do that are not run of the mill, everything from stretching themselves into funny shapes to having that handy bag from which *anything* might be pulled.

And what cartoon hero or villain would be complete without his mail order catalog? From the pages of the *Ace Catalog*, your character can order improbable goods and have them arrive faster than FedEx. Need a catapult or an electronic robot dog? Just place your order and wait.

Being a roleplaying game, there are experience points to be had — or "plot points," as they are called in this instance. One inspired design choice is that you can earn points for making others, especially the game master, laugh. It is the RPG equivalent of bringing down the house and essential for a comedy game. So, too, the way the game treats its characters' health. In *Toon*, death is inconsequential. You don't die, you "fall down" and have to sit out three minutes of play — a precursor of the death penalties in today's online games such as *World of Warcraft*, where after your demise you miraculously appear as a ghost and have to spend time running back to your body.

Now, *Toon* is not perfect. It has more rules than it needs, although at the time it seemed rules-lite. In a game where timing and spontaneity are king, stopping to look up a rule is deadly. It's also not a game most groups would play for years on end. It just doesn't lend itself to elaborate ongoing storylines, character growth, and rich world detail. But when your model is the standard, self-contained six minutes of mayhem of the classic Warner Brothers cartoon that's hardly surprising. Most telling of its weaknesses is that it needs just the right group, from GM to players, to make whole thing work. In the wrong hands — the shy, the deliberate, the rules lawyers, the just plain dull — a game of *Toon* is the equivalent of the incompetent stand-up comedian, a night of pain and suffering for all.

At its best, though, *Toon* is an exhilarating, terrifying freefall of fun. From the simplest of plot points ("Get the mouse!") games spin wildly and hilariously out of control. It is cooperative and competitive at the same time as players seek to make each other laugh *and* top the last joke — it's not what you actually get done that matters, it's the style that counts. Failing funny still counts as winning. It is the gamer's handbook to improv. Sure, it needs a GM ready to throw out the notes, even throw out the rules, but when that happens *Toon* transforms the evening from a roleplaying game into a total party experience.

Even so, why does *Toon* matter? What is it about a game that most of you have never heard of that warrants this attention? Two reasons are relatively obvious.

First it launched a trend for comedy RPGs. In the years that followed other titles came out — *Ghostbusters*, *Paranoia*, *Tabloid*, and more. It showed that comedy as a genre could work in the RPG form. Comedy games owe their existence to the appearance of *Toon*.

Second, it was the first of a wave of rules-lite games. While it didn't start that trend (several other rules-lite titles were underway at the same time), it was one of the first to hit shelves and showed that roleplaying games didn't need massive rules and overstuffed boxes to be fun. All that was really necessary was a spirit true to the essence of the subject — a spirit conveyed by the rules, setting, and even the writing style. *Toon* was one of the earliest and best examples of this, with its rules set that worked so brilliantly to encourage an evening of cartoon mayhem.

By far the most important reason why *Toon* matters, though, is something it embodied, an offshoot of its rule-lite approach. *Toon* was an evolution in roleplaying and it helped us — players, GMs, and especially designers — to see more clearly the essence of roleplaying. Although it had rules and structures, *Toon* succeeded best when players ignored all that. In many ways it reminded us what the essence of roleplaying was and can be. Stripped down to a circle of people, a few dice, and some healthy imagination, *Toon* is spontaneous storytelling, a shared experience where the product doesn't matter, only the interplay of the moment. *Toon* made it clear how a theme and a few mental props can create a complete game experience. Other roleplaying games might show us the connections between myth and history, but *Toon* goes right to the heart of what gaming is really all about — theater and improvisation.

So, go. Find. Buy. (Used copies of the game can be found on the secondhand market, but the publisher, Steve Jackson Games, is also selling PDFs from its website, for the technologically savvy among you.) Don't let this opportunity fade just because you've never heard of *Toon* before. Get your own copy and unleash the power of animated chaos on your gaming circle!

Make them die laughing — it's worth plot points, after all.

DAVID "ZEB" COOK has somehow managed to make a long-term career as a professional game designer, against all better sense and reason. Since the early 1980s, Zeb (no, he doesn't mind if you call him Zeb) has worked in both the electronic games and paper games industry on titles such as *Stargate Worlds* MMO, *City of Villains* MMO, *Fallout II*, the second edition rules for *Advanced Dungeons & Dragons*, *Planescape*, *Conan*, and much more. Over the years, he swears he has worked on every type of game out there — MMORPGs, RTS, CRPGs, paper roleplaying games, board games, card games, and even some real oddities (anyone remember the *Bullwinkle and Rocky Roleplaying Party Game*?), in genres covering fantasy, superheroes, science fiction, pulp, TV, historical genres, and just plain weird. Somehow, he also managed to find time to write a few novels and short stories, and swears one day he really will write that book about game design he's always talked about. He even knows what a Bohemian ear-spoon is.

Mike Pondsmith on

TRAVELLER

KEY DESIGNER: MARC W. MILLER

GAME DESIGNERS' WORKSHOP (FIRST EDITION, 1977)

IF MARC MILLER HAD never written *Traveller*, I would have never become a game designer. So it's *his* fault that your *Cyberpunk* character was killed last week.

From the trio of simple black books in the initial boxed set, to the profusion of modules, supplements, deck plans, figures, and spaceships that would expand the line incredibly, *Traveller* has been the premier science fiction roleplaying game. Over the years it has forged a legacy that includes not only legions of diehard fans, but also a fair number of game designers who have taken inspiration from those three little black books (or, as *Traveller* fans call them, the "LBBs"). That's hardly a surprise. In my not-so-humble opinion, *Traveller* — and here I mean the first edition, not the many worthy variations that have followed in its footsteps — embodies the epitome of clean, elegant roleplaying game design.

Let's take a look at the box containing those first three books for a moment. It sports no flashy cover with spaceships rocketing through the galaxy — no blaster-waving space stud idly cradling an underdressed, overstacked alien female in one arm. Its cover, like those of the books it holds, is dead black, with just a spare bit of type — an interrupted transmission from a damaged spaceship drifting in the Deep Abyss. "This is Free Trader Beowulf, calling anyone," the desperate message reads. "Mayday, Mayday . . . we are under attack . . ." These simple, terse words instantly catapult the reader into a scenario that imagination makes far more exciting than any heroic space art could convey — a ship under attack by unknown forces, alone against the universe. You want to be there, holding off the enemy with your body pistol while air whistles out of the rents in the *Beowulf*'s hull. The box cover doesn't titillate you — it *challenges* you.

The rulebooks contained inside are just as challenging, and rewarding. *Traveller* was the first true science fiction RPG in a world of *D&D* wannabes and fantasy flavors-of-the-month. Its roots go back to the classics of science fiction: Asimov's Foundation series, Anderson's Polesotechnic League books, Niven's

Known Space cycle. *Traveller*'s spaceships work using physics and hard science; its chemical slug throwers trump space-opera ray guns and its heroes are smugglers and merchants instead of superheroic Galactic Patrolmen. For those of us who aren't fantasy-fans — for those who lust after the stars instead of elven forests, *Traveller* is the Real Thing.

You start out a *Traveller* character by rolling the usual fistful of six-sided dice, but once your numbers are rolled up, the mechanics add a novel premise: your character isn't a typical callow youth starting out on his or her first big adventure away from home. No, *Traveller* characters are *experienced*. To create a character, you have to actually generate his entire life up to the moment when you begin playing him in an actual game, choosing and trying different career paths over years of trials and travails as the character is developed. (Heck, until the second edition, you could even kill your character off in the process!) On top of that, instead of abstract levels and classes, you actually now have *skills*. The result of the character-generation process is a seasoned spacer who *knows* stuff, and has a *reason* to know it, instead of a generic "5th-level thief" with a 20 percent in "pick locks." This process also gives the character a background that allows you to add roleplaying depth to your portrayal; even your brand-new character can begin conversations with, "Ah, that reminds me of the time I was wounded while serving in the Marines on Jagland Beta 9. . . ."

Combat is also elegant and well balanced; you beat a simple target number (8) on two six-siders. Modifiers can shift the outcome of the roll, but even these will only be brought into play if the game master desires that extra level of complexity. While more fully expanded with the later *Snapshot* rules, this basic "hit the target" number system would become the model for many game systems to follow. Damage is also clearly defined. There are no simple hit points; instead, you allocate damage done to your character between his strength, endurance or dexterity scores, thereby controlling just what effects a hit will have on him. While this might seem odd to a player of more traditional RPGs, you soon realize that this system allows you to subtly tailor the kind of character you have — if he's tough, you chew through his dexterity first; if he's weak but skilled, you knock down his endurance instead of dexterity.

Combat isn't just limited to people, though. In *Traveller*, you can also get mano-a-mano with starships — from the ubiquitous Type T Scout ships everyone starts with, all the way up to such gigaton ships as the High Lightning class from the *Azhanti High Lightning* supplement. *Traveller*'s vector movement system gives combat the feel of real space action, while its weapons allow players to engage in the type of head-to-head laser battles that are the hallmark of sci-fi cinema. Plentiful deck plans from a variety of publishers and rules allowing players to design their own layouts mean that you can tackle that enemy ship in deep space, wipe out its defenses, then move to a savage boarding action all with one set of rules.

Traveller was also unique in its day as the first RPG that really gave the game master *tools*. The rules encourage game masters to get in there and get their mental hands dirty — the tools for making ships, planets, animals, and aliens are all laid out in lucid, precise text, just begging to be used.

Need a spaceship? The second of the LBBs, *Starships*, shows you how to build the ship you want, customized and ready to be improved. (And a lot of players and GMs spend almost as much time on their ships as they do on their characters!) Until the advent of *Mekton* and *BattleTech*, the ability to build large, complex vehicles was the hallmark of *Traveller*, and the capabilities were further expanded with the addition of the *High Guard* book that followed the initial rules release. And though decades have passed in the gaming world, *Traveller* remains among the gold standards for "build your own spaceship" systems.

But ships are just the start of the toolset. Need a planet? *Worlds and Adventures*, LBB number three, gives you frameworks for building the planets and star systems you need, complete with believable ecosystems. The rules are also great for adapting the strange new worlds you'd read about in your favorite science fiction epics. (I still have my now-20-year-old notes for a *Traveller* version of Poul Anderson's Merseia.) You can even develop new alien races with the animal rules, and many enterprising game masters have done just that.

But the real gem of *Traveller* is the Imperium — the setting in which the whole game takes place. A classic, sprawling empire of millions of stars, it offers players a background that can encompass almost any science fiction world they can devise. The setting's aliens — Vargr, Aslan, and Droyne — are just Nivenesque enough to be interesting; the nobility is just enough of an Asimov/Anderson fusion to host both jaded fops and idealistic leaders.

The Imperium's flexibility was demonstrated quite nicely when *Star Wars* exploded onto the pop culture scene not long after *Traveller*'s release. It didn't take much to morph the Imperium into Darth Vader's Dark Empire — just read the lightsaber and blaster article in the *Space Gamer* and you were good to go. The psionics rules to power the Force were already written up in *Worlds and Adventures*.

Yep, *Traveller* even got *there* ahead of George Lucas.

Traveller's influence on hobby gaming is legendary. From its loins came off-spring in the form of dozens of innovative game companies and their products. FASA, which would go on to publish such classics as *BattleTech* and *Shadowrun*, began life as the Freedonian Aeronautics and Space Administration, publisher of licensed *Traveller* material. Hero Games' *Champions* drew from *Traveller*'s idea of a point building system. R. Talsorian's *Lifepath* character history and target number resolution systems (as well as the homage of "black box *Cyberpunk*") were inspired by the many *Traveller* games I was a proud part of.

It can be argued, in fact, that almost every major science fiction-styled RPG owes a debt to *Traveller* — if not for specific design elements, then for providing the benchmark of what a good sci-fi RPG should be.

And without its inspiration, I would probably still be a child psychologist studying delinquent kids for the State of California.

So, like I said, it's all Marc Miller's fault.

The son of a psychologist and an Air Force officer, MIKE PONDSMITH has somehow managed to make a pretty good living since the 1980s as a game designer, even though his mother didn't originally think he could. He is usually blamed for creating the hit games *Cyberpunk*, *Mekton*, *Teenagers From Outer Space*, and the Origins Award-winning *Castle Falkenstein*, as well serving a far-too-long stint as a design manager at Microsoft Game Studios. Although insanely busy doing the stuff he loves, he still finds time to kick his son's butt in the occasional *Mekton* game.

Zev Shlasinger on

TWILIGHT STRUGGLE

KEY DESIGNERS: ANANDA GUPTA, JASON MATTHEWS
GMT GAMES (2005)

IT USUALLY TAKES YEARS to determine whether or not a game can be considered a classic, but *Twilight Struggle*, arguably, deserves this honor for its richness of theme, innovation of gameplay, and the sheer coolness factor of fighting the Cold War in under three hours.

Twilight Struggle focuses on the two major players of the Cold War, the United States and the Soviet Union: not surprisingly, this is a two-player game. The object of the game is to spread and extend influence around the world, without causing a thermonuclear war. As influence in countries swings one way or the other, players gain victory points for controlling individual countries, as well as controlling or dominating continents. When the scales tip too much in one direction — 20 points worth — that player wins.

The game offers an educational look into this historical era and does so in a fun, but tension-filled game of interactive action. Not only does the map give you a geography lesson but the cards themselves are pulled from history. Their titles tell the story: Cuban Missile Crisis, Camp David Accords, East European Unrest. And they all have historically appropriate effects on the action. Take the Camp David Accords, for example: this card first gives the U.S. player a victory point — makes sense, since Jimmy Carter helped initiate the peace talks and saw them to the end. The card also gives the U.S. player an influence point in Israel, Jordan, and Egypt. Again, this follows historical reality, as the two agreements that made up the Accords helped the U.S. improve relations with these nations. Finally, the Accords card blocks the playing of the Arab-Israeli War card, enforcing the peace now agreed to by these nations.

There is a lot that one can do in this game, and while the array of options in any given turn may seem overwhelming at first, the learning curve is short. It's not that difficult a game — okay, it's not easy, either— but with a concise explanation of the rules, anyone can get playing immediately. Once a novice get the basics down, he will be able to expand his options rather quickly. The only downside is that *Twilight Struggle* can be a relatively long game, usually lasting two to three hours, so it requires a time commitment. Fortunately, you only need two people to make that commitment to stage a session.

Gameplay is card driven. There are three decks, each focusing on a particular time period of the Cold War. After a certain number of turns have elapsed, a new deck is introduced and combined with the deck or decks already in play. The cards depict historical events, as described earlier, but each one also has a number in the top left corner, representing its operation points. These are points a player can spend to increase influence around the world, causing coups and realignments in various countries. All the cards' effects involve influence in some fashion, since that's what the game is about.

The important thing to note about the cards is that they do not benefit each superpower equally. You have to be careful what card you play, as it can benefit your opponent more than you. If, as the U.S. player, you wish to play a card associated with the U.S.S.R., you need to make sure that your use of its operation points will far outweigh the benefit its event will give to your opponent. For example, the U.S.S.R.-associated card De Gaulle Leads France causes the U.S. player to lose two influence in France and gives one influence there to the U.S.S.R. player. The U.S. player has to carefully consider if he can afford the loss in that particular area in order to gain the card's operation points for use elsewhere.

It's the balancing act required by the cards — weighing their worth in operation points over their value, positive and negative, as events — that provides the game's tension and much of its fun.

If the heart of *Twilight Struggle* is cards, then influence would be its reason for existence. The game is about influence: who has it and where. There are scoring cards that award points for different levels of sway — presence, domination, or control — within a continent. In the beginning of the game, scoring is focused on three areas of operation: Europe, the Middle East, and Asia. As the game progresses, more and more parts of the world come into play. In the mid-game, for example, Central and South America draw the superpowers' attention. This slowly widening conflict means that players must carefully consider where to extend influence. Do they concentrate on one continent to gain control (for the most points in that area) or spread themselves across several continents to get points from multiple areas? Just as important is when that influence is extended. Taking advantage of too many early scoring opportunities can sometimes come back to limit or undermine longterm plans. Ignoring them can give your opponent a lead.

Twilight Struggle also factors in the possibility of thermonuclear war, a very real possibility during the Cold War. The game reflects this ever-looming threat in the form of DEFCON (defense readiness condition) levels. Various actions, such as coups in battleground countries or certain card plays, drive the DEFCON level up or down. But you don't want it going down to DEFCON 1. If a player becomes too aggressive and brings the DEFCON level down that far, a nuclear war ends the game and grants his opponent an automatic win (though, really, everyone loses in a thermonuclear war). This mechanic provides a built-in control against reckless play, but also simulates the brinkmanship of the Cold War, as each player provokes the other just enough to spread influence, but not enough (probably) to trigger an all-out war.

All in all, *Twilight Struggle* gives you a compact history lesson about the Cold War, nicely encapsulating the struggle between the two superpowers and those caught (accidentally or not) between them. Coupled with that is the game's accessibility and the design's cleverness, all of which make *Twilight Struggle* stand out among the crowd of recent political wargame releases.

I'm willing to bet those strengths are enough to rank the game as a classic years from now, too, though only time will tell.

ZEV SHLASINGER is president of Z-Man Games, Inc., a publisher of board, card, and roleplaying games. Some of the titles published by Z-Man Games include the *Shadowfist* CCG, the B-Movie card game series, *Primordial Soup*, *Parthenon*, and *Cartoon Action Hour*. Z-Man Games has won several awards, including the Origins Vanguard Award for *Warchon*. Zev has been a gamer since he was eight, starting off with *Clue*, *Monopoly*, *Careers*, and *Stratego*. From *Stratego* he jumped to *Risk*, then *Axis & Allies*, and from there, *Star Fleet Battles*. He is also no stranger to RPGs and CCGs.

Kenneth Hite on

UNKNOWN ARMIES

KEY DESIGNERS: GREG STOLZE, JOHN SCOTT TYNES
ATLAS GAMES (FIRST EDITION, 1998)

THE "OCCULT UNDERGROUND" OF *Unknown Armies* owes more to Tim Powers and James Ellroy than it does to Umberto Eco or Anne Rice. It's a world of skeevy, desperate Tarantino characters who become increasingly unhinged and suffer for it, and come back for more because they cannot conceive of anything more important than stealing G. Gordon Liddy's shot glass to work a magic housebreaking ritual. And those lowlifes are potentially the most important people in the world, because they're the only ones willing to change it.

And how do they change it? That's up to the players, who work together, first of all, to determine the narrative structure of the game: what story do they want to tell? They might be working for an occult-obsessed billionaire who wants to remake the heavens in his own image, or they might be a gang of wannabe "dukes" defending their magical turf from him. They might be the staff of a tabloid TV show looking for fringe happenings to exploit, or the elite enforcers of the Vatican scheming to keep magick from the masses. Whoever they are — from would-be do-gooders to empire-building cultists — the ground is shifting under their feet. The old magicks are irrelevant and outdated; the secret world has moved on as "normal" has shifted into new patterns. As John Tynes put it, with *Unknown Armies* "it was time to invent some new mythologies instead of the endless necrophilia — the Templars and so on — that comprises many writers' approaches to classical occultism."

The core of these new mythologies is in the game's tagline: "A roleplaying game of power and consequences." If you want to wield power, there will be consequences. Some of them are written into the game's backstory — the afore-mentioned magickal enforcers and greedy billionaires. Most of them are embedded in the rules. All magick comes at a price. For example, entropomancers, whose magick comes from chaos and chance, have to take life-threatening risks to build up extra luck for a gunfight. Alcohol-fueled dipsomancers must abandon sober judgment to drink the souls of the dead. A mechanomancer sacrifices pieces of his personality to build robot clockwork servitors, and a flesh-working adept must hurt himself to injure others. And those are just for minor charges; major magicks require major departures from the sane and normal. The avatars have it even harder. They must conform to an archetypal pattern — Demagogue, Executioner, Messenger, Savage — and ruthlessly shed the rest of their humanity to wield archetypal power. If they do it better than anyone else, then they ascend, becoming the new archetypes to which the universe conforms. Both adepts and avatars must abandon human perspectives in exchange for (just maybe) being allowed to redefine those perspectives.

Mechanically, *Unknown Armies* is merely excellent. Stolze and Tynes' occult-horror RPG serves as the bridge between the reliable percentile dice system (skills run from 0 percent to 100 percent, roll your skill number or less to succeed) of *Call of Cthulhu* and the strongly character-focused, narrative-driven small press games of the 21st century. The core of the rules is a tweaked percentile system: the closer to your skill number you roll, the better the result. However, it's what you can do to determine and change the numbers that gives the game its power. Skills are broad or narrow as the player desires, definable as anything from "ungodly strong" to "Hittite ritual lore" to "card sharp," limning the character precisely, more words than numbers. (This freeform skill system comes from Jonathan Tweet's RPG *Over the Edge*.) You can "flip" your obsession skills — things you care most about — so that a sorry 82 becomes an excellent 28 when the chips are really down. If your obsession is either combat or magick, rolling a matched success — a 44, say — gives you a "cherry," an extra benefit.

But it's not all rewards and cherries. The game has a harsh commitment to personal consequences; as the rules put it, "If you're playing a sociopath, even unintentionally, then a sociopath is what your character will become." In most games, your character can rack up more kills than Ted Bundy and still be the same jolly fellow he was back at the tavern. In *Unknown Armies,* performing or witnessing acts of violence, terror, or unnatural magick will either harden you into callous apathy (and lose you those obsessions) or break you down in failure. It's this tension, the forced choice and the mandatory consequence, that moves the game up into the realm of truly great roleplaying experiences. Both the slide into madness and the consequent dramatic tension derive, of course, from *Call of Cthulhu,* for which game John Tynes wrote nigh-legendary sourcebooks in the 1990s.

Greg Stolze designed the mental stress and madness rules to reflect his own experience: "I spent some time right out of college working for a group of social workers and therapists who specialized in traumatized children. I learned more about mental stress on that job than I ever wanted to know." The result provides one of the most ruthless, emotionally realistic roleplaying experiences available. The back cover asks "What will you risk to change the world?" In *Unknown Armies,* a character must risk himself just to get a chance at the big score.

Unknown Armies has no majestic gods or lordly vampires behind the scenes. (Its vampires are pathetic inbred Rumanian hillbillies with bad skin.) Its secret conspiracies, even the nice ones, are built of twisted dreams, overweening error, and curdled ambition, not any grand design or airy theory. Its archetypes all began as human beings, and any of them can be replaced by a more obsessed human being. When enough utter monomaniacs (333) have ascended, they redefine the world so completely that all creation restarts. And that's all. *Unknown Armies* is thus ruthlessly humanocentric, almost the photographic negative of the similarly harrowing and rigorous *Call of Cthulhu.* Where the latter game posits powerless humans trying desperately to save the world from insane reality, *Unknown Armies* tells us that the only reality is what human beings choose to make of it, and frightens us with the thought that only insane people care enough to really change it. But for all that, it remains a game of alchemical optimism at its heart — from madmen and loners on the margins of society, a better world can come. If they want it enough to fight all the other madmen and loners to the death, and risk losing the rest of themselves, that is.

KENNETH HITE is an Origins Award-winning game designer, developer, editor, and author whose credits include 60-plus roleplaying games and supplements, from the *Star Trek Roleplaying Game* to *RuneQuest* fourth edition to *GURPS WWII: Weird War II* (as well work on some *Unknown Armies* sourcebooks, and in its second edition). His current projects include a series of Lovecraftian gaming PDFs released by Ronin Arts. His long-running *Pyramid* column "Suppressed Transmission" covers High Strangeness; he reviews games and surveys the RPG industry in his other column, "Out of the Box," at Paizo.com. He lives in Chicago with his wife Sheila and the apparently mandatory cat.

Sandy Petersen on

UP FRONT

KEY DESIGNER: COURTNEY F. ALLEN

AVALON HILL (1983)

UP FRONT IS A card game of squad-level combat in World War II. It is perhaps an unusual candidate for any collection of best hobby games. It was published near the end of the wargame heyday, and was deeply out of step with its peers. It has numerous flaws — the rules are badly organized and difficult to learn. It has so many obscure rule exceptions and modifications that it is literally impossible to remember them all. Hence, in almost every game played, someone unknowingly breaks some rule.

Unlike most other wargames, you lack omniscience, and even control. At the start of a scenario, you have no idea what the terrain of the battlefield will be like. You often lose control over your units, or frustratingly cannot get them to do what you want. For instance, a unit will not shoot unless you have a Fire card in your hand the unit can use. Sometimes you are forced to sit idly for turn after turn, discarding cards, while your opponent's plan advances implacably.

And yet — it is arguably the most fun tactical wargame ever created.

Let's look at what goes into playing *Up Front*, and then see why it is such a great game. I still play my 24-year-old set!

Two types of cards are used in the game, plus a variety of counters. One set of cards represents soldiers or armored vehicles. Thus there is a card for Private Peterson (no relation), Private Hamblen, and so forth. The soldier's card gives his morale rating (of primo importance) and has a chart showing how effective his weapon is at different ranges. You start with a squad of soldiers, chosen from among the 40-odd unit cards, and lay them out on the tabletop, after dividing them into two to five teams.

You also get a hand of cards, which do the bulk of the game's work. These cards may have an action for a section to perform (Fire, Rally, and so on); they may represent terrain ranging from stone houses to rivers; or they may represent special one-off powers, such as temporarily creating a hero (the Hero card), or allowing a target to hide behind a tree (the Concealment card), or even ordering

342 ★ HOBBY GAMES: THE 100 BEST

a random sniper attack (the Sniper card). The Hero card is multi-use — it is one of the few cards that can be played at any time (i.e., during your opponent's turn). It either doubles the hero's firepower, or enables him to instantly recover from a Cowering card, which can enable you to save a unit from impending doom.

Like any card game, the cards you use control the course of action — you can play one card per team. Some actions (such as entrenching or infiltration) can be performed without a card, but you still only get one action per team. Most armies (Germans being a notable exception) can either play cards, or discard them — not both; so if you drew a bad hand and want to discard, you have to use up one or two turns to do this. It generally takes multiple turns to get one of your team to accomplish a task. For instance, let's say you want one of your teams to move forward and dig in. You need to play a Movement on one turn, then play a Woods card (the terrain you want them in) on the next turn. Then you might try to dig in on the third turn (a special action that, if successful, gives that team some fire protection). That's three turns to Move-Woods-Entrench. The turns move extremely quickly, and this gives your opponent a chance to react to what you're doing.

The cards serve multiple purposes. Every card contains numbers that are used to randomize results in various ways, so you never roll a die. To see if your team managed to entrench, you flip a card from the draw pile, and if it has a 0 on it, you succeeded.

At the end of the turn you fill up your hand. As you play, you look to fulfill the victory conditions — usually something along the lines of "get four soldiers close to the enemy." When the deck runs out for the third or fourth time (depending on the scenario), the game automatically ends

What makes *Up Front* so good?

★ Fast-Playing.

★ Interactive.

★ Two-Stage Death.

★ Variation.

FAST-PLAYING: Turns in *Up Front* are extremely quick. The most actions you can possibly take is five (if you've subdivided your squad into five teams). In most turns you take far fewer actions than that — often just a simple discard. So you need not sit around waiting for your enemy to move a million counters — a notable improvement from most wargames.

INTERACTIVE: The basic interaction is simple — when he shoots at you, you try to play a Concealment card. But there is more to it than this. When you see one of his squads move, you start thinking about discarding a (bad) terrain on him — yes, you can play certain cards on the enemy player to hinder his troops. When you notice that his frightened soldiers are not rallying, you should realize he may not have a Rally card in hand — and plan to focus fire on that team before he manages to draw the right card. Every move your opponent makes causes you to think about many possibilities.

TWO-STAGE DEATH: It's almost impossible to kill a soldier in *Up Front* with a single shot. Typically, the first hit causes him to Cower, which renders him useless until you can Rally him with a card. The second hit on a Cowering soldier, in effect, kills him. The fact that your units die this way is actually a huge part of the game's fun — as you play, you do not immediately run out of units or, at least, you do so at a slow rate. You do, however, see your team become less effective. Moving to a hilltop is more difficult — instead of just Move-Woods-Entrench (to use my earlier example), you might need to Move-Rally-Woods-Entrench. This can be a challenge, particularly if you don't have one of the needed cards in your hand. Since a typical hand is only four to six cards, this often happens. To retain a needed Rally card, you may have to Move your team without a terrain card, hoping that one comes up in the next draw, so your team can find something safe to jump into before the enemy takes advantage of their movement in the open. Or you must trust to Concealment cards.

This two-stage death is simple in concept, but it affects play by forcing you to take chances (such as a Move without terrain), and it means that your plans are always impacted by your foe's decisions. There is a sort of "friction" as the game progresses, and it makes the conflict feel very realistic. Winning is not a matter of having the better plan — it is a matter of who can get their plan, bad as it may be, to work.

VARIATION: It's literally impossible to have a game of *Up Front* between identical forces. The various armies play by different rules, plus your squads have different levels of morale and are equipped with different weapons. They're even different sizes. A Russian squad only has a four-card hand, whereas the American squad has six cards. But the Russians can discard his entire hand at one time, whereas the

Americans can only discard two cards. Plus, more of the deck's cards can be used as Concealment for a Russian. These two nations play quite differently. With only four cards in his hand, a Russian player rarely has everything he needs for his next plan, and must trust more to luck. The Americans, with their huge six-card hands, can make better plans, but their hand is almost unwieldy — it's hard to discard a bad hand for them, so when things go wrong, the Americans cannot react quickly.

IF YOU CAN FIND a copy of *Up Front*, and you like tactical combat at all, check it out. Or even if you just like card games. In either case, you won't be disappointed. This is a game that surpasses its flaws, and turns some of them into strengths. And, oh yes, if you can find someone else who knows how to play the game, have him teach you — the rules organization is discouraging at first glance.

The original *Up Front* included the German, American, and Russian armies. The *Banzai* expansion, released in 1984, added the Japanese and British. The *Desert War* expansion, from 1985, added the Italians and French. There have been some unofficial expansions over the years, as well.

The original, Avalon Hill edition of *Up Front* can be quite difficult to come by. I have been informed, however, that Multi-Man Publishing is planning to reprint the game. If so, this is good news indeed.

SANDY PETERSEN's interest in the fiction of H.P. Lovecraft has colored much of his work in the hobby game and computer game industries. He was the primary designer for the first edition of *Call of Cthulhu* in 1981, as well as the author of many subsequent background and scenario products for the game. He also authored several critically acclaimed *RuneQuest* supplements for Avalon Hill and Games Workshop, and served as co-designer for West End's *Ghostbusters* roleplaying game. Sandy's computer game credits include *Sid Meier's Pirates!* and *Sword of the Samurai* (for Microprose); multiple levels for *Doom*, *Doom II*, and *Quake* (for id Software); and *Rise of Rome*, *Age of Kings*, and *The Conquerors*, all for Ensemble Studios' Age of Empires series.

R. *Hyrum Savage on*

VAMPIRE:
THE ETERNAL STRUGGLE

KEY DESIGNERS: RICHARD GARFIELD, L. SCOTT JOHNSON, ROBERT GOUDIE

WHITE WOLF (THIRD EDITION, 2006)

VAMPIRE: THE ETERNAL STRUGGLE, affectionately known to its fans as *VTES* or *V:TES*, is a multi-player trading card game originally designed by Richard Garfield and first published by Wizards of the Coast in 1994. At release, the game was titled *Jyhad*; however, that was quickly changed to capitalize on its connection to the popular *Vampire: The Masquerade* roleplaying game. Currently the game, in its third edition, is published by White Wolf/CCP.

In *VTES*, players assume the roles of ancient vampires called Methuselahs, members of rival clans of undead and denizens of the horror setting known as the World of Darkness. The goal of each Methuselah is to defeat all opponents and thereby control the city in which they reside. Because they are vampires, blood is the currency of the game. Recruiting younger vampires, directly attacking a rival Methuselah, or any number of other actions all require blood. To represent this, each Methuselah starts play with an amount of blood called a pool.

Each players use cards from his deck, and pays for each card with blood from his pool. If at any time a player's pool is reduced to zero, he's out of the game. Instead of the static life level found in traditional trading card games, *VTES* forces a player to spend his life points, a creative way to tie two required card game components — life and resources — into a single mechanic.

In designing the game, Richard Garfield didn't just return to what had worked in his most famous creation, *Magic: The Gathering*. He crafted an entirely new game based on fundamental design principles that he had learned from his earlier work. In doing so, he effectively created an entirely new way to play trading card games.

VTES is the first truly multi-player trading card game. The player's goal is to destroy the player to his left, who is called the prey, while at the same time defending himself from the player to his right, called the predator. This interaction mechanic is elegantly structured to make the competition manageable. At the same time, *VTES* plays to the strengths of more traditional multi-player games by allowing negotiation and "kingmaking." Players who appear to be losing can ally in order to help one of them win. They can work together in combat, even agree to no longer attack each other, until one of them is in a position to seal a victory. These deals can be struck in the open or agreed to before play begins. This political component ties nicely to the representation of the vampires' society in the *Vampire: The Masquerade* roleplaying game and novels.

Unfortunately, as with any multi-player game that invites negotiations and kingmaking, this player interaction mechanic can backfire. An uncooperative or vengeful player can choose to give up his own chances of winning just to get revenge upon someone else. Overcoming this sort of situation can be seen as one of the skills necessary to win, but it can be frustrating.

Still, because *VTES* requires at least three players, with most sessions including four or five, games feel less confrontational than traditional one-on-one trading card duels. There's more opportunity for discussion and conversation, even apart from the aforementioned deal-making. The social atmosphere can keep the game interesting and fun, even when a player is losing. And since every battle does not involve every player, the game feels less like relentless conflict. In this, playing *VTES* is more a board gaming experience than a card gaming one.

The variable paths to victory within the game are another important facet of *VTES*'s success. These include something never seen before — direct player vote. Other trading card games have featured alternate victory conditions, such as the ring victory or honor victory in *Legend of the Five Rings*. However, *VTES* has such wide and varied alternate victory paths that multiple types of decks and play styles can succeed. Stealth is one avenue to victory, traditional direct attack another, and the blood highway (putting out more vampire cards than the other players) is yet another. Equally interesting is that each vampire clan or faction can build variants of any of the deck types; a Ventrue voting deck is very different from a Tremere voting deck, with the Ventrue relying more on direct tactics and the Tremere on subterfuge, while a Gangrel beatdown deck has a different feel than a Brujah beatdown deck. Again, these differences smartly reflect the clan identities established in other World of Darkness products.

Combat between vampires in *VTES* feels incredibly visceral. Cards allow for each combat to continue past the initial round, so instead of the standard binary trading card game situation — I'm alive or dead — combats in *VTES* are protracted, which makes them feel like roleplaying game battles. Vampires retain damage from round to round, too, and must therefore be nursed over the course of the game to remain in play. Thus, players must constantly decide how much of their blood pool they want to invest in their minions and how much they want to save for other uses.

Sessions of *VTES* take a long time to play, with a typical four- or five-player game lasting about two hours. This can make it hard for players to arrange games. The time factor has also impacted the way official tournaments of *VTES* are run at conventions — they are typically only two or three rounds with a final. The game's length, coupled with its sometimes-daunting negotiation mechanic, has probably led to its relatively weak professional competitive following.

Beginning players of *VTES* can find the game overwhelming, with its multitude of vampire clans and the richly detailed setting that underpins so many of the cards. Even when you don't have to know a Tremere from a Gangrel, it can feel like you should. The game's brilliant design, though, makes it a rewarding experience for players who refuse to be frightened off. And that incredibly immersive atmosphere provides not only an intriguing introduction to the World of Darkness, but helps make *Vampire: The Eternal Struggle* a perfect mix of trading card game and roleplaying game, and a worthy choice as one of the best hobby games of all time.

When not reading comic books or designing things "that go bump in the night," R. HYRUM SAVAGE is the product manager for hobby games, as well as the Marvel and DC Comics trading card games, at Upper Deck Entertainment in Carlsbad, California. His credits include lead design on the forthcoming third edition of the *Chill* roleplaying game. He was also one of the creative forces behind *Forbidden Kingdoms*, the two-fisted d20 pulp adventure game. He currently lives in the San Diego area with his wife, three children (one more due shortly), four cats, a snake, a turtle, and a beta fish.

George Vasilakos on

VAMPIRE: THE MASQUERADE

KEY DESIGNER: MARK REIN•HAGEN

WHITE WOLF (FIRST EDITION, 1991)

FROM THE FIRST LOOK, the cover intrigues you — a red rose upon a green marble backdrop and the title *Vampire: The Masquerade* rendered in ghostly gray and white. Simplicity at its finest, and mysterious, too. A typical roleplaying game cover would sport an eye-popping painting by a popular fantasy or science fiction artist, a colorful scene promising adventure in a world not your own. But not *Vampire*. *Vampire* seduces you like a mysterious woman in the night whispering promises of something more. So you glance around to see if anyone is looking, and then move closer to investigate.

As you do, she bares unexpected fangs and jumps out at you!

The art. As you skim through the *Vampire* rulebook, startling, evocative artwork pounces from the pages. The images — most in stark black and white, some with subtle tones and washes — suggest danger. Not the blunt and predictable sort of adventure touted by the garish drawings in other roleplaying games, but threats faced along a path of haunting, perilous sensuality. The works, from such masters of the horror illustration as Timothy Bradstreet, slip into your consciousness and draw you fully into the world of *Vampire: The Masquerade*.

Created by Mark Rein•Hagen and first published by White Wolf Game Studios in 1991, the *Vampire* roleplaying game is set in a grim, dark world, much like our own, but secretly populated with creatures of the night. In the game your character is not the stalwart knight saving the kingdom from invading goblins or the scruffy starship captain holding back the onslaught of alien bugs. He's not even the monster hunter, intent on destroying the things in the dark. No, this time you play the monster. You are an ever-mysterious and brooding vampire struggling to maintain the shreds of your humanity, even as you navigate the twisted political hierarchies of the undead. Your society forbids you from revealing what you are to the mortal world, so you dance around them at night in, as the game's subtitle implies, a masquerade.

Vampire is set in the modern day — in any city you choose. Not some galaxy far, far away. Not some pseudo-medieval fantasy realm on the other side of a clothes closet. In *Vampire*, it's now. Today. This makes it easier for players to step across that barrier of the imagination, to connect more quickly and more fully to the game world and a character. You may have trouble picturing a dwarf battling a tentacled monster at the gates of a lost mine in Middle Earth, but can certainly envision a troubled outsider trying to survive in New York or Los Angeles or your own hometown — or, rather, a slightly warped reflection of that real location, as it exists in the game's setting. This background world is called, evocatively, the World of Darkness.

In establishing the look of the World of Darkness, Rein•Hagen — as well as the game's artists and graphic designers — tapped into the growing Goth culture of the late '80s and early '90s. The Goth influence gave the game an original feel, but also made it attractive to people who had never considered roleplaying before or had grown out of the hobby. This fresh customer base was key to *Vampire*'s initial success and a boon to the industry as a whole. But it was not just the artwork and graphic design that kept them interested in the line.

Vampire explores themes that were hardly ever found in roleplaying games before its release. The point of the game is not for your character to bash monsters and grab their stuff. Characters are concerned with establishing a sense of self, of creating an identity for themselves within their immediate circle of undead brethren and within the larger setting. To encourage this sort of gameplay, *Vampire* needs a very different set of rules than the ones typically utilized in RPGs.

Enter the Storyteller System. This simple, but elegant engine focuses players on telling a story by minimizing rules and eliminating a lot of the dice from the gaming table. The die-rolling mechanic requires only a 10-sided die. Your character has different traits that have a value between zero and five. These are recorded via little circles on your character sheet that you fill in like the circles on a standardized test. But a character's identity is not established by these numbers. They are loose guides, really, and nowhere near as important to gameplay as your character's less numbers-bound attributes.

When you create your character, you're asked to choose some general concepts to define him (whether the character will be a hedonist, martyr, and so on), and, more importantly, a specific clan to which the character will belong. These clans are vampire "families" with very detailed histories and radically different philosophies, political structures, and even physical appearances. Each of the seven clans presented in the first-edition rulebook represents a general style of play. If your character is going to be a strong-minded scrapper, he's probably a Brujah. If he's going to be the artsy type, someone who loves to throw parties, he's a Toreador. A deformed creature of the night, instantly recognizable as something not quite human? Clan Nosferatu is for you.

During character creation, players can also give their characters various physical and mental advantages and disadvantages. Many of the abilities you "buy" for your character this way twist the rules and provide support for your chosen gameplay style. You can use a character's willpower to add dice to rolls during crucial situations. Then, if the same character has a conniver demeanor, he might get a willpower point back when he tricks someone into doing something for him. In this way the mechanical rules, the dice-rolling and point generation, are made subservient to roleplaying. The assembled flaws and advantages also help to make each character an individual.

So, too, the character's clan designation. The seven clans are varied enough to provide players a hook, a detailed set of goals and philosophies that make it easy to understand a new character from the very first session. Moreover, the complicated web of clan interactions and the guiding concept of the Masquerade itself emphasize the importance of stealth and diplomacy over blind brawn. Vampires cannot last long in the World of Darkness through might alone; subtlety — and therefore roleplaying — takes precedence over combat.

Vampire changed gaming. In the early '90s, even as computer games were beginning to lure players away from traditional RPGs, *Vampire* reminded pen and paper game designers that they still had something unique to offer. What separates tabletop gaming from computer/online gaming is the fact that players can develop their character in ways more substantial than adding a badge and a few new pixels. Players are given a lot more freedom with pen and paper games, and the face-to-face gaming experience, but designers have to create games that allow, even encourage, players to use that freedom.

Vampire did just that. And, with its heavy emphasis on art and graphic style, it showed that gaming rulebooks are more than just textbooks. They can — and should — have personality. *Vampire* reminded us that a roleplaying experience should be more than just a violent dungeon crawl; it should be a storytelling journey in which you explore and develop a character. Before *Vampire*, roleplaying games seemed to be about nothing more than getting to the next experience level or overcoming the big boss at the end of a long quest. *Vampire* made it about you. Your character.

It's hard to imagine the hobby gaming industry today without the influence of *Vampire*.

Vampire: The Masquerade was only the beginning, of course. It introduced players to the Storyteller System and the intriguing World of Darkness. In the years that followed, White Wolf released many other core books for the setting — *Werewolf: The Apocalypse*, *Mage: The Awakening*, *Changeling: The Dreaming*, *Wraith: The Oblivion*, even a game where you finally got to play the monster hunters. Each new title expanded World of Darkness, but maintained an emphasis on developing characters and telling good stories.

But it all began with that intriguing green marbled book with the red rose.

GEORGE VASILAKOS is president and art director of Eden Studios. Formerly the art director for New Millennium Entertainment, George acquired the rights to the *Conspiracy X* roleplaying game when that company dissolved. He then formed Eden Studios to reinvigorate the line and publish other gaming-related projects. In the past, George has been an art director and graphic designer for Last Unicorn Games, Wizards of the Coast, and Decipher, working on the *Star Trek* and *Lord of the Rings* RPGs. He was the inspiration behind the *Knights of the Dinner Table, HACK*, and *Abduction* card games, and *All Flesh Must Be Eaten*, a roleplaying game of zombie survival horror. Recently, he directed all the graphics work on the *Buffy the Vampire Slayer, Army of Darkness*, and *Angel* roleplaying game lines for Eden Studios. George lives in Loudonville, New York. He loves online games, comics, and movies, as well as his tolerant wife, two hellspawned sons, Theo and Dimitri, and his lovely daughter Sophia.

Kevin Wilson on

VINCI

KEY DESIGNER: PHILIPPE KEYAERTS

DESCARTES EDITEUR (1999)

ONE OF THE MOST popular types of board game is the empire-building game. Typified by such entries as Avalon Hill's *Civilization* and the more recent *Tempus* from Café Games, there are dozens — perhaps hundreds — of board games that allow you to build up an empire, usually researching new technologies such as pottery and aviation to power up your civilization or earn extra victory points. *Vinci: The Rise and Fall of Civilization* is one of the best games in this genre.

As with another empire-building game, Dicken and Kendall's *History of the World*, *Vinci* places you in command of a series of civilizations that rise up to power, go into decline, and then vanish into the mists of time. How well you do in the game is determined by your civilizations' overall performances rather than being tied to a single empire. Indeed, becoming too attached to a particular civilization is often a losing strategy.

Vinci is a masterpiece of simplicity. Unlike most games of this sort, which can take four hours or longer to play, *Vinci* can be played from start to finish in under two hours and still handles up to six players. It accomplishes this by taking a fresh look at the genre and eliminating every bit of complexity or bookkeeping that isn't fun. New civilizations appear fully developed, so there's no need to go through the painful early stages of building up your empires. There are no complicated die-rolling systems for combat — to conquer a territory you simply commit the proper number of troops to that area and you're done. Most interestingly, civilizations do not research new technologies or work their way up a "tech tree," a feature of the empire-building genre that I would have claimed was absolutely essential before playing *Vinci*. Instead, each civilization has two key technologies or attributes that grant them special abilities and define their character for the duration of their lifespan. The goal of the game is simple — accumulate the most victory points by the end — but only through the careful utilization of your civilizations' advantages can you achieve it.

At the start of the game, six civilizations are created by assigning two ability tokens to each at random. These tokens can represent anything from messengers (which allow a player to leave gaps in their empire as they expand) to slavery (which awards the player points as he conquers and enslaves enemy troops on the board) or even barbarians (which give no special ability, but provide the player with a lot of troops). These abilities form the core of the game, and the combinations that can occur are exciting to see and keep things fresh and interesting each time you play. Combining field general (temporarily gain seven extra troops each turn for purposes of attacking only) and slavery, for instance, might create an offensive juggernaut reminiscent of the Mongols that marches around the board gobbling up troops left and right. Another civilization might combine astronomy (which allows the player to attack across water spaces) and barbarians, creating a Viking-like empire that shuttles its hordes across the water in huge raids on their neighbors.

However, not every combination of abilities is created equal. Some civilizations will simply have better powers than others. The way this is balanced in play is through the "civilization menu." Once the civilizations have been created, they are placed in order on a track, or menu, until chosen by a player. For instance, the Viking raiders listed above might be the first civilization on the menu, with the Mongols next down the line. When it is a player's turn to select a civilization, he can either choose the Vikings for free or, if he's pursuing an offense-focused strategy, he can pay two victory points to skip the Vikings and move down the menu to the Mongols instead, and so on. Any victory points spent this way are placed on the civilization that was skipped and are awarded to the player who later chooses that civilization. In this way, undesirable power combinations gradually gain value until chosen, while a particularly potent ability combo will wind up costing the player some points if he wants to get it before one of the other players snaps it up.

Additionally, the abilities are further balanced by how many troops they provide to the player. Particularly nasty abilities (such as currency, which awards one extra victory point per territory controlled) only provide a couple of troops with which to conquer the board, while weaker abilities, such as messengers or astronomy, can come with a whole army. This is important because you need a lot of troops in order to spread out and control territory, which is the main way you gain victory points. Aside from a couple of terrain considerations, such as attacking down from a mountain or into a dense forest, the only way to conquer a territory is to assign enough troops there to overwhelm any enemy forces.

This leads into the trickiest part of the game — deciding when to abandon your civilization and move on to a new one. Doing so places the old civilization into "decline," which means that it can't actively defend itself anymore, but you still gain points for the territory it holds. You can only have one empire in decline (any earlier empires are removed from the board), so choosing the right moment to put a civilization into decline and selecting your next batch of abilities is critical to your overall performance. If a set of abilities isn't working out, you need to be flexible enough in your strategy to abandon it for another.

If there are any legitimate complaints to be made about *Vinci*, it could be said that the gameplay can encourage kingmaking and bash-the-leader tactics. Because victory point totals are public information, situations can arise where one of the other players has the game pretty much sewn up going into the last turn, leaving you with only an outside chance at winning. Nonetheless, *Vinci* remains an incredibly strong design, and it's easy enough to play with hidden victory points to avoid this element of the game.

Although currently out of print, you can still find inexpensive copies of *Vinci* on the Internet if you look around — a quest that is definitely worth the time you'll invest. *Vinci* is a tremendous light strategy game that captures the feel of conquering your way across Europe at the head of a marauding band of Gauls without having to deal with the minutiae of where to build your new aqueduct and how many archers to train this turn. It is highly recommended for gamers who enjoy titles such as *Civilization*, but who simply don't have as much energy or free time as they once had to invest in them.

Kevin Wilson has been a game designer since the late 1990s. He is the co-designer of the 7th *Sea* and *Spycraft* roleplaying games, as well as the author of numerous other RPG books, such as *Spellslinger* and *Wonders Out of Time*. In addition, he has designed several board games, including *Doom*, *Warcraft*, *Descent: Journeys in the Dark*, and *Arkham Horror* second edition (with Richard Launius). Kevin received a B.A. in Cognitive Science (Artificial Intelligence) from U.C. Berkeley in 1997, and was active in the interactive fiction community at the time. He wrote several works of interactive fiction — including *Once and Future* and *The Lesson of the Tortoise* — and founded the annual Interactive Fiction Competition and the Internet magazine *SPAG*, both of which are still active today. Kevin currently lives near the Twin Cities with his utter lack of cats.

R.A. Salvatore on

WAR AND PEACE

KEY DESIGNER: MARK D. MCLAUGHLIN
AVALON HILL (1980)

WAR AND PEACE IS another in the classic Avalon Hill line of large-scale turn-based strategy wargames. Akin to *Third Reich* and the company's various Civil War battle games, *War and Peace* takes place during the Napoleonic wars. From the perspective of a history buff, that's an era I've never found remotely interesting. I much prefer earlier Dark Age and medieval settings or later time periods — the latter half of the 19th century to mid-20th century.

Still, when asked to come up with a hobby game that I consider one of the best ever, the title that immediately leapt to mind was *War and Peace*. That alone should say something, I expect.

There's a new mantra among video game designers, elevated by the success of *World of Warcraft*: easy to learn, hard to master. In my gaming experiences as a player, I live by that philosophy. I want to pick up a book or a box and actually *be playing* the game within a short amount of time — an hour or two at the most. The idea of spending days learning enough of the basics to even begin play does not interest me at all. I guess that's why I prefer *AD&D* first edition to the newer and more complex versions.

War and Peace fits this mold. On its surface, it's a simple game. Your goal is to stop the French from conquering the world, or, if you're playing the French, conquer, conquer, conquer! Combat flows swiftly, with easy resolution — not quite as simplistic as *Risk*, but still transparent enough so that any neophyte will have a good idea as the armies line up if he's likely to get his butt kicked or have a decent chance of scoring the victory. There are variables, of course, such as the power of the commander involved, but they remain at a minimum, allowing for an easy flow of gameplay, and again, for that quick start.

The game is designed for two to four players, but you can squeeze six into the open, full-war format. In this setting, players taking the lesser powers, such as Spain and England, might find themselves more dependent upon their alliances, but don't be fooled. Playing England, with a minimal ground army and a solid navy, but one that, because of the nature of the campaign, remained off to the side of the main action, I still managed to sneak forces into Paris, not once, but twice, capturing the city and forcing Napoleon (poor Roger) into exile.

For the bigger game, when the war is run in full, players are offered open choices. There's no script to be followed, except that (optionally) the aggressor French have to reach certain benchmarks. For this format, more people equates to more fun. There's nothing quite like the look on the face of the Austrian player as he's getting sandwiched between the French and the Russians. A massive army east, a massive army west, and he sits there with (comparatively) miniscule resources and a tough decision: with whom do I side?

That brings us to the mini-games, the scenarios of the various pivotal battles of the Napoleonic wars, complete with explanations of how the real historical events played out. One round of Waterloo and it's pretty easy to understand why the French lost! The scenarios also show the flexibility of *War and Peace*. You can play for hours on the wider scale, or play in various limited battles that can be finished within an hour.

Okay, so you've probably heard much of this before regarding the many wonderful board games out there. So what was it that set *War and Peace* apart for me? Sleepless nights. It's that simple, really. The game's level of complexity fit my brain perfectly, in that I could break off from a session and go to bed at night with the visual of the board completely in mind. I'd lay there for hours going over an opponent's supply lines, for example, trying to figure out how I could commit forces quickly to disrupt them. From there, I'd go on to design a strategy for hammering the front line forces so as to place their attrition rate (as they would be unsupplied) into the stratosphere.

Like the pacing of a novel, games move at varying rates and with varying amounts of information-dumping. Any good turn-based game requires a player to strategize several moves ahead, achieving small objectives that will lead to larger conquests. From chess to *Risk* to *Stratego* to *War and Peace* to *Third Reich*, the interdependent complexity of those strategic steps will vary, of course, as will the comfort level of each gamer. We all have a different optimal level of information collection and manipulation; it's why there is never going to be a universal "favorite" author or game. At a game design company, a conversation with an artist, a programmer, and a designer about the same subject will invariably result in three distinct discussion foci.

So for me, it's *War and Peace*. I've played them all and that's the one that had me lying in bed for hours and hours, working up multi-turn strategies for blasting my enemy's supply lines, or creating a back-alley run to Paris. That's the game, with its simple elegance yet multitude of tactics, that offered to me exactly the right amount of information to juggle. Neither overwhelming nor underwhelming, too hot nor too cold, too big nor too small, too soft nor too hard, *War and Peace* fit this duck's bill.

R.A. SALVATORE began writing shortly after receiving his Bachelor of Science degree in Communications/Media from Fitchburg State College. His first break came in 1987 when TSR, publisher of *Dungeons & Dragons*, offered him a novel contract based on a proposal for the Forgotten Realms shared-world setting. With over 11 million books sold in the U.S. alone, and nearly four dozen books to his credit, many of them bestsellers, Salvatore has become one of the most important figures in modern epic fantasy. He is currently working with 38 Studios, LLC. as creator of worlds for their first game project. Salvatore makes his home in Massachusetts with his wife and children; their dogs Oliver, Artemis, and Ivan; and three elderly cats, including a black tortoise shell named Guenhwyvar. His gaming group of 26 years still meets on Sundays to play everything from *Dungeons & Dragons*, to *World of Warcraft* and other massively multi-player online games.

WARHAMMER 40,000

KEY DESIGNERS: RICK PRIESTLY, ANDY CHAMBERS, GAV THORPE

GAMES WORKSHOP (FOURTH EDITION, 2004)

I ENCOUNTERED *WARHAMMER 40,000* first while patronizing a local comic book shop and later working at it. Each week, I'd peruse the walls for the latest comic releases and also glance through the gaming products. I was a big RPG player as a teenager and religiously bought just about every *D&D* and *Champions* product. Time and time again, I found myself picking up this strange book entitled *Warhammer 40,000: Rogue Trader*. To be honest, I had little clue what it was about. Clearly, the game was set in some sort of dark future. Brutal images of mechanized soldiers battling exotic aliens across harsh battlefields covered every page. The incredible art evoked a mythology like nothing I had seen before. Over time, the game's rulebooks seem to multiply: *Chapter Approved, Slaves to Darkness, The Lost and the Damned, 'Ere We Go!, Freebooterz. . . .* I knew that these books had some sort of tie to the small miniatures rack in the back of the store, but I wasn't certain precisely what that connection was.

During the '90s I worked at that same store, and by then, *Warhammer 40K* had really taken off. Instead of just a few displays of miniatures, half the walls in our store were covered with Games Workshop racks. Every weekend, customers would cover eight-foot tables with terrain and play all day with armies of miniatures painted with a kaleidoscope of colors. Here I learned the game's basic vocabulary: *bolter, lasgun, hellgun, shuriken catapult, ork boyz, overwatch,* and yes, *Space Marine.* The pictures I had seen in the *40K* rulebooks came alive in these battles; the indelible image of powered armor formed years before now strode in the form of a bite-sized warrior across the tiny battlefield. I wanted to join the fray, but, alas, finances prevented me. *40K* was not the game for a poor, starving grad student, nor is it now. (I should also note in passing that complaining about *40K's* cost is almost a metagame unto itself for players.)

Hosts of imitators and wannabes attempted to follow *Warhammer*'s trailblazing. They saw the game's immense popularity and naturally wanted a piece of its success. I started gaming with these other products, but the more I played, the more I found myself attracted to the dark future of *40K*. No other miniatures could compare to the sleek Eldar Jetbike, the ponderous Space Marine Dreadnought, or the horrific Tyranid Hive Tyrant. Eventually, I succumbed and purchased the then-current version of the core rules: *Warhammer 40,000*, third edition.

One of the easiest traits to admire about *40K* is that it's simultaneously alien and familiar. Alien, because the game takes place in the far future where "in the grim darkness there is only war." Familiar, because the actors in this drama are all well known from the fantasy genre. Space Marines, the dominant image, are space knights on a crusade for mankind. Orks maraud the galaxy for no other reason than combat. The winsome Eldar (i.e. elves) are an ancient race on the downside of their existence. They seek only to preserve their fragile civilization. Most pure sci-fi games that fail do so due to a lack of familiarity. Players can't embrace too strange a game universe because there's no concept to latch onto. *40K*, on the other hand, provides many such familiar themes.

As soon as I first grabbed a handful of d6s, I knew I was hooked. Over the course of a single game, *40K* players roll hundreds of dice. The outcome of each firefight in a battle is decided by the careful maneuverings of miniatures and the roll of the dice. In every game I'd squat down to view my opponent from my tiny army's point of view; I'd spot the glint of an enemy's armor peaking over rubble across an empty field. Eagerly, I'd grab my dice — color coordinated with my army, of course — and blast away. I counted each hit and wound with glee, only to lament each point my dreaded foe's armor deflected.

What fascinates me above and beyond the actual gameplay is that every single bit of *40K* is open to debate. Take the rules, for example. They're extremely simple. The *40K* rulebook doesn't claim to cover every possible scenario or situation. Instead, it exhorts players to resolve their differences calmly. If no such compromise prevails, players are to roll a d6 (really) and see who comes out on top! Naturally, such open-ended rules produce no small amount of analysis. I've never played a game of *40K* that didn't involve some situation where my opponent and I invoked precedents or parallels to prove out our point. I note this not as a criticism, but rather as praise. Such earnest rules discussions permeate gaming tables, conventions, and Internet discussion forums. Because the rules are rarely clear cut about corner cases, rules "lawyers" come out in force to argue strenuously. This guarantees that *40K* ever remains on our lips.

Of course, the game is only a portion of the actual hobby; it's probably the assembling and painting of figures that consumes much of my time. *40K* certainly has its canonical color schemes and army lists, but Games Workshop encourages its players to forge their own styles there, too. Want a bright orange Space Marine? Go for it! Or how about an all-black Eldar force? Sure! Games Workshop shows off these variegated styles in the pages of its monthly publication, *White Dwarf*, in order to promote this individuality. *40K* provides an entire universe for gameplay, but the individual players give it local character. Fans endlessly compare their forces and painting schemes everywhere *40K* is played.

Beyond the rules and the miniatures lurks another area of strength: the background world. *40K* possesses an incredibly rich mythology. Most intriguing about the lore is the absence of good guys. There are no white hats, just different points of view. Yes, the Space Marines are on a crusade, but the Imperium doesn't seem like all that nice of a place. Humanity is ruled by an oppressive monarchy, whose ruler lies in a permanent catatonic state. Society is so rigid that technological innovation has ground to a halt. The government controls and manipulates the great mass of people. Various agencies ruthlessly destroy any deviance or dissent. Even the visually vile, such as the forces of Chaos, have their good side. After all, many of them are Space Marines who despaired at humanity's dismal condition. They embraced freedom and turned to dark gods with the hope of toppling the Emperor. Despite their often-daemonic behavior, the Chaos Space Marines see the dangers of the Imperium much as we, the impartial viewer, see them.

Frankly, with all the things that *Warhammer 40,000* has to offer, I don't see it going out of style. At least, not for another 38,000 years.

JACK EMMERT is a longtime gamer, whose earliest memories of the hobby stretch back to *Chainmail*. His teenage years were spent reading comic books and playing *AD&D*. During his student years, Jack wrote several pen and paper RPG supplements to make ends meet. After a lengthy stint in the ivy-covered towers of academia, Jack co-founded Cryptic Studios. He designed the hit MMORPGs *City of Heroes* and *City of Villains*. Currently, he is the chief creative officer and directs the design of all games from Cryptic Studios. This includes the much-anticipated *Marvel Universe Online*.

Chris Pramas on

The Warlock of
Firetop Mountain

Key Designers: Steve Jackson, Ian Livingstone

Puffin Books (first edition, 1982)

2007 MARKS THE 25TH anniversary of the release of *The Warlock of Firetop Mountain*, making it the perfect time to reflect on the impact and legacy of this seminal work. *The Warlock of Firetop Mountain*, by Games Workshop founders Steve Jackson and Ian Livingstone, was a pioneering release that popularized the solo gamebook and successfully brought the roleplaying game experience to a wider audience. This book alone sold over two million copies and it was only the first of the Fighting Fantasy series. *The Warlock of Firetop Mountain* spawned 58 more Fighting Fantasy books in the original series, a support magazine, a board game, an ambitious spinoff series, several computer games, two traditional roleplaying games, and a series of fantasy novels. Then there was the legion of imitators, another sure sign of success. Not bad for a slim paperback less than 200 pages long.

In *The Warlock of Firetop Mountain* you play a heroic adventurer in a fantasy world. The titular warlock, Zagor, is said to have a legendary treasure and you, of course, want to make it your own. The warlock lives in a dungeon lair full of monsters, tricks, and traps that many have died trying to penetrate. By choosing your path carefully, making smart use of equipment and magic, and overcoming challenges, you can best Zagor and win his treasure.

On first inspection *The Warlock of Firetop Mountain* is not unlike Bantam's Choose Your Own Adventure books. That series began in the late '70s with Edward Packard's *The Cave of Time* and set up a basic formula that is followed to this day in solo adventure books. In brief, you are the story's protagonist and throughout the book you make your way through a series of scenes. At the end of each scene, a decision must be made. In the Choose Your Own Adventure books, these choices are usually binary: "Do you keep the bag of money or give it to the police?" Depending on what you choose, a new scene is presented. If you choose to keep the bag of money, for example, you might have to evade goons sent to recover it. Several endings are provided, so your choices impact how the story resolves.

Jackson and Livingstone took that framework and added a game system inspired by the tabletop roleplaying games of the day (some of which — most notably *Tunnels & Trolls* — already featured solo adventures). This immediately gave the reader a lot more to do in the story than pick X or Y. The Fighting Fantasy System is simple compared to contemporaries such as *Advanced Dungeons & Dragons* and *RuneQuest*, but it introduces almost all of the core concepts of roleplaying games. Readers get to generate characters, resolve challenges with dice rolls, manage a character sheet and equipment, and make life-or-death decisions for their characters. And unlike traditional RPGs, the player doesn't have to share the spotlight with other players. The reader gets to be the star and win all the glory.

The Fighting Fantasy formula created books that were midway between novels and tabletop roleplaying games. Throughout the 1980s this proved to be a sweet spot for two important reasons. First of all, *The Warlock of Firetop Mountain* and its follow-ups pushed central concepts of hobby gaming into mass-market bookstores. Up until that time such games were largely confined to specialist hobby shops and conventions. The Fighting Fantasy books put a roleplaying game experience into a format that bookstores would embrace. By doing so they introduced a huge number of young people to the world of hobby games. Fighting Fantasy books topped the kids' charts for many years in the U.K., too, making the line one of the few truly successful introductions to gaming to make it in the mass market.

The Warlock of Firetop Mountain also succeeded in appealing to existing gamers. Traditional roleplaying games have many strengths, but they require a group of players and a game master. Even when players are participating in a successful RPG campaign, there's still a lot of downtime between sessions. The Fighting Fantasy books gave gamers a roleplaying activity they could do on their own. They could choose when to play and for how long. The books were also portable, so they could be played nearly anywhere. In this way, gamebooks gave roleplayers a way to stay connected with their hobby between sessions or when they couldn't find a group to play with. This was, incidentally, exactly the case with me when I was a young gamer. I had already been playing games such as *AD&D* and *Traveller* when I came across the first book in Steve Jackson's

Sorcery, an epic four-part Fighting Fantasy spinoff series, in a bookstore at my local mall. The fact that I was roleplaying two or three times a week didn't make me any less impatient for the books in the series to be released so I could finish the story.

The series that *The Warlock of Firetop Mountain* initiated came to an end in 1995 with the publication of the 59th Fighting Fantasy book. In 2002, the line was picked up by a new publisher, Wizard Books, which has re-released older titles and published some new ones, too. However, like tabletop RPGs, solo gamebooks have declined in popularity, and for similar reasons. The mind space that game-books occupied has been largely taken over by video games, which can provide a similar experience but in a much more immersive way. This has certainly not been lost on Jackson and Livingstone, who announced in 2006 that the Fighting Fantasy books would become the basis for a new series of Nintendo DS and PSP games. It seems *The Warlock of Firetop Mountain* is still a tough old bastard.

CHRIS PRAMAS is an award-winning game designer, writer, and publisher. He is best known as the designer of *Warhammer Fantasy Roleplay*, second edition, and the creator of *Freeport: The City of Adventure*. He is also the founder and president of Green Ronin Publishing. Pramas got his start as a freelance designer, writing for such games as *Over the Edge*, *Feng Shui*, and *Underground*. He later spent four years as a staff designer at Wizards of the Coast, ending his tenure there as a creative director. Today, in addition to his work with Green Ronin, Pramas is a content designer for the *Pirates of the Burning Sea* massively multi-player online game at Flying Lab Software. Although a New Englander by birth and a New Yorker by experience, he has lived in the Pacific Northwest for the past 10 years and has no plans to move again.

THE WARLORD

KEY DESIGNER: MIKE HAYES
SELF-PUBLISHED (RED BOX EDITION, 1966)

THE YEAR WAS 1970. I was a 19-year-old undergraduate student at the University of Keele in Staffordshire. Though supposedly studying Biology and Psychology, my time was spent mainly hanging round a table football machine in the Students Union garbed in a long and very tatty fur coat from a local Oxfam shop. I wore gold-rimmed John Lennon specs and shoulder-length hair, as was the fashion in the flower power era. My parents took very few photographs of me in my hippie days. . . .

My academic performance was unexceptional. But my one proud achievement was as founder and president of the University of Keele Games Society. It was the first board games society ever established at a British university. Every Sunday afternoon the 30 or so members would meet to play *Buccaneer*, *Formula One*, *Monopoly*, and *Risk*. At that time, Avalon Hill wargames had barely reached British shores. And Gary Gygax was still mending shoes for a living.

At the time I had just discovered *Diplomacy*. The game had taken over the Games Society. I was *Diplomacy*'s number one evangelist at Keele, spreading the word to anyone who would listen. One evening I cornered fellow biologist John Parker. John Parker had a guru-like status within Keele's hippie community. He was one of the few students to own a stereo hi-fi. Every night we would pile into his room to listen to Grateful Dead and Quicksilver Messenger Service albums at an unsociably high volume. He knew everything cool and "happening" in music and underground culture. Whatever you told him about, he knew something better. That evening I enthused about *Diplomacy*. John was unimpressed. "You should play *The War Game*," he scoffed. "Now *that's* a great game."

My curiosity was aroused. I insisted John show me this *War Game*. Next day he took me round to visit some final year students. They were the current guardians of a battered copy of a game that had been handed down around the campus over the years. It was actually called *The Warlord*.

I managed to borrow the Keele heirloom for a weekend and set about making my own copy. The map was hand-drawn on poster card, with wooden *Risk* pieces as armies. *The Warlord* quickly took over from *Diplomacy* as the Games Society's obsession. Everyone I played it with agreed it was the best game they had ever played. But you needed a student lifestyle to be able to enjoy it. A typical game lasted eight hours or more.

The Warlord was invented by Mike Hayes, a Geography lecturer at the University of Sheffield. Unable to find a publisher for his masterwork, he brought in the components — cheap plastic tiddlywink counters (armies), LEGO pieces (nuclear missiles), and hand-cut plastic tiles (radiation zones) — and assembled copies of *The Warlord*, which he sold himself. Mainly in academic circles, I think.

This title is my candidate for Best Game of All Time. As a game design it is "perfectly simple." For an overview, think "Nuclear *Risk* in Europe." A huge map comes in four sections depicting Europe and North Africa, broken into regions of different colors. As in *Risk*, a turn consists of placing a number of new armies on the board and then launching attacks. Successful attacks capture opposing army counters as hostages. At the end of a turn, hostages are converted into stages of nuclear missiles. At the end of each turn, a player will have expanded his borders a little and will have placed a nuclear deterrent deep within his home territory.

Undoubtedly the game's most innovative feature is its combat system, which is brilliant in its simplicity. Instead of rolling a die, you secretly *select* a number, between one and the number of armies with which you're attacking. The defender must try to guess your chosen number. If he guesses wrong, you win and remove one of his defending armies. But if he guesses *right*, that's the number of armies *you lose*. And as this clever little rule generates a "He knows that I know that he knows . . ." situation, the game inspires much anguish and many sweaty foreheads for the players.

Nuclear missiles earned after a successful attacking phase also create terror amongst the players. At the end of a turn an attacker cashes in his captured hostages for missile stages. Missiles cannot be exploded until a player's next turn. This gives anyone who thinks a missile might be aimed at them a turn to capture it or face potential annihilation. When a missile explodes, the region it explodes in becomes radioactive and is impassable for the rest of the game. Units are removed from all territories bordering on the radiation zone. And if a missile is within the devastation zone, it chain-reacts and blows up on its spot. . . .

Fast forward to 1975. I had graduated and was now sharing a flat in

Shepherd's Bush, West London with two friends from school, Ian Livingstone and John Peake. Frustrated with our jobs, we resolved to start our own company. And as it happened, our little company — Games Workshop — began to do rather well. Ian and I had discovered yet another obscure game which had taken over our lives — *Dungeons & Dragons*.

As Games Workshop prospered, we expanded into publishing. In 1980 we launched a range of four boxed titles under the advertising slogan "The British Empire Strikes Back." (George Lucas later forced us to abandon our *Star Wars*-type ads.) One of the four was *Apocalypse*, a re-work of the second (Blue Box) edition of *The Warlord*. Mike had changed the game considerably with the Blue Box version, introducing sea areas and super missiles. Personally, I always preferred the pure-and-simple original to the later developments.

By now the Red Box version was long out of print. Foolishly, I had never bought a copy. But I still had my original handmade version from Keele, right? Ten years ago I tried to find the game to play with our Games Night group. It was then that I remembered I had stored my hand-drawn *Warlord* boards in the loft of a previous house and forgotten all about them during the move. I was devastated.

For years a copy of Red Box *Warlord* was top of my "Games to Get" list. As so few had ever been produced, though, it was looking like a hopeless task. Even Mike himself couldn't put a copy of the original game together for me.

But my quest finally ended at Spiel '99 in Essen, Germany. An English dealer, Second Chance Games, had shelves packed with obscure titles, many of which I remembered fondly from the Games Workshop days. Perched high on a shelf in the corner, was a large red box. *The Warlord*! There it was!

Andy Ashcroft, owner of Second Chance Games, wouldn't accept less that £125 for *The Warlord*. "Sorry," he said. "I can't go any lower than £125. This is a very rare game. I've already been offered £115 by another dealer. And I've heard that Steve Jackson is looking for this game. . . ."

★ ★ ★

STEVE JACKSON began his career in games in 1974 as a freelance journalist with *Games & Puzzles* magazine. In 1975 he and school friend Ian Livingstone founded Games Workshop. The company established a chain of retail shops and went on to manufacture Citadel Miniatures. Games

Workshop also published *White Dwarf* magazine and its own range of games, including *Warhammer*. Jackson and Livingstone also collaborated on a highly successful series of Fighting Fantasy gamebooks (1982 Puffin Books, 2002 Wizard Books) which have sold over 15 million copies to date. In the mid-'90s Steve Jackson spent 2.5 years as a games journalist with the London *Daily Telegraph* before setting up computer games developer Lionhead Studios with industry legend Peter Molyneux. Lionhead's first game, *Black & White*, sold over two million copies. Currently he is Professor of Games Design at Brunel University, West London.

John Wick on

WIZ-WAR

KEY DESIGNER: TOM JOLLY
JOLLY GAMES (FIFTH EDITION, 1991)

NOTHING EVER GOES RIGHT in *Wiz-War*. Nothing ever goes as planned. In this game, you don't make plans, you make *contingencies*.

Consider this. Four wizards trapped in a dungeon. Each has two treasures and each has three enemies who know only one of them can escape. *Bloodbath* isn't a bloody enough word. Maybe *bloodtorrent*. This is one of those games you don't play with your friends. Not the fragile ones, anyway. And you *definitely* don't want to play it with your girlfriend. Aristophanes never imagined the kind of revenge such carelessness would cause.

And it isn't enough that these wizards have fireballs and lightning bolts at their command. Click-clackering skeletons, carnivorous trolls, vampiric shadows, and the ever-so-charming Democratic Monster are all at their beck and call.

Poor Democratic Monster. He's never given a chance to know who's side he's on. Every 10 seconds or so, another wizard grabs his consciousness and twists it around, forcing him to attack the one who used to be his ally. And in 10 seconds time, everything switches again. He shambles the corridors, cursing Washington and Franklin and Jefferson, lamenting on the moral ambiguities of "liberty."

But I digress.

Tom Jolly released *Wiz-War* in 1985. The original edition came out in a plastic bag. I didn't play that one. The first time I saw the game, it was in a small brown box. Little did I know that over 20 years later, that little brown box would still be bringing me such joy. I had little faith when I first saw it. A doubting, skeptical man was I, playing it first at a convention in Los Angeles. Between working security and talking up D.J. Trindle — then assistant editor of *Shadis* magazine — for a freelance gig, I stumbled across the little brown box in open gaming. I saw cardboard pieces. I was nowhere near impressed or intrigued, but I had nothing else to do and the guy who owned the game was so enthusiastic. I sat down, picked the red wizard (who looked like Marty Feldman from *Young Frankenstein*), and I listened carefully to the rules.

"Roll one d4 for movement," he told me. The other players listened intently. I was looking through the paper rules booklet, not even stapled. He continued.

"You move your wizard. You can pick up one thing. If you do, it ends your movement."

"What about the treasures?" the girl playing the green wizard asked, looking at the two matching treasures.

"You can only carry one treasure at a time," he said. "And if you drop two treasures on a power point, you teleport out of the dungeon."

"And that's how you win?" asked the guy playing the blue wizard.

"You can also lose," the guy who owned the game said, "by getting killed. You have fifteen hit points. If you lose them, you die and your treasures disappear."

He pointed at the two large decks of construction paper cards. "Draw two cards each turn. You can only use one attack card. You can use all the other ones you want."

That's what we needed to know. The game began.

It started slow. I had a handful of cards, most of which were pretty boring. I discarded them quickly, looking at as many cards as I could. As I drew new cards, the titles started to make me giggle. Cards like Go Away! and Ugly and Big Rock caught my eye. I also saw a card called Create Wall that didn't seem very useful. I discarded it quickly.

Then, as I was looking at my new cards, I heard this exchange:

"Lightning bolt! Six! Add! Five!"

"Reverse!"

"Anti-Anti!"

"Aw, man!"

I looked up and the mad majesty of Wiz-War was suddenly revealed to me.

The system of card interaction Tom Jolly designed for *Wiz-War* would be seen again later in another game about dueling wizards. Combinations of cards designed to create a true sense of *attack-parry-riposte* is what makes Tom's game so much fun. Every card has a counter, every counter has a counter-counter, and every counter-counter has an escape hatch that nobody ever sees coming.

The wizards summon supernatural allies to their aid, adding even more dangers to the dungeon. Not only that, but certain cards even fiddle with the board, moving entire sectors around, throwing the whole maze into utter chaos, forcing players with solid strategies back on their heels, trying to regain their balance.

And let me tell you something for free, friends. I never thought I'd dread the combinations of words *create* and *wall* so much until I played *Wiz-War*. And if this little piece ever inspires you to pick up Tom's game, I advise you now to keep your eyes out for that combination of words. When the opportunity arises, you'll know exactly when to use it.

Since I first played *Wiz-War*, I've become a designer myself, and Tom's game has taught me a lot. I learned about how the element of chance can influence the outcome of a game. I learned about building drama, climax, and anti-climax, and I learned that the key to making a good game is giving the players *choices*. The more you can put the player in a situation where he has to make difficult decisions, all of which seem like valid strategies, the better.

Most importantly, I learned that just because a game is funny doesn't mean it also can't be an exercise in cutthroat strategy. And, if anything in this essay is true, it's this: *Wiz-War* is a damn funny game that will make you cry.

Most recently, I was at DarkCon, a game convention in Phoenix, Arizona, where I was invited to play *Wiz-War*. I declined. "There are two games I don't play with friends," I said. "One of them is *Diplomacy* and the other is *Wiz-War*."

They insisted. They told me they were cool about it. They told me they were tough. They insisted they were strong. I nodded, sat down, and 20 minutes later, someone stood up and shouted, "Screw you, John Wick!"

I love this game.

JOHN WICK has designed roleplaying games, board games, and collectible card games about samurai, pirates, orks, Templars, and housecats. He is a Master Mason and eats a hot dog for Discordia every Friday. More about his games can be found at www.wicked-dead.com.

AFTERWORD

by James F. Dunnigan

SOMETHING ODD HAPPENED HALF a century ago. Grownups began to play board games, big time. Before that, these games were considered kid stuff. Adults could indulge, but aside from card games — canasta was big in the '50s, anyone remember canasta? — it was not respectable for grownups to get down and game. I was always something of a historian, and having been around way back when, I took note of this transformation.

Here's what happened. Geeks happened. Especially geeks who didn't think of themselves as geeks. The geek thing was really all about education. What most people don't realize (historians love to use that phrase) is that the parents and children of the 1950s and '60s were the first generations of what I call "the overeducated." The idea that everyone should go to high school is only about a century old. The concept of college for the masses was a post-World War II fantasy that panned out. At the end of the 20th century, someone did the math and realized that the majority of scientists who ever lived are alive now.

In the 1960s, when I got into the game business, there was a growing number of geeks, but there were no computers yet to absorb so much of their time. There were more kids going to high school and college than ever before, and all that additional education created a taste for new pastimes. The geeks needed something to entertain, to exercise that educated and developed mind. Games were the solution. Not the traditional games, but games that made you think a little harder, that required some math skills, games that were a little more challenging. In a word or three, games for geeks.

The 3M Corporation caught wind of this and came out with their snazzy Bookshelf Games. While most of these were original designs, such as Sid Sackson's *Acquire* (1962) and *Executive Decision* (1972), several were repackaged games of antiquity, such as chess and backgammon. Publishing these games was considered a bold move at the time, but 3M always was an entrepreneurial company, and their board games for adults were a hit.

But what about the geeks? They got wargames from Avalon Hill, the brainchild of Charlie Roberts, who was — well, still is — an entrepreneur. He was also a military history buff (as many adults, and teenage males, are). He thought, why not wargames? These were nothing new, but wargames had previously been for professionals, not for a mass market. Charlie realized that wargames were basically chess on steroids. Thus the wargames Avalon Hill produced were relatively simple, played quickly, and caught on with a large civilian audience, games such as *D-Day* (1961), *Stalingrad* (1963) and *Afrika Korps* (1964).

They also imparted a real historical experience. They immersed the player in the historical situation. Geeks loved it. While the wargame experts in the Pentagon — we're talking super geeks here — looked down on the commercial wargames, most military people ate it up. This was especially true with the young guys. Remember, this was the first generation of officers where the majority of them had college degrees. The draft was still around, and there were lots of college grads in the ranks, as well. There were lots of wargames being played on military bases, though the older generation of officers and NCOs didn't quite know what to make of it. Geeks with guns?

I get blamed for a lot of things that went down during this period, but the one thing I will take credit for is pushing the idea that there were a lot more game designers out there than anyone realized. I looked at those early Avalon Hill games and understood that the mechanics were pretty simple, but could benefit from some better organization. When Tom Shaw, who ran Avalon Hill after Charlie Roberts left in the early '60s, asked me to do a game for them, he mentioned that the rules should just follow the format of the last game. That was a sensible, "organic" approach. However, the game they asked me to do was about World War I naval warfare — published in 1967 as *Jutland* — while the last game they had published — 1966's *Guadalcanal* — was on World War II land warfare. It was okay. I love solving problems.

Over the next few years I put together a game designer's tool kit and invented the profession of *developer*. As I envisioned it, the developer was akin to the director of the movie, with the designer being the screenwriter and the art department handling the cinematography. In my system, the "screenwriter" had more authority, and often had the final say. (This system evolved when games went to computers, with the programmer, initially, taking the place of the developer, and usually having the final say. Currently, a game's producer is the one with the last word on everything.) What I did was create procedures and easy-to-understand lists of what had to be done, and when, and by whom, as a game was being perfected.

My partner at Simulations Publications, Inc., Redmond Simonsen, integrated graphics creation with all this, and further refined the game rules development process.

Avalon Hill had used the word *developer* before, but left it up to the guy with that role — usually a local high school or college student working part time — to use his wits and improvise. I preferred to organize. Big time. Very geekish.

You had a problem. You solved it.

During my time at SPI, I made this point to wargamers via editorials and talks at game conventions. I kept hammering away at the idea that, if you could play these board wargames, you could design them. This resonated with many players, especially those who were used to making their own modifications to existing games. That was easy to do with board games, and was so popular that, a decade later, as computer games proliferated, programmers (or at least their bosses), felt compelled to give gamers the ability to make modifications. Back at SPI, we published hundreds of games designed by people who took me at my word, and many of those designers are still at it. Convincing people they could do it, that was big. The geeks were unleashed.

During the 1970s, there were several other major developments. First, people discovered those wargame mechanics could be used for non-historical stuff. It's a fact of life in the publishing business that fiction outsells non-fiction. So we soon had popular fantasy and science fiction roleplaying games and all manner of other types of games, covering whatever great ideas the growing number of designers could imagine.

Then came the personal computers. I had been using computers since the 1960s (that's another story), and eagerly took to PCs. I could see where things were going — that eventually most of what we now call hobby games would be run on computers. When I discussed this at game conventions, the gamers in the audience lit up. The geeks were getting their computers, and they were loving it.

Another, rather more unnoticed, development in the 1970s was the rise of the "simple strategy game." I noted at the time that some of these had an audience far beyond the usual geek market. This concept was eventually embraced, in a big way, by European designers, thus giving us what we now tend to call "German games." Games for people who are geekish, but not heavily into math and military history.

But the 1970s ended on a down note for me. A decade of pretty intense market research (plus some fancy math, and tying up the company minicomputer on weekends to crunch the numbers) showed that there was not much future in the wargame, or "historical games," business. There were just not enough geeks of that stripe left to sell games to, at least the ones that interested me. PC games and non-historical games provided access to other potential markets — some non-geeks, some geeks of a different stripe — but that's not what I was there for. So I went off to greener pastures in financial modeling, writing, embarrassing government officials, and punditry.

The wargame business has continued to decline in terms of units sold, but not when it comes to new ideas. Each year, interesting original titles find their way to print (though those wargames are likely to be called "strategy games" now, and are but a small niche in the overall games market). And designers in other parts of the industry continue to invent new types of games — collectible card systems, mass-market designs. They keep looking for those problems and solving them. . . .

Half a century ago, the hobby gaming world, as we now know it, was new and unformed. We were explorers in an unmapped mindspace, creating markets and mischief, where none had existed before. The hundred games that have been examined in this book are but a few (rather good) examples of the thousands of games produced since the late 1950s. All done by people who, like me, believed that you could just do it.

In 1966, Avalon Hill asked JAMES F. DUNNIGAN to design a game. After that game, *Jutland*, was released in 1967, they promptly asked him to do another, *1914*. A year later he began his own game publishing company (Simulations Publications, Inc., or SPI), which he would end up running for 11 years. Over the course of his career, he has designed more than 100 historical simulations and authored such titles as *How to Make War* and *The Complete Wargames Handbook*. He left SPI in 1980 to write more books, get into modeling financial markets, and pursue all manner of interesting projects. He has been a lecturer to the State Department, the CIA, and the U.S. Army War College. He lives in New York City.

APPENDIX:
FINDING HOBBY GAMES

by Bill Bodden

MANY OF THE GAMES you've read about in *Hobby Games: The 100 Best* are readily available and easy to find. Others may prove more difficult to track down, even for the most dedicated hobby enthusiast. Hobby games haven't achieved the same level of collectability as, say, comic books or baseball cards; this can be both a blessing and a curse in the case of rare games. On the one hand, the asking price for even the most elusive title is not likely to be as high as that demanded for *Fantastic Four* #1. On the other hand, a copy of that elusive game may be harder to come by. In fact, only a few thousand copies may have ever been printed.

Finding hobby games currently in production is easy; open up your local phone book and search the yellow pages under the heading "Games." However, most of the titles discussed here are not going to be sold at national toy chains or "big box" retailers, so you'll be looking for a specialty hobby shop. If there's no game store of that type where you live, or a even a comic book shop that sells a few games, you can probably find one in a nearby town or city. It'll be worth the effort to search it out and stop by. In addition to many of the games covered in this book, a well-stocked specialty hobby shop will be able to introduce you to many other excellent games. The majority of stores will also happily special order something for you if they don't have it.

Conventions are another excellent venue in which to seek out games. Besides the dealer's room, larger conventions (such as Gen Con and Origins) often run auctions that can include a wide variety of material, both common and rare. The Gen Con auction in particular has a storied history, and is regarded within the gaming community as a good place to search for out-of-print titles of all sorts. In fact, the Gen Con auction has grown so large that an "auction store" runs parallel to it, where certain items may be purchased for a fixed price.

While you're at the convention, don't be shy about trying out new games in the demo area and at the manufacturers' booths. There are a great many wonderful games in the world, and the perfect one for you and your friends may be hiding just down the next aisle. Talking to manufacturers is also a great way to learn about new editions of classic games, or upcoming work from the designers represented in *Hobby Games: The 100 Best*.

The next step, after you've exhausted all the local possibilities, is to widen your search. There are hundreds upon hundreds of Internet sites dedicated to hobby gaming. BoardGameGeek.com focuses on board games of all sorts, RPG.net on roleplaying games, Grognard.com on wargames, and TheMiniaturesPage.com on, as you might guess, miniatures. Many others are dedicated to specific game lines or companies or individual designers. Most of these sites are frequented by fellow game enthusiasts who will be happy to share their knowledge with you.

Several of the sites mentioned above boast excellent game-related databases that list, among other things, the history of a game's publication and the various editions and printings it has gone through over the years. This information can be invaluable to you in your search. In fact, the larger fan sites also feature message boards through which members can trade or sell games. You aren't likely to find bargains here, since these boards are frequented by dedicated collectors, but you will be dealing with people who know a lot about what they're selling.

Some stores specialize in rare and out-of-print games. Such specialists can often be found displaying their wares at larger regional or national conventions or advertising on fan sites. Expect to pay a premium price for titles obtained through such businesses, not only for the time and effort they've put into finding the game, but also for the cost of storing an out-of-print title for several years. Many also have waiting lists and search services, for titles they don't currently stock.

eBay and other online auction sites are a viable alternative for tracking down copies of obscure or out-of-print games. The variety offered on these sites can be tremendous and the prices competitive, but buying games this way does have inherent risks; strongly consider purchasing only from a seller with a high positive feedback rating and don't be afraid to ask questions about the item you're bidding on. You may find exactly what you're looking for on the first try, but if not, don't despair; new items are listed by the thousands every day.

A few terms to keep in mind when participating in live or online auctions:

MINT CONDITION: The package has either never been opened, or if opened, the game has never been used. This game is in like-new condition, and will be priced accordingly.

PUNCHED: This term refers to a game's cardboard counters. When new, these pieces come in die-cut sheets of varying sizes. To use the pieces, a player has to "punch" them out, or remove them from their sheets. When a game is described as punched, it's always important to be certain all the counters are present. Some wargames and board games have hundreds of small counters — "monster" games such as *Terrible Swift Sword* can includes thousands — and once they're separated from their sheets, they're easy to loose.

UNPUNCHED: As above. This refers to a game that, while the box may have been opened, the pieces are still in their original, factory-direct state. An unpunched game has never been used, and tends to command a substantially higher selling price than a punched version of the same game.

NEW EDITIONS PRESENT AN unexpected peril in your search for a particular game. A new edition may appear to be the game you want, but it may be substantially different in terms of rules, components, or playability from the version released even a few years before. For example, *Dungeons & Dragons* has undergone five major rules revisions, as well as several smaller revisions. While the differences may appear cosmetic to the uninitiated, they can matter when you gather around the kitchen table to play.

If you're looking for an older or rare game, do some research before buying the latest edition. Changes to a game need not be as radical as the various *D&D* rules overhauls to impact play. Just a slight alteration in the way points are tracked, the board design, or the types of counters used can change the gameplay quite a lot, which means that revised editions are not always universally acclaimed as an improvement over the original. On the other hand, new editions can fix nagging problems that have annoyed players for years. (For revised editions of board games and wargames, some particularly savvy publishers include both the "classic" rules and the new ones.) In the end, though, it's up to the buyer to learn what, if any, differences exist between the old edition and the newer revised one.

Tracking down hobby games can be a challenge, but one that's well worth the effort. There are many resources available — many of them local — to help you bring your quest for that elusive game to a successful and satisfying conclusion.

BILL BODDEN has been part of the hobby games industry since the late 1980s, including stints as a retailer, a wholesale buyer, and a manufacturer's rep. Bill is the sales manager for Green Ronin Publishing, has had gaming-related work published by Sabertooth Games/Black Library and Mongoose Publishing, and is a freelance writer and a regular contributor to *Scrye* and the industry trade magazines *Game Buyer* and ICv2's *Guide to Games*. Bill lives in Wisconsin with his wife and their four cats, and doesn't get to game nearly as often as he'd like.